M000033940

The
Appalachian
Frontier

The Appalachian Frontier

AMERICA'S
FIRST
SURGE
WESTWARD

John Anthony Caruso

With a New Introduction by
John C. Inscoe

Maps by Francis J. Mitchell

THE UNIVERSITY OF TENNESSEE PRESS / Knoxville

The Appalachian Echoes series is dedicated to reviving and contextualizing clas-
sic books about Appalachia for a new generation of readers. By making available
a wide spectrum of works—from fiction to nonfiction, from folklife and letters to
history, sociology, politics, religion, and biography—the series seeks to reveal the
diversity that has always characterized Appalachian writing, a diversity that promises to confront and challenge long-held stereotypes about the region.

Copyright © 2003 by The University of Tennessee Press / Knoxville.
All Rights Reserved. Manufactured in the United States of America.
First Edition.

This book is printed on acid-free paper.

Library of Congress Cataloging-in-Publication Data
Caruso, John Anthony.
The Appalachian frontier: America's first surge westward/
John Anthony Caruso; maps by Francis J. Mitchell; with
a new introduction by John C. Inscoe.— 1st ed.
        p.cm.—(Appalachian echoes)
Originally published: Indianapolis: Bobbs-Merrill, 1959.
Includes bibliographical references (p.) and index.

ISBN 1-57233-215-8 (pbk.: alk. paper)

1. Southwest, Old—History.
2. Appalachian Region—History.
3. Frontier and pioneer life—Southwest, Old.
4. Frontier and pioneer life—Appalachian Region.
5. Tennessee—History.
6. Kentucky—History—To 1792.
I. Title.
II. Series.

F396.C32 2003
976'.02—dc21   2002075984

For
my daughters
JOHANNA *and* CAMILLE
and their GRANDFATHER
ALIDOR HOUCKE-COLLART
three addicts of Western lore

Contents

Maps

Foreword

WHILE THE IDEA OF A CONTINUING OR STATIC FRONTIER HAS long remained an enduring staple in the stereotypes surrounding this region, not until the last twenty-five years or so have historians begun to seriously examine the actual frontier. Works such as Robert D. Mitchell's *Commercialism and Frontier: Perspectives on the Early Shenandoah Valley* (1977) and *Appalachian Frontiers: Settlement, Society, and Development in the Preindustrial Era* (1990), as well as other accounts, are usually focused on particular areas or topics in the region, however, and do not attempt to offer a comprehensive overview. John A. Caruso's *The Appalachian Frontier: America's First Surge Westward*, while representing an older, narrative type of history, does indeed cover the entire history of settlement from the seventeenth century up to the advent of Tennessee's statehood in 1796. The virtue of this narrative approach, however dated, is that it combines social, political, and economic history in a single, comprehensive overview that I believe still holds great interest to both scholars and general readers.

In *Southern Rights: Political Prisoners and the Myth of Confederate Constitutionalism,* Mark E. Neely argues that East Tennessee, regarded as economically and culturally "backward" in the nineteenth century, was in fact advanced politically, with very high voter participation and political leaders of exceptional caliber. Surely some explanation of the sophistication of later nineteenth-century political parties in Tennessee must be connected with the earliest efforts of people in this area to establish self-government. Caruso's analysis of the Watauga Association in 1772 and the abortive "lost state" of Franklin, East Tennessee's first effort to establish an independent state, clearly establishes this lineage.

Caruso's descriptions of Daniel Boone, the Long Hunters in Kentucky, the siege of Boonesborough, and the perpetual battles between settlers and Indians all remind us that, at one point in the late eighteenth century, much of the region of Appalachia was indeed unified in a continuing struggle to settle new lands in what would become West Virginia, Kentucky, western North Carolina, and Tennessee. The lifestyle of most of the immigrant groups, Germans and Scots-Irish predominately, even at this early stage demonstrated a wide diversity in patterns of religion, settlement, and customs that belie later stereotypes. Caruso also includes full descriptions of land developers, speculators such as William Blount and Richard Henderson, early industrialists, and other economic elites not commonly associated with the frontier in current misperceptions of early Appalachia.

What really preserves the interest of Caruso's book for contemporary readers, however, is his frequent use of personal anecdotes describing the varied reactions of his human characters in this drama. In one such story, Daniel Boone returns after a harrowing escape from Shawnee captivity to discover his wife and children have moved to another settlement during his long absence. The "poignant despair of an abandoned home," however, is broken when the family cat, also abandoned, recognizes him and jumps in his lap. Such stories, repeated countless times, served on the frontier to reaffirm settlers' common humanity. Whether they were true or not, the repetition of certain themes and the varied texture of the reported reactions of the participants offer a key to understanding how these frontiersmen viewed themselves and their relation to neighbors and family. Historian Elliott J. Gorn argues in another context, for example, that fight narratives articulated a fundamental contradiction of frontier life—how the abandonment of "civilized" ways ultimately led to an expansion of civilized society.

Likewise, Caruso's treatment of Native Americans is remarkably sympathetic, revealing their often justified anger and frequent frustration at being cheated and steadily pushed off their own land. Caruso yet again uses anecdotes to good effect, so that individuals—Nancy Ward, Blackfish, Dragging Canoe—come to life and emerge with their personalities intact. At the same time, Caruso does an excellent job both explaining and showing the complex effects of the almost constant fear of sudden Indian attacks most white settlers endured. The stories of Daniel Boone's rescue of his daughter, kidnapped by hostile Indians, and John Kirk's savage retribution for the murder of his family resonated deeply within all European settlers on this eighteenth-century frontier. It is interesting to note here that the image in the nineteenth-century American mind of Tennessee and Kentucky was primarily that of this earlier frontier period, replete with mythic figures such as Daniel Boone and Davy Crockett. Later pejorative stereotypes of Appalachia, imposed on the public's mind in the 1870s and 1880s by local color writers such as Mary Noailles Murfree, did not erase this earlier image.

John Inscoe in his new introduction has done a superb job of contextualizing Caruso's *The Appalachian Frontier*, noting in particular its strengths and weaknesses in light of recent scholarship on Appalachia. His own most recent book, *The Heart of Confederate Appalachia: Western North Carolina in the Civil War*, written with Gordon McKinney, is a fine example of this new scholarship on Appalachian history at its best. In point of fact, this introduction could stand alone as excellent historiographical analysis of the current state of Appalachian scholarship. Finally, Caruso's book fits very well into John Alexander Williams's new interpretation of Appalachian history, *Appalachia: A History*. Williams argues that myth is critical to understanding both the sense of place in the region and the region's own self-image within American national identity. Caruso's narrative of Daniel Boone, an American and Appalachian hero, illustrates in an exemplary fashion this dual role of folk narrative in both defining and shaping the contextual limits of Appalachia's history.

DURWOOD DUNN
Tennessee Wesleyan College

Introduction

THE CONCEPT OF FRONTIER HAS ALWAYS BEEN CENTRAL TO OUR understanding of preindustrial Appalachia. For modern scholars of the region, in fact, it has been an image far too lingering, even too central, in how the southern highlands have continued to be perceived. Long after the rest of America's eastern half had moved well beyond its frontier status in terms of a settled populace and a fully developed market economy, the image of frontier still clung to Appalachia. The mountain South remained in both popular and scholarly perceptions a remote, primitive, and undeveloped wilderness; its residents were termed "our contemporary ancestors" or "yesterday's people." Sometimes they were romanticized as simple, quaint, and innocent; more often they were denigrated as backward, violent, ignorant, and poor.[1]

In recent years, historians of Appalachia have worked hard to overcome its stigma as a perpetual frontier. In 1977, Ronald Eller chided his fellow scholars for their willingness to buy into the myths of the region "as a vanishing frontier, and its people as frontiersmen, suspended and isolated." He bemoaned the marginalization and even the absence of the region's past in broader treatments of southern or American history by scholars who were "guided by the tacit assumption that nothing significant ever happened in the mountains."[2] Well over a decade later, anthropologist Allen W. Batteau noted at the beginning of his book *The Invention of Appalachia:* "Appalachia is a creature of the urban imagination. . . . [It] has provided American society with colorful characters for its fiction, perfect innocents for its philanthropy, and an undeveloped wilderness in which to prove its pioneering blood."[3]

While current scholars have done much to challenge the idea of its perpetual or lingering frontier status, Appalachia was, of course, for much of the eighteenth century, one of America's most significant frontier regions. It was on this more traditional frontier, both in concept and time period, that John Anthony Caruso focused in this book, first published in 1959. Prior to the American Revolution, most of the piedmont of Virginia and the Carolinas continued to qualify as frontier in status, characterized still by sparse settlement, new waves of settlers, and relative remoteness from more densely populated and commercially connected coastal areas. But by the mid-eighteenth century, attention turned more and more to the mountains beyond the piedmont. The Appalachians came to take on new significance, not only for the settlers moving into its valleys and coves, but also for its political, military, and strategic importance as the European power struggle for a North American empire intensified.

It is a big story that Caruso tells here, and in hindsight, a fairly traditional one. While much of this story was familiar at the time, it is striking to note how many elements of the history laid out by Caruso have been lost or ignored by those historians who have responded to Eller's call for a "new history" of Appalachia. The fascination with frontier remains strong in this more recent work although it has been cast in new and very different contexts. The very titles of a number of recent works on southern Appalachia reflect the term's continued viability: Robert Mitchell's *Commercialism and Frontier,* a study of mercantilism in the eighteenth century Shenandoah Valley; his subsequent *Appalachian Frontiers,* a seminal essay collection exploring the identities and experiences of early settlers in various parts of the mountain South; and Wilma Dunaway's *The First American Frontier,* a vast and provocative interpretation of southern Appalachia's economic development over the course of the colonial and antebellum eras.[4] Other significant work on the southern highlands produced in the forty-odd years since Caruso's book was published, covering a wide range of topics, approaches, and parts of the region, have made the concept central as well.[5]

These new scholars use the term "frontier" to describe something different from Frederick Jackson Turner's concept, that it was simply "the outer edge of the wave—the meeting point between savagery and civilization."[6] There now seem to be several divergent, yet overlapping, ways in which historians of early Appalachia understand the nature of the frontier experience and interpret its significance.

One of these rests on the idea of the frontier as not so much a dividing line between civilized and uncivilized, or settled and unsettled, but rather as a series of mixing zones, where, according to one description, "different cultures, environments, experiences, economies, motives, and perspectives come into contact."[7] Yet other historians have embraced this "revisionist notion" of what constitutes a frontier by calling attention to "zones rather than binary dividing lines . . . contested spaces rather than a stage in the progress of the world according to Europeans."[8] The interplay of different peoples, distinguished by race, ethnicity, religion, or class, was basic to the American—and by extension, the Appalachian—frontier experience.

In the southern highlands as elsewhere, these "contact points" took a variety of forms—from conscious conflict to the far more subtle, even unperceived, exchanges of ideas, values, cultural traits, or lifestyles. We have become far more conscious of both social hierarchy and social diversity as integral to the earliest white settlement of the highlands. We now recognize that Appalachia's first white settlers included slaveholders and slaves; that generalizations of ethnic distinctiveness, such as Scots-Irish individualism and German clannishness, contain grains of truth, but that "accommodation, adaptation, exchange, and coexistence among such groups played a more important part in the cultural dynamics of the region"; and that mixed race identities and full-scale assimilation were as basic to Indian-white contacts—from Cherokees to Melungeons—as were trade and conflict.[9]

A second line of analysis has used the exigencies of space and time to compartmentalize the frontier stage of development within Appalachia, usually categorizing it either geographically, chronologically, or both. In his *Appalachia's Path to Dependency,* Paul Salstrom divides the highland South into three economic and topographic subregions—Older Appalachia, Intermediate Appalachia, and Newer Appalachia—based not only on initial white settlement of each, but more significantly, on the three different time periods in which the frontier closed and a different stage of social and economic viability began.[10] Wilma Dunaway, on the other hand, stresses initial settlement patterns in characterizing the frontier status of the same region. She divides the European settlement of Appalachia (or resettlement, as she characterizes it in acknowledging the displacement of its earlier Native American residents) into four historical stages: the pre-1763 settlement of the eastern slopes of Virginia's Blue Ridge and the Ohio Valley; two definable stages of expansion before and after the American Revolution; and finally, the inroads made by white newcomers into the areas vacated by Cherokee Removal in the late 1830s.[11]

A related corollary to these redefining efforts is a challenge to the idea that the highland frontier implied merely a subsistence economy and way of life. In one of the most seminal revisionist studies of the region, *Commercialism and Frontier,* Robert Mitchell demonstrated that strong entrepreneurial impulses were inherent in the earliest stages of the Shenandoah Valley's settlement. These manifested themselves in a variety of ways: rampant land speculation, thriving trade linkages between frontier mercantile establishments and eastern seaboard ports, early road networks that linked communities both within the region and to those well beyond, and rapid increase in marketable agricultural surpluses and home manufactures. Subsequent studies of preindustrial Appalachia—David Hsiung's work on the interconnectedness of early market centers in northeastern Tennessee; Kenneth Noe's book on the socioeconomic and political impact of the railroad on southwestern Virginia; John Inscoe's on the influence of slaves and slaveholders in western North Carolina; Barbara Rasmussen's on absentee land speculation in five counties of West Virginia; Durwood Dunn's on market dynamics at the community level in Cades Cove, Tennessee; Mary Beth Pudup's on town and county elites in southeastern Kentucky; and John Stealey's and Charles

Dew's on early extractive industries of salt mines and iron forges, respectively—all testify to the validity of Mitchell's model for the region and together portray the social and economic dynamics of Appalachia's formative years as far more complex and varied than once assumed.[12]

In light of the vast new scholarship that interprets early Appalachia in such different terms, what does Caruso's work still have to offer readers? John Anthony Caruso was the product of a very different era in terms of both scholarship and national mood. Born in 1907 in the small coal-mining community of Fairchance, in western Pennsylvania, he was the son of immigrants—his father had been an olive picker in Italy, and his mother was Spanish. He was born only a year after his mother's arrival in America while his father worked in a coal mine, earning seventeen cents a day. Education came late for Caruso; he was thirty-eight years old when he earned his undergraduate degree. In the meantime, he had traveled in Mexico and developed an interest in it that would eventually become his dissertation—on the Pan-American Railroad—and his first book—*The Liberators of Mexico* (1954). He earned his Ph.D. at West Virginia University in 1949 and spent his entire career there until his retirement in 1974. He was one of the last students of Charles Henry Ambler, a prominent historian of West Virginia who himself had been a student of Frederick Jackson Turner at the University of Wisconsin. Despite his early interest in Latin America, Ambler's influence led Caruso to turn to early American history and Appalachia. "I decided I wanted to write American history," he once said. "After all, I am an American."[13]

The initial product of that decision was *The Appalachian Frontier*, published in 1959. It was the first in a series of similar volumes he wrote on other American frontiers. Two years after its publication came *The Great Lakes Frontier* (1961), then *The Southern Frontier* (1963) and *The Mississippi Valley Frontier* (1966). Caruso culminated the series a decade later with *Jefferson's Empire: The Golden Age of the American West*, though it remains unpublished. He was at work as well on a biography of William Clark (Lewis's partner) at the time of his death. Caruso also worked as a consultant for the National Geographic Society during the 1960s and *U.S. News and World Report* during the 1970s, both of which valued the breadth of his scholarship as well as the popular appeal of his work.[14] He retired from West Virginia University in 1974, and continued to live in Morgantown until 1997, when he died at the age of eighty-nine.

All four of Caruso's frontier histories were published by Bobbs-Merrill, a major commercial publisher. They were aimed at a general, nonacademic audience and proved significant successes for both author and publisher. *The Appalachian Frontier*, in fact, was nominated for the Pulitzer Prize in history in 1960. It is not hard to see what appealed so to readers of that era. As one reviewer noted of the book upon its publication, Caruso's "chief concerns are men and movements, personalities and politics . . . but he devotes considerable space to the buckskinned private in the army of pioneerdom."[15] That range of topics and perspectives, along with Caruso's knack for descriptive detail and lively storytelling, proved to be a winning formula that readers today will still appreciate.

It was also at an interpretive level that *The Appalachian Frontier* proved so appealing to its first readers. Coming of academic age in the 1940s and 1950s, Caruso was part of the age of consensus in terms of how leading American historians had come to see the national experience. In the aftermath of the Great Depression and the Second World War, the "American Century" had reached its zenith. At mid-century, the Cold War thrust a formidable new challenge onto the country in the menace of Communism, both at home and abroad, and it inspired scholars to seek in the nation's history the roots of its unique character and value system. This so-called consensus school of history stressed the continuity in the American past and a common sense of purpose that shaped the unfolding of its history, especially during the nation-building eras of the late eighteenth and early nineteenth centuries.

Westward migration and the pioneer spirit that infused it were integral components in shaping the American character and were certainly those that most captured the popular imagination.

It is no coincidence that the 1950s was the decade in which both Daniel Boone and Davy Crockett emerged as icons to a new generation of moviegoers and the very first generation of television viewers and in which westerns as a genre, on both big and small screens, enjoyed their greatest popularity. One of the greatest of these epic westerns, *The Alamo,* starring John Wayne as Crockett, hit movie screens in 1960, just months after *The Appalachian Frontier* first appeared in bookstores.

Caruso's book was very much a product of its age. As its subtitle, *America's First Surge Westward,* suggests, the migration into and beyond the southern highlands was the beginning of a continuum in the conquering of the continent, a movement clearly meant to be celebrated and revered. Those who led that westward surge were heroes to be admired and emulated. Robert L. Kincaid, in the original introduction to the book, proclaimed it to be the story of "hardy traders, hunters, adventurers and homeseekers" who endured "hardships and terrors in the unknown wilderness." He gave special acknowledgment to the "heroic leaders familiar in the annals of this western migration [who] come alive in this book." Kincaid echoed the very satisfying and comforting theme that Caruso's narrative confirms throughout: "The new Republic was on its way. The Appalachian barrier was hurdled. The Mississippi basin became the home of a dominant, resourceful people who gave to American life the bone and sinew of greatness."[16]

This celebratory tone of American nation-building is also evident throughout Caruso's narrative and a clear reflection of the age of consensus in which he wrote. His interpretation owes much to the ideas of Frederick Jackson Turner—perhaps via his own mentor, Charles Ambler. Specifically, Turner viewed the continual nature of the American frontier as a major leveling force in shaping the democratic character in which the nation took such pride, a process Caruso clearly saw at work in Appalachia. While acknowledging up front the ethnic diversity of the Europeans who made up the first generation of Appalachian settlers, he also noted that "each group, irrespective of its origin or its national background, evinced typically American characteristics engendered by a blending of European heritage with frontier influences." He reiterated this theme more explicitly later in his narrative, writing of German and Scots-Irish settlers: "The poverty and dangers they shared in common made them equals; they developed no sense of superiority one over the other. Each settler, therefore, respected his neighbors' property and religious beliefs— in principle if not always in practice."[17]

If such sentiments seem to modern sensibilities rather simplistic and romanticized, other aspects of Caruso's story demonstrate a more complex set of dynamics at work. They also remind those of us currently studying the region's formative years of certain aspects of that experience that seem to have been obscured or marginalized in more recent Appalachian scholarship.

First and foremost, as the book's subtitle suggests, it is important to remember that Appalachia was always part of a much grander scheme of historical development, politically, militarily, and geographically. Those of us immersed so deeply in the study of the region and its people sometimes tend to forget that the white settlement of the mountain South in the eighteenth century was not merely the chronological foundation of the Appalachian experience. As Caruso so vividly demonstrated, it also represented a vital—even defining—stage in the American progression across the continent. That vast range of mountains from the Alleghenies, Cumberlands, and Shenandoahs to the Blue Ridge and Great Smokies, constituted a formidable hurdle, even barrier, for those who had set their sights not so much on the southern highlands as on what lay beyond them.

These challenges provide the core of much of Caruso's story. By focusing as much on the movement across the Appalachian mountains as with settlement within them, he set a far more vast stage than that upon which current scholars of the region generally focus. In so doing, he conveyed a more nuanced sense of the sporadic nature of migration and settlement and of the push and pull factors that drove or drew—and he provides ample evidence of both—those first white highlanders to stake their claims in the southern mountains.

Events and individuals well beyond the highlands were, for Caruso, key forces in these developments. He thus devoted a full chapter to the French and Indian War, the culmination of a century-long struggle between two of Europe's three most powerful nations. Although it was fought in areas far from the southern highlands, that conflict was a vital determinant of how and when the highlands would be settled and by whom. While the military aspects of the American Revolution were less crucial to trans-Appalachian development—Caruso stated that "the struggle of the thirteen colonies for independence was almost as remote to the frontiersmen as if it were taking place on another planet"—he did recognize the variety of ways in which that war's outcome shaped the political and economic destiny of southern highlanders. "In conquering the wilderness," he noted, "they were unconsciously helping to build that political edifice for which their warring brothers in the east were laying the foundation."[18]

In other ways, too, Caruso cast a wide net to explain the forces that shaped southern Appalachian development and identity. Events unfolding far to the east—forts established in the mid–seventeenth century near present-day Richmond and Petersburg; tensions arising from the presence of Palatinate immigrants to London; Indian policies initiated by Virginia's last colonial governor, Lord Dunmore; and the Regulator movement in piedmont North Carolina—all of these disparate factors proved to be vital components of the Appalachian story as Caruso told it.

By the same token, developments taking place far west of the mountains were integral to Appalachia's fate, as Caruso made clear in the latter part of his narrative. He elucidated the struggles involved in settling Harrodsburg, Kentucky, and Nashville, Tennessee (both established, interestingly enough, earlier than comparable settlements in the mountains to the east); John Sevier's ill-fated Muscle Shoals project, an attempt to win land grants from Creek Indians in what would later be northern Alabama; and James Wilkinson's schemes to establish a trade monopoly between Kentucky and Spanish New Orleans.

Caruso's book also reminds us of the extent to which the settlement of Appalachian and trans-Appalachian areas was based on military actions both within and beyond the region—an aspect of the history often overlooked in more recent analyses of the eighteenth-century highlands. Not only as part of the broader war for empire, but at a variety of other levels and in other contexts, violent conflict was a pervasive part of how and why the Appalachian frontier developed as it did. Several battles and campaigns merit extended coverage in Caruso's narrative: the clash between British troops and Shawnee Indians in 1774 at Point Pleasant along the Great Kanawha River in what would later become West Virginia; the Revolutionary War showdown between Cornwallis's British forces and Wataugan frontiersmen at Kings Mountain, South Carolina; the siege at Boonesborough, Kentucky, where Daniel Boone's leadership ensured the repulsion of Shawnees again in 1778; and campaigns against both Creeks and Cherokees by militia from the short-lived State of Franklin.

Caruso's perspective on the frontier encounters between whites and Native Americans fully reflects the time period in which he wrote: conquering whites "won" the continent by forcibly, yet admirably, overtaking—through negotiation or violent struggle —the lands of Indians who unsuccessfully resisted such encroachments. And yet, from our more multicultural sensibilities today, there are some redeeming aspects of Caruso's coverage of the Indians in his story. Many of them emerge as full-fledged characters whose motives and viewpoints are laid out as fully as those of their white antagonists. Several Indian leaders (with names not readily recognizable in today's Appalachian histories) figure prominently here: Chief Logan, half-French and half-Mingo, whose blood vengeance escalated the conflict along the Ohio River that would come to be known as Lord Dunmore's War; Shawnee chief Cornstalk, also central to that western Virginia clash, whose later murder by impetuous American soldiers led to serious repercussions farther west in Kentucky; Oconostota, a Cherokee leader who reluctantly ceded Kentucky lands to the whites moving onto it through the Wilderness Trail; and Blackfish, a Shawnee leader who kidnapped Daniel Boone and forced upon him a Shawnee name and honorary status as his adopted son.

In other ways, too, *The Appalachian Frontier* grapples with realities well beyond the romanticized pioneer sagas and Turnerian celebrations of frontier democracy. Caruso's analysis foreshadows the work of Mitchell and others, for instance, in that it recognizes the profit motives that drove much of the impulse to settlement in and across the mountains. While frontiersmen Daniel Boone, George Rogers Clark, and John Sevier are certainly the most familiar figures in Caruso's narrative, he devoted even more attention to men like Richard Henderson, James Robertson, and William Blount, whose efforts to settle Kentucky and Tennessee had as much to do with financial contracts, commercial transactions, land speculation, and legal challenges as they did in overcoming Indians and wilderness hardships.

If such economic impulses are integral to Caruso's story, so too are the politics through which so much of the struggle for Appalachian lands was played out. In fact, one of Caruso's major strengths as a historian lay in his tendency to politicize much of what happens throughout the book, an aspect of the Appalachian experience overlooked in many recent social and economic assessments. One is struck, for example, in the early part of the book by the prominence of political debates and ambitions in colonial and state capitals such as Williamsburg and New Bern in struggles over power and policy far to the west. The dispute between Richard Henderson and George Rogers Clark over the governance of Transylvania in Kentucky was resolved not through gunfights, sieges, or even threats of violence, but rather through petitions, lobbying, and rational discourse before the Virginia assembly in Williamsburg.

Even more significant were the efforts made by trans-Appalachians to break the bonds that linked them to those very distant Tidewater capitals. Their attempts to create new and self-governing polities in and beyond Appalachia drive much of the story in the book's latter chapters. The Wataugans who settled in what would become northeastern Tennessee embodied merely the first of several such efforts. Caruso noted that the articles of government that they established for themselves in 1770, known as the Watauga Association, had both direct and indirect antecedents in the Regulator movement and did what the Regulators never could: create "the first free and independent government, democratic in spirit and representative in form, ever to be organized on the American continent."[19]

As such, it also served as a precedent for similar efforts elsewhere along the Appalachian frontier. In Transylvania, the leaders of Boonesborough, Harrodsburg, and other Kentucky settlements came together in 1775 in an attempt to establish a representative government to prevent the "chaos and confusion" that its lack could easily have generated on this rapidly growing region. In the Cumberland country of central Tennessee, the North Carolina legislature created a military district at the close of the American Revolution, with county courts, commissions, and other trappings of local government following close behind. Simultaneously, other Tennesseans—those of the original Watauga settlement—sought to sever their ties with North Carolina and create their own state, a move that failed due to the vigorous opposition of its mother state, thus identifying Franklin ever since as the "lost state."

There were cumulative effects in the unfolding of these events, and Caruso's narrative demonstrates the interconnectedness of the developments he described, as well as the patterns that define the various struggles he chronicled. It is no coincidence that several of these events share a cast of characters: James Robertson, Richard Henderson, John Sevier, and James Wilkinson are among several major players in this saga who show up at various places and in varying roles throughout the era.

The culmination of all of these movements, both the successes and failures, was statehood for Kentucky and Tennessee, and it is with detailed accounts of those processes that Caruso ended his book. Not only were these the culminating political manifestations of frontier settlement in Appalachia, but they also represented the first in what would become a vital and recurring stage throughout American frontier history. The quest for statehood was, sooner or later, an important part of the demographic and economic progress of all frontier territory across the continent. In several cases, such as Missouri, California, and Kansas, it was that very process that resulted in national controversy and sectional tension.

Caruso traced these complex political movements in clear and thorough detail, but he never separated them from the other struggles that so shaped the power plays of legislative assemblies, governors, commissioners, and other political leaders, official or renegade. He wove their stories seamlessly into those of the many other struggles simultaneously at play—tensions with Indians, the entrepreneurial grabs for trading rights and real estate, and the mere challenges of daily life in these wilderness settings.

All the while, Caruso made this a lively, readable account, filled with dramatic stories of interesting individuals and groups: John Sevier's escape from the Morganton, North Carolina, courthouse in the midst of his trial for treason; the abduction of Daniel Boone's daughter, Jemima, and two other girls, and the mission to rescue them from their Cherokee captors; the frenzy of conversion experiences, or "falling exercises" at evangelical camp meetings, at one of which three thousand Kentuckians succumbed; the Wataugans' assault up the sharp slopes of Kings Mountain and their unceremonious treatment of the corpse and belongings of the British commander, Patrick Ferguson, a casualty of their attack; a nearly one-thousand-mile river voyage by John Donelson's flatboat, the *Adventure,* during which Indian attacks led to the drowning deaths of several women, children, and slaves.

As modern scholars continue to rediscover and reinterpret Appalachia's early history in all its richness and complexity, Caruso's more conventional narrative still offers perspectives and insights into that turbulent past well worth their own rediscovery. This vigorous, multifaceted history demonstrates that nearly twenty years before Ron Eller worried about those scholars who assumed "that nothing significant ever happened in the mountains," at least one scholar was very much aware of how much had happened in early Appalachia and how significant it was for the nation at large.

JOHN C. INSCOE
The University of Georgia

Notes

1. The term "yesterday's people" comes from a book of that title by Jack Weller (Lexington: Univ. Press of Kentucky, 1965). "Our contemporary ancestors" is also from a title of a much cited essay: William G. Frost, "Our Contemporary Ancestors in the Southern Mountains," *Atlantic Monthly* 83 (March 1899): 311–19. For a recent overview of the stigmas and stereotypes to which Appalachia has been subjected, see Dwight B. Billings, Gurney Norman, and Katherine Ledford, eds., *Back Talk from Appalachia: Confronting Stereotypes* (Lexington: Univ. Press of Kentucky, 1999).

2. Ronald D Eller, "Toward a New History of the Appalachian South," in Stephen L. Fisher, J. W. Williamson, and Juanita Lewis, eds., *A Guide to Appalachian Studies,* special issue of *Appalachian Studies* 5 (Autumn 1977): 75.

3. Allen W. Batteau, *The Invention of Appalachia* (Tucson: Univ. of Arizona Press, 1990), 1.

4. Robert D. Mitchell, *Commercialism and Frontier: Perspectives on the Early Shenandoah Valley* (Charlottesville: Univ. Press of Virginia, 1977); Robert D. Mitchell, ed., *Appalachian Frontiers: Settlement, Society, and Development in the Preindustrial Era* (Lexington: Univ. Press of Kentucky, 1991); Wilma A. Dunaway: *The First American Frontier: Transition to Capitalism in Southern Appalachia, 1700–1860* (Chapel Hill: Univ. of North Carolina Press, 1996). Other essay collections that followed Mitchell's *Appalachian Frontiers,* often with essays by the same scholars, include Michael J. Puglisi, ed., *Diversity and Accommodation: Essays on the Cultural Composition of the Virginia Frontier* (Knoxville: Univ. of Tennessee Press, 1997); David C. Crass et al, eds., *The Southern Colonial Backcountry: Interdisciplinary Perspectives on Frontier Communities* (Knoxville: Univ. of Tennessee Press, 1998); and Kenneth E. Koons and Warren R. Hofstra, eds., *After the Backcountry: Rural Life in the Great Valley of Virginia, 1800–1900* (Knoxville: Univ. of Tennessee Press, 2000).

5. Among the most significant of these works are Rodger Cunningham, *Apples on the Flood: The Southern Mountain Experience* (Knoxville: Univ. of Tennessee Press, 1987); David C. Hsiung, *Two Worlds in the Tennessee Mountains: Exploring the Origins of Appalachian Stereotypes* (Lexington: Univ. Press of Kentucky,

1997); Paul Salstrom, *Appalachia's Path to Dependency: Rethinking a Region's Economic History, 1730–1940* (Lexington: Univ. Press of Kentucky, 1994); and Barbara Rasmussen, *Absentee Landowning and Exploitation in West Virginia, 1760–1920* (Lexington: Univ. Press of Kentucky, 1994). Several works explore similar themes in the nineteenth century, including Mary Beth Pudup, Dwight B. Billings, and Altina L. Waller, eds., *Appalachia in the Making: The Mountain South in the Nineteenth Century* (Chapel Hill: Univ. of North Carolina Press, 1995); Durwood Dunn, *Cades Cove: The Life and Death of a Southern Appalachian Community, 1818–1937* (Knoxville: Univ. of Tennessee Press, 1988); and Koons and Hofstra, *After the Backcountry.*

6. Frederick Jackson Turner's "The Significance of the Frontier in American History" was given as a lecture in 1893 and first published in the *Proceedings of the Forty-first Annual Meeting of the State Historical Society of Wisconsin* (Madison, Wis., 1894). It has been reproduced in many other volumes since. On the significance of Turner's essay, see Ray Billington, *The Genesis of the Frontier Thesis* (San Marino, Cal., Huntington Library, 1971); and Richard Hofstadter, *The Progressive Historians: Turner, Beard, Parrington* (New York, Knopf, 1968).

7. Michael J. Puglisi, "Images and Realities of Cultural Diversity on the Virginia Frontier," introduction to Puglisi, *Diversity and Accommodation*, 14; and Gregory H. Nobles, "Breaking into the Backcountry: New Approaches to the Early American Frontier, 1750–1800," *William and Mary Quarterly*, 3d ser., 46 (1989): 641–70, esp. 642–43.

8. Andrew R. L. Cayton and Fredrika J. Teute, "Introduction: On the Connection of Frontiers," in *Contact Points: American Frontiers from the Mohawk Valley to the Mississippi, 1750–1830* (Chapel Hill: Univ. of North Carolina Press, 1998), 2.

9. Quotation from Puglisi, *Diversity and Accommodation*, book jacket. See the essays in that book and in Mitchell, *Appalachian Frontiers*, for a good sampling of recent scholarship on these themes.

10. Paul Salstrom, "Newer Appalachia as One of America's Last Frontiers," in Pudup, Billings, and Waller, *Appalachia in the Making*, 78, map.

11. Dunaway, *The First American Frontier*, 54–55, maps 3.1 and 3.2.

12. In addition to the works of these authors cited above, see David C. Hsiung, "How Isolated Was Appalachia? Upper East Tennessee, 1780–1835," *Appalachian Journal* 16 (1989): 336–49; Hsiung, "Seeing Early Appalachian Communities through the Lenses of History, Geography, and Sociology," in Crass et al, *The Southern Colonial Backcountry*, 162–81; John C. Inscoe, *Mountain Masters: Slavery and the Sectional Crisis in Western North Carolina* (Knoxville: Univ. of Tennessee Press, 1989), esp. Chapter 2; Mary Beth Pudup, "Social Class and Economic Development in Southeast Kentucky, 1820–1880," in Mitchell, *Appalachian Frontiers*, 235–60; John E. Stealey III, *The Antebellum Kanawha Salt Business and Western Markets* (Lexington: Univ. Press of

Kentucky, 1993); and Charles B. Dew, *Bond of Iron: Master and Slave at Buffalo Forge* (New York: W. W. Norton, 1994). For essays drawn from these works and others on the use of slaves in extractive industries in early Appalachia, see Inscoe, *Appalachians and Race: From Slavery to Segregation in the Mountain South* (Lexington: Univ. Press of Kentucky, 2001).

13. Norman Julian, "A Life Well-Written, Well-Spent," a profile of Caruso in the *Dominion Post,* January 9, 1991. I am grateful to Caruso's daughter, Camille Caruso Weiss, herself a historian at West Virginia University, for sharing this clipping and her own memories of her father with me, which together provided the sources for much of the biographical information laid out here.

14. Caruso was one of the contributing authors to one of the National Geographic Society's best-selling volumes, *America's Historylands: Landmarks of Liberty* (Washington, D.C.: National Geographic Society, 1962), which sold over a half million copies.

15. J. T. Winterich, review of *The Appalachian Frontier* in *Saturday Review,* June 13, 1959, 22.

16. Introduction by Robert L. Kincaid to Caruso, *The Appalachian Frontier* (Indianapolis: Bobbs-Merrill Co., 1959), 7–8.

17. Quotations from pages 23 and 42 of this volume.

18. Both quotations from page 235.

19. Quotation from page 109.

Come my tan-faced children
Follow well in order, get your weapons ready,
Have you your pistols? have you your sharp-edged axes?
    Pioneers! O pioneers!

For we cannot tarry here,
We must march my darlings, we must bear the brunt of danger,
We the youthful sinewy races, all the rest on us depend,
    Pioneers! O pioneers!

O you youths, Western youths,
So impatient, full of action, full of manly pride and friendship,
Plain I see you Western youths, see you tramping with the fore-
    most,
    Pioneers! O pioneers!

Have the elder races halted?
Do they droop and end their lesson, wearied over there beyond
    the seas?
We take up the task eternal, and the burden and the lesson,
    Pioneers! O pioneers!
        "Pioneers! O Pioneers!"
        WALT WHITMAN

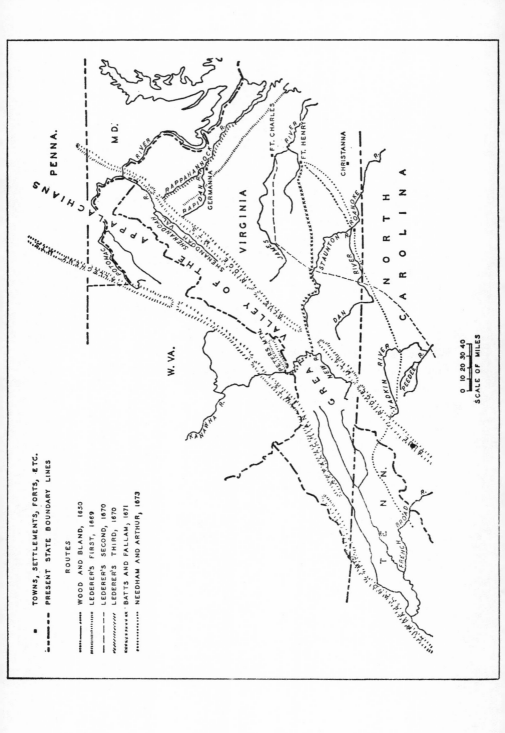

TOWNS, SETTLEMENTS, FORTS, ETC.
PRESENT STATE BOUNDARY LINES

ROUTES

WOOD AND BLAND, 1650
LEDERER'S FIRST, 1669
LEDERER'S SECOND, 1670
LEDERER'S THIRD, 1670
BATTS AND FALLAM, 1671
NEEDHAM AND ARTHUR, 1673

0 10 20 30 40
SCALE OF MILES

1

Explorers
in the Back Country

IN THE FIRST HALF OF THE EIGHTEENTH CENTURY STREAM AFTER stream of German and Scotch-Irish immigrants poured into the frontier known as the Old West. Here, in the back country of New England, the Great Valley of southeastern Pennsylvania, central and western Maryland, the Piedmont of Virginia and the Carolinas, and the Valley of Virginia, they had to adopt a pattern of life entirely isolated from European influences. Here they formed the first pioneer society with characteristics which are regarded as typically American.

The southern section of the Old West, where the first settlements were made, had singular geographic features, as though it were a stage especially set for actors about to begin some unique and fascinating drama. It started at the Fall Line where navigation on coastal rivers halted before cataracts and, south of the Roanoke, before pine barrens that rose hundreds of feet above the level countryside. Beyond these barriers spread the Piedmont of Virginia and the Carolinas. Its rich soil, its swift streams, its mild climate and its boundless forests were irresistible attractions to the farm-loving Germans and to the adventurous, land-hungry Scotch-Irish. In the west rose the Blue Ridge Mountains. The pioneers, pressing their advance in this new land of Canaan, passed through gaps in the mountains to emerge on the Great Valley of the Appalachians where they cleared the wilderness and raised their humble cabins. In the far distance the jagged peaks of the Allegheny Front ended the Old West and temporarily shut in the pioneers from the rich and mysterious country of Kentucky and Tennessee beyond.

White explorers, hunters and fur traders had tramped into the Old West a full century before the German and Scotch-Irish immigrants appeared. The first exploration of the Old West goes back to the middle of the seventeenth century when that Frontenac of Virginia, Captain Abraham Wood, commanded Fort Henry at the Falls of the Appomattox on the present site of Petersburg. Fort Henry was one of several strategic points built to protect white settlements against possible Indian depredations. But though their immediate purpose was defensive, they were to the Tidewater, as the Virginia plain was called, what St. Louis and Chicago later became to the Great Plains: points of departure for traders and explorers into the interior. In Wood's day, Fort Henry was a combination of frontier town and military and trading post, much like Chicago in the early nineteenth century. Just across the river lay the principal village of the Appomattox Indians, "who furnished Wood with messengers, hunters, porters, and courageous and faithful guides." The Indians bartered furs for such articles as guns, powder, bullets, tomahawks, kettles, blankets, cutlery, brass rings and other trinkets.

In August 1650 Wood, with three companions on horseback and two white servants and an Indian guide on foot, advanced to the forks of the Roanoke in search of choice lands which Wood hoped to sell. One of the party, Edward Bland, a merchant from Charles City County, kept a diary of the journey in which he recorded the discovery of "exceeding rich Land, that beare two Crops of Indian Corne a yeare and hath timber trees above five foot over, whose truncks are a hundred foot in cleare timber, which will make twenty Cuts of Board timber a piece, and of these there is abundance."

They journeyed in this fertile country for about a hundred and twenty miles to the present site of Clarksville, Virginia, near the North Carolina line. The Indians grew less and less friendly as they advanced. Bland wrote that a Tuscarora chief urged them to turn back before they should reach impassable marsh and swamp country. They replied in the spirit of true explorers that

they "were resolved to go through," that they were afraid
neither of him nor of his tribe and that they had no choice but
to advance, "for we were commanded by our King."

Their avowed loyalty, however, fled before the mere rumor
of a plot to destroy them. After paying a nervous visit to the
falls of the Roanoke and to a place where Indians killed huge
sturgeon, they packed their belongings and turned homeward.
Bland called the region "New Brittaine" because he concluded
from discovering a westward-flowing river that he and his comrades had journeyed beyond the limits of Virginia. In four days
they were back in the safety of Fort Henry.

The next organized effort at western exploration came two
decades later under Governor William Berkeley of Virginia.
Both he and his lieutenant, Abraham Wood, were primarily
businessmen who, under the guise of sponsoring western exploratory parties for the Crown, sought to enrich themselves in the
Indian fur trade. In order to expand this trade as much as possible, Berkeley willingly sacrificed his popularity with the agricultural elements of the colony. In 1669-1670 he sent out three
expeditions under a learned German physician, John Lederer,
one across the Rapidan River to the mountains, another to Saura,
an Indian village on the Pee Dee River, and the last up the Rappahannock.

Lederer's journal of his explorations, translated from the original Latin by his friend, Sir William Talbot, contains statements
which scholars of the Old West have questioned for many years.
In the underbrush of Virginia, for example, he saw "leopards"
and "lions," though he admitted that these animals were "neither
so large nor so fierce as those of Asia and Africa." He reported
the height of a ridge as so "extraordinary" that he climbed, presumably on horseback, from "the first appearance of light" until
"late in the evening" before he reached the summit. Next day
he saw from a peak of the Blue Ridge "the Atlantick-Ocean
washing the Virginian-shore." He wrote of Amazonian women
who "shoot arrows over their husbands shoulders," men who
fought with silver tomahawks, and a tribe of Indians whose

women "delighted in feather ornaments, of which they have great variety; but peacocks in most esteem, because rare in those parts."

The editors of Lederer's journal, Alvord and Bidgood, declared that such statements "make pleasant reading," but "sound like the tales of Baron Münchausen." Most academic writers held this view until another scholar, Lyman Carrier, came to Lederer's defense. After carefully studying the journal and the region in which the explorer had traveled, Carrier charged Alvord and Bidgood with failing to make "full use of the evidence at their disposal" and with falling "into the common error of modern historians" of labeling false or inaccurate what they cannot readily understand. He then offered explanations of the dubious statements. "The American lion," which is also called "mountain lion, puma, catamount and cougar, formerly ranged the Atlantic slope . . . as it does the western mountains today. Several native members of the cat family could qualify as small leopards." As for the ridge, might not Lederer have exaggerated its height by inadvertently climbing it in circuitous manner and by judging from the amount of time he required to reach the summit? In believing that he saw the Atlantic from a peak of the Blue Ridge, Lederer simply indulged the optical illusion that "has deceived many others since that time." For purposes of propaganda, Indians often deprecate their enemies by accusing them of using their womenfolk as warriors. Finally, the metal hatchets and peacock feathers are easily explained—Indians had been purchasing such articles for years from Spanish traders in the Gulf Region.

Lederer contributed much to the exploration of the Old West. He may have been the first white man to see the Valley of Virginia. He was also the first man to make a map of the region between the Atlantic coast and the Blue Ridge Mountains. Covering about twenty-five thousand square miles, it showed the Rappahannock, Pamunkey, James and Roanoke rivers—all more or less in their proper sources. This was a remarkable achievement for a man who was obliged to obtain his information from his own observations and from Indians he chanced to interview during his journeys. Yet, ironically, Lederer's map was ignored in Virginia for another century in favor of an incomplete and inaccurate map made by one Augustine Herman.

Lederer's journal contains excellent descriptions of some of the places he visited and keen observations of Indian psychology. Here, for example, is his advice in trading with Indians:

you must be positive and at a word; for if they perswade you to fall anything in your price, they will spend time in higgling for further abatements, and seldom conclude any bargain. Sometimes you may with brandy or strong liquor dispose them to an humour of giving you ten times the value of your commodity; and at other times they are so hide-bound, that they will not offer half the market-price, especially if they be aware that you have a designe to circumvent them with drink, or that they think you have a desire to their goods, which you must seem to slight and disparage.

This was valuable advice, for already Berkeley had made fur trading one of the principal industries of the colony.

In the following year Berkeley and Wood prepared another expedition for the purpose of finding "the ebbing and flowing of the Waters on the other side of the Mountains." The new venture was led by Captain Thomas Batts, a successful planter from a well-known English family, and two other gentlemen, Thomas Wood, perhaps a relative of Abraham Wood, and Robert Fallam, who kept a brief, clear, and accurate journal of the expedition.

During the journey Wood became seriously ill and remained behind, but Batts and Fallam advanced along the Staunton River to the Blue Ridge Mountains and emerged in the valley of the New River where, having exhausted their food supply, they called a halt. They had reached the point where the New River breaks through Peters Mountain at Peters Falls in Giles County, Virginia, near the West Virginia line.

Early next morning they took possession, in the name of their King, Charles II, of the land drained by the waters flowing westward into the Ohio River. They also commemorated their discovery by branding four trees, one with their own initials, two others with those of Berkeley and Abraham Wood, and the last with the royal insignia. Mindful of the purpose of the expedition, they persuaded themselves that the slight movement of the water was caused by the ebb and flow of the tide. Returning home, they jubilantly announced that they had discovered a route to the Pacific Ocean.

The English based their claim to ownership of the Ohio Valley on this expedition. Yet, ironically, says Alvord,

... the event which redounds so much to the credit of Englishmen, and substantiates so completely the claims of the mother country to that particular territory for which she made war on her rival at such a cost of blood and money, is practically unknown and has even been frequently denied by historians. The names of Frontenac, Joliet, Marquette, and La Salle are familiar to every schoolboy, while those of their English competitors in exploration, who were in every respect their equals in daring and enterprise, have remained till this day in obscurity, almost in oblivion.

Two years later Abraham Wood, who had been promoted to the rank of general, sent James Needham, a "gentleman," and Gabriel Arthur, an illiterate but courageous young man, to trade with the Indians in the back country of Carolina. Needham and Arthur advanced toward their destination by the Great Trading Path, which crossed an island in the Staunton River. This island the Occaneechi had fortified in order to control the fur trade of the region by acting as middlemen between the Virginians and the tribes farther west. They did not want to lose their profits by allowing Needham and Arthur to trade directly with the Cherokee and other tribes. The two were forced to return to Fort Henry; but General Wood persuaded them to resume the expedition. This time they succeeded, through the influence of an independent trader named Henry Hatcher, in gaining passage to a Cherokee village, perhaps on the French Broad River, where they were welcomed by a chief of the tribe. After a short rest, Needham with eleven Cherokee returned to Fort Henry, leaving Arthur with the villagers to learn their language.

A month later Needham with his Cherokee friends and an Occaneechi guide named Indian John set out for the village with the intention of taking Arthur back to Fort Henry. One night, as they encamped at the ford of the Yadkin, Indian John quarreled with Needham, shot him through the head, ripped open his body, tore out his heart, and, holding this up as he turned eastward, shouted defiance at the whole English nation. He then sent the frightened Cherokee home to kill Arthur, while he himself rode off to his people on Needham's horse.

The Cherokee hurried to their village and reported what had happened. Seizing on the absence of the chief, who was friendly to the English, some friends of the Occaneechi bound Arthur to a stake and began to heap dry reeds around him. Just then the chief appeared with gun on his shoulder and killed the Indian who was lighting the pyre. Promising to escort Arthur home in the spring, he contrived to safeguard his life by sending him out with a war party, which roamed as far south as the Apalachee country in West Florida, where it unsuccessfully raided a small Spanish mission before it trekked northward to the valley of the Great Kanawha in the present state of West Virginia.

Homeward bound, the war party fell in with some hostile Indians, who wounded Arthur in the thigh and captured him, but who, finding from his long blond hair that he was a white man, returned his weapons and treated him kindly. Finally the band made its way back to its starting point, whence Arthur, accompanied by the chief and eighteen of his people laden with furs, eventually returned to Fort Henry.

Both Needham and Arthur made valuable contributions to American exploration. Needham, by reaching the French Broad River, became the discoverer of Tennessee, while Arthur was perhaps the first white man to see the valley of the Great Kanawha.

On the trail of these explorers followed ambitious fur traders. In expeditions which sometimes included as many as a hundred pack horses, each equipped with merrily tinkling bells, they advanced from the Fall Line forts farther and farther into the wilderness. Some went as far as the New River; some crossed the Blue Ridge and hunted in the Shenandoah Valley, and some followed Needham's route to the Carolina Piedmont, where they exchanged guns and trinkets for furs with the Cherokee. The more adventuresome pressed as far south as the foothills of the

Alleghenies and traded with the Creek and the Chickasaw.

From every direction they returned with glowing descriptions of the choice lands they had found. Inspired by these tales, groups of small Virginia farmers packed their meager belongings and moved westward with their cows and sheep, which they grazed in the open meadows and canebrakes while they built cowpens, cleared fields, grew corn and raised crude cabins for protection and shelter.

They were soon joined by homeseekers from the Tidewater, where plantation farming had crowded them out. Governor Alexander Spotswood, one of the ablest leaders of colonial Virginia, actively encouraged them. He herded the Indians in the colony into a huge reservation, which he called Christanna. There he took care to provide the Indian children with Christian training and a practical education. Indian elders gratefully laid presents of furs at his feet, while young men and women, wrapped in crimson blankets and painted with blue and vermilion, bowed to him in reverence.

Spotswood also founded a colony of Germans at Germanna, on the banks of the Rapidan, for the purpose of developing the production of iron. For this enterprise he was pleased to be known as the Tubal Cain of America.

Such a man as Spotswood was naturally curious about the country beyond the mountains, which Virginia claimed by right of her ancient charter. Moreover, he had learned, perhaps from the surveyor Colonel William Byrd, that the French had taken possession of the Great Lakes region, where they carried on a lucrative fur trade, and had established themselves at Kaskaskia and on the lower Mississippi.

Possessed of a robust and "restless spirit only slightly concealed under an air of dignity," Spotswood resolved to see things for himself. His military experience complemented his adventurous temperament. He had been wounded at Blenheim, had fought at Malplaquet, and had risen at the age of twenty-eight to the rank of quartermaster-general.

In August 1716 Spotswood assembled at Germanna two companies of rangers and a small group of mounted "gentlemen" with their servants and Indian guides. The expedition was to assume the form of an exploratory picnic. The gentlemen had abundant provisions, which included several cases of Virginia wine—both white and red—Irish usquebaugh, brandy, stout, two kinds of rum, champagne, cherry punch and cider. The blast of a trumpet early on the morning of August 30 called them to their horses.

The governor, dressed in green velvet riding clothes, Russian leather boots and a hat bedecked with a brilliant plume, led his companions along the banks of the Rapidan toward its source. Five days later they reached the Blue Ridge Mountains. Up they clambered for three more days, crossing small streams, killing rattlesnakes and suffering such discomfort as that of being stung by hornets, until they halted on one of the loftiest peaks of the mountains.

The occasion called for proper celebration. Spotswood delivered an eloquent address and drank the health of the King and that of the royal family; then he led his companions down the western slope of the peak. The descent proved hazardous. The little streams they followed led to precipices which often frightened and stalled their horses. But their perseverence was eventually rewarded; they came on a smiling valley watered by a clear and beautiful river which Spotswood called the Euphrates— a name which later yielded to that of Shenandoah. Crossing the river, they buried in its bank a bottle which contained a paper claiming the region for their King, George I.

The valley abounded with wild turkeys and deer and cucumbers and currants and grapes. On these they feasted and then, assembling and loading their guns, drank to the health of the King in champagne, and fired a volley; drank to the Princess in Burgundy, and fired a volley; drank to the royal family in claret, and fired a volley; drank to the governor, and fired a volley. In this convivial mood the gentlemen turned their horses homeward, leaving some of the rangers to continue west to the Warriors' Path where Iroquois often hunted or sent arrows in their jealousy against Shawnee, Tuscarora and Catawbas.

Later Spotswood glowingly described "World's End," as he called the country he had visited. To encourage settlement in the western valley, he pictured it as an agricultural paradise abounding with health-restoring mineral springs. He also presented to each of the gentlemen who had accompanied him a miniature golden horseshoe on which was inscribed *Sic Juvat Transcendere Montes*. It is pleasurable to cross the mountains—and to have relived the expedition with the adventurous governor and his Knights of the Golden Horseshoe.

Before long Spotswood had acquired immense estates for himself and his friends. His appetite for property increased with every acre he secured. In 1720 he influenced the Virginia assembly to pass an act which divided the Piedmont of Virginia into two counties, Brunswick and Spotsylvania, where the landowners enjoyed religious toleration and exemption from taxes or quitrents for a period of ten years. Spotswood and his associates put this act into operation despite the refusal of the Crown to approve it unless land grants were limited to 1,000 acres.

By the middle of the eighteenth century these large landowners or planters controlled the Virginia and Carolina piedmonts. Most of the grants, which ranged from ten to forty thousand acres, were owned by Tidewater planters. A few, however, were in the hands of such powerful noblemen as Lord Fairfax and the Earl of Granville, court favorites of Charles II and James II respectively. Fairfax owned the portion of Virginia between the Rappahannock and Potomac rivers; Granville owned most of northern Virginia.

These speculators and others employed a liberal number of agents in a variety of duties. They assigned lands, collected quitrents, and distributed pamphlets which promoted the western country as "the best, richest, and most healthy part" of America. Some owners attracted immigrants by making slight improvements in their properties and by maintaining agents in the eastern ports to persuade new arrivals to settle on their grants. Some speculators held their lands until they became valuable; others insisted on renting and encouraging settlement, only to demand an exorbitant fee for what improvements they had made. Sometimes hastily drawn boundaries resulted in the discomfiture of the farmer, who found that he was forced to repurchase his land at a higher price after ownership was finally established.

Such was the section of the Old West in which the German

and Scotch-Irish immigrants planted the first settlements. Among them were small groups of New Englanders, Welsh and French Huguenots. In ensuing years they were joined by thousands of others from all parts of the east and from Europe. Some of the original settlers and some of the newcomers settled permanently in the Old West; others, or their descendants, moved in large or small groups across the Alleghenies to the frontier southwest of the Ohio River, known as the Appalachian Frontier or the Old Southwest, where they founded new settlements and eventually established the states of Kentucky and Tennessee.

Each group, irrespective of its origin or its national background, evinced typically American characteristics engendered by a blending of European heritage with frontier influences. How and why these characteristics developed and led to the making of the social order known as American democracy entails the fortunes of the migratory groups in the Old World and in the New. Let us, therefore, follow them.

The

Immigrants

Most of the german immigrants were natives of the Palatine, in southwestern Germany, who had fled to America from devastating wars, religious persecution and burdensome taxes. The first group left the Palatinate in 1708 under their minister, Joshua von Kocherthal. This group numbered ten men, ten women and twenty-one children whose ages ranged from six months to fifteen years.

On passes procured by their leader from the English representative in Frankfort on the Main they went to England, where Queen Anne encouraged them by granting them an allowance of a shilling a day. This generous example was soon imitated; rich families gave them clothing and tools, while the government decreed them citizenship without charge.

When Kocherthal applied in their behalf for transportation to America, the Lords of Trade decided to send them to the colony of New York, where they could serve as buffer folk against the Indians or be employed in the manufacture of such naval stores as tar, pitch and high masts, which the Mistress of the Seas greatly needed. On arriving in New York at the end of 1708 the Palatines proceeded to the mouth of Quassaic Creek, some fifty-five miles north of New York City, where Governor Francis Lovelace gave each of them fifty acres and, in addition, granted Kocherthal five hundred acres for a glebe and two hundred and fifty acres for his family. Here they established Newburgh, named in honor of the residence in the Palatinate of the House of Pfalz-Neuberg.

News of Kocherthal's success drifted back to the Palatinate, where new oppressions and the privations of an unusually severe autumn and winter combined to touch off another and much larger wave of emigration. Each new month proved more rigorous than the last. In November firewood would not burn in the open air. In December wine and liquor froze into solid masses of ice, trees and vines withered at the roots, and birds dropped dead as they flew. In January 1709 men claimed that their saliva congealed before it touched the ground. Before the month ended most of western Europe was buried in ice and snow. All the rivers, including the swift Rhone, were frozen; all along the coast the sea was solid enough to bear heavily laden carts.

Persecuted by their rulers and ruined by the wintry blasts, many Palatine husbandmen and wine dressers resolved to leave their wretched country. Kocherthal's success in gaining the assistance of Queen Anne encouraged them to adopt the same course and seek English shores. Soon the whole Palatinate seemed to have migrated to London. By the fall of 1709 over thirteen thousand Palatines overflowed the city, filling taverns and public squares in Blackheath on the southern side of the Thames, where sixteen hundred tents from English military stores were erected to shelter them. Queen Anne made them liberal donations, provided them with food, presented them with a thousand German Bibles and distributed coal among them at Christmas time. A collection was taken up for them throughout the kingdom. This yielded nearly £2,000, and Parliament appropriated £35,000 more for their subsistence and transportation.

Curiosity drew half of London to Blackheath to see those hardy and simple foreigners who reportedly subsisted on brown bread, roots and the cheapest of meats. The practical Palatines fashioned inexpensive toys and sold them by the thousands. Rumors of Palatine brawn spread throughout the kingdom. The diarist Narcissus Luttrell heard of an elderly German who wagered an Englishman that he could walk three hundred miles in Hyde Park within a week. The German won the wager and then walked an extra mile for good measure.

The government took a more serious view of their presence. What was to be done with them? Only a handful could find

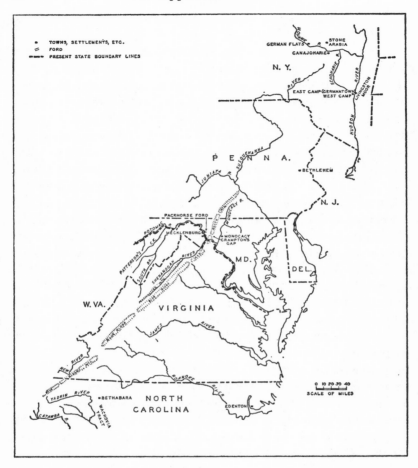

employment. The working people of London frankly distrusted them. They accused the Palatines of eating the bread which belonged to Englishmen and of working for smaller wages. Even beggars felt that the Queen's bounty belonged to themselves. Shopkeepers regarded Palatines with a jealous eye. Two thousand infuriated Londoners who were armed with axes, scythes and hammers attacked a Palatine camp and, much to the Queen's chagrin, struck down, threatened and robbed all who failed to run away. When an epidemic of smallpox struck London, the Palatines were accused of infecting the air.

At last the British authorities adopted a singular policy. The Catholic immigrants, numbering over three thousand, were returned to the Palatinate. The Protestants, however, were distributed throughout the empire. Some were sent to Ireland, some to the Carolinas. But the majority of them were transported to New York, whose governor, Colonel Robert Hunter, proposed to employ them in the production of naval stores.

As a site for the experimental work camp Hunter selected a tract on Livingston Moor, which had been recommended to him by the proprietor, Robert Livingston, as very suitable for his purpose. There, in the autumn of 1710, they were settled in two villages—East Camp, now Germantown; and West Camp, which name still survives.

The experiment was a failure from the very beginning. The local farmer hired to supervise production knew nothing about extracting pitch from virgin pine, so the Palatines found other employment. They established a school for the instruction of the few children who had survived the voyage; they built huts for shelter; they sowed grain; several hundred of them volunteered in an expedition against Montreal. Hunter grew more and more weary of supporting them. At last, having exhausted cash and credit—and having failed to receive his salary for five years—he informed them through his overseer that they must shift for themselves.

The Palatines despaired, for winter was approaching and winter had always brought starvation. In their extremity they sent a deputation of three men under John Conrad Weiser to purchase land from the Indians. The Indians not only sold the Palatines the land they desired but guided them through the forest, pointed out edible roots and herbs to them and provided the mothers with fur robes on which to rest and sleep.

The purchased land lay in the valley of the Schoharie, which they reached by blazing a trail fifteen miles long through the forest. Here fifty families settled during the first year. The next year another group, breaking through snow three feet deep, joined their comrades in Schoharie, swelling the population of the settlement to over a thousand.

They endured a poverty that belied their diligence. They

plowed their land with sickles, ground corn in stone mills like their Indian friends and, having at first neither horse nor cow, carried their belongings into the valley on their backs like the gold miners of the Klondike some two centuries later. On their backs, too, they carried salt and wheat seed from the village of Schenectady about twenty miles away.

To the common trials of pioneer life was added the unsleeping hostility of the government. Three times their land was granted away; three times they repurchased it. Then, exasperated by the dishonesty of the local speculator, they waited for the Albany sheriff who had been sent to eject them. Under the direction of Magdalena Zeh, a woman of Amazonian strength, they seized the sheriff, knocked him down and threw him into a ditch where a sow was wallowing. After inflicting many other indignities on him, they threw him on a rail and rode him through several settlements. Finally they deposited him on a small bridge across a stream along the old Albany road, a distance of six or seven miles from their starting point. There Mistress Zeh seized a club and beat the sheriff until two of his ribs were broken. Friends later rescued him and nursed him back to health.

Despite the experience of the unfortunate sheriff, dishonest speculators continued to wage a war of recrimination against the Palatines for several years. At last the beleagured Schoharie settlers decided to send Weiser and two other men to lay their cause before the Lords of Trade in London. This recourse proved unfortunate. In Delaware Bay pirates captured the three men, tortured and flogged Weiser until they extorted from him the money provided for the mission and then turned him and his companions free.

On arriving in London they were thrown into prison on the ground that the Palatines whom they represented, had, in taking possession of Schoharie, appropriated a tract which belonged to others. Weiser remained in London for five years, endeavoring to obtain for his people a title to the lands they had settled with so much peril and hardship. The appeal proved vain. Hunter returned to England and argued the case with such vehemence that finally Weiser gave up in despair. Returning to Schoharie, he advised his people to leave the colony and settle in Pennsylvania, where he was confident they would obtain more hospitable treatment.

Not all of them were of the same mind. Some of them decided to stay on their clearings and buy their land again from the government; some accepted the offer of the new governor, William Burnett, to settle on lands elsewhere. The latter group, under the leadership of John Christopher Gerlach, emigrated to the Mohawk Valley, where—with other Palatines—they founded the towns of Herkimer, German Flats, Mannheim, Oppenheim, Minden, Palatine Bridge, Canajoharie, and Stone Arabia. For thirty years the Mohawk was as German as the Rhine.

The majority of the settlers of Schoharie decided to accept Weiser's advice and seek refuge in Pennsylvania. Under the guidance of their Indian friends, they cut a road through the forest from Schoharie to the headwaters of the Susquehanna, where the women and children floated down the river in rafts and canoes and the men marched along the road with their cattle.

At the juncture of the Swatara and the Susquehanna, they ascended the former stream. Between the sources of the Swatara and Tulpehocken Creek, on the rolling countryside so reminiscent of their native Palatinate, they selected land and settled. The limestone soil and the abundance of streams promised them rich agricultural reward for their patient industry. In ensuing years some of them advanced northward to the Juniata and southward through the low gaps of the South Mountains to the Great Valley of southeastern Pennsylvania. As they moved southward they found less and less prejudice from other newly arrived immigrants, the Scotch-Irish. Quitrents were cheaper too; Pennsylvania charged £15 for each hundred acres, Maryland only £5, and Virginia speculators in the Shenandoah Valley even less.

In 1726 the first German families attracted by these conditions crossed the South Mountains through Crampton's Gap and followed the Monocacy into the Potomac Valley, where they built such towns as Monocacy and Frederick. Others crossed the Potomac by Old Packhorse Ford, over which Indian hunters and warriors had passed since time immemorial, and founded a settlement which they named Mecklenburg but which inscrutable history rechristened Shepherdstown in honor of Thomas Shepherd, whose original name was Schaeffer and who settled there in 1734.

The first Palatine to settle in the Valley of Virginia was Adam Müller, who changed his name to Miller. In 1726, when a Knight of the Golden Horseshoe told him of the fertile and beautiful country beyond the Blue Ridge Mountains, he forthwith resolved to see it with his own eyes. Entering the Valley through Swift Run Gap, he built a cabin near the present site of Elkton. The land pleased him so much that he hurried back to Pennsylvania to fetch his family and to spread word of his good fortune among his former neighbors. They and some of their friends followed him. Within a few years nine plantations containing fifty-one persons, young and old, were flourishing along the Shenandoah River near Massanutten Mountain.

Farther north, five miles below the present town of Winchester, another Palatine, Justus Hite—or Joist or Yost Heid, as he variously spelled his name—built in 1731 a cabin destined to become the center of German migration that eventually helped to fill the back country of Virginia. With Hite and his family came his three sons-in-law, their families and a few of their friends. Each man in this group founded a separate settlement. Among them was Peter Stephan who, with other settlers, laid out Stephansburg which changed its name several times before it adopted its present one of Stephens City.

By 1740 waves of migration, each larger than the one previous, spread to the Great Falls, at the junction of the Shenandoah and Potomac rivers, and then swept through the Valley in all directions. In the next two decades immigrants poured through the gaps of the South Mountains to Patterson's Creek, then to the South Branch of the Potomac as far as the New River region, then to the Greenbrier, and eventually to the Great Kanawha—converting, as they advanced, a trackless wilderness into a continuous agricultural paradise. On the eve of the American Revolution they had reached the mountains of Kentucky and were ready with the Scotch-Irish to bring permanent settlement to the Appalachian Frontier.

Of all the migratory groups in the Old West none surpassed the courage and faith of the Moravian Brotherhood, which established Wachovia, the first permanent settlement in the back country of North Carolina. The Moravians were followers of that Morning Star of the Reformation, John Huss, who in 1415 "sealed his faith with a martyr's death." Originally they called themselves *Unitas Fratum*—the Unity of Brethren—but eventually they became known as Moravians, because most of them came from Moravia, the central province of present Czechoslovakia.

Their rule of faith and practice was based on the Old and New Testaments as God's word, "which he spake to all mankind of old time in the prophets, and at last in his Son and by his Apostles, to instruct us into salvation, through faith in Christ Jesus." Their leader in America was perhaps the best-known personality of the sect, Count Nicolaus Ludwig von Zinzendorf. He, like Saint Francis of Assisi, forsook the comforts of wealth to pursue evangelical work.

In 1741 Zinzendorf established a permanent organization in Bethlehem, Pennsylvania, and soon set out to bring religion to the Delawares and Shawnee in the Wyoming Valley of that colony. Armed only with the shield of faith and the gospel of peace, he advanced among the savages and announced that he came to dispel the darkness of their souls with the light of Christ. The Indians received him suspiciously. Legend says that one day while he sat writing in his tent, some Delawares stole up with the intention of killing him. Suddenly they saw two deadly snakes crawl into the tent from the opposite side, approach Zinzendorf, and pass harmlessly over his body. Thereafter the Delawares regarded him as a protégé of heaven. None of them dared disturb the Moravian settlements for several years.

In 1751 Zinzendorf bought 100,000 acres in North Carolina from Lord Granville, who wanted mines discovered, land cultivated and towns and cities established on his vast estate. Hearing that the Moravians were thrifty and industrious settlers, he was happy to make them a liberal offer. On their part, they sought an estate where they could worship God without the restraint they had endured in Pennsylvania and where they might sell farmland to members of the Brotherhood. Zinzendorf chose Bishop August Spangenburg, a learned, devout and intensely practical man, to make surveys in the Granville tract and select the site of the purchase. The prelate and five other Brothers left Bethlehem and arrived sixteen days later at Edenton, North Carolina, where they remained for several days. Spangenburg was so ill with fever that he fainted as he rode his horse and grew so weak that he had to be assisted to mount and dismount. Nevertheless, he refused to remain in Edenton until he was well. "The Lord," he said, "will give me the necessary health and strength. I will have to pass through much weakness, you will have to exercise much patience, but the Lord will help me through."

Prostrated with malarial fever, two of the Brethren remained behind, and eventually returned to Pennsylvania; but Spangenburg led the remaining three doggedly toward their goal. Several days later they arrived in the Catawba Valley, where they were joined by a surveyor and two hunters who supplied them with game. But the deeper they pushed into the wilderness the harder their journey became. Indians constantly eyed them with suspicion. Mountains rose all around them like huge waves in a storm. Confronted with an "indescribably" high peak, they once were obliged to remove the baggage from the horses to keep them from being hurled backward. Taking firm hold of the reins, they coaxed the trembling animals forward while they dragged the baggage after them as they climbed on hands and knees. Near the summit darkness overtook them; unable to put up their tents, they slept under the trees.

The Lord soon showed them a chestnut grove where they found water and forage for their horses. Patiently crossing a stream full of large rocks, they entered a broad valley, only to encounter a blizzard that drove them like dry leaves in all directions and almost swept them off their feet. Even the stoical Spangenburg complained—he had never known so strong a wind. He took refuge in his faith; it assured him that tomorrow would be no worse, and might be better.

And in the morning the Lord let His face shine upon them. Warmed and cheered by a flood of sunlight, they put more of the mountains behind them; but before the day ended they faced new difficulties. For two weeks they were "completely lost," walled in on all sides, while they and their horses trembled from hunger and cold, and Brother Antes suffered "unendurable pain" from cold in a cut on his arm. But the Lord never forsook them. To their grateful joy He sent them three hunters, one of whom, Owen, invited them to his hut, cheered them and nursed Brother Antes' wound.

Resuming their journey with renewed courage, on December 27 they came upon "a body of land" in Anson County, about ten miles from the Yadkin. Spangenburg rejoiced, for at last they had reached the promised land, the terrestial paradise "reserved by the Lord for the Brethren."

Before them spread a wide prairie abounding with springs that "never fail in summer," fine creeks, stone for building purposes, and meadows even more beautiful than those they had seen around Nazareth, Pennsylvania. Spangenburg had fourteen sections surveyed—a total of 73,000 acres—measuring ten miles wide and eleven miles long. Later he added enough to increase the amount to nearly one hundred thousand acres. He named the tract Wachovia, because its well-watered fields reminded him of Wachau, a former estate of the Zinzendorf family in Austria which derived its name from *wach*, meaning stream, and *aue*, meaning meadow. Soon after it was surveyed Spangenburg returned to Pennsylvania and then sailed to England where he reported to Lord Granville. Presently this nobleman and James Hutton, Secretary of the Moravian Brotherhood, came to an agreement on financial terms and signed a deed of property.

The Brotherhood soon took steps to establish a colony on its newly acquired possession. It assigned this task to twelve Brethren who, under the leadership of Brother Gottlob Königsdorfer, left Bethlehem early in October 1753 with their goods stored in a large wagon drawn by six horses. During the expedition Brother Bernhard Adam Grube kept a diary which reveals on almost every page the simple Christian faith that, translated into resigned patience and unremitting industry, enabled them to surmount the obstacles they everywhere encountered. Water was scarce, food not easily obtained. The Brethren were often obliged to travel many miles before they could find pasturage for their horses; sometimes, if they were fortunate enough to pass by a farm, they bought oats—after they had helped the farmer thresh it. In the wilderness they often went without bread and meat and grain. Not always were they received with open arms. The folk they encountered were often suspicious of them or full of wonder at the sight of the huge wagon, strong horses and men bound for a distant region.

The Brethren usually rose before dawn and, buoyed by singing their prayers, traveled several miles in their lumbering wagon before they halted for their breakfast of broth. On this meager repast they journeyed until nightfall, overcoming incidents which varied with the condition of the road, the elevation of the ground and the state of the weather. Then they made camp, usually near a house or beside some stream, ate their supper, recounted their experiences, reverently heard Brother Gottlob say the evening service, and went to sleep in the care of Jesus. All of them reposed on the ground save Brother Gottlob who, ascending a little closer to heaven than his charges, "rested well" in his hammock between two trees.

Many and almost insurmountable were the difficulties that daily slowed their advance. Once their wagon proved too heavy for a bridge which collapsed just as the horses and the fore part of the vehicle were safely across. Sometimes their horses, straying during the night, delayed their early morning start. Sometimes the wagon, loaded with their belongings, was too heavy for the six horses to draw over a steep hill. Then they were obliged to carry the goods on their shoulders to the summit, sometimes in rain or snow, sometimes in bitter cold or oppressive heat. At the summit they faced the problem of descending. They carefully spragged the wheels of the wagon and held back with "all their might" by the tree trunk they had fastened to the rear—still they came down so rapidly that most of them lost their footing and rolled and tumbled pell-mell. Their discomfort left them unruffled. "No harm was done," wrote Brother Grube, "and we thanked the Lord that He had so graciously protected us, for it looked at times as if it could not possibly be done without accident, but in spite of stump and stone we got down safely."

As they crossed the James River, rain fell in torrents, drenching them to the skin. One night Brother Gottlob had to forgo the comfort of his hammock to help his charges dig trenches around their tent, which was in danger of being washed away by the rain-swollen streams. When the weather cleared, "we spent most of the day drying our blankets and mending and darning our stockings." The rain soon changed to snow. "The farther we went the more snow we found, and travel was difficult," for they followed the "Upper Road," which lay along the hills of the Blue Ridge in such an angle that "we could hardly keep the wagon from slipping over the edge of the mountain." Often they were obliged to cut down trees so that the wagon could pass, or clear the road before they could get by a bad place.

On November 17 they at last arrived on the fringe of Wachovia. They were grateful to find that, as ever, the Lord had provided for them. This time the celestial gift was in the form of a deserted cabin "large enough that we could all lie down around the walls." In this mansion, descended miraculously from heaven, they held a lovefeast in imitation of the early Christians while wolves padded and howled outside. And in that Pentecostal hour the tongue of fire descended upon Brother Gottlob, inspiring him to thank the Lord with this little poem:

> We hold arrival Lovefeast here,
>   In Carolina land,
> A company of Brethren true,
>   A little Pilgrim Band,
> Called by the Lord to be of those
>   Who through the whole world go,
> To bear Him witness everywhere
>   And naught but Jesus know.

The texts for the day were strikingly appropriate: "I know where thou dwellest," even in the wilderness. "Be ye of the same mind one with another," they prayed and then laid them down to rest. Brother Gottlob, as usual, hung his hammock above their heads.

Soon Brother Gottlob returned to Bethlehem, leaving Brother Jacob Loesch in charge of the colony. This resolute man soon sent his charges to explore and clear the land. It proved both beautiful and fertile. Near a clear creek which flowed through a wooded plain surrounded by low hills, they cleared with their crude implements over eight acres on which they planted winter wheat, flax, millet, barley, oats, buckwheat, turnips, cotton and tobacco. Later, at the request of Brother Hans Martin Kalberlahn, a Norwegian who acted as the colony's physician, they added such medicinal herbs as fennel, caraway, parsley, poppy, sage and anise.

The next two years were brimful of work. They cut roads, raised vegetables and grain, built houses and shops and made journeys that covered hundreds of miles.

But they devoted their best hours to the herculean task of building a mill a mile downstream. They felled giant trees; they quarried and shaped and dressed suitable millstones; they built a dam; they forged metal bearings for the wheel; they constructed the race. And before the end of their second year in Wachovia the mill was grinding away. Around it sprang up a hamlet which the Brethren called Bethabara in memory of that place on the Jordan where John baptized Jesus. Soon roads were leading to it from all directions; the forest receded as Bethabara grew; a tannery, a pottery, a carpenter shop rose among the dwellings. During the French and Indian War the Brethren welcomed refugees and soldiers from both sides.

The Brethren always set a bowl or plate for hungry travelers. And Kalberlahn never denied his medical or surgical skill to any ailing person who was given lodging in the "strangers' house" until he or she was well enough to return home. But Kalberlahn did not confine his unresting duties to Bethabara; he traveled on horseback as far as a hundred miles to deliver a baby or treat a case of smallpox or mend a broken arm.

Once, on New Year's Day, he became a hero of a different sort. The Brethren discovered fire on the roof of their house, and Kalberlahn, rushing to help put it out, severely burned his feet. On the same day a man was injured on the head while cutting down a large tree. The Brethren carried him to Kalberlahn who, despite his own suffering, wasted no time in treating his patient. The skull was not fractured, and the man recovered before his physician.

Nothing epitomizes the Moravian spirit better than the short entry in Spangenburg's diary for Christmas Eve 1753. "We had a little love-feast; then near the Christ child we had our first Christmas Eve in North Carolina, and rested in peace in his hope and faith." In the surrounding forest wolves howled and panthers screamed throughout the night.

Moving with the Germans in the Old West were immigrants from the British Isles: English, Scotch Highlanders, Irish, Welsh, and Scotch-Irish. Among them were the ancestors of such famous Americans as Daniel Boone, James Robertson, Thomas Jefferson, Davy Crockett, Sam Houston, John Caldwell Calhoun, James Knox Polk, Jefferson Davis, Abraham Lincoln and Stonewall Jackson. Representing the militant and expansive movement of American life, these names foretell such epic achievements as the Louisiana Purchase, the Lewis and Clark Expedition, the annexation of Texas, the Mexican War and the acquisition of California and Oregon. Andrew Jackson and Abraham Lincoln personify such frontier ideals as universal manhood suffrage and social equality for all men.

The most numerous and significant of the British immigrants in the history of the American frontier were the Scotch-Irish. These were the descendants of Scotch Highlanders, Lowland Scots and Englishmen who had migrated in successive groups to that region of northern Ireland known as Ulster. The earliest group settled, with the permission of James I, on the huge estates of the outlawed earls of Tyrone and Tyrconnel. The fertility of the soil, the favorable terms by which land could be bought and the advantages derived from a number of circumstances attracted other groups to Ulster until, by the end of the seventeenth century, that region became predominantly Scotch-Irish.

Zealous Presbyterians, they built many fine churches of their denomination, while they converted a number of remote towns into renowned emporiums. Their commercial success, however, eventually caused their undoing. Their exports of cattle became so large that they excited the alarm of English landowners who complained that the competition of the Ulster pastures had lowered English rents. Confronted with this condition, Parliament felt obliged to pass laws absolutely prohibiting the importation to England from Ulster of all cattle, sheep, swine, beef, pork, bacon, mutton and even butter and cheese.

The Scotch traders also complained, forcing Parliament in 1667 to boycott Irish cattle, beef, all kinds of grain and, subsequently, horses. When even these repressive measures failed to allay English resentment, Parliament passed acts in 1670 and again in 1696 excluding Scotch-Irish vessels from the American trade and prohibiting any importation directly from the colonies to northern Ireland.

In the face of this restraint, the Scotch-Irish found an outlet for their industrial activity in manufacturing. Even there Parliament dealt them a staggering blow. In 1699 it passed an act prohibiting them from exporting manufactured wool to any country whatever. The crushing blow came five years later. An act excluded Presbyterians from all civil and military offices and forbade their ministers from celebrating marriages on pain of heavy fines and imprisonment.

Such were the tyrannies that had impelled the Scotch-Irish to seek new homes in America. Through Lewes and Newcastle, through Philadelphia and Boston, they moved in steady streams up the Mohawk and Cherry valley frontiers, and then down to Pennsylvania. Like the Germans, they were too poor to buy lands. Instead, they sought isolated spots on the frontier, where they squatted unmolested or defied the few rent collectors who invaded their domains. When they were challenged for titles they replied that Pennsylvania had solicited for colonists and that they had come accordingly. They even squatted on Conestoga Manor, a tract of 15,000 acres which the Penns had reserved for themselves. When they were told to move on they replied that this would be contrary to the "laws of God and nature" and that so much land should not be idle "while so many Christians wanted it to work on and to raise their bread." And they stayed. Indeed, they even encouraged others to join them. In 1725 one of them wrote to a friend in Ulster that every member of his family was pleased with the colony "and wod If we were in Ireland again come here Directly it being the best country for working folk & Tradesmen of any in the world."

Toward the middle of the century the Scotch-Irish began to move westward in thousands, following a trail that paralleled the banks of Octorara Creek and then turning northward along the Susquehanna and its tributaries. Finding that the Germans had already occupied the best lands, they had to satisfy themselves with the hillier country beside the Juniata River and west of the Cumberland Valley. By the middle of the century these bold and indigent strangers had occupied the whole mountainous region as far as the frontier post of Bedford.

After they had taken up the lands of interior Pennsylvania they turned southward into the free lands of Virginia and North Carolina, into the valleys of the Shenandoah, the Yadkin and the Catawba. In a single year more than four hundred Scotch-Irish families with horse wagons and cattle settled in the back country of North Carolina. The immigration was so great that the colony more than doubled its population within twenty years.

The Scotch-Irish represent a striking example of the powerful influence which hereditary and environmental factors exert on the psychological make-up of a people. Their ancestors had been compelled to hunt over perilous terrain and sometimes in rigorous weather in order to supplement their inadequate food supply. At the same time they often engaged in sanguinary feuds which family hate or a mutual desire for plunder or revenge kept alive from generation to generation. This pattern of life developed in them a self-reliance and a physical endurance acquired by their descendants, who were thus enabled to respond with admirable effectiveness to the formidable challenge of the American frontier. They had undying confidence in their own manhood. In action they were as bold and intrepid as the Romans; in Indian fighting they won the admiration even of the Shawnee, who acknowledged them as superiors.

The Scotch-Irish also acquired a defiant, aggressive and grasping nature which compensated for feelings of insecurity and inferiority doubtless engendered by centuries of precarious existence. They seldom neglected an opportunity to better themselves. They kept the Sabbath and everything else they could lay their hands on. And they manifested an indomitable spirit of personal independence which impelled them to resist any encroachment on their individual rights. They were impatient of the slow process of the law, resentful of governmental restraint imposed on them without their consent. While they supported royalty with their heads, their hearts desired that the people should be the ultimate repository of political power.

Though life had made them hard-boiled and sometimes cruel, they yearned, like the rest of humanity, for society and sympathy, sentiments which circumstances compelled them to gratify in their own hearthstones for it was there that

. . . the mother and children, under an ever-present sense of their dependence upon his protection and counsel, gathered around the husband and father, as their hero and their oracle, with mingled emotions of love, gratitude, veneration, and pride; while he, in return, regarded the protégés of his prowess with those feelings of tenderness natural to the sacred relation he sustained toward them, deepened and intensified by a realization of their absolute dependence upon his strength and their confidence in his courage.

This strong feeling of domestic affection—this clannishness, strengthened by time and constant necessity of mutual assistance —was one of the traits of the Scotch-Irish pioneers that spelled their success.

Originally they were stanch followers of John Knox, though later in the American wilderness many of them found the Baptist or Methodist faiths better suited to their religious needs. The bleak surroundings—which had engendered in their Scotch forefathers a disdain for political authority—incited in them a profound feeling of superstitious awe.

Their rude imaginations became impressed by the viewless presence of a vast, invisible, intangible, mysterious being, whose character they invested with the same savage attributes as their own. They saw his terrible chariot in the black mass of whirling clouds, and heard his angry voice in the roaring storm. They caught the gleam of his vengeful weapon in the lightning's bolt that shivered the gnarled oak, and saw the outpouring of his omnipotent rage in the rushing torrent that dashed the granite buttress of the mountain from its base; and when the wintry night wind shrieked its wailing dirge around their lonely hovels, they told their children, in the subdued tones of ignorant awe, of his wrath which they could not appease, and his power which they could not withstand.

Inspired by the preaching of John Knox, who understood their psychological needs, they repudiated prelacy and papacy alike for a religion in which no minister or other ecclesiastic could be foisted on a congregation without its own consent, and in which not even its humblest member could be deprived of any congregational right without the privilege of appealing to its highest tribunal which was composed of representatives chosen by the people. Thus they embraced popular government in religion as they had in politics. Their stubborn attachment to democratic principles inspired the saying among them that, when God made the Scotch-Irish, He put a bone in them that never lets the knee bend save to Himself.

In Ulster they had found themselves pressed on every side by politically powerful Episcopalians and by numerically superior Roman Catholics. These circumstances engendered in them a hatred for everything English and a dread of Catholicism. More than ever, they conformed only to the Word, and even this they handled in the rude, practical manner so characteristic of them. Typical of their ministers was the Reverend Matthew Clark of Kilrea, a veteran of the siege of Londonderry. Once, preaching from Philippians 4:13, the Reverend Clark began with the words: "'I can do all things.' Ay, can ye, Paul? I'll bet a dollar o' that!" Whereupon he drew a Spanish dollar from his pocket and placed it beside his Bible on the pulpit. Then, with a look of surprise, he continued: "Stop! Let's see what else Paul says: 'I can do all things through Christ, which strengthened me.' Ay, sae can I, Paul; I draw my bet!" And he returned the dollar to his pocket.

The reactions of the German and the Scotch-Irish immigrants to their experiences determined the nature of American character. Because they had been oppressed they believed in freedom; because they were underprivileged they believed in social and political equality. They resented the leisurely life and wealth of the East. They hated what the East championed—class distinction and privilege—and championed what the East denied them—universal manhood suffrage, social equality and religious toleration which, incidentally, spawned new creeds. Adaptability was the price of survival: they became emphatically practical, versatile and ingeniously mechanical. They "preferred the useful to the beautiful and even required the beautiful to be useful."

The poverty and dangers they shared in common made them equals; they developed no sense of superiority one over the other. Each settler, therefore, respected his neighbor's property and religious beliefs—in principle if not always in practice. At the same time their feelings of inferiority and insecurity made them bold, persistent, aggressive and boastful, while their frustrations engendered a restlessness that plunged them into constant and feverish activity. They sought quick and direct and forceful solutions to problems that required reflection and patience. Yet their response to their environment converted these shortcomings into the very virtues they needed to survive and succeed on the frontier. And there they expressed, in word and deed, their unmistakably American character.

The French

and Indian War

For sixty-five years France and England had warred intermittently with all the venom of business rivals over possession of the territory between the Mississippi River and the Allegheny Mountains. The prizes they sought included fisheries, land and the fur trade for which they fought the first three of the wars in vain. Now, in 1754, they resumed hostilities in the French and Indian War, which, in its broader European phase, is known as the Seven Years' War. The American phase began as a dispute over possession of the Ohio Valley and gradually involved a large part of North America.

The French claims to the interior of the continent originated in 1671 when Daumont de Saint Luggon, swinging aloft his sword in the presence of awed Indian allies, proclaimed the sovereignty of France of "all the countries, rivers, lakes, and streams . . . both those which have been discovered and those which may be discovered hereafter, in all their strength and breadth, bounded on one side by the seas of the North and the West, and the other by the South Sea." Coincidentally, Batts and Fallam a few months later proclaimed the same territory for England. Thus with a few words a Frenchman and two Englishmen were instrumental in plunging their countries and several others into a series of intercolonial wars which in the end converted such widely scattered regions as the plains of India, the hinterland of Prussia and the forests of North America into bloody battlefields and which at the peace table changed the course of world history.

In 1673 Louis Joliet, the son of a wagonmaker of Quebec, and

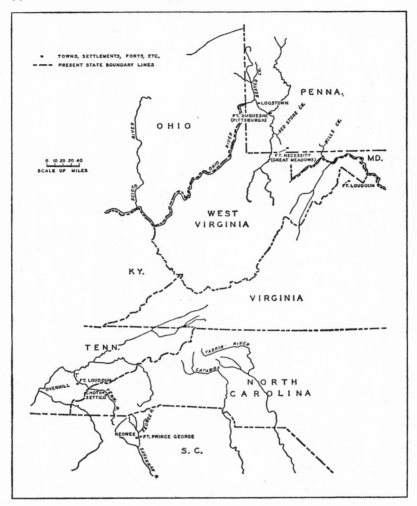

Jacques Marquette, a Jesuit priest, descended the Mississippi from the mouth of the Wisconsin to a point beyond the mouth of the Ohio and planted France in the heart of North America. A few years later La Salle dreamed of securing the region for his king by building across the Lake Country and down the Mississippi a chain of forts which would hem in the English colonies to the east and at the same time would serve as depositories of the royal fur trade.

When La Salle's dream faded with his tragic death on the banks of the Trinity, his mantle fell on the chivalrous shoulders of Pierre La Moyne, Sieur d'Iberville, who with 200 men in 1699 built Fort Maurepas on Biloxi Bay. For some years the impoverished young Louisiana colony was run unsuccessfully by a wealthy merchant, Antoine de Crozat, and then by John Law's glittering bubble, the Company of the Indies. Eventually returned to the Crown, it began to grow strong and to prosper despite the opposition of the Montreal merchants who prevailed upon the Crown to export all furs from the upper Mississippi through the St. Lawrence rather than down the river.

Meanwhile, in 1718, on a malarious plain infested by snakes and alligators, John Baptiste La Moyne, Sieur de Bienville, brother of Iberville, laid the foundations of the present metropolis of New Orleans. Within twenty years the golden lilies of France were waving over the territory from New Orleans northward to the Ohio and the Missouri. Thousands of settlers planted themselves along the Mississippi, establishing Fort de Chartres in 1720, St. Philippe in 1723, Prairie du Rocher in 1733 and Vincennes—which was to figure prominently in the campaigns of George Rogers Clark—in 1734. On the Alabama River the French built Fort Toulouse to establish trade with the Creek Indians.

By the middle of the eighteenth century France began to realize her dream of an unbroken empire stretching from New Orleans to Quebec and fortified by a chain of strongholds and trading posts connecting fur centers on the Mississippi with those on the St. Lawrence. Thanks to her skill and diligence, she was confident that she had stemmed the swelling tide of English colonization. At Niagara a fort commanded the entrance to the heart of North America. One at Detroit guarded the territory from Lake Erie to the north. Another at St. Mary's stood sentinel to warn of any hostile approach to Lake Superior. Still another at Michilimackinac guarded the narrow channel between Lake Huron and Lake Michigan. A fort at Green Bay and one at St. Joseph debarred these two routes to the Mississippi by the Wisconsin and Illinois rivers. Fort Ouiatenon on the Wabash and Fort Miami on the Maumee protected the trading highway from Lake Erie to the Ohio. Kaskaskia and Cahokia in the Illinois Country were armed emporiums of the Indian trade.

France had now only to prevent the English from overrunning the Ohio Valley whose strategic importance she had realized as early as 1721 when her difficulties with the Fox Indians forced her traders to shift their routes from the portage between the Wisconsin and Illinois to that between the Maumee and Wabash. They discovered that the new route shortened considerably the distance between the Canadian and the Louisiana settlements.

The first British traders in the Ohio Valley were perhaps Carolinians and New Yorkers, whose visits were sporadic and inconsequential. Next came Pennsylvanians who had followed Shawnee and Delawares in their migration westward to Kittanning and Logstown, near Economy, Beaver County, Pennsylvania. For deer, elk, buffalo and beaver skins the Pennsylvania traders exchanged rum, guns, gunpowder, lead, lace, thread, jewelry, women's stockings and other articles which they had bought from such merchants as Jeremiah Warder of Philadelphia and Joseph Simon and Levi Andrew Levy of Lancaster.

Thanks to their aggressive and enterprising leader, George Croghan, a Dubliner who had migrated to America in 1731, the Pennsylvanians soon dominated the trade in the upper Ohio Valley. Croghan shortly opened trading centers at Pine Creek, Logstown and Beaver Creek, while his men with their pack horses came and went on trails that spread out like the sticks of a fan to the country of the Miami Indians and that of the Illinois Indians at the mouth of the Scioto. Croghan had reached French domain, but he was still unsatisfied. In 1748 he climaxed his prosperity by building a palisaded fort at the Miami village of Pickawillany, deep in French territory.

Virginia claimed the Ohio Valley under the charter of 1609 and by the Batts and Fallam discovery of 1671. Many of her leading citizens were resentful of what they regarded as the encroachments of Pennsylvania traders on her domain. To forestall them as well as to stem the French advance, Colonel Thomas Lee and twelve others, including Lawrence and Augustine Washington, half brothers of George Washington, George Mason and John Hanbury, a Quaker merchant residing in London, petitioned the Board of Trade in England to organize a trading and speculating enterprise which became known as the Ohio Company.

Anxious to strengthen English control in a region which France also claimed, the Board of Trade approved the request and granted the company a tract of 200,000 acres free of quitrents for ten years, and promised it an additional award of 300,000 acres on condition of settling a hundred families on the original tract and of building and garrisoning a fort for their protection. Governor Robert Dinwiddie, who became a member of the company, hoped it would serve as a powerful weapon in checking the French advance while it encouraged British progress. He knew that it would secure a good share of the Indian trade which hitherto had been monopolized by Croghan and his men.

Moreover, possession by the company of a tract of land in a region disputed among the colonies would strengthen the claims of Virginia. To facilitate its success, Dinwiddie planned to reconcile the southern and northern Indians, who, though allies of the English, were constantly at war with each other. The company failed to secure the required number of immigrants, but it became a keen competitor of the Pennsylvania traders. Its agent, Christopher Gist, established a storehouse at Wills Creek, now Cumberland, Maryland, and explored much of the region.

France wasted no time in taking steps to regain lost ground. In 1749 La Galissonière, the French governor, sent Pierre Joseph Céloron de Blainville to renew possession of the Ohio Country, to ascertain the attitude of the Indians and to expel the British traders. In pursuance of these aims, Céloron descended the Ohio, burying at important points along the river lead plates claiming the region for France. This exploit aroused the indignation of the Indians, who interpreted it as evidence that the French meant to deprive them of the region. They therefore sided with the British traders with whom Céloron left, for the English governors, messages warning them against future trespasses in French territory. When the governors ignored these warnings, the French in 1752 established forts at Presque Isle, on the present site of Erie, Pennsylvania, farther south on French Creek at Waterford and at Fort Venango—now Franklin, Pennsylvania—at the junction of French Creek and the Allegheny River.

On learning of these activities, Dinwiddie sent a small party under twenty-one-year-old George Washington to warn the French that they were on Virginia territory. The party, which included Christopher Gist as interpreter, made its way to Fort Le Boeuf at Waterford where the French commander, Legardeur de St. Pierre, received Washington courteously but told him that in taking possession of the region he was merely following the orders of his superior. After a similar experience at Fort Venango, Washington returned home to report that force alone would drive out the French.

Dinwiddie promptly struck back. In January 1754 he sent a construction crew of thirty-three men to forestall the French by building a fort at the forks of the Ohio. Three months later the governor, thinking that the fort was completed, sent Washington with 150 men to garrison it. At Wills Creek the young Virginian met the construction crew, who informed him that on April 17 a large force of Frenchmen had landed before the unfinished fort, planted cannon against it and summoned the ensign in charge, Edward Ward, to surrender. Ward had complied and had been permitted to depart with his men. The French demolished the unfinished fort and began a more elaborate one which they named Fort Duquesne in honor of the governor of Canada.

Washington regarded the seizure of a King's fort by the threat of cannon as an overt act of war. Henceforth he acted as though hostilities between England and France had begun. Though he knew he was greatly outnumbered, he decided to march against the enemy, 140 miles away. On May 24 he reached Great Meadows, a grassy valley where traders pastured their pack horses. Considering the place "a charming field for an encounter," he set his men to throw up an entrenchment while he sent out scouts to search the forest for French troops. They found none.

Two days later Christopher Gist, who had recently settled on Laurel Hill, near present Uniontown, Pennsylvania, brought word that during his absence on the previous day fifty Frenchmen had intended to burn his house but had been dissuaded by the two Indians left in charge of it. Washington vainly sent seventy-five men to find the enemy. That evening a friendly chief named Half King who was encamped near by with a few warriors sent Washington word that he had found the tracks of two men, presumably made by French scouts, leading into the forest. Washington resolved to find the enemy himself. Leaving the main force to guard Great Meadows against the possibility of a surprise attack, he led forty men toward Half King's wigwams. Through heavy rain, through a forest "as black as pitch," they moved along a path so narrow that they sometimes lost it and sometimes tumbled over one another in the dark. When at sunrise they reached their destination, they numbered only thirty-three; seven of their comrades had been lost and left behind in the forest.

Washington and Half King decided to proceed against the French without delay. Following the tracks of the French scouts found the day before, they pushed into the forest until they came to a rocky hollow or quarry in which the French had concealed themselves. In the ensuing fight, which lasted less than fifteen minutes, the young French commander, Coulon de Jumonville, and nine of his comrades were killed. One was wounded, and the remaining twenty-one in the French party threw down their guns. Some of the Indians knocked the wounded on the head and then scalped them. One Englishman was killed and three, including an officer, were wounded.

Expecting to be attacked any time by a superior force, Washington returned with his prisoners and men to Great Meadows and sent to his superior, Colonel Joshua Fry, for reinforcements. At the same time he began to build Fort Necessity, a simple square enclosure with a knee-deep trench. While this work progressed Christopher Gist brought word from Wills Creek that Fry had been killed in a fall from his horse. Thus Washington, at twenty-two years of age, found himself the commander of the expedition.

The three companies of Virginians left in Wills Creek now joined him, bringing nine small guns and the swivels on which to place them so that they could be fired in any direction. Next arrived a company of South Carolina regulars under Captain James Mackay. Because he had been commissioned by the King,

Mackay thought himself superior to any officer commissioned by the governor. Insisting that his command represented a separate force, he chose his own camp site and refused to exchange salutes and countersigns. Washington discreetly avoided a controversy; instead, he calmly assembled his Virginians and began a road to Red Stone Creek, where he hoped to build a fort and hold it until the arrival of reinforcements should enable him to march to the forks of the Ohio.

Washington advanced very slowly with his men and wagons and swivels to Gist's where he held a council with forty Indians who warned him that he would soon be attacked by overwhelming numbers. Their curiosity in examining the fort and their expostulations in discussing the French, however, aroused Washington's suspicions; and when, despite their many avowals of friendship for the English, they hurriedly retired, he realized that they were spying for the French. Even Half King deserted him. Finding that Washington had no presents to give him and had very meager provisions for his warriors and their families, he moved off with them on the pretext that he was not in good health. Washington had to use his own inexperienced men as scouts to prevent surprise by the French.

The next few days brought him disheartening news. He heard that the French were to march from Fort Duquesne with 800 white troops and 400 Indians. Washington, accepting this unfounded rumor as reliable information and fearing an attack might come at any moment, held another council in which he and his officers agreed to retreat to Great Meadows, where they felt confident they would have a better chance of victory. Washington had neither bread nor bacon and only a quart of salt to preserve his scant meat supply. His retreat would give him better access to needed supplies while it would force the French to traverse thirteen more miles of bad road over mountain country before they could strike at him.

The task before him required the utmost of his fittest men. Washington had, a few days before, sent back to Great Meadows all but two of the wagons and most of the horses to convoy expected supplies. The two wagons, a few scraggy horses, and the officers' mounts were all he had to move the nine swivels, the ammunition and the baggage. Furthermore, he could count only on his Virginians, for Mackay forbade his men to lift a finger either in clearing the road or in dragging the swivels.

When Washington found that the wagons did not suffice for the ammunition, he ordered his mount to be loaded with powder and shot. His officers quickly followed suit. Then, in sweltering heat, the retreat began. His strongest men dragged the swivels over the roughest road of the Alleghenies. Over rut and rock and stump they pulled like dray horses, every grade a despair, every furlong a torture, in a journey which, though short in mileage, seemed endless. Two days later, bedraggled and hungry and exhausted, they reached Great Meadows—not to rest but to strengthen their rampart to meet the attack they hourly expected.

It soon came. At dawn on July 3 a sentinel, shot in the heel—perhaps by an Indian scout of the French—alerted the fort. Common danger drove Virginians and Mackay's regulars together for the first time. Aroused from sleep they sprang from their beds while their commanders ordered them to prepare for action. A heavy rain was falling as they slipped into the trenches. The French, yelling and firing aimlessly, charged 500 strong from the edge of the forest. Their leader was the dead Jumonville's brother, Coulon de Villiers, who, because he burned with revenge, had been sent from Fort Duquesne with orders to capture Washington and drive the English from the territory.

From tree and stump, from stone and bush, the French poured a withering fire at the defenders, at their horses and cows, and even at their dogs, in desperate endeavor to deprive them of transportation and food. Hour after hour the rain whipped down. It churned the trenches into soft mud, soaked the cartridge boxes, half drowned the soldiers and almost silenced the muskets and swivels. It showed no more respect for the French who—unable to use their arms effectively, distrusting their Indian allies and fearing the arrival of enemy reinforcements—toward dusk asked for a parley.

At first Washington, suspecting a scheme to get into and examine the trenches, refused. But when the French asked him to send an officer to receive a proposal, he hesitated no longer. Negotiations conducted by Captain Jacob van Braam, a Dutchman who understood the French language imperfectly, eventually led to terms of capitulation. The English were granted honors of war and were permitted to march out with drum beating, taking with them one of the swivels and their property. They were protected against insult from the French and their Indian friends. The prisoners taken in the tussle with Jumonville were freed, and two officers, Van Braam and Robert Stobo, were retained as hostages. Of Washington's 300 fighting men, thirteen had been killed and fifty-four wounded. Mackay left no record of his losses. Villiers, returning triumphantly to Fort Duquesne, claimed the battle cost him only twenty men in killed and wounded.

Since the Indians had killed the horses, the defeated men began to march back to Wills Creek on foot on the morning of July 4, leaving the swivel and most of their baggage behind and carrying their wounded and sick on litters or on their backs. The Indians pursued and plundered them, destroying Dr. Craik's medicine chest and thus preventing him from effectively treating the sick and wounded. Three or four days later they arrived in Wills Creek. Washington and Mackay went to Williamsburg where they informed Dinwiddie of their defeat. The governor, blaming it on the delay of the regulars and North Carolinians and on the inability of Croghan to provide promised supplies, upheld Washington and made plans to prosecute the struggle with greater vigor. The French and Indian War had openly begun.

At the beginning of the war Governor Dinwiddie, in conjunction with Governor William Dobbs of North Carolina, took measures to convert the Indians of the region from potential enemies to active allies. In recent years the Cherokee and Catawbas had been more friendly toward the English than toward the French, though they resented both as encroachers of their country. The whack of the white man's ax or the crack of his rifle was like a knell warning them of the eventual doom of their race. They grew more and more resentful with every buffalo the white man killed, every tree he felled, every acre he cleared, every cabin he built.

In the summer of 1755 they learned that General Edward

Braddock, starting for Fort Duquesne with 1,400 redcoats, 450 Virginia militiamen under Washington and 50 Indian scouts, had met tragic defeat at the hands of 600 Frenchmen and 200 Indians. The tribes of the Old West quickly sided with the victors in an effort to rid themselves of the English encroachers once and for all. In the fall of 1755 Dinwiddie and Dobbs decided to gain the Indians' friendship and enlist their support by sending commissioners to formulate treaties with them.

The Virginia commissioners, Colonel William Byrd, third of that name, and Colonel Peter Randolph, met the Cherokee at the Broad River in North Carolina and delivered a message from Dinwiddie warning them against the French:

I advise you to be on your Guard against them, their Speeches are made up of Falsehoods and unjust Reports, let none of them remain among you, and by no Means allow them to build any Forts on the [Tennessee River] in the upper Cherokee Country, for their Intentions are with evil Design against you and your brothers the English.

The Cherokee chief was Attakullakulla, the most celebrated and influential Indian among all the tribes then known. He was a mere wisp of a man of about eighty, who weighed little more than a pound for each year of his life. The white men called him Little Carpenter, because his deep, artful and ingeniously diplomatic gifts enabled him to fit the pieces of a treaty together as skillfully as a carpenter fits pieces of wood. To Dinwiddie's advice Little Carpenter replied with a threat: "If no Steps are taken for our Security, the French will extinguish the Friendly Fires between us." In return for a present of goods and the promise of a strong fort, Little Carpenter pledged four hundred warriors within forty days.

In the late spring of 1756 the North Carolina commissioners, Chief Justice Henley and Captain Hugh Waddell, met King Heygler of the Catawbas at Salisbury. Following the example of the Cherokee, Heygler petitioned Governor Dobbs to send him ammunition and to build his people a strong fort to secure "our old men, women and children when we turn out to fight the

Enemies on their Coming." Henley agreed to provide the ammunition and promised to urge his superior to have the fort built
as soon as possible. Whereupon Heygler, a master of dry irony,
made another request:

I desire a stop may be put to the selling of strong liquors by
the white people to my people especially near the Indian nation.
If the White people make strong drinks, let them sell it to one
another, or drink it in their own families. This will avoid a great
deal of mischief which otherwise will happen from my people
getting drunk and quarreling with the white people. I have no
strong prisons like you to confine them for it. Our only way is
to put them under ground and all these [he pointed proudly to
his warriors] will be ready to do that to those who shall deserve it.

That spring and summer Dinwiddie and Dobbs concerted their
plans to build the promised forts. Captain Waddell with a construction crew was sent to the Catawba country where, near the
mouth of the South Fork of the Catawba River, he set his men to
build a fort for that tribe; but before the building was completed
Dobbs ordered him to discharge his men and return home.
French agents and South Carolina traders who desired to retain
the Catawba trade for their own colony had prevailed upon King
Heygler to request Dobbs to desist from building the fort. Some
years later South Carolina built for the Catawbas a fort at the
mouth of Line Creek, on the east bank of the Catawba.

Meanwhile Dinwiddie had sent Major Andrew Lewis with
sixty workmen to Chota, the chief town of the overhill Cherokee,
where Little Carpenter gave him a cordial welcome. Major Lewis
immediately began construction of a fort; but the nearer it approached completion the cooler grew Little Carpenter's friendship until he began to equivocate about sending the warriors he
had pledged. The truth was that he had momentarily opened
his ears to French agents who promised him goods free of charge
and succeeded in convincing him that the English had come
with irons to tie his people hand and foot, enslave the women
and children and take the Cherokee lands for themselves. Lewis
suspected that Little Carpenter had formed some scheme against
the English. He pictured the Cherokee chief as "a great villain"

who would "do everything in his power to Serve the French."

One day Lewis walked inadvertently into a great council of the headmen of the overhill towns. The assembled Indians had agreed to write to Captain Robert Demere, who was coming with several hundred soldiers to garrison the fort, ordering him to return to Charleston. Speaking of the few soldiers who had already arrived, Little Carpenter heatedly said that he "would take their Guns, and give them to his young men to hunt with, and as to their clothes they would soon be worn out and then their skins would be tanned, and be of the same colour as theirs, and that they should live among them as Slaves." Lewis reminded him of the treaty solemnly negotiated the previous spring. In reply Little Carpenter and other chiefs requested Lewis to tell Dinwiddie that "they [the Cherokee] had taken up the Hatchet against all Nations that were Enemies to the English." This subterfuge failed to impress Lewis. He was not surprised when he could secure only ten Cherokee—seven men and three women—to accompany him back to Virginia. In the fall of the same year the fort was completed.

Meanwhile South Carolina had begun a fort in the Cherokee country, apparently to prevent the wavering Cherokee from yielding to the wishes of the French. The fort—named in honor of Lord Loudoun, commander-in-chief of all the English forces in America—stood on the left bank of the Little Tennessee, seven miles from the Virginia fort. Its completion in the early summer of 1757 gave the English control of the surrounding region. The commander of the garrison, Captain Paul Demere, brother of the commander of the fort at Chota, won the friendship of the Cherokee by giving them numerous presents, by rewarding them for scalps and by constantly assuring them of safety from French attacks. Out of gratitude many of the Cherokee joined the Virginians against the French while smaller groups participated in raids against the French and French Indians on the Ohio River.

By this time the French and Indian War had widened into the world conflict known as the Seven Years' War. The declaration of war in May 1756 brought Russia, Austria and Poland to the side of France while Frederick the Great of Prussia stood with

England. By entrusting the European phase of the war to the efficient armies of her ally, England was able to concentrate her forces against the French colonies in North America and India. In the next two years, however, nearly all her military efforts ended in defeat, thanks to Lord Loudoun. He spent much time in writing dispatches he never sent and, in the opinion of one who knew him, was like St. George on a tavern sign—always on horseback but never moving on.

On the contrary, the enterprising but poorly supplied French commander, the Marquis de Montcalm, made most of every opportunity. In the summer of 1756 he swooped down with 3,000 men on Fort Oswego, an important key to the Indian trade on the Great Lakes, and after storming it for three days forced the garrison of 3,000 men to surrender with considerable supplies. In the following summer Montcalm struck at Fort William Henry, at the southern end of Lake George, forced it to surrender, burned it and returned to his headquarters at Fort Ticonderoga. A year later the French commander won another great success when he defended the fort against 13,000 Redcoats. The soul of the British force expired, however, when General William Howe was killed. Under cover of darkness, General James Abercromby withdrew, counting 1,944 killed, wounded and missing. Montcalm lost only 377. The year ended with the Indians spreading desolation along the Mohawk Valley and sending the settlers scurrying to the safety of Albany and Schenectady.

Gradually the martial picture changed. Thanks to the vigorous efforts of William Pitt, who had dominated the British government since the fall of 1757, England easily wrested victory from France. So enthusiastic was Parliament in voting sums for the prosecution of the war that, said Walpole, "You would as soon hear 'No' from an old maid as from the House of Commons." Pitt speedily removed supine and incompetent commanders who owed their positions to birth or prestige and replaced them with such gifted and vigorous young men as Jeffrey Amherst and James Wolfe. Thereafter England marched from victory to victory.

The harmony between the frontiersmen and the Cherokee was of short duration. As they marched homeward from military service in the spring of 1758, a small group of young Cherokee braves seized some stray horses. The owners, hastily forming a party, went in pursuit of the thieves and killed twelve or fourteen of them. The relatives of the slain sought revenge by killing a number of settlers in various places on the Virginia frontier. Little Carpenter—now pro-English with the advent of English victories—protesting his friendship for the English, cautioned his people against thinking ill of them and disavowed the crimes in the name of the Cherokee nation.

Eventually his advice was accepted and peace returned to the frontier. Some Cherokee, including Little Carpenter, showed their friendship for the English by joining the expedition which General John Forbes had prepared against Fort Duquesne. But these warriors quickly became dissatisfied. The whites insulted them as they passed through Virginia, and General Forbes himself treated them harshly. Little Carpenter complained that the general had not furnished them "so much as with a little paint." Small wonder that two days before Fort Duquesne fell Little Carpenter and nine other Cherokee deserted the expedition. Forbes had them pursued, disarmed and sent home.

In the spring of 1759 Governor William Henry Lyttelton of South Carolina heard that Cherokee had attacked several white settlements in the colony and had renewed negotiations with the French. Late in April a party of young men from the village of Settico fell upon North Carolina settlers in the region of the Yadkin and Catawba rivers and returned with twenty scalps. Lyttelton then sent Little Carpenter a reminder of his pledges of friendship toward the English and demanded satisfaction for the murders committed by the young men of Settico. This message was delivered at a conference between many of the overhill warriors and Captain Demere in the guardhouse of Fort Loudoun.

Little Carpenter replied that he was powerless to secure the arrest of the headmen of Settico, because they were kinsmen to Oconostota, one of the most influential chiefs of the tribe. Oconostota was a wrinkled old man who had been "president" of his nation for over half a century and who, as agent and envoy extraordinary to the King of England, had once crossed the "big river." In London he had dined with George III and had successfully completed his mission. The high standing he enjoyed had gained him the confidence and good faith of his people in all and everything he would advance in support of their rightful claims. In view of these circumstances Little Carpenter could promise nothing save that he would do his best to maintain peace between his people and the English.

So long as Little Carpenter remained in the Indian towns he succeeded in restraining the young men from making further attacks. But during his absence in September they again went on the warpath and severed communication between Fort Loudoun and Fort Prince George, which had been built in 1753 near the important Indian village of Keowee. When news of these new attacks reached Lyttelton, he immediately fitted out an expedition to compel the Cherokee to keep peace. On October 26 he gathered an army of 1,500 men and proceeded from Charleston to Fort Prince George, where Little Carpenter and other warriors met him and professed their desire for peace. In reply the governor demanded that the Cherokee surrender the twenty-four young men suspected of having committed the recent crimes. If they rejected his wishes, he said, he would destroy their warriors and starve their women and children.

Little Carpenter strained every effort to meet Lyttelton's demand, but he was able to bring to the fort only two of the wanted men. The rest either had been rescued by their friends or had fled across the mountains. Meanwhile smallpox and desertions had so reduced Lyttelton's army that he was constrained to reach a satisfactory settlement with Little Carpenter. He requested the chief to surrender twenty-two men, saying that a hostage would be confined in the fort for each one undelivered. Moreover, he demanded that the English traders be permitted to return to their homes in the Cherokee towns and that all Frenchmen who ventured into Cherokee country be killed. Having confirmed these terms by treaty, Lyttelton set out for Charleston, leaving as hostages twenty-two of the most prominent of the Indians who had accompanied him, regardless of his promise to give them safe passage back to their homes.

The Cherokee saw no reason why innocent men should be imprisoned and requested Captain Demere to release them. When Demere refused, they attacked the fort but were driven off.

They then sought vengeance by killing a number of traders in the neighborhood, while their comrades in the lower towns raided settlements in the Carolinas and Georgia, scalping men, women and children and driving the survivors to the more thickly settled regions.

On February 16, 1760, Oconostota came to the riverbank opposite Fort Prince George and asked to speak to Lieutenant Coytmore, the officer in charge. Previously he had asked for the release of the hostages and had been refused. Now, as Coytmore with two of his men came down to the riverbank, the chief waved a bridle he carried in his hand. At this preconcerted signal a volley blazed from patches of tall grass, killing Coytmore and wounding his attendants. The garrison, enraged by this treachery, killed the Indian hostages. From the surrounding hills Oconostota and his warriors poured volleys of musketry into the fort all day and throughout the night, but they wrought no damage. The garrison returned the fire, destroying the near-by town of Keowee.

Word of the murder of the hostages brought the whole Cherokee nation into the war against the English. Ignoring Little Carpenter's pleas for peace, bands of infuriated and painted young men vainly attacked Fort Loudoun. The chief, still protesting his friendship for the English, shook his wise head and retired into the woods with his family.

On hearing of the new atrocities, Lyttelton sent an appeal to Major General Jeffrey Amherst, newly appointed commander of the British forces in America. Amherst immediately ordered Colonel Archibald Montgomery with 1,300 men to South Carolina. In April 1760 Montgomery crossed Twelve-Mile River into Cherokee country, burning all the Indian villages in the valley of the Keowee and killing and capturing more than a hundred of their warriors. When they still refused to make peace, he marched against their middle towns.

The savage yells of the red men mingled with the loud huzzas of the kilted Highlanders who, waving their Scotch bonnets, dashed against their enemies and drove them from the field. Nevertheless, Montgomery, burdened with the wounded, lacking means of removing his baggage and fearful of ambuscades, silently withdrew his forces. He returned to Keowee, and from there went to Charleston and New York. By leaving Captain Demere and his devoted band to their fate he acknowledged ignominious failure.

The defenders at Loudoun scorned all thought of surrender. When their bread was gone, they killed and roasted and ate their dogs and horses. Sometimes the Indian women defied the protests of their warriors to bring in a few pots of pork and beans. Gradually the beseiged garrison weakened from disease and lack of food. For two months they had heard nothing from the English; they abandoned all hope of being relieved. They believed they had been "forsaken by God and man." At last some of them deserted while others threw themselves on the mercy of the Indians.

In these circumstances Captain Demere saw the futility of prolonging the hopeless contest and on August 7 surrendered the fort. The Indians seemed generous with their terms of amnesty. The soldiers were to march out of Fort Loudoun with their drums, arms, as much powder as the officers thought necessary and what baggage they could carry. They were to be provided with horses and with an Indian escort to hunt for them, and they were to proceed unmolested to Virginia or to Fort Prince George, while the sick and the lame were to be nursed in the Indian towns until they should recover. They were to surrender all cannon and unnecessary ammunition.

The next day the garrison evacuated the fort and the Indians took possession, moving their families into the barracks and officers' houses. As many of the garrison as could march—men, women and children—soon started for Fort Prince George. Accompanied by Oconostota and most of the overhill warriors, they felt confident that no harm would befall them. But as they advanced their captors gradually withdrew until they found themselves alone at dusk. Next morning, when they resumed their march, they were fired upon by Indians hidden in patches of tall grass. Demere was wounded with the first volley. When another officer returned the fire, the Indians raised the war whoop, surrounded them and poured arrows and endless volleys of small arms fire into their ranks. Demere, three other officers, twenty-three privates and three women fell dead.

Seeing the hopelessness of fighting, the survivors surrendered. An Indian seized a certain Captain Stuart and carried him across the creek to safety. He and those of the garrison who remained—some one hundred and twenty in number—were made prisoners, taken to Chota and compelled to dance before a vast throng of rejoicing Indians. Only Little Carpenter deplored the scene. With all he could command of worldly goods, he purchased Stuart from his captor, lodged him for a few days in Fort Loudoun and then, on the pretext of going hunting, took him, his servant and an old doctor to the camp of the Virginians on the Holston River. The Indians sent other prisoners to the French in New Orleans. Many were ransomed by the South Carolinians in the course of the next few months.

The Indian triumph was short-lived. In the following year Colonel James Grant laid waste the lower and middle towns, and the Cherokee sued for peace. In accordance with the terms of the treaty, Little Carpenter gathered as many of the prisoners as were willing to quit the Indian country and returned them to their homes. The Cherokee agreed to surrender Fort Loudoun to anyone who might be sent to take possession of it, but it was not regarrisoned and was shortly destroyed.

The long duel for empire had now reached its last phase. It was on July 26, 1758, that 12,000 redcoats under Amherst and Wolfe captured the French stronghold at Louisbourg, while John Bradstreet swept across the Mohawk Valley to Lake Oswego, crossed it, and captured Fort Frontenac, which he destroyed together with seven of the nine ships he found in the harbor.

Bradstreet's victory was magnificent, for it brought Lake Ontario under British control, isolated Fort Niagara, cut off French communication with the Ohio River and permitted General John Forbes with 6,000 men to advance on Fort Duquesne. The French, deserted by their Indian allies and reduced to 500 men, blew up the fort and scattered by land and water. The final blow came in the following year on the Plains of Abraham above the city of Quebec where the vanquished Montcalm and the victorious Wolfe alike met death. The next year the fall of Montreal yielded all Canada to the English. As the war drew to a close Spain entered it on the side of France, but too late to revive her sinking ally. Indeed, Spain lost Cuba and the Philippines. But the new king, George III, wanted peace. Pitt resigned, and by the beginning of 1763 the warring powers were ready to discuss terms.

With a scratch of the pen France surrendered to Great Britain an empire which had taken her two centuries to secure and develop. By the definitive Treaty, signed on February 10, 1763, she gave up all her possessions save two colonies in India, a few West Indian islands and two fishing posts in the Gulf of St. Lawrence. She also ceded Canada and all her possessions east of the Mississippi save the Island of Orleans. England, unaware of the fact that the Philippine Islands had fallen to her forces before the preliminary treaty was signed, restored them to Spain and exchanged Cuba for Florida. France compensated Spain for her losses by ceding Louisiana west of the Mississippi and the Island of Orleans.

Great Britain now faced the responsibility of organizing the territory she had acquired. To this difficult task she gave her prompt and earnest attention. The Proclamation of 1763, promulgated by George III on October 7, divided the territory acquired from Spain into the provinces of East Florida and West Florida and organized the Canadian possessions into the Province of Quebec. To each of these jurisdictions she appointed a governor with full power, though she guaranteed to the inhabitants the same civil rights enjoyed by the thirteen English colonies. She also promised that each of the three provinces would eventually be granted representative government of the same type as that which existed in the crown colonies.

In dealing with Indian affairs the proclamation departed drastically from England's old policy. The endless wilderness of North America teemed with savages whom she must keep under control. Hitherto each colony had supervised its own relations with the Indians, a policy which had given unscrupulous traders ample opportunity to cheat them of their furs and speculators to rob them of their lands. The proclamation eliminated the possibility of such recurrences. Now only imperial agents could purchase lands from the Indians.

The vast region west of the Allegheny Mountains was set off as an Indian reservation. No settler was permitted west of the watershed which separated the sources of rivers flowing westward to the Mississippi from those flowing eastward to the Atlantic Ocean. No lands could be purchased from the Indians; no white settlements could remain in the reservation which was divided roughly at the Ohio River into two departments with an Indian superintendent over each.

This barrier, however, was only a temporary arrangement. Great Britain foresaw that imperial agents would grant charters to land companies from time to time, and that this would necessitate the opening of new areas of colonization. Indeed, the proclamation served only as a challenge to the restless and curious and adventure-loving Americans to hunt and explore in the mysterious and forbidden land beyond the line. Before the decade was over the Long Hunters had crossed the mountains into the country of Kentucky.

The Long

Hunters in Kentucky

THE IROQUOIS CALLED THE COUNTRY *Ken-ta-ke*—"PRAIRIE" OR "meadow land"—which, in various spellings, became its permanent name. Teeming with deer, buffalo, bear, elk and wild turkey, it attracted Cherokee, Shawnee, Seneca and Catawba hunters from a considerable distance north of the Ohio and south of the Cumberland. Their fierce jealousies often impelled the rival tribes to turn their arrows against one another, prompting the Cherokee, who claimed the land, to dub it the Dark and Bloody Ground—a legend disputed by many historians.

From the comfortable distance of Philadelphia, however, Benjamin Franklin could praise it as one of the finest sections in North America. No region, he wrote, equaled it for the extreme richness and fertility of its soil, its healthy temperatures, its mild climate, its limitless hordes of wild game, its facility of trade with the Indians and its "vast convenience of inland navigation or water carriage."

The first English explorers and hunters of consequence in Kentucky came with two great land companies which were organized almost simultaneously. One of these, the Loyal Land Company of Virginia, founded in London in June 1749, secured a grant of 800,000 acres north of the North Carolina boundary and west of the Alleghenies. The company chose Dr. Thomas Walker, a physician and experienced surveyor from Albemarle County, Virginia, to inspect the country and to select the location of the grant. Leading five companions, Walker in the spring of 1750 reached a gap in the mountains which he named Cumber-

land in honor of the duke who, four years earlier, had routed
the forces of the Young Pretender at Culloden Moor.

From Cumberland Gap Walker followed Yellow and Clear
creeks along the Warriors' Path to a river which he also named
Cumberland. On one of its banks, about four miles below the
present town of Barbourville, two of his companions, Henry
Lawless and John Hughes, built the first log cabin raised by
white hands between the Cumberland and Ohio rivers.

Walker and his men are remembered only for their discovery
of Cumberland Gap, but what they missed in achievement they
more than made up in adventure. Once a bear bit one of them
and wounded three of their dogs; at another time, they barely
escaped a charging buffalo. An elk killed one of their dogs, and
rattlesnakes frequently bit their horses. Despite such hazards they
killed enough game and animals to arouse the envy of a Nimrod
and then returned home only to find that the Loyal Land Company had dissolved.

The other organization active in exploring Kentucky was the
Ohio Company, whose large grants between the Monongahela
and Kanawha rivers and, later, on both sides of the Ohio we have
previously discussed. The Ohio Company agreed to settle 300
families and to erect a fort near the present city of Pittsburgh
and another near the mouth of the Kanawha. It instructed its
agent, Christopher Gist, to seek and survey good level ground
as far as the Falls of the Ohio—the present site of Louisville.
Descending the Ohio in the spring of 1751, Gist landed on the
Kentucky side and visited Shawnee Town where he was well
received. Some days later, advancing toward the Falls, he met
Hugh Crawford, a licensed trader, who presented him with two
teeth of a mastodon found in what became known as Big Bone
Lick. The amazed explorer learned that

the Rib Bones of the largest of these Beasts were eleven Feet long,
and the Skull Bone six Feet wide, across the Forehead, & the other
Bones in Proportion; and that . . . several Teeth . . . were upwards
of Five Feet long, and as much as a Man could well carry: that
he had hid one in a Branch at some Distance from the Place, lest
the French Indians should carry it away—The Tooth which I

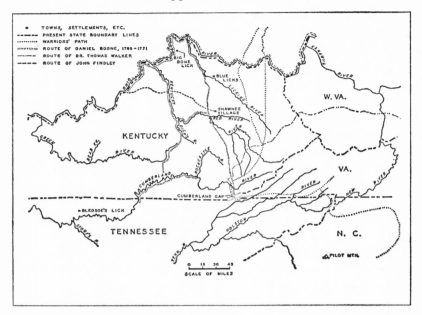

brought in for the Ohio Company, was a Jaw Tooth of better than four Pounds Weight; it appeared to be the furthest Tooth in the Jaw, and looked like fine Ivory when the outside was scraped off . . .

Gist's amazement at these prodigious relics soon changed to fear of present danger. Learning that Indians were in the vicinity, he fled southward, crossed the Licking, Kentucky and Red rivers and Walker's route and eventually returned to the Kanawha.

The next year a Pennsylvania trader of Irish descent, John Findlay—or Finley, as his name was sometimes spelled—descending the Ohio with three or four companions as far as the Falls, accompanied a party of Shawnee to their town of Eskippakithiki, eleven miles east of what is now Winchester. He was still in the village when some traders from Pennsylvania and Virginia who were returning from the Catawbas assembled there in January 1753. The traders began to quarrel over their barter outside the village and soon fell into the hands of straggling Indians. Findlay and a companion, protected by the friendship of the villagers, returned to their homes.

The incident is important because Findlay learned from the traders, who must have followed the Warriors' Path to the country of the Catawbas, about Cumberland Gap. His stories of this gateway to Kentucky and of other places he had seen inspired Daniel Boone sixteen years later to undertake an expedition in behalf of the Transylvania Company.

The outbreak of the last French and Indian war brought the expeditions in Kentucky practically to a halt. And they did not resume appreciably until, nine years later, the Treaty of Paris drove the French from the continent, cowed their Indian allies and gave England the region between the Alleghenies and the Mississippi. Then white men, feeling secure from the Indian menace, advanced into the Old Southwest in greater numbers than before.

Typically American in their restlessness and love of adventure, the dauntless hunters and traders evinced little or no regard for the forbidden line drawn by the Proclamation of 1763. In this they merely reflected the attitude of some of the most influential men in the colonies. "I can never look upon that proclamation," wrote George Washington, "than as a temporary expedient to quiet the minds of the Indians." Aspiring to western lands himself, Washington later expressed the conviction that the proclamation

must fall . . . especially when those Indians consent to our occupying the lands. Any person, therefore, who neglects the present opportunity of hunting out good lands, and in some measure marking out and distinguishing them for his own, in order to keep others from settling them, will never regain it.

Most of those who trekked into the wilds of Kentucky immediately after the war lacked the genuine qualities of the pioneer. They hungered, not for new homes and knowledge, but for the excitement of the chase and for the profit they hoped to obtain from sales of peltries. Such was Captain James Smith, who in the summer of 1766 led four men—one of whom was a young mulatto—through Cumberland Gap and hunted with them along the Cumberland and Tennessee rivers. Such again were Isaac Lindsay and his four companions, who in the same year conducted a successful safari in the vicinity of Stone's River.

In 1769 men of more responsible temperaments began to arrive in Kentucky. These men loved exploration more than adventure, knowledge of the country more than material gain. Known as Long Hunters because of the duration of their absence from home, they pushed deep into the Dark and Bloody Ground and returned from it with graphic and detailed information without which settlement might have been delayed and possibly frustrated. To this group belonged Benjamin Cleveland of the upper Yadkin Valley. In the midst of their extensive explorations from 1769 to 1772 Cleveland and his men met a group of Cherokee who deprived them of their supplies and their clothes and sent them home. To keep himself and his men from starving, Cleveland was obliged to kill his faithful hunting dog which, he said later, provided him with the sweetest meat he had ever eaten.

In the summer of 1770 Uriah Stone began an expedition which, though fraught with failure and even tragedy, resulted in discoveries that were to prove invaluable to newcomers. Each of his men was equipped with two horses, traps, a large supply of powder and lead, a small hand vise and bellows, files and screw plates with which to repair rifles that "got out of fix." After exploring in various sections of Kentucky they encamped near a buffalo trail in present Sumner County. Two of them, Isaac Bledsoe and Casper Mansker, traveling on the trail in opposite directions, each discovered a salt lick to which he gave his name.

In the flat surrounding his lick Bledsoe said he saw thousands of buffaloes. These animals paid him no heed until the wind blew; then, scenting him, they broke and ran in droves. The other members of the expedition had less romantic adventures. Indians, always lurking around them, attacked them in their camp, taking their peltries and shooting one of them, Robert Crockett, from ambush. After sustaining several such experiences the hunters journeyed to Spanish Natchez, and in the spring of 1771 they returned home.

A few months later Joseph Drake and Henry Scaggs organized

a party of forty men from the New River and Holston valleys. Dressed in hunting shirts, leggings and moccasins, and well supplied with horses, ammunition, dogs, blankets and salt, they pushed deep into Kentucky. Scaggs wrote later that he saw thousands of buffaloes, elk and deer, with "wild turkies scattered among them; all quite restless, some playing, and others busily employed in licking the earth." The buffaloes and other animals had eaten away the soil so deep "that they could, in places, go entirely underground."

After some weeks twenty-six of the men tired of the wilderness and returned to their homes in Virginia; fourteen elected to remain. Of these all but three soon departed on a long trip of exploration. One day a band of straggling Indians under the half-breed, Will Emery, attacked the camp, capturing two of the men and carrying away the peltries which the party had accumulated in months of hunting. The other man managed to escape. The explorers, returning to camp to discover that their friends and peltries were gone, left emphatic record of their frustration on a barkless poplar:

2300 Deer Skins Lost   Ruination By God

Too angry to admit defeat, the hunters resolved to retrieve their losses around Bledsoe's Lick. What they saw there filled them with amazement. Within four or five miles of the lick the cane had grown so thick that they thought they had come to the wrong place. What had caused this phenomenon? On examining the lick itself they discovered the answer. Around the lick, for several hundred yards, they found countless buffalo skulls and bones; indeed, the flat around the lick was bleached by them. Some years later Isaac Bledsoe told William Hall, a pioneer chronicler, that the French *voyageur*, Timothé de Monbreun, had hunted around the lick shortly after its discovery. He had killed buffaloes for their tallow and tongues. With the help of a companion he had loaded a keel boat and descended the Cumberland.

The Drake and Scaggs expedition had significant results. The elaborate and detailed information which Scaggs brought back doubtless influenced Richard Henderson and his associates to accelerate their plans for colonizing Kentucky. Already their future scout, Daniel Boone, the greatest of the Long Hunters, was in the Dark and Bloody Ground extensively and systematically exploring the country.

Daniel Boone is the childhood friend of countless Americans. Some know him well, others little; but to all he is the embodiment of what they want and admire most for themselves: love of adventure and of unseen places, physical prowess, resourcefulness and moral courage in the face of danger, rich and ample reward for services rendered and an independence of action that scorns all authority not emanating from the people.

Boone was born in Berks County, Pennsylvania, on October 22 (Old Style; November 2 New Style), 1734. His parents, Squire Boone and Sarah Morgan, were Quakers of wavering conviction. By defending the right of two of their children to "marry out," they were excommunicated as "worldlings." Their crime was that they had too steadfast a respect for reality. To them Quaker pacifism seemed wise in preachment but unwise in practice. Life in the wilderness of Berks County was full of hazards; it needed a fighter to surmount them; and the Boones, while giving lip service to Quakerism, kept feet on the ground and finger on the trigger.

Daniel was a fighter from childhood. When two girls disturbed his sleep under a tree by emptying a pan of fish entrails on him, he sent them home with swollen faces and bloody noses. The complaint of their mother brought Sarah Boone to the defense of her son: "If thee has not brought up thy daughters to better behavior, it is high time they were taught good manners."

Daniel disliked his father's occupations, farming and blacksmithing: drudgery is irksome to a restless soul. All his life he seems to have sought escape from civilized responsibility as though it revolted his nature. He was happy only in the wilderness, and the wilderness taught him the three things he knew, and knew infinitely well: hunting, exploring and Indian psychology. Of formal education he had little, but in it he revealed traits of an original mind. His handwriting was an audacious scrawl; his spelling, unorthodox; his sentences, free of prevailing syntax. Legend says that one of his uncles who undertook his education failed to improve his spelling and complained to his father. "Let girls do the spelling," replied Squire Boone, "and Daniel will do the shooting."

To Daniel shooting was almost as vital as breathing. And circumstances soon removed him to surroundings where good shooting was indispensable to keeping alive. In 1742 his sister Sarah shocked Quaker godliness by "marrying out" to the father of her unborn child. Five years later Daniel's brother Israel took a bride who also was not a Quakeress. When Squire was called to account for the "disorderly marriage," he replied emphatically that his son should have the right to marry whom he damned pleased, whereupon the Quakers disowned him. Squire found in this circumstance an opportunity to better his lot. Deciding to move to better land, he sold his property and in the spring of 1750 took his family westward across Pennsylvania and then by slow stages down the Cumberland Valley and finally to the Yadkin Valley in North Carolina. In 1753 he purchased land three miles west of the present town of Mocksville in the vast tract that the King had granted to the Earl of Granville and upon it built a cabin.

In 1755 Daniel served as a wagoner in Braddock's campaign, during which he became acquainted with John Findlay, who was destined to serve as his guide in Kentucky. On the day of defeat when his wagons were surrounded, Boone slashed the harness, leaped onto one of his horses and dashed into the forest.

During these years Daniel grew to that romantic figure with which every schoolboy is acquainted. His contemporaries describe him as a man of average height with broad shoulders, dark hair, friendly blue eyes arched with fair eyebrows, thin-lipped wide mouth and nose of a slightly Roman cast. Such was Boone when in 1756 he fell in love with and married Rebecca Bryan.

The bride, "whose brow," says a sentimental chronicler, "had now been fanned by the breezes of seventeen summers," was the daughter of Joseph Bryan, a recent backwoods settler. According to the same writer, she was "like Rebecca of old, 'very fair to look upon,' with jet black hair and eyes, complexion rather dark, and something over the common size of her sex." Her expression was that of "childlike artlessness"; her address, "pleasing"; and her deportment, "unaffectedly kind." "Never," concludes our chronicler, "was there a more gentle, affectionate, forbearing creature, than this same fair youthful bride of the Yadkin."

Theirs was doubtless a typical frontier wedding. The bride customarily rode to church on a pillion behind her father's saddle. After the ceremony the pillion was removed and strapped behind the bridegroom's saddle. Wife and husband then rode off on their honeymoon, which they enjoyed in the company of their friends. The wedding party, gathering in the cabin where the couple was to spend the night, prepared a feast which usually included venison and corn bread. The jug made the rounds; the fiddlers drew the dancers to their places; and ribald hints on the pleasure of procreation provoked hearty applause and guffaws.

In the course of the evening the bride climbed the ladder to the loft of the cabin, where her girl friends, following her one by one, put her to bed. When the girls descended the young men performed the same office for the bridegroom. Late in the night the celebrants sent food up the ladder for the newlyweds and left them to their nuptial pleasures.

Their marriage lasted fifty-six years, until Rebecca died at the age of seventy-three. In that expanse of time she had many opportunities to prove her patience and loyalty. Once Daniel was absent for two years on a hunting trip. At another time she heard he was dead. Still another time, she saw him wounded by a tomahawk. For a good part of her married life she was not quite sure whether her husband was alive or dead. Yet such was her confidence in his ability to extricate himself from any difficulty that she patiently awaited better news. Invariably it came. As Daniel used to say, all you needed to enjoy happiness was "a good gun, a good horse, and a good wife," and during his long life he was fortunate enough to have all three.

For Daniel the ideal life was that of a Nimrod dwelling in an earthly paradise full of deer and bear and buffalo. Such was the joy of Epaphronditus Bainford, whom William Byrd met in 1728 along the North Carolina frontier while running the dividing line between that colony and Virginia. "This Forester," wrote Byrd, "Spends all his time in ranging the Woods, and is said to make a great Havock among the Deer, and other Inhabitants of the Forest, not much wilder than himself." Boone, too, played havoc with wild game in the bottoms of the creek near his home. Many bears, attracted by the nuts that dropped generously from numberless beech trees, roamed into the region. Daniel and his father killed ninety-nine of these animals in a single hunting season. Thereafter the stream became known as Bear Creek.

Soon Indian warfare flared along the frontier, bringing Daniel's hunting temporarily to an end. When the Cherokee began to raid the Yadkin Valley, the Boones and the Bryans fled from their farms with other settlers. Daniel and Rebecca jumped into a two-horse wagon and drove to the vicinity of Fredericksburg, Virginia. Here Boone probably met George Washington, hunted animals and Indians and hauled tobacco to market.

Perhaps, too, he accompanied John Forbes, when in 1758 that general led his army across Pennsylvania for the purpose of retrieving Braddock's defeat and driving the French out of Fort Duquesne. In his old age Boone said that while serving as wagon master with troops campaigning in Pennsylvania he killed an Indian by throwing him off the "Juniata Bridge" to the rocks forty feet below. Forbes's expedition is the only one known that could possibly have crossed the Juniata River.

By the fall of the following year Daniel was again in the Yadkin Valley, where for fifty pounds he bought 640 acres from his father. Eventually he was able to resume his hunting trips. After the Cherokee were subdued in 1760, Boone struck deeper into the wilderness.

Awareness of ability often engenders pride which loves to commemorate its owner in long-lasting inscription. Boone left record of his hunting prowess on many trees. Near a cave surrounded by happy hunting grounds in what is now Washington County, Tennessee, he left on a beech tree an inscription known to all:

> D. Boone
>
> Cilled A. Bar on
> tree
>
> In the
> Year   1760

The beech tree yields easily to inscription. Its soft, smooth surface allows the hunting knife to carve deeply in its trunk, and although its slow growth stretches and distorts letters and figures, it protects them from obliteration. For the pioneers it served the purpose of commemorative stone or medal, danger signal, good and bad news, relief from boredom, outlet for pent-up emotion and legal document. The discovery of a spring, the tracing of a lost companion, the triumph of a hunt, the marking of a claim— all these found expression in the pliant and preserving wood of the beech. "Fifteen hundred skins gone to ruination." Thus it once consoled a group of Long Hunters who, after an arduous season, unfortunately encountered an overwhelming number of Indians in their path.

For the pioneer hunting was at once a sport, a livelihood and an occupation. He lay in wait at salt licks; he watched from behind trees; he ranged the wilderness. Boone usually started out either early in the morning when the dew had softened the dead leaves or at moonrise when the deer were feeding. He also loved to trap. If he sought beaver, he would bait a twig rubbed with castor found in the perineal glands of that animal. The beaver, attracted by the scent, would swim up and touch the bait with his nose and catch his forepaw in the trap. Struggling for his freedom, he would drag himself into the water and, pulled under by weight, would drown. Boone needed no bait to trap otter. This animal simply fell victim to a trap placed at an "otter slide," where it habitually plunged into the water.

The pioneer found prosperity only in the forest. Deer was his most profitable game. He would "hoppus" a buck or a doe across his shoulders to his cabin, where he could either jerk the venison in the sun or preserve it with wood ashes and saltpeter. The skin he often converted into leggings and breeches. In a fair hunting season he realized about four hundred dressed deerskins, a fourth of which, averaging two hundred and fifty pounds, he could load on his horse in a single trip back home. Each skin was classified "buck" or "doe" and brought him from forty cents to four or five dollars, depending on its quality and on the market.

The pioneer needed every dollar he realized from a successful hunting season. A thousand dollars a year in our modern currency barely sufficed to defray his expenses. He paid perhaps seven pounds for a "rifle-gun," powder horn, shot pouch and "patchen pouch" for wadding. A trip to the wilderness made several "rifle-guns" necessary and a full set of gunsmithing tools including a hand vise and bellows, files, and screw plates. This was not all. He also needed several horses, traps and ammunition and other articles—all of which were very expensive.

In the next few years Boone roamed many miles away from home. Sometimes he threaded his way deep into the wilderness of North Carolina where the mountains exhibit their variegated colors ranging from amethyst or deep purple to pale mistlike gray—depending on mood of day or time of year. In the spring the hollows and the moist, open spaces at the foothills flame with azaleas and rosebay, while the lower woods gradually thicken with mountain laurel and rhododendron—all white and pink— which by June invade the higher slopes and summits. In this enchanted region Boone saw Blowing Rock overlooking an immense primeval forest studded with green hills; he saw Mount Mitchell with its eternal hood of snow; he saw the Grandfather, perhaps the oldest mountain on earth; he saw Pilot Mountain towering amid luxuriant growth, so called because it served the Indians as a guide in their ceaseless wanderings. At Linville Boone watched the cataract taking its shimmering leap into the gorge.

Sometimes he hunted in company. Once in the Holston Valley he and Nathaniel Gist, son of the famous explorer and guide, were attacked by a pack of hungry wolves whose dens were in caves adjoining the camp. The animals also fought their dogs, killing some and crippling others. Eventually Boone and Gist eluded the wolves and returned home by different routes.

In the fall of 1763 a new field of adventure opened up to Boone. By the Treaty of Paris East Florida had become English. The need for settlers impelled its governor to issue a proclamation offering a hundred acres to any Protestant immigrant. This generous offer and the fascination which tales of a strange land always held for Boone directed his thoughts southward. He bade Rebecca farewell and joined by friends and his brother Squire, who had just turned twenty-one and had recently married, set out.

The promised land proved unpromising. Boone and his friends found the weather wet and the game scarce; they shivered while they nearly starved to death. They explored Florida from St. Augustine to Pensacola where Boone, according to legend, bought a house. If the house existed, he was destined never to occupy it. On his return home Rebecca threw cold water on what little ardor he yet retained for the new colony, and it sizzled out of his thoughts.

One day late in 1768 or early in 1769 John Findlay drove a scraggy horse and wagon down Yadkin Valley, selling pins, needles, threads and Irish linens. When he was not hunting and exploring somewhere on the far-flung frontier, he eked out a living by peddling what few household articles the backwood folk could not produce. From the Pennsylvania settlers at Salisbury or at the Forks of the Yadkin, he learned that Boone was living in the region. He knew Daniel but had not seen him since they had served as wagoners in Braddock's expedition more than ten years before.

Findlay was soon sitting by the fire in Boone's cabin, regaling his old friend with tales of Kentucky. His Irish fancy grew more and more exuberant as he unfolded his repertoire of experiences. Kentucky—there was the paradise for a hunter! There you saw deer at every lick; there you found buffalo on every trail, thousands of them, so that you had to be careful to avoid being crushed by them when they stampeded and made the earth for miles around rumble with their hoofs. There at the Falls of the Ohio you saw wild geese and ducks so plentiful that you did not have to shoot them! And there was real land—lush, green, fertile —endless acres, in every direction, all for the taking!

The Indians? Well, they were dangerous, but they did not bother a trader; indeed, they welcomed you just as they had welcomed him when just last year he had gone down the Ohio. Why, he had even gone inland on a hunting expedition with them and had set up his trading post in the middle of Kentucky, exchanging goods with them as fast as they could bring in their pelts. Then with his canoe loaded to the brim he had paddled up the Ohio as far as western Pennsylvania, where he had changed his pelts for good hard cash!

Findlay told Boone that he planned to return to Kentucky and that he wanted a skillful woodsman to accompany him. Would Daniel like to go along? Enthralled by the stories of adventure and success he had just heard, Daniel jumped at the opportunity. Things had not gone well for him in the backwoods of North Carolina. The farm had provided him and his family with such a scanty livelihood that he had been obliged to borrow money from several principal families of the county. When he was unable to repay it at the promised time, they had sued him in the local court at Salisbury. That had disgusted him—all the more because he felt unhappy where he was; he longed for the wilderness, his natural abode. Now the golden opportunity had come; he would make a name for himself; he would undertake an expedition into Kentucky!

But such a trip needed financial backing. Where was he to obtain it? He decided to appeal to the one man he knew who had long dreamed of establishing a land company in Kentucky— Richard Henderson, recently appointed an associate judge of the newly created Superior Court of North Carolina. Henderson was destined to figure prominently in Boone's career as well as in the history of the Old Southwest. He was the prototype of the American capitalist of a later day: exceedingly ambitious yet intensely practical, as most of the leading frontiersmen have been. A man of indefatigable energy and wide imagination, he had educated himself; had assisted his father, Samuel Henderson, the High Sheriff of Granville County; and had, after reading law for a short time in the office of John Williams, been admitted to the bar. His oratorical gifts soon won him a large and lucrative practice. His legal circuit often brought him to Salisbury where he became well acquainted with Squire Boone and Daniel, who regaled him with bizarre and fascinating tales of western exploration. These only increased Henderson's desire to establish a colony in Kentucky.

Henderson had already befriended Boone. When Daniel was sued for debt Henderson had acted as his lawyer. In order to collect his legal fees Henderson in turn had been obliged to sue Boone. But, admiring the rugged scout's past services in western exploration, Henderson was unwilling to press action against him. Instead, he continued litigation from court to court. In March 1769 Boone was summoned to appear in court at Salisbury. The hunter seized the opportunity to lay before Henderson designs for an extended exploring trip into Kentucky with Findlay as his guide. Henderson gave his consent. He hired Boone to explore the whole country north of the Kentucky River.

On May 1, 1769, Boone and Findlay began the journey to Kentucky. Accompanying them were Daniel's friend and brother-in-law, John Stuart, and three "camp-keepers," Joseph Holden, James Mooney and William Cooley—all of whom were equipped with blankets or bearskins, household utensils and enough rations to last them until they reached good hunting grounds. The six men passed through Cumberland Gap, followed the Warriors' Path and eventually reached the west branch of the Rockcastle River. At first Boone explored alone in the country north of the Kentucky; then he and Findlay explored in the Elkhorn Valley.

For six months the party saw no Indians. But in December while Boone and Stuart were crossing a canebrake on a buffalo trail near the Kentucky River, they encountered a band of mounted Shawnee returning from a hunting trip in the Green River country to their homes north of the Ohio. Taking the two white men prisoner, the Shawnee conducted them to their own camp where they took everything of value, including rifles and ammunition. They had no intention, however, of killing or even of detaining the explorers. They wanted only the pelts which they regarded as their own property.

A few days later, therefore, the Indians' leader, Captain Will, provided Boone and Stuart with moccasins, a doeskin for patch-leather, a small "trading gun" and enough powder and shot to kill food for themselves on their way to the settlements and released them.

"Now, brothers, go home and stay there," said Captain Will as he bade them farewell. "Don't come here any more, for this is the Indians' hunting ground, and all the animals, skins and furs are ours. If you are so foolish as to venture here again, you may be sure the wasps and yellow jackets will sting you severely."

Boone and Stuart had no intention of heeding Captain Will's warning. Pursuing the Indians to their camp during the night, they retrieved four or five of the horses and put many miles between themselves and their former captors. In the morning, confident that he had eluded them, Boone stretched himself on the ground to rest while the horses were feeding. Imagine his consternation when he looked up and saw Captain Will and his band galloping toward them. The white men were captive again before they had time to think of getting away. Tying a horse bell around Boone's neck and compelling him to caper about for their entertainment, they asked in broken English, "Steal hoss, ha?"

Then, informing them that they would be released as soon as they had crossed the Ohio, the Indians marched Boone and Stuart northward. By that time, the Shawnee reasoned, their horses would be safe from further attempts to steal them. In this hope they were disappointed. A few nights later Boone and Stuart dashed into a canebrake. The excited Indians made sure their horses were secure and then, shouting madly, surrounded the canebrake in the hope of catching Boone and Stuart should they emerge. The two men stayed where they were and eventually escaped.

Hurrying back to their camp, they found it abandoned. Their companions, having given them up for lost, had started back for the settlement. Boone and Stuart soon overtook them, but the others had had enough of adventure. Findlay journeyed north-ward to visit relatives in Pennsylvania, while Holden, Mooney and Cooley returned to their homes on the Yadkin. Not long after their departure, Squire Boone, loaded down with supplies and accompanied by a friend, Alexander Neely, came on his brother and Stuart. Henderson and his associates in the land company they hoped to establish, having heard nothing of Boone, had surmised that he and his companions must have run short of ammunition, flour, salt and other necessary articles. Desiring Boone to continue his explorations, they had sent Squire with the supplies. Squire and his friend resolved to follow Daniel and Stuart wherever they went.

The explorers encamped near the mouth of the Red River and soon provided themselves with what they needed for the winter. Neely had brought along a copy of *Gulliver's Travels* and had begun to read it to his companions. One day while he was regaling them with the account of Glumdelick and its inhabitants, the Luldegruds, they saw Indians approaching. These were promptly driven off, whereupon Neely rejoiced at the defeat of what he called "the Luldegruds." Flattered by this metaphor, they forth-with commemorated their victory by giving the creek that flowed near their camp the name of Luldegrud which it still holds.

All winter long they hunted and trapped. Boone and Stuart, being the best of friends, usually hunted together, but once they decided to separate and meet again at camp in two weeks. Stuart crossed to the south side of the Kentucky River in a small canoe he and Daniel had built. Daniel anxiously awaited his return. At first he attributed Stuart's prolonged absence to the swollen river, but when the water subsided and his friend still failed to return, Daniel decided to search for him. He found Stuart's trail; he found a recent fire; he found his friend's initials carved on a tree; but he found Stuart nowhere.

Five years later while Boone was blazing the Wilderness Trail for the Transylvania Company, he found his brother-in-law's remains in a hollow sycamore near the crossing of the Rock-castle River. Stuart's initials on a brass band of his powder horn provided grim proof of the identity. Stuart's left arm was broken;

the bone still bore the discoloration of a bullet; the skull showed no traces of the scalping knife. What had caused his death—Indians, an accident, attacking wolves? The wilderness has kept its secret to this day.

Stuart's disappearance discouraged Neely, who returned to the settlements, leaving the Boone brothers alone in the wilderness. They stayed until May 1770, when, their ammunition running low, Squire Boone again departed for the settlements to obtain supplies. Left all alone, Daniel ranged the woods as far north as the Ohio, acquainting himself with the Kentucky and Licking valleys. He visited the Big Bone Lick where he examined the fabulous fossil remains of the mammoth and the mastodon, and then went to the Blue Licks where he saw with amazement and delight thousands of shaggy buffaloes gamboling, bellowing and making the earth rumble beneath the tramping of their hoofs, just as Findlay had described. One day while he stood on a cliff near the junction of the Kentucky and Dick's rivers, he suddenly found himself hemmed in by a party of Indians. Seizing his only chance of escape, he leaped into the top of a maple tree growing beneath the cliff, slid sixty feet below and made his getaway to a chorus of guttural "Ughs" from the dumbfounded Indians.

At last he made his way back to camp where on July 27, 1770, Squire rejoined him. His brother had traveled to and from the settlements undisturbed, had sold their furs, paid off his debts, provided for both families and had brought back new supplies. The brothers immediately started eastward to hunt. Legend says they reached the Kentucky River and settled in a cave near the mouth of the Marble Creek in Jessamine County. Soon they moved to another cave on Harmon Creek in the same county.

When their ammunition and supplies ran low, Squire made another trip to the settlements. Daniel, thinking Squire was too slow in returning, went east to meet him and luckily encountered him along the way. The brothers resumed their explorations, advancing as far as the valleys of the Green and Cumberland rivers, where they hunted and spent some time with Casper Mansker and his companions. Then, their pack horses loaded with pelts, they set out for home; but when in May 1771 they reached Cumberland Gap, they bumped into a party of Indians who robbed them of all their earthly possessions. Daniel Boone scarcely regarded this as a reversal of fortune. He had realized his dream—he had seen Kentucky. His descriptions of the golden land he had explored made Henderson all the more eager to establish a colony there when his judgeship should expire two years hence.

The Regulators
of North Carolina

LUSH MEADOWS, DEEP FORESTS OF OAK AND HICKORY, BROKEN fields of red clay watered by numerous small streams, plateaus studded with snow-capped mountains shining in the sun—this was the back country of North Carolina which in the middle of the eighteenth century embraced the sparsely settled counties of Orange, Granville, Rowan, Anson and Dobbs.

The first settlers in the region built their cabins before 1740 along the lower western valleys of the Yadkin, Haw, Tar, Catawba and Deep rivers, occupying the region between the present cities of Raleigh and Morganton. The succeeding years saw them arriving in ever increasing numbers—German, Scotch-Irish, Highlander, Welsh and English immigrants from New England, New Jersey, Pennsylvania and Maryland. In 1765 Governor Tryon reported that more than a thousand pioneer wagons passed through Salisbury on their way to the back country.

The settlers lived a life of poverty and hard work. Most of them were destined to go to their graves ignorant of plank floors, feather beds, riding carriages and side saddles. Many districts had no schools. Most of the children went from high chair to field and forest where labor in all kinds of weather left many of them with rheumatic fever and the facial ravages of old age before they reached their prime.

To this bare and hard existence was added the burden of oppressive government. Coming from a more liberal colony, the average backwoodsman resented the political institutions of

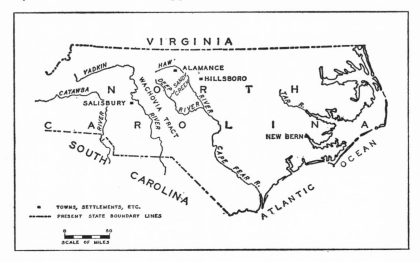

North Carolina because they gave him no voice in public affairs. Cut off from communication or sympathy with the governing classes of the province, his impulsive nature led him in time of stress to seek redress of grievances by forceful means.

The executive branch of the colonial government consisted of the governor, who represented the royal prerogative, and his council who, appointed by the King on his recommendation, nearly always displayed gratitude for their positions. The governor in council named the justices of the superior and inferior courts. In addition, he appointed the officers of the militia and selected the sheriff from among freeholders whose names he had obtained from each inferior or county court, which was the sole unit of local government. Its justices executed their commands through the sheriff and his liberal number of deputies.

The legislative branch of the government consisted of an assembly of two houses: the upper house, composed of the members of the council; and the lower house, composed of deputies elected by freeholders. Elections were held by the sheriff. In the absence of political parties influential men in the county named the candidates, who were usually elected. The effects of this system are easily seen. A few men in each county controlled the political offices, whose effectiveness depended on the personal honesty of their incumbents. Oddly enough the system worked well in the eastern counties, but in the back country where social and economic conditions were quite different officers often proved tyrannical and mercenary. To counteract the stench of this Augean stable the people eventually adopted as cleansing agent an association known as the Regulators.

The county court levied taxes and the sheriff collected them. Taxes were apportioned by the poll; the wealthy planter in the east paid no more than the poor farmer in the west. In the back country money was scarce. Business was conducted largely through barter, and the farmers seldom kept money in their homes. What little cash they needed they usually obtained from one of the few men in the region who practiced the business of lending small sums.

When the sheriff came for the taxes—and for mercenary reasons he contrived to come unexpectedly—the farmer would propose that they go and get the tax money from one of the lenders. The sheriff would not only refuse the request but would proceed to distrain on some of the farmer's property, for which service he took a sizable fee. The farmer would then hasten to the lender, borrow the needed money and hurry after the sheriff; but this officer had departed by a route different from that he had promised to take.

The farmer, going to the county seat, would find that his property had been sold to some friend of the sheriff for much less than its value. From such an experience the farmer adduced that governmental officers were in collusion for the purpose of robbing him. He became convinced that the county seat was full of men who had amassed large sums of money at the expense of poor farmers like himself.

Debt and taxation often took the farmer's horse from the plow and stripped his wife of her homespun dress. In Orange County not far from the present town of Chapel Hill, a sheriff who was distraining and selling property came to the house of a farmer but found him absent. Disappointed in his design but determined to satisfy his demands somehow, he forced the farmer's wife to take off her dress, slapped her on the buttocks, told her to make herself another and sold the dress at auction for her husband's tax.

In Granville County rapacious officers picked flaws in the titles of properties, compelling their owners to remedy pretended or insignificant defects by taking out new patents. In other back counties officers would resolve a service into two or three and demand a fee for each. Lawyers and court officials postponed cases in order to obtain more fees.

Under these conditions American hatred for oppression quickly asserted itself. In 1765 the enraged people found a champion in George Sims, a militant journalist whose *Address to the People of Granville County* exposed the vicious methods by which dishonest lawyers, and especially Samuel Benton, clerk of the County Court, extorted fees from their victims. In his homespun style, understood by all, Sims shot ironic darts with deadly aim:

We will suppose ourselves all to be men, who labour for our livings, and there is a poor man among us, who has dealt for 4 or 5 pounds in such things as his family could not possibly do without, and in hopes of being spared from the lash of the law till he can sell some of his effects to raise the money; he gives a judgment bond to his Merchant, and before he can accomplish his design his bond is thrown into Court, and Benton the poor mans Burgess has it to enter on the Court docquet and issue an execution the work of one long minute. Well, Gentlemen, what has our poor neighbour to pay Mr. Benton for his trouble? Why, nothing but the trifling sum of forty one shillings and five pence. Well he is a poor man and cannot raise the money. We will suppose Mr. Benton condescends to come to terms with him. Come (says he) and work. I have a large field and my corn wants weeding (or something like that). I will give you 1/6 a day, which is the common wages of a labourer in these times till you pay it off because you are a poor man, and a neighbour I will not take away your living. Well how many days work has our honest neighbour to pay Mr. Benton for his trouble and expense in writing about a minute? Why, he must work something more than 27 days before he is clear of his clutches. Well the poor man reflects within himself. At this rate says he when shall I maintain my own family. I have a wife and a parcel of small children suffering at home and I have none to labour but myself, and here I have lost a month's work and I do not know for what, my merchant not yet paid, I do not know what will be the end of these things; however, I will go home, and try what I can do toward getting a living. Stay neighbour, you must not go home, you are not half done yet, there is a damned Lawyers mouth to stop before you go any further, you impowered him to confess that you owed £5, and you must pay him 30/ for that, or else go and work nineteen days for that pick-pocket at the same rate, and when that is done, you must work as many days for the Sheriff, for his trouble, and then go home and see your living wrecked and tore to pieces to satisfy your merchant.

The leader of this hierarchy of public thieves was William Tryon, who became governor of the colony in the same year that Sims published his essay. Like Stratford in the days of Charles I, Tryon epitomized his public policy by the word "thorough." He worshiped money with the passion of a Croesus. While he averred that the aim of his administration was to preserve the prerogative of his royal master, his real ambition was to amass a private fortune. In this he could rely on the full support of his officers, who were even more experienced than he in the art of fleecing the public.

Tryon felt obliged to defend his lieutenants as representatives of his government against the growing criticism of the people. Vain as Rehoboam, he taxed the colony £20,000 in order to build himself a magnificent palace at New Bern. The Venezuelan patriot, Francisco Miranda, saw this edifice in 1783 when time had marred some of its beauty and said it had no equal in all South America.

Isolated from and out of sympathy with the dominant classes of the province, the backwoodsmen only awaited a leader who would inspire them to organize against their oppressors. They found one in Hermon Husband, a well-to-do, industrious, shrewd and honest Quaker from Maryland who was a member of the assembly from Orange County. His assiduity as a pamphleteer and his activities as a writer, agitator and legislator in pressing for redress of their complaints won him the entire support of the men of the back country. Although he always claimed he had never officially joined them, Husband inspired the backwoodsmen to form an association called the Regulators—a title borrowed from a group of men who had organized in South Carolina to suppress robbers and to correct many abuses in the back country of that province.

The North Carolina association first resorted to action in Orange County in April 1766 when the sheriff declared that he intended to distrain two shillings and eight pence for each delinquent tax. The Regulators replied by drawing up a paper which is typically American in character: they expressed their unwillingness to pay oppressive taxes, determined to stand by their constitutional rights, resolved to seek redress of grievances through their representatives in assembly and to vote corrupt officials out of office and promised one another to abide by majority rule.

A full decade before the Declaration of Independence these crude and unschooled frontiersmen forecast its spirit in their own program "for regulating Publick Grievances and Abuses of Power in the following particulars, with others of like nature that may occur":

That we will pay no taxes until we are Satisfied they are agreeable to Law and Applied to the purpose therein mentioned, unless we cannot help and are forced.

That we will pay no Officer any more fees than the Law allows, unless we are obliged to do it, and then to show a dislike to it & bear open testimony against it.

That we will attend our meetings of Conferences as often as we conveniently can or is necessary in order to consult our representatives on the amendments of such Laws as may be found Grievous or unnecessary, and to choose more suitable men than we have heretofore done for Burgesses and Vestrymen, and to petition His Excellency our Governor, the Hon'ble Council and the Worshipful House of Representatives, His Majesty in Parliament, &c., for redress of such grievances as in the course of this undertaking may occur, and inform one another & to learn, know and enjoy all the Privileges and Liberties that are allowed us and were settled on us by our worthy ancestors, the founders of the present Constitution, in order to preserve it in its Ancient Foundation, that it may stand firm and unshaken.

That we will contribute to collections for defraying necessary expenses attending the work according to our abilities.

That in cases of difference in judgment we will submit to the Majority of our Body.

To all of which we do solemnly swear, or, being a Quaker or otherwise scrupulous in Conscience of the common Oath, do solemnly Affirm that we will stand true and faithful to this cause until We bring them to a true Regulation according to the true intent & meaning of it in the judgment of the Majority.

The Regulators sent printed copies of this paper to all the officers in the colony. At the same time they refused to pay the taxes demanded by the sheriffs, while Husband undertook to act as sheriff of Orange County by collecting in it the exact amount of tax lawfully due from every Regulator. When Husband's name was called in the assembly as a member from Orange, Governor Tryon in a haughty voice demanded to know why the King's subjects in that county had refused to pay their taxes. In reply Husband threw a bag containing money on the table before Tryon. "Here, sir," he said, "are the taxes which my people refused your roguish sheriff. I brought it to keep it from dwindling, seeing that when money passes through so many fingers, it, like a cake of soap, grows less at each handling. The people have sent it down by their commoner and I am now ready to pay it over to the treasurer if he will give me a receipt to show my people that the money has been paid."

Tryon eyed him with contempt and wanted to have him arrested on some pretext. Summoning his council, he asked it for advice concerning the propriety of issuing a warrant against Husband. The council disapproved. Nevertheless, at Tryon's request, one of its members issued warrants against Husband and another leading Regulator, William Butler, both of whom were charged with "Traiterously and feloniously conspiring with others in stirring up an Insurrection."

On May 2, 1768, on Tryon's orders, Edmund Fanning, colonel of the Orange County militia, with twenty-seven armed men seized Husband and Butler and took them to Hillsboro, where they were given a brief trial and thrown into jail. They were told that they would be tried again in New Bern and that there they would surely be convicted and hanged. Fearing for their lives, they sent for Fanning, who got them to sign a paper in which they promised to refrain thenceforth from criticizing the laws of the colony and from voicing Regulator grievances. They were released under bond to appear for trial at the following term of court.

Though Husband kept his promises, he failed to calm the people. Indeed, their resentment grew with every new dishonest act. They were especially incensed against Fanning and John Frohock, clerk of the court of Rowan County, both of whom had recommended imprisonment and even death for prominent members of their organization. Fanning, a New Englander who had been educated at Yale, was a man of eloquence and superior ability. For some years he had served as one of the leading men in the assembly. Unfortunately, he belonged to the office-holding class, and, like his associates, he stretched his authority as much as possible in order to make money. Like them, too, he believed he had a legal right to take all he could get. In this belief he was no better and no worse than his colleagues. His frankness and haughty manner, however, gained him the particular hatred of the Regulators, who regarded him as the prototype of the officers from whose hands they had suffered.

Rednap Howell, a witty and satiric versifier who came to North Carolina from New Jersey, taught the children of the back country to chorus the infamy of dishonest officials in more than forty humorous ballads and jingles. In the following stanzas he attributes the theft of a horse to John Frohock, misspelled "Frohawk." The verses show Frohock and Fanning in cynical confab:

> Says Frohawk to Fanning, "To tell the plain truth,
> When I came to this country I was but a youth;
> My father sent me, I wa'nt worth a cross:
> And then my first duty was to steal a horse.

I quickly got credit and then ran away,
And haven't paid for him to this day."

Says Fanning to Frohawk, " 'Tis folly to lie,
I rode an old mare that was blind in one eye.
Five shillings in money I had in my purse,
My coat it was patched, but not much the worse.
But now we've got rich, as 'tis very much known
That we will do very well if they'll let us alone."

On another occasion when Howell learned that Fanning had ordered "some double gold lace for a hat and some narrow double gold lace for a jacket," he wrote the following:

When Fanning first to Orange came
    He looked both pale and wan.
An old patched coat upon his back,
    An old blind mare he rode on.
Both man and mare wa'nt worth five pounds
    As I've been often told,
But by his cavil robberies
    He's laced his coat with gold.

What were "his cavil robberies"? The fee bill allowed the register two shillings and eight pence for recording each conveyance "or any other writing, or giving a copy thereof." A deed, for example, was regarded as more than a mere conveyance; it contained also the certificate of the examination of a feme covert, the certificate of the examiner and the oath of execution. The people regarded a deed as a single conveyance; Fanning regarded it as four. He therefore claimed that he was entitled to four fees, one for each service.

Such a man as Fanning will employ any weapon at his command to shield himself from the popular resentment which he feels he has aroused. In May 1768 Tryon told the Regulators that if they should send him a petition containing their grievances and then return peacefully to their homes, he would use all the power of his office to obtain justice for them. When the Regulators met to prepare the petition, however, Fanning, fearing it might prove offensive to his interests, requested them through Husband to accept one written by himself; no other petition, he said, would "go down with the governor."

The colonel warned Husband that if this request was ignored, he would represent his case which was scheduled to be tried in September as one involving treason. Confused by this threat, the Regulators resorted to the expediency of appointing a committee which would lay before Tryon and his council all the papers of their organization together with a request to pardon anything they had done contrary to the King's peace and government. At the same time they procured affidavits to support charges against the sheriff, clerk and register in twenty cases of alleged illegal fees and sent them to the governor.

Tryon frowned on this procedure, darkly hinted treason and championed Fanning, though he promised to prosecute any person found guilty of taking illegal fees and to issue a proclamation against the same abuse. This proclamation, posted in Hillsboro, brought no relief. Indeed, Husband claimed that it resulted in higher fees than before. The people retaliated by refusing to pay their taxes. In a message to Tryon they explained that officers paid no attention to his proclamation.

"Seeing that these sons of Zeruiah are like to prove too hard for your excellency, as well as for us," they said, "we have come to the resolution to petition the lower house, as the other branch of the legislature, in order to strengthen your excellency's hands."

The Regulators soon heard that Tryon intended to reply to their threat to his prerogative by sending against them a force which included Indians. To forestall this purported intention, the Regulators gathered about twenty miles from Hillsboro on August 11, 1768, and selected a deputation of eight men to interview the governor. Tryon replied that he had no intention of enlisting either the militia or Indians against them, that he was always ready to secure justice for them, that Fanning had agreed to submit the charges of illegal fees to the next superior court—by whose decision he promised to abide—and that the sheriff's accounts in Orange County had been examined and approved.

Tryon also set August 20 as the day on which the Regulators

were to be permitted to examine the public accounts. But when this date approached he sent them a letter stating that their measures were illegal and that they had made every man of "property and probity" in the country believe they intended to stage an insurrection rather than seek legal process against those whom they accused. In the circumstances, he said, he felt he should adopt measures to protect the next term of court, when Husband and Butler were to be tried. And he demanded that twelve prominent Regulators meet him on August 25 at Salisbury and become surety in bond of £1,000 that they would make no attempt to rescue Husband and Butler. The Regulators refused this demand on the ground that they had no plans to rescue their friends; all they asked was that the governor should dissolve the assembly, a procedure which they thought would stop every complaint. Tryon ignored this plea. Instead he called nearly fifteen hundred soldiers to protect the Hillsboro court.

Before this array of force the Regulators were not prepared to stand. Assembling on September 22 about half a mile from the town, they sent a proposal to Tryon seeking to know on what terms their submission would be accepted. Tryon replied that if they would surrender five of their leaders from Orange, two from Anson and two from Rowan, lay down their arms before the army and promise to pay their taxes in the future, they would be pardoned. Husband and Butler were excluded in the nine acceptable persons. The Regulators refused these terms but, undecided about what they should do, quietly returned to their homes.

At their trials both Husband and Butler were charged with inciting the King's subjects to riot. Husband was acquitted, but Butler was sentenced to six months' imprisonment and to pay a fine of £50. The officers were tried next. Every precaution was taken to prevent Regulators from making a possible attempt to obstruct justice. Troops asked the business of every man who wished to attend court. If a man admitted an intention to testify against the officers, he was sent away. If he insisted on staying, he was ordered to leave town.

Nevertheless, some of them returned and succeeded in testifying against Fanning and other officers. Their efforts, however, proved vain. Fanning convinced the jury that in taking a fee for each service on a deed he had simply conformed with the decisions of certain justices of the county court. In consequence the court held that he was innocent of "tortuous taking," a ruling which constrained the jury to impose on him a merely nominal penalty: he was fined a penny for each offense. On being convicted, he immediately resigned his position as register.

By this time the Regulators were active in nearly all the back counties. In Rowan they tried to prosecute John Frohock for extortion, but the grand jury was packed. Its members, the Regulators found, were not the same as those who had originally been chosen. Such cases were numerous. The Regulators naturally deduced that the laws favored the officers and that, therefore, they should be changed.

In a pamphlet addressed to the people Husband recounted their grievances and urged them to arouse themselves from their own "blind, stupid conduct" by electing honest members to the lower house in the next assembly. When it met in October 1769 the lower house showed itself sympathetic toward the people. It passed a bill to regulate legal fees, and it introduced an act which provided means for recovering small debts. This good beginning, however, was soon nullified by an event unrelated to it.

On November 2 the lower house unanimously passed a resolution on a question then at issue between the colonies and the Royal Government. Tryon disapproved of the resolution and dissolved the assembly. In the succeeding elections for delegates to the lower house the Regulators showed surprising strength: two from their organization were elected, one of whom was Husband. Tryon hastened to repair this loss by making Hillsboro a borough, which promptly returned Fanning to the assembly.

No sooner had this body resumed its duties when in September 1770 it received alarming information concerning Regulator activity in the Hillsboro district. Failing to obtain relief of grievances through petitions to the governor, the assembly and the court, they had resolved on force. They prefaced this with an elaborate petition to the superior court, demanding unprejudiced juries and public accounting of taxes. Their frame of mind is clearly disclosed in these sentences:

Our only crime with which they can charge us is vertue [*sic*] in the very highest degree, namely, to risque our all to save our country from rapine and slavery in our detecting of practises which the law itself allowed to be worse than open robbery. . . . As we are serious and in good earnest, and the cause respects the whole body of the people, it would be a loss of time to enter into argument on particular points, for though there is a few men who have the gift or art of reasoning, yet every man has a feeling and knows when he has justice done him as well as the most learned.

The presiding judge, Richard Henderson—the future proprietor of Transylvania—agreed to take their petition under careful consideration until the following Monday morning. On that day Hillsboro was filled with a vociferous army of men. When the court convened at eleven o'clock, the Regulators crowded into the courtroom "as close as one man could stand by another," many of them armed with switches, cowskin whips and clubs. Their spokesman on this occasion was Jeremiah Fields, who told Henderson they were determined to have their cases tried and had come down to see justice done. They charged the court with injustice at the preceding term, objected to the appointment of jurors by the common court and expressed their determination to have the panel changed and another appointed in its place.

After some parley Henderson yielded to their demands. But they had already become an unruly mob. When the session resumed, several of them fell on John Williams, Henderson's law partner, who escaped a beating by taking refuge in a near-by store. They next threatened to strike Henderson while he endeavored to placate them from the bench window. Instead, they turned on Fanning. Dragging him by his heels from the bench where he sought refuge, they beat him until he managed to break away and flee to a store. Pursuing him, they threw dirt, brickbats and stones at the building. They broke all its windows, but they failed to draw Fanning outside. Then they turned their wrath on Henderson, who gradually succeeded in appeasing them by promising to hold court until the end of the term. Permitting him to adjourn court, they conducted him "with great parade" to his lodgings. After exacting a promise from Fanning to surrender next day, they permitted him to go home.

Henderson had no intention of keeping his word. That evening at about ten o'clock he made his escape by a back way, putting Fanning in a desperate situation. The next morning Regulators threatened the colonel with death, but they reconsidered and permitted him to run out of town as fast as his legs would go. They spent their fury by burning his house, his furniture and practically all his personal belongings.

Enraged by Henderson's perfidy, the Regulators took possession of the court, called over their cases and, in futile protests over conditions they were powerless to remedy, made profane entries in the records: "Damned rogues"; "Fanning pays costs but loses nothing"; "Negroes not worth a damn, Cost exceed the Whole"; and in a case of slander, "Nonsense, let them argue for Ferrell has gone hellward."

On the night of November 12, 1770, they avenged themselves on Henderson by burning his brother's barn and stables, destroying several horses and a quantity of corn and two days later burning the residence of the judge himself. Governor Tryon offered £100 reward for clues leading to the arrest of the incendiaries, who, however, were never apprehended.

Amid all this alarm and confusion the assembly met in early December. Tryon's first object of vengeance was Hermon Husband. He was arraigned before the lower house and expelled on a charge of "false and seditious libel" for publishing a circular letter bearing the signature of a leading Regulator named James Hunter and addressed to Maurice Moore, a judge of the supreme court and a member of the assembly. Tryon also had him arrested and imprisoned without bail to keep him from returning to the Regulators. A few weeks later the assembly passed legislation for suppressing riots. This law, an emergency act which was to expire in one year, empowered the attorney general to try charges involving rioting in any superior court, declared an outlaw any person who failed to obey a court summons within sixty days and authorized the governor to use the militia to enforce the law.

The Regulators resolved to take measures to gain Husband's release. In February 1771 they gathered in the woods and reasserted their principles. Like good Americans, they averred that all laws contrary to God's law of equality were null and void and that all officers who exacted illegal taxes and fees from the poor were guilty of a worse crime than open robbery. They asked that extortioners be brought to trial and "the collectors of the public money called to proper settlements of their accounts." Emboldened by their own words, they prepared to march on the jail at New Bern to rescue their leader.

Unwilling for the present to precipitate a civil war, Tryon freed Husband when he learned that the Regulators were approaching. This stopped their march but did not soften their anger. They decided to pay a visit to the superior court at Salisbury. On March 6, 1771, about four or five hundred of them encamped in the woods west of the Yadkin River.

"The lawyers are everything," they complained. "There should be none in the province."

"We shall be forced to kill them all."

"There never was such an act as the Riot Act in the laws of England." Down with England!

To an officer who requested them to explain their presence they said: "We come with no intention to obstruct the court, or to injure the person or property of any one, but only to petition for a redress of grievances against officers taking exorbitant fees."

"Why, then, are some of you armed?"

"Our arms," they replied, "are only to defend ourselves."

Though they were informed that no court would be held on account of the disturbances, the officers, finding them "peacefully disposed beyond expectation," agreed to settle their differences with them by arbitration on the third Tuesday in May. After each side had chosen referees, the Regulators marched through Salisbury, gave three cheers and quietly returned to their homes.

Tryon was bent on revenge. Displeased with himself for having been obliged to set Husband free, he dismissed the term of court and called another for March 11. The sheriffs of the several counties in the district were directed to elect as jurymen only "gentlemen of the first rank, property, and probity in their respective counties." Thus Tryon took means to obtain jurors and witnesses suited to his purpose.

On the appointed day the court opened. With willing witnesses and a unanimous grand jury, sixty-one indictments were found for felonies or riots against leading Regulators in Orange County, many of whom lived two hundred miles away and who had been at home during the riots of which they were accused.

Tryon next received the grand jury at his palace and informed it of his intention to lead an armed force against the "insurgents." The jury joined the council to applaud his purpose. The governor obtained the necessary funds, which the assembly had refused to provide, by creating a paper currency by drafts on the treasury. Before leaving New Bern he ordered Hugh Waddell—now a general—to march to the Yadkin with a detachment of 250 men and to collect forces all along the road to his destination, where he was to await a convoy from Charleston, South Carolina, with a supply of powder for Tryon's army.

On May 1, 1771, the governor himself, with somewhat fewer than a thousand men, marched westward and eight days later encamped at Hillsboro. On the same day General Waddell, while awaiting the convoy from Charleston, received word that it had been seized and that the ammunition he expected had been blown up by nine young Regulators disguised with blackened faces.

Deciding to try to join Tryon, Waddell sent messengers to Hillsboro to advise him of the capture of the convoy. On the next day he broke camp and started for Hillsboro, intending to join Tryon at the Haw River. Hardly had he crossed the Yadkin, however, when he received a message from the Regulators warning him to halt or retreat. Finding his men inclined to desert rather than fight the Regulators, he retreated toward Salisbury. The Regulators pursued him, engaged him in a skirmish and, surrounding his detachment, took most of his men prisoners. They permitted him to escape with a few of his men.

On May 11 Tryon moved from Hillsboro to relieve Waddell. Marching through Regulator country, he crossed the Haw River where he received small reinforcements and proceeded to the Alamance River which he reached on May 14. Learning that a large group of Regulators had gathered on the hills about five miles farther on, he marched his men toward them in two columns.

The Regulators numbered about two thousand, half of whom were armed. They had no desire for battle; indeed, they hoped that a show of force would frighten the governor into granting their demands. In the interest of peace they addressed to him a petition which was delivered by Dr. David Caldwell, a preacher. Tryon replied:

I lament the fatal necessity to which you have now reduced me by withdrawing yourselves from the mercy of the crown and from the laws of your country. To require you who are now assembled as Regulators, to quietly lay down your arms, to surrender up your leaders, to the laws of your country and rest on the leniency of the Government. By accepting these terms within one hour from the delivery, of this dispatch, you will prevent an effusion of blood, as you are at this time in a state of REBELLION against your King, your country, and your laws.

The Regulators refused the terms. In vain did Dr. Caldwell try to persuade them to withdraw, pointing out that they had no cannon, no military training, no ammunition and no commanding officers to lead them into battle.

At this juncture an old Scotchman called out to the minister: "Doctor Caldwell, get out of the way or Tryon's army will kill you in three minutes!" The preacher hastily cleared the field.

Hermon Husband, too, had deserted. Though he had bravely faced threats, imprisonment and torture, he shrank, like a true Quaker, from violence. He had come along in the hope of helping to reach a compromise, but when he saw no hope he mounted his horse and quietly rode away. Realizing his danger, he fled to his old home in Maryland, and from there to western Pennsylvania where he remained for the rest of his days.

To the last minute the Regulators hoped to avoid bloodshed. About noon on May 16 they sent Robert Thompson, an amiable but outspoken man, to speak to Tryon once more. During their conversation Thompson must have uttered some plain truths, for Tryon killed him with a gun he had snatched from a militiaman. Soon perceiving his folly, he decided to placate the Regulators by sending a flag of truce toward their side of the field; but they, enraged by his murderous act, began firing with deadly aim. Tryon then angrily mounted a white charger, shouting, "Fire! Fire!" Seeing his men hesitate, he bellowed, "God damn it, fire! Fire on them!"

To which a Regulator replied, "Fire and be damned!" The battle was joined.

At first the Regulators controlled the situation. They sought the protection of trees, rocks and fences while they fired. Their sharpshooters found easy targets in Tryon's men who, fighting in the open fields, were unable to do more than shoot. Worse followed for the governor. Captain Montgomery led a charge of his mountain boys that routed Tryon's force and compelled it to abandon two cannon. But Montgomery soon fell while Tryon succeeded in rallying his troops.

The Regulators, lacking officers with authority to give orders, became confused. Unable to fire their cannon, they fled from the field in bands of hundreds. In less than two hours the battle came to an end. Nine men had been killed on each side while Tryon counted sixty-one wounded and his opponents a larger number. About fifteen Regulators were taken prisoners. One of these, James Few, a carpenter who had been outlawed for participating in the Hillsboro riots, was executed on the spot.

From Alamance Tryon led his troops to Sandy Creek, where he exacted an oath of allegiance from the people. He also issued a proclamation pardoning all persons who should submit to an oath of allegiance. Six thousand met this demand within a month. Tryon soon returned to Hillsboro where the prisoners were court-martialed. Twelve were convicted of treason, and half of these were condemned to death. Among them was Benjamin Merrill, a former captain in the Rowan County militia, who repudiated the Regulators just before he was led to the scaffold. He was hanged by his neck, cut down while he was still alive, and disemboweled, decapitated and quartered. "And may the Lord have mercy on your soul," the judicial sentence had added.

Another condemned man, James Pugh, remained steadfast in his principles. Mounting the barrel which served as the scaffold, he berated Tryon with Scotch-Irish vehemence for several minutes. He had turned to address Fanning when the barrel was overturned.

Thus ended in failure the attempts of the Regulators to secure reform in local government. Should they submit to the continued oppression, or should they accept the alternative of moving westward? Some of them, regarding the hopelessness of their condition as a greater evil than the danger of the wilderness, packed their belongings and mingled with the tide of emigration that was crossing the mountains into the western country of the colony which later became the state of Tennessee. Morgan Edwards, who visited this region in 1772, wrote that fifteen hundred—most of them of Scotch-Irish stock—had departed since Alamance, and that many more intended to follow as soon as they could dispose of their farms.

Was Alamance the first battle of the American Revolution? Several local historians, eager to make the most of every historical event falling within their state, have answered in the affirmative. A more objective writer, John Spencer Bassett, saw no connection in the two events. In fact, most of the Regulators were Tories. While they hated Tryon, they remained loyal to the King. They had aimed against the oppressive agents of the government, not against the government itself. If the movement had never happened, said Bassett, "the armies of Washington and Clinton, of Greene and Cornwallis, would have fought out their battles much the same as they did fight them."

Nevertheless, historians cannot overlook the fact that the movement was an authentic expression of western principles, and therefore of American character. It provided an "object lesson

for the whole country." The Regulators, wrote George Bancroft with some grains of truth,

. . . form the connecting link between resistance to the Stamp
Act and the movement of 1775; and they also played a glorious
part in taking possession of the Mississippi valley, towards which
they were carried irresistibly by their love of independence. It
is a mistake if any have supposed that the Regulators were cowed
down by their defeat at the Alamance. Like the mammoth, they
shook the bolt from their brow and crossed the mountains.

Though they failed, they showed that the colonists were capable
of armed resistance; and that British armies, however formidable
in other circumstances, would be rendered weak in a hostile
country. Tryon's campaign, finally, developed the military organization of North Carolina. This was shown during the Revolution when that colony's troops won the battle of Moore's Creek
which, though small in comparison with other victories, prevented the Tories in the southern colonies from joining the
British.

The

Wataugans

IN THE SPRING OF 1770 A GRIMY TRAVELER, WEARY FROM HIS long and difficult journey across the mountains, found rest and friendship in John Honeycut's crude cabin on the banks of the Watauga River in present eastern Tennessee. The stranger had come to "spy out" good land on which he hoped to settle with his family and some friends. He was a fair-complexioned man of twenty-eight with light blue eyes and dark hair. In demeanor he was taciturn, but his face, though somber, showed a strength that was impressive. From his native home in Brunswick County, Virginia, he had recently moved to Orange County, North Carolina, where he is said to have sympathized with the Regulators, though he took no active part in their dissatisfaction with the government. He had no formal education; just before his departure his wife had been teaching him his letters and how to spell. The stranger's name was James Robertson.

He had crossed the mountains alone with a rifle in his hands and a good horse under him. Honeycut welcomed him with frontier hospitality and helped him build a hut and plant Indian corn. Early in August Robertson started back to his home in Orange County. Like most hunters of the early frontier, he lived on game and the small amount of parched Indian corn he carried in his saddlebag. He soon lost his way. Finding himself among impassable cliffs, he abandoned his horse. Rain fell repeatedly on his powder, rendering most of it useless. When his strength permitted he struggled up a summit and climbed a tree to observe the mountain ranges with the intention of blazing as direct a path as the rhododendron and laurel thickets would permit. Descending, he began to cut the thickets with his knife only to

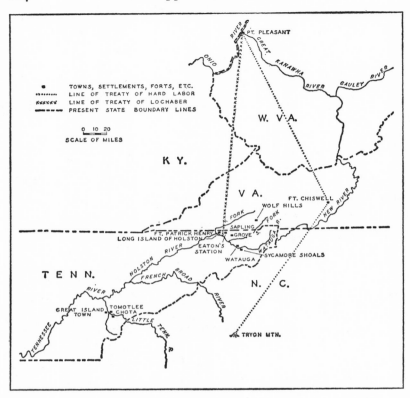

discover that he had recrossed his path. In a moment of despair he threw himself on the ground, hoping that he would never rise; but the next hour he stumbled on with renewed courage. His food supply exhausted, he sustained himself for fourteen days more on what few berries and roots he could find. Yet he would have starved to death had not two hunters fed him and reluctantly permitted him to ride one of their horses.

At last Robertson arrived at home. Enchanted by his colorful accounts of the Watauga country, sixteen persons, including his brother Charles, agreed to accompany him to that region. They started out in the early fall to give Robertson time to gather and store the corn he had planted and to lay in a winter's supply of deer and bear meat. They moved westward in the usual pioneer manner—the men walking with their rifles on their soulders, the oldest children driving the milch cows, and the women and young children riding on horses already burdened with household goods and farming implements. Arriving in the Watauga country, the group separated. Each family cleared a piece of ground and built a cabin around Sycamore Shoals where Elizabethton, Tennessee, now stands. This became the center of the Watauga settlements.

Robertson's steadfastness, restless energy and unusual common sense soon won him the admiration of the settlers in the region. His dour determination transcended all obstacles. His personality was embodied in the house he built on an island in the Watauga River. It was sturdy, roughhewn and more spacious than the other dwellings. The log veranda which ran the full front length of the house suggested his quiet dignity, while the huge stone-and-clay fireplace with its logs blazing in the winter time symbolized his ardent faith and dauntless courage in the face of adversity. His furniture was as simple as his needs.

One of Robertson's neighbors was Evan Shelby, a Marylander of Welsh stock, who had shown himself a gallant soldier under Braddock, under Washington at Great Meadows and Fort Necessity and under Forbes in his march to Pittsburgh. After the close of the French and Indian War Shelby had married and become an Indian trader. During his travels he heard about a trader and farmer from western Virginia named William Bean, who in 1768 had raised his cabin on the Watauga and who, after spending several months in the wilderness, had returned like a Marco Polo to his old surroundings, regaling everyone he met with tales of the golden land he had visited. Shelby had forthwith packed his horse, bidden his family farewell and ridden into the twilight zone. On reaching the Holston he had settled on an estate which he called Sapling Grove—the present site of Bristol, Tennessee—where he engaged in merchandising, farming and cattle raising.

In January 1771 he announced his arrival in a letter to his sons, Isaac and John, who had just returned home from military service: "This is Too Litt you know that wee are all saffe arrived at our habitation on Holston after a Jurney of three weeks and three days upon the Road wher wee found all things in Good orders and wee Seem well satisfyed with the Cuntry. . . ." He had nothing of importance to report, he said, save " . . . that sartain officers is to have their quatto [quota] of Lands upon these waters which will I hope be a means of setleing of this Cuntry with a much Better sort of Peopel than it wood a been settled with but I always thought if the officers had their choice they wood Sooner Chews ut hear than on the Ohio for without any Dout the advantages hear must be more than ever Can be Expected Their. . . ." Shelby then urged his sons to purchase " . . . all officers and Soldiers Right you Can Possible Git So that Git them to go with you to the Collonels of the Redgments and to git a proper Sartifycatt that the warrants may be obtained. . . ."

Shelby predicted that the country would be settled, that the settlers would be men of property and that the region would soon become a county. Impelled by these convictions, he returned to Maryland, sold his lands there and moved with his family to the banks of the Holston.

Another leading settler of the region, John Sevier, symbolized the heroic life of the frontier. The son of a Huguenot gentleman who had settled in the Shenandoah Valley, his proclivities were a blend of all those found in genuine pioneers: he was at once settler, speculator, adventurer, trader, Indian fighter and lawmaker. His personal qualities were no less admirable. He was a gentleman from sole to crown—elegant in manners, handsome of face and figure and dignified in carriage. He was gay and pleasure-loving. Mediocre men became jealous of his gifts, only to be charmed by his fascinating demeanor. His influence over his fellow Wataugans was almost boundless. His tact, his courtesy, his generosity had quickly captured their esteem, and he was soon to win their admiration by his skill and blind daring in Indian fighting.

So subtle were Sevier's persuasive powers that he could convert the most recalcitrant pioneer to his views by making him believe that these had originated with himself. His great knowledge of human nature was not derived from books—for which he cared little—but from keen observation of men and events, yet he was far from unlettered. His correspondence with Madison,

Franklin and other influential contemporaries shows a practiced and sometimes even a graceful style.

Early in the 1760's John Sevier settled in Long Meadows where he devoted his time to farming. Eager to improve his fortune, however, he established the town of New Market where he became a tavern keeper, farmer and merchant. In 1770 he deserted New Market for Millerstown—now Woodstock in Shenandoah County. John—always searching for land on which to build a better home for his family—and his brother, Valentine, visited the Watauga country several times during the next two years. Soon John's father and other brothers, catching the infection of his enthusiasm for the frontier, settled with him on the north side of the Holston in the Keywood settlement. Later John moved with his family to the Watauga.

By this time several groups of cabins dotted the wilderness in eastern Tennessee. The first settlement consisted of about a dozen cabins on Long Island in the Holston River. The second lay south of the Holston at Sycamore Shoals on the Watauga. The third, lying on the present site of Rogersville, was named Carter's Valley in honor of its first settler, John Carter, a Virginian who built a store and traded with Indians, white settlers and frontiersmen who were on their way down the Holston, Tennessee, Ohio and Mississippi rivers to settle in the Natchez region.

What circumstances had started this new great tide of migration? Many of the Wataugans were Regulators who had fled westward across the mountains after the Battle of the Alamance. Other settlers came as the result of the treaties concerning the western boundary of white settlement which North Carolina and Virginia and the British government concluded with the Cherokee. By the Treaty of Hard Labour John Stuart, Superintendent of Indian Affairs for the Southern Department, and the Cherokee in 1768 drew a boundary line back of the Carolinas and Virginia beyond which white men were forbidden to settle. But the appearance of settlers in the upper Holston Valley to the west of the line soon necessitated another agreement.

Accordingly, on October 18, 1770, by the Treaty of Lochaber,

South Carolina, the line was extended to leave no white settler on Cherokee lands. The Indian boundary now began from the intersection of the North Carolina and Cherokee lines some seventy-odd miles east of Long Island, ran westward to a point six miles east of Long Island and then northward to the junction of the Great Kanawha and Ohio rivers. When John Donelson and Alexander Cameron surveyed this line late in the following year, they discovered that the Wataugans had settled, not within the bounds of Virginia as they believed, but within those of North Carolina. By the King's orders and by the Treaty of Lochaber, this land had been reserved for the Indians.

Cameron ordered the Wataugans to leave, but since their crops were then in the ground they persuaded him to allow them to remain until the following spring. When that season arrived, "some of them went away, but others and more people came in their room" and brought their goods with them. Feeling that their tenures were insecure, however, they decided to purchase the land from the Cherokee. With American self-reliance they met for deliberation and counsel and deputed James Robertson and John Been "to treat with their landslords, and agree upon articles of accomodation and friendship." The negotiations succeeded. For about six thousand dollars in merchandise and some muskets and household articles, the Cherokee leased to the Wataugans for a period of ten years all the country on the river.

The whites and Indians decided to celebrate their new understanding with athletic games. At Watauga on the chosen day they held a race, wrestling matches and other sports in which they mixed in very friendly fashion. But toward evening some ruffians from Wolf Hills, who had been lurking in the surrounding forest, killed one of the Indians, whereupon his comrades left the spot in great anger. The settlers immediately saw in the disgraceful deed the possibility of Indian revenge. Robertson calmed their fears by volunteering to go to the Cherokee villages and settle the matter. While John Sevier made preparations to build a palisaded fort, Robertson set off alone through the wilderness for his destination, over a hundred and fifty miles away.

The mission was, of course, very dangerous, but the Cherokees, learning that Robertson was coming to see them, decided to let him alone. His knowledge of Indian psychology and his ready tact saved the situation. At his request the chiefs called a council in which he assured them of the anger and sorrow of the Wataugans and of his determination to try to arrest the criminals and punish them severely. The Indians were so pleased with his sincerity that they agreed to forget the matter and take no vengeance on their innocent white brothers. Robertson then quietly returned home.

Among the Wataugans were a few criminals who had put the mountain wall between themselves and justice. The rest were "honest, industrious, enterprising men" bent on earning a livelihood. Realizing that neither North Carolina nor Virginia would recognize their right to live within Indian country, they felt "apprehensive" that they "might become a shelter for such as endeavored to defraud their creditors"; moreover, they wanted to record deeds, wills, and "do their public business."

They resolved, therefore, to form a government of their own. This move was doubtlessly inspired by Robertson, who was acquainted with the principles of the Regulators in North Carolina. The Wataugans decided to adopt written articles of agreement known as the Watauga Association, the first free and independent government, democratic in spirit and representative in form, ever to be organized on the American continent.

Lord Dunmore, governor of Virginia, referred to the Wataugans as "actually a set of People in the back country of the Colony bordering on the Cherokee Country, who finding they could not obtain titles to the Land they fancied . . . have appointed Magistrates and framed Laws for their present occasions and to all intents and purposes erected themselves into though inconsiderable yet a Separate State." Dunmore thought the Wataugans had set a bad example "to the people of America of forming governments distinct from and independent of His Majesty's Authority."

Indeed, the Watauga settlers were expressing that inherent American characteristic for political independence and local government which ultimately resulted in the establishment of our states. This trait persisted in every region until the entire Union was formed. Unfortunately, the original articles of the Watauga Association are lost. All we know of them is derived from historians who lived many years later; knowledge of them would have disclosed the particular psychological needs of the men who fashioned them.

The framers of the Watauga Association established a court of five members in which was vested executive, legislative and judicial powers. James Robertson, Charles Robertson, John Sevier, John Carter and Zachariah Isbell had responsible and mature legal judgment, though they lacked legal training. Charles Robertson was a man of probity and sound reasoning, Carter was the oldest settler in Watauga and Isbell was a former magistrate with broad legal knowledge. The historian of early Tennessee, Samuel Cole Williams, mindful that Sevier did not settle permanently in the Watauga country until the end of 1773, concluded that he was not one of the original members of the court. With this opinion Sevier's best biographer, John Driver, does not agree, pointing out that Sevier "had already obtained possession of the land to which he later moved and that he had remained there for a time during the year in which the Association was formed."

The name of the sheriff who executed the mandates of the court is unknown. The court's decisions were final, for it was at once a common pleas court, an appellate court and a supreme court. In addition it was department of interior and department of state. It not only controlled internal affairs but also had the power to secure lands by making treaties with the Indians. In short, it enjoyed sovereign power.

Needless to say, its functions were numerous. These included the recording of deeds and wills, the settling of disputes, the issuing of marriage licenses and the conducting of vigorous warfare against lawbreakers. For six years the court acted as a censor of morals and interfered, with straightforward effectiveness, to right wrongs for which a more refined and elaborate system of jurisprudence would have provided only cumbersome and inadequate remedies.

In April 1775 Lexington initiated the American Revolution. Soon afterward the revolutionary Provincial Congress of North Carolina established a committee of safety in each of its six districts. The Wataugans, immediately identifying themselves with the revolutionary cause, instituted similar action. Uncertain whether their settlements lay within the jurisdiction of Virginia or within that of North Carolina, and fearing that neither colony would grant them protection because they had violated the Proclamation of 1763, they organized themselves into an independent district which they named Washington in honor of the commander of the Continental Army.

The Watauga committee of safety contained thirteen members, including James Robertson, Charles Robertson, John Sevier, Jacob Brown, William Bean, Robert Lucas and John Carter, chairman. It resolved to "adhere strictly to the rules and orders of the Continental Congress, and in open committee acknowledged themselves indebted to the united colonies for their full proportion of the Continental expense." It established a militia with Carter as colonel.

As the revolution spread southwestward John Stuart, acting on the orders of General Thomas Gage, took steps to induce the Cherokee to give their support to the British cause. Complying with this request, Stuart sent his brother Henry to the overhill Cherokee towns. In April 1776 Henry arrived at his destination with thirty loads of ammunition to learn from Alexander Cameron that the chief difficulty would not be in securing Cherokee promises of aid, but would be in restraining the young warriors from making an immediate attack on men, women and children—whether Tories or Revolutionists—who had settled in the Watauga region which the Cherokee claimed as their rightful hunting grounds.

The orator and resolute chief, Dragging Canoe, had always hated the Americans and had vehemently opposed the selling or leasing of ground to them. He now declared that his young men complained constantly that Virginians and North Carolinians had settled on their lands without their consent and that they "were almost surrounded by white people." Stuart replied that the encroachments "were made contrary to the Kings Orders,

that affairs were in such a situation at this time that they seemed
to trample on his Authority and that we could not do anything
with them but that we hoped things would not continue long
so." He also reminded Dragging Canoe that the Indians, in leasing land to the Wataugans, had acted contrary to the advice of
their superintendent. To which Dragging Canoe replied that the
Wataugans had negotiated only with a few old men who, unable
to hunt, had been reduced by poverty to leasing their land.
Most of his young men, the chief asserted, would support him in
recovering the Cherokee hunting grounds.

The more the Cherokee talked of attacking the white settlements, the more Stuart tried to dissuade them. The ignorant settlers, he told them, believed that they had legally purchased the
land and that, therefore, no Cherokee should object to their
settling it. He promised to try to induce the settlers to move.

Stuart was as good as his word. In May 1776 he sent a trader
named Isaac Thomas with a letter to the Wataugans who, though
alarmed, resolved to stay where they were. If they could not
prevent an attack, they reasoned, they could at least delay it.
Accordingly, they sent Thomas back to the Cherokee with conciliatory messages. The Indians generously allowed them twenty
days more.

But circumstances made war inevitable. One night in May a
mounted stranger delivered a letter at Charles Robertson's gate
and sped away. The letter, addressed to the Wataugans and
bearing Henry Stuart's signature, said that the King of England
had no desire "to set his friends and allies, the Indians, on his
liege subjects," that those who should agree to become his soldiers
would "find protection for themselves and their friends," and
that a British army would land on the coast of West Florida,
advance into Cherokee, Creek and Chickamauga country and
crush the rebellious colonists with innumerable Indian allies. The
original letter soon disappeared, but copies of it were circulated
widely among the settlers, filling them with hatred for its purported author, his brother, Alexander Cameron and the Cherokee.

Amid this consternation Henry Stuart vehemently denied

authorship of the letter. Isaac Thomas, he declared, had disclosed to him that it was written by Jesse Benton, who, together with other Wataugans, desired "to involve the Settlements of Virginia and North Carolina in an unjust War with the Indians" in defense of the lands they had taken unlawfully. Stuart doubtless spoke truth. Nothing in his report of the Cherokee controversy can be construed as evidence of chicanery. Indeed, many of its details corroborate the testimonies of several independent witnesses.

The Wataugans, on the contrary, had everything to gain by involving themselves in a war with the Cherokee. They had settled the region in violation of the Proclamation of 1763; they could hope to retain their lands and assuage their guilty feelings only by pretending that the Indians, incited by British agents, planned to attack them. They, therefore, were happy to pledge their full support to the American Revolution.

They hastened to convince the revolutionaries of Virginia that the Indians intended to attack only the supporters of the revolutionary cause. When Anthony Bledsoe, a member of the Committee of Safety of Fincastle County, advised the Wataugans to remove themselves from Cherokee lands, their spokesman, William Cocke, replied that they and the Holston settlers would stand by "the glorious Cause in which the americans have Successfully begun the war in defense of Liberty & property." And he prayed that the Virginia assembly, "Esteemed throughout america for Equity & humanity will no longer look upon us as a Separate people but will willingly afford us such assistance as may Inable us to defend Our Selves from an Enemy that only wish to destroy their unalterable friends." They sent a similar appeal to North Carolina.

Meanwhile the Cherokee prepared for war. During the early summer they mended guns, made arrows and moccasins and beat large quantities of corn into flour. Henry Stuart and Cameron attempted to restrain them by warning them that "an indiscriminate attack" without British approval and assistance "would be the means of drawing on them the King's displeasure and of uniting all parties against them." The old chiefs agreed, but Dragging Canoe and his young men were determined on war; they accused Stuart and Cameron of warning the white men of an impending attack. Stuart then saw the futility of attempting to dissuade them from their purpose and prepared to return to his brother in Mobile. Before he departed he urged Dragging Canoe to refrain from killing Loyalists and women and children and to end hostilities at his brother's command.

Word of Cherokee intentions reached Little Carpenter's niece, Nancy Ward, beloved priestess in the annual ceremony of the Pretty Woman. Because her daughter loved a settler, Joseph Martin, she resolved to send warning to the white men. Summoning Isaac Thomas, who was living among the Cherokee, she informed him that 700 warriors planned to fall on the Watauga and Holston villages. Thomas took this information to the settlers who quickly sought protection in their small stockaded forts.

The men, assembling to the number of 170, marched to the fort at Eaton's Station and sent out scouts to ascertain the enemy's whereabouts. The scouts soon returned with word that the Indians were approaching the fort. What should they do? Should they stay cooped up like turkeys in a pen? Or should they attack the redskins? William Cocke convinced them that the Indians would not storm the fort but would, with small parties, massacre the women and children in the settlements.

Hesitating no longer, they advanced on July 20 to a place known as Island Flats, a large tract of level and wooded land lying near Long Island on the Holston, where they discovered a small party of Indians, fired on them and sent them into headlong flight. Unable to overtake the Indians, they turned at dusk toward the fort. Suddenly they found themselves attacked in their rear and in grave danger of being surrounded. To meet the savage onslaught, they extended their line under Captain James Shelby.

The Indians mistook this for a movement of retreat. "The white men are running away!" they yelled. "Scalp them!" A huge brave bumped into a Lieutenant Alex Moore, who shot him in the knee. The brave, still standing, hurled his tomahawk; it missed. Moore sprang at him with a large butcher knife. The

Indian grabbed the blade; it cut deep into his hand. He gripped it like a vise. A pool of blood rose in the palm of his hand and spattered both men as it trickled to the ground. The two men clinched, each with his free hand. Moore threw the brave to the ground, pulled his tomahawk from his belt and sank it into the Indian's skull. Just then Dragging Canoe fell with a serious wound. His braves, becoming demoralized, hurriedly picked up their dead and wounded and fled, marking the retreat to their villages with streams of blood. Thirteen scalped Indians lay on the field. Four white men were seriously wounded, but all of them recovered.

At dawn on the following day a formidable force of Indians under Old Abraham attacked the Watauga fort. The women had just gone out to milk the cows when in the gray light they saw the Indians galloping toward them. All of them ran screaming to the safety of the fort save pretty Kate Sherill, who found that its nervous defenders had inadvertently locked her out. Sevier, seeing her plight, leaped to the top of the stockade, shot her foremost pursuer, and, leaning over, seized her by the hands and lifted her to safety. Some months later her gallant rescuer, who had been a widower for several years, became her husband.

The men, about forty in number, placing themselves under James Robertson with Sevier as second in command, leveled their rifles through the loopholed stockade and picked off a goodly number of redskins. In less than an hour the attack was beaten back. Nevertheless, the Indians beseiged the fort for several weeks, during which time several settlers were killed or captured.

One day James Cooper and Samuel Moore, a boy in his teens, went out to find boards to cover a hut. When they saw Indians approaching, Cooper jumped into a creek to escape their arrows and bullets, but the water was shallow and he was killed and scalped. Moore was taken to an Indian village where he was tortured and burned. Cooper's cries reached the fort, and Sevier prepared to hasten to his rescue; but Robertson, suspecting a feint and needing all the men he commanded to protect the women and children from possible massacre, persuaded him to remain.

Another prisoner of the siege was the wife of the settler William Bean. She, too, would have been burned had not Nancy Ward, exercising a prerogative as the Pretty Woman, pronounced her pardon.

The revolutionary authorities of Virginia, the Carolinas and Georgia were now prepared to conduct separate campaigns against the Cherokee. The delegates of North Carolina in the Continental Congress determined "to carry fire and Sword into the very bowels of their country and sink them so low that they may never be able to again rise and disturb the peace of their neighbors."

Late in July a party of Georgians under Major Samuel Jack burned two Cherokee towns. In August General Andrew Williamson led an army from South Carolina against the Hiwassee villages, which they found evacuated. Nevertheless, he destroyed all the buildings, corn and cattle. In September General Griffith Rutherford marched with a North Carolina army into the middle towns and valley settlements. He and Williamson joined their forces and carried fire and sword to every village of the region, compelling the Indians to flee to the overhill towns.

Virginia ordered Colonel William Christian to raise an army and march against the Indians. Forthwith Christian addressed a circular to the militiamen of the surrounding region, requesting them to gather at Long Island in the Holston River. Within a few weeks he realized 1,800 men, including pack horse men and cattle drivers. All of them save a company of horse-riflemen were infantry, armed with flintlocks, tomahawks and butcher knives. Leading his troops across the Holston to near-by Double Springs, Colonel Christian halted for several days to enable some Wataugans to join him. When these men arrived Christian led his force toward the French Broad River, which the Cherokee vowed they would permit no white man to cross.

That night when Christian encamped a trader appeared and informed him that 3,000 Cherokee awaited his arrival at the river and would dispute his passage over it. Christian then took every precaution against a surprise. And in the morning he sent the trader back to the Cherokee with word that he would never stop until he crossed not only the French Broad but also the Tennessee. He resumed his advance. Guided by Isaac Thomas, the army marched on a narrow path along several creeks until it approached a ford of the French Broad.

The hearts of the Cherokee became as water when they learned that the white men were as thick as the trees. They sent Christian a trader waving a white flag attached to his rifle. The colonel gave orders to pay no heed to the man. And the trader disappeared to tell his friends that the white tide was about to engulf them. To give the Cherokee the impression that he intended to stay on the place for several days, Christian, on arriving at the French Broad, had his men set up tents and build many fires. That night he forded the river with a strong detachment and came up with the intention of surprising the encamped Cherokee from behind. But the colonel found the wigwams empty. The Indians had retreated to Long Island, the key that opened the gate to their country, where they had resolved to make a stand.

A trader who lived among them, however, dissuaded the Indians from their purpose. The Great Spirit, he said, had made the one race from white clay and the other from red. The former was destined to conquer; it could not be stopped from invading the Cherokee country. Better to retreat to their villages beyond the mountains. The Cherokee accepted his advice, abandoned all their defensive measures and scattered to their homes.

Meanwhile Christian pressed his advance. Two villages—Tamotlee and Great Island Town—fell to him without offering resistance. The surrounding fields provided him with ample corn and potatoes, while the deserted huts made comfortable bivouacs for his men. Not a Cherokee could they find, so they put the torch to fields and villages. Then Christian sent out three or four of his men with white flags and requested Chief Raven of Chota, Little Carpenter and Dragging Canoe to make peace on such terms of submission as he should demand. If they refused he would destroy their towns and pursue the fugitives as far as the Creek nation.

Dragging Canoe, who was recovering from his wound, refused to surrender; but Raven and Little Carpenter, having opposed war from the beginning, were happy to comply with whatever terms Christian might offer them. They met him in Chota, where they made peace. They promised to surrender all prisoners, return the horses, cattle and goods they had stolen, give up all Tories residing or hiding out in their villages and send delegates representing the entire tribe to sign a formal treaty at a designated place and time. Christian then destroyed two villages that were loyal to Dragging Canoe and the one that had burned the boy, Samuel Moore.

Returning to Long Island, Christian broke camp and disbanded most of his men. The remainder were sent to garrison Fort Patrick Henry, opposite Long Island, against the possibility of an attack by Dragging Canoe and his followers. Virginia and North Carolina kept 400 rangers in the woods between the Watauga settlements and the Cherokee villages. But for the present Dragging Canoe planned no trouble. Accompanied by his followers and some white traders and adventurers, he withdrew to the Tennessee River where they founded new villages and formed themselves into an independent tribe known as the Chickamauga.

In April 1777 nearly a hundred Cherokee, including Oconostota and Little Carpenter, came to Fort Patrick Henry. From there Colonel Christian conducted the chiefs and their attendants to Williamsburg, Virginia, for a conference with Governor Patrick Henry and the Virginia assembly. The chiefs asked for protection from further encroachments in return for their neutrality during the Revolution. The Virginians agreed to protect and guarantee their lands and requested them to meet in July at Long Island to sign the formal treaty.

At this place on July 20 Oconostota, Little Carpenter and other chiefs signed two treaties, one with the commissioners of North Carolina and the other with those of Virginia. The Indian representatives hoped that the whites would be requested to move from the Watauga country. Instead they learned that they must surrender more land to them. To the Indians' angry protests Waightstill Avery, head of the North Carolina commission, replied as follows: "We are now about to fix a line that is to remain through all generations, and be kept by our Childrens children; and we hope that both Nations will hereafter never have any more disputes."

Colonel Christian, one of the Virginia commissioners, added this assurance: "We agree with you that the line shall be like a wall, high and strong that none can pass over or break down." With this understanding the Indians surrendered the region as far south as the Watauga settlements extended. Both Virginia and North Carolina maintained agents in the Cherokee country until the terms of the treaty were discharged in every detail. The agent for North Carolina was James Robertson, who went to reside in Chota.

By now the Wataugans enjoyed the protection of North Carolina. In November 1776 that state had annexed the Washington District and had authorized it to send its four representatives, one of whom was John Sevier, to the Provincial Congress at Halifax. In the spring of 1777 this body passed laws which provided the district with courts of common pleas and quarter sessions, justices of the peace, a sheriff and a militia with John Carter as colonel. On December 18, 1777, North Carolina established Washington County, whose boundaries were those of the present state of Tennessee. The Wataugans thus completed a new chapter in the westward advance of American nationality.

Lord Dunmore's
War

THE FRONTIER ADVANCED IRREPRESSIBLY. THE AMERICANS, DEFY-
ing every attempt of the English government to limit them to
territory prescribed in its Indian treaties, trespassed the rich valley
of the Clinch and its tributaries and pushed into Kentucky and
along the banks of the upper Ohio. They came to hunt and then
to settle in lands which the Shawnee and the Cherokee claimed
as their hunting grounds.

The chiefs of these tribes had often warned white men to stay
away. Captain Will had expressed the wish of his race when in
1770 he had uttered his admonition to Boone and his party. But
an insatiable hunger for bottom lands more fertile and extensive
than their own drove pioneers on, leaving them indifferent to the
growing resentment of the aforementioned tribes. The English
government, aware that trouble was brewing and that war might
eventually ensue, maintained Shawnee representatives at Fort
Pitt.

The Shawnee had good reason to complain. Throughout the
summer and fall of 1773 separate groups of surveyors appeared
in several regions of the Virginia frontier to lay out tracts for
homesteaders already on the ground and for placements for government grants to veterans of the French and Indian War.

At Fish Creek—near present Moundsville, West Virginia—a
young and adventurous Virginian, George Rogers Clark, built a
cabin. From there he with a small party made exploratory expeditions down the Ohio and subsequently undertook the task of
surveying the interior of Kentucky.

At about the same time Lord Dunmore, governor of Virginia,

granted that zealous aspirant of western lands, George Washington, permission to have 10,000 acres surveyed for him on or near the Scioto River or on the Falls of the Ohio. Whereupon Thomas Bullitt, official surveyor for the colony of Virginia, went with a party to Chillicothe where he met the great Shawnee chief, Cornstalk, who warned him that the aggression of the whites was "designed to deprive us of the hunting of the country, *as usual* . . . the hunting we stand in need of to buy our clothing." Bullitt, seeing justification in the argument, refused to continue the survey. Learning of this, Dunmore recalled him in the fall of 1773. The lands which Washington sought were finally surveyed under the supervision of Bullitt's successor, John Floyd, in the spring of the following year.

The Shawnee, hoping that the English government would do them justice, protested the white aggressions to Alexander McKee, deputy of Sir William Johnson, who was the Superintendent of Indian Affairs for the Northern Department. The King's orders, they remonstrated, restricted settlement to the Great Kanawha River, but this boundary agreement was being violated and their hunting grounds overrun. Though they frowned upon the retaliatory acts of their young men, they admitted they were powerless to restrain them, "for when they are disappointed in their hunting, and find the woods covered with the White People . . . they are foolish enough to make reprisals without waiting to apply to the great men that shou'd redress their complaints and regulate the conduct of their White Brethren toward them."

In the face of the treaties it had ratified the British government could hardly deny the justice of these arguments. Lord Dunmore was therefore reprimanded for allowing and even encouraging the aggressions. In his reply to Lord Dartmouth he confessed his inability to restrain the frontiersmen. He had learned from experience. He wrote:

. . . the established Authority of any government in America, and the policy of Government at home, are both insufficient to restrain the Americans; and that they do and will remove as their avidity and restlessness incite them . . . they do not conceive that Government has any right to forbid their taking possession of a

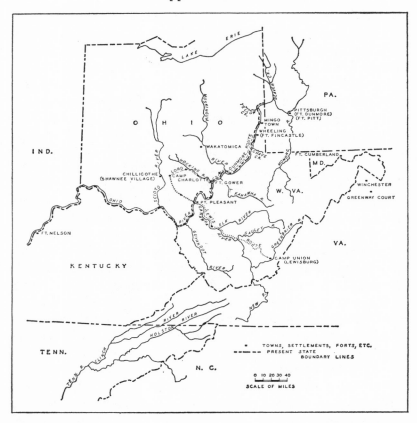

Vast Tract of Country, either uninhabited, or which Serves only as a Shelter to a few Scattered Tribes of Indians. Nor can they be easily brought to entertain any belief of the permanent obligation of Treaties made with those People, whom they consider, as but little removed from the brute Creation.

The white men cared little that their invasion would mean eventual starvation for the Indians. Most of them were hunters who believed, as did Boone, that the privations they endured should be compensated by the profitable sale of their peltries. But Sir William Johnson saw them with an Indian's eye. The white hunters were, he said, "idle fellows . . . to lazy to cultivate lands," attracted by the plenty of game they found to employ "themselves in hunting, in which they interfere much more with the Indians than if they pursued agriculture alone, and the Indian hunters . . . already begin to feel the scarcity this has occasioned, which greatly encreases their resentment."

The Shawnee wanted no trouble with their white brothers. This is shown by the generosity which Captain Will extended toward Boone and his companions in 1770. But nobility of feeling made no impression on the hunters. Captain Will, they felt, had robbed them outrageously, and he should be punished in proportion to the magnitude of his crime.

The whites justified their invasion of the Ohio Valley by the Treaty of Fort Stanwix by which the Six Nations of New York and Pennsylvania had ceded lands south of the Ohio as far west as the Tennessee River. This confederacy—which sought British protection in its effort to dominate all the other tribes of Canada, the Great Lakes and the Ohio Valley—had made the cession in order to keep intact their old holdings in New York and Pennsylvania.

The Shawnee had protested the Treaty through the Seneca, the westernmost tribe of the confederacy. To the Six Nations the Ohio Valley meant little directly; to the Shawnee it meant much. But the Seneca refused to listen to the protest and therefore declined to pass it on to the rest of the confederacy. And the Shawnee had to bow to the circumstances because they were not native to the region but had settled on it with the permission of the Six Nations.

The Shawnee would have accepted the Treaty with less bitterness had the authorities been able to check the abusive conduct of the frontiersmen. Lord Dunmore reflected long on what should be done with these backwoodsmen. Should they be allowed to hold their lands and unite with the Indians? He dreaded the consequence. Should they be permitted "to form a Set of Democratical Governments of their own, upon the banks of the Old Colonies"? This he believed the English government would not allow to be carried into execution. He had no choice but to take the frontiersmen "Under the protection of Some of His

Majesty's Governments already established." Thus Dunmore
surrendered unconditionally to the frontiersmen.

At the beginning of 1774 Colonel William Preston, surveyor
for Fincastle County, which then included the territory south
of the Ohio below the mouth of the Great Kanawha, instructed
the officers and soldiers who had obtained land warrants from
Lord Dunmore to meet his deputy surveyor, John Floyd, at the
mouth of the Great Kanawha on April 14 for the purpose of
locating their lands.

On the appointed day forty-three men assembled at the designated place and cautiously proceeded down the river. The Shawnee decided to defend their hunting grounds. While three of the
white men were prospecting for land near the mouth of the
Little Guyandot, they were captured and held for three days.
Given their freedom, they were warned that henceforth any
Virginian found on the Ohio would be killed. Whereupon the
expedition scattered, some of the men later returning home by
water from New Orleans and others by the Wilderness Trail.

Meanwhile another party of pioneers met further up the Ohio
at the mouth of the Little Kanawha. The party intended to
descend the Ohio and establish a settlement in Kentucky. Among
them were George Rogers Clark and Captain Michael Cresap, a
trader and farmer from western Maryland who had failed in business and had moved to the Ohio Valley. In pursuance of their
plans the party received word that an advanced group of their
hunters had been fired upon near the mouth of the Great Kanawha. This was a warning from the Indians, but the whites
accepted it as a challenge; they pressed forward, intent on surprising and destroying one of the Shawnee towns. They selected
Cresap as leader of the enterprise, but he advised them to desist
from their intentions, warning them that it would precipitate a
general war for which they perhaps would be justly blamed. He
recommended that they return to Wheeling and wait until they
should learn what arrangements, if any, Virginia had made with
the Indians for the peaceful occupation of the region. The hunters accepted Cresap's advice.

In those days Virginia claimed all of western Pennsylvania,

especially Fort Pitt and the valley of the Monongahela. Her representative there was Dr. John Connolly, justice of the peace of Augusta County, an energetic but irascible man who made his headquarters at Pittsburgh. Connolly was occupied in organizing a militia, in reconstructing the fort which had been dismantled in 1772 and which he renamed Fort Dunmore, and in negotiating with the Indians to gain support for the surveying and settling ventures being conducted in Kentucky under the official auspices and protection of Virginia. He gave no encouragement to the frontiersmen arrived in Wheeling. Convinced that the Shawnee were ill-disposed toward the whites and that war between the two groups was inevitable, Connolly advised Cresap by letter to use his influence with his men to cover the country with scouts until the settlers should fortify themselves.

On receiving this message Cresap resolved on warfare. He erected a new post; he called a council of war and read Connolly's letter to his men; he summoned all the Indian traders and solemnly declared war. The frontier soon blazed with attacks on Indians within striking distance of Wheeling. The first of these attacks was made upon a canoe containing a Shawnee, a Delaware and a white man named Stephens.

As the canoe descended the Ohio shots rang out from the dense underbrush along the riverbank. The Indians fell, but Stephens was rescued from the river by Cresap's men who, oddly enough, happened to be near by. Stephens naturally believed that Cresap's men had killed the Indians, though Cresap himself professed innocence of the matter. The next day he received word that five canoes full of Shawnee were descending the river from Pittsburgh. Collecting fifteen men, he pursued and overtook the Indians near Grave Creek. The Indians abandoned their canoes. A skirmish ensued, in which one of the Shawnee and a white man were killed. The settlers took a considerable amount of booty from the abandoned boats.

The skirmish was merely the prelude to one of the most inhuman episodes in the epic of the pioneers. At Mingo Town—up the river from Wheeling and near the present town of Steubenville, Ohio—was located a permanent camp inhabited largely by women, children and old men who belonged to the Six Nations but who called themselves Mingo. Their leader was Tah-gahjute, who had assumed the name of Logan in honor of his friend, James Logan, secretary of the province of Pennsylvania.

Chief Logan was the friend of the white men. His father was a Frenchman who when quite young had been kidnaped and adopted into the Oneida tribe. For many years Logan lived in Shamokin—now Sunbury, Pennsylvania—where he became a chief of great influence among the Indians of the Susquehanna. During the French and Indian War he had maintained a strict neutrality and had, by taking refuge in Philadelphia, avoided the wiles of Indians friendly to the French.

Obliged to abandon his ancestral home, Logan lived in various places in Pennsylvania until, in 1772, he removed to the Ohio. He was fond of saying that he had two souls, one good and one bad, and that when his good soul prevailed he was kind and humane, but that when his bad soul ruled he was perfectly savage and delighted in seeing blood flow. Cresap's men had once resolved to attack Logan's camp but had changed their minds and returned home.

No such qualm tormented Daniel Greathouse, a border ruffian who often visited the farm of a settler named Joshua Baker on Yellow Creek across the river from the camp. There Indians often bought liquor and other articles for the elders and milk for the papooses. On May 3, 1774, four Mingo, two men and two squaws, came to the farm while Greathouse and a group of frontiersmen were present. The Indians were in an angry mood, for on the previous day three whites had shot two Mingo on the Indian side of the Ohio not far from their village.

Greathouse and his friends, however, soon restored their spirits with firewater and invited them to a game of shooting at the mark. One of them, Logan's brother, put on a military coat belonging to one of the white men and, swaggering around, exclaimed, "I am white man."

Offended by this claim, the owner of the coat asked the Indian to return it. When the drunken Indian ignored the request, the white man shot him and three other Indians dead. During the day Indians twice crossed the river either to join or to inquire for their comrades. Each time they met with gunfire. By the end of the day eight Indians had been killed. One of the dead was Logan's sister-in-law, who was carrying her papoose by John Gibson, later a revolutionary hero and the secretary and acting governor of Indiana Territory.

Logan's bad soul now ruled and thirsted for bloodshed. He did not know who was responsible for the crimes, but he blamed Cresap as the leader of the white men. Full of anger and fire-water, of which he was uncommonly fond, he gathered a small band of Mingo and led them against the settlement. That day he took thirteen scalps, among them those of six children.

Three times Logan repeated his forays, ambuscading and defeating a group of Virginians who had pursued him and murdering McClure, their leader. Then his anger subsided almost as quickly as it had risen. He forbade his men to torture one of the prisoners whose life he saved at the risk of his own. Then calling the prisoner to his wigwam, Logan gave him some gunpowder ink and dictated a note to him. This he tied to a war club and left in the cabin of a settler whose entire family had been scalped. The note, "written with ferocious directness," was "a kind of public challenge or taunt to the man whom he wrongly deemed to be the author of his misfortunes." It said:

To CAPTAIN CRESAP—What did you kill my people on Yellow Creek for. The white People killed my kin at Coneestoga a great while ago, & I though[t nothing of that]. But you killed my kin again on Yellow Creek, and took m[y cousin prisoner] then I thought I must kill too; and I have been three time[s to war since but] the Indians is not Angry only myself.

The Shawnee still opposed war. Cornstalk, having pledged his faith to shield the Pennsylvania traders who happened to be sojourning in Shawnee country, sent five of his men to guide their return to town from camp. When they arrived Cornstalk appointed a party in charge of his brother to conduct them to Pittsburgh. With them he sent a warning letter to McKee, informing him of the recent murders but announcing his determination to keep the Shawnee quiet until "wee see whether it is the intention of the white people in general to fall on us." Cornstalk also requested McKee to inform the governors of Virginia and Pennsylvania of the peaceful disposition of his people and to urge them to put a stop to such crimes as had been committed by white men.

McKee had no influence with any of the officials mentioned in the letter. Indeed, Connolly not only refused to receive the Shawnee messengers but ordered their arrest. The traders, fearing bloodshed should Connolly be obeyed, spirited the messengers across the river just as militiamen appeared to take them into custody. The messengers, unaware of Connolly's orders, descended the Ohio on their return home. When they encamped at Beaver Creek they were suddenly surprised by militiamen who killed one of them and then retreated "in a most dastardly manner."

Still most of the Shawnee opposed war. They overlooked the crimes of the whites and even requested them to ignore "what our young men may now be doing." But the relatives and friends of the murdered Shawnee clamored for revenge. Hoping to appease them, the headmen of the tribe called a meeting at their important village of Wakatomika on the Muskingum. It was in vain—the bereaved Indians could not be restrained; they were determined to take thirteen white lives for the thirteen friends and relatives they said the white men had murdered. They joined the Mingo under Logan, who in June 1774 conducted them in a series of raids against innocent and unsuspecting families on whom they fully satisfied their vengeance.

At the outbreak of hostilities the frightened settlers deserted their cabins for the safety of the east. In a letter informing George Washington of the massacre of Logan's people, Valentine Crawford, who resided at Jacob's Creek in Westmoreland County, Pennsylvania, said that all of the settlements west of the Monogahela had been ruined. "There were more than a thousand people crossed that river going Eastward in a single day," he wrote. Two days later William Crawford, brother of Valentine, wrote to Washington that the settlers were "much alarmed, many hundred having gone Eastward over the Allegheny Moun-

tains, and the whole country is vacated as far as the Monongahela."

Word of the Mingo and Shawnee raids soon reached Governor
Dunmore at Williamsburg. Desiring to protect the frontiersmen
and sensing the futility of pacific hopes, he relayed the information he had received to the House of Burgesses and called out
the militia of western Virginia. The House of Burgesses replied
as follows:

It gives us pain . . . to find the Indians have made fresh encroachments and disturbances on our Frontiers; we have only to
request that your Excellency will be pleased to exert those powers with which you are fully vested by the Act of Assembly, for
making provision against Invasions and Insurrections, which we
have no doubt, will be found sufficient to repel the hostile and
perfidious attempts of those savage and barbarous Enemies.

Accordingly, Dunmore considered two possible plans of operation, one of which he would adopt and direct in person. He
planned either to conduct the campaign on the Ohio, or, that
proving impossible or inadvisable, to invade the Ohio wilderness
and strike at the Shawnee capital on Pickaway Plains in the valley
of the Scioto. His army was to consist of two wings or divisions,
one of which, the right or northern, he was to command in person. The other, composed exclusively of mountain men from the
counties west and southwest of the Blue Ridge, was to be under
his most experienced officer, Andrew Lewis, the veteran of the
French and Indian War, who was now a colonel.

Before he left Williamsburg with his division Dunmore ordered Major Angus McDonald with a body of 400 to build a
fort at the creek that runs through the present city of Wheeling, West Virginia, and to cross the Ohio and destroy the
Shawnee village of Wakatomika. McDonald began construction
of the fort, which he called Fincastle, and then, leaving it under
Captain William Crawford who had come from Pittsburgh with
200 men, descended the Ohio to the mouth of Fish Creek—now
in Marshall County, West Virginia. At that point he crossed

the river into Shawnee country, burned Wakatomika which the Indians had deserted, destroyed 500 bushels of old corn and cut down seventy-five acres of growing corn.

Unable to meet the Shawnee in battle, however, McDonald returned to Wheeling, then proceeded to Greenway Court where Dunmore had established temporary headquarters, and apprised him of his failure. In view of this unfortunate turn of events the governor resolved to adopt the plan of invading the Ohio wilderness. From Greenway Court he marched to Fort Cumberland, crossed the mountains to the mouth of Red Stone Creek in Westmoreland County, Pennsylvania, and arrived at Pittsburgh where he was joined by John Connolly with 200 men.

Now leading 1,300 men, Dunmore floated down the Ohio to Wheeling, ordered Crawford with his troops to the mouth of the Hocking and then continued down the river to Harris' Ferry in Wood County, West Virginia, thirteen miles below the present city of Parkersburg. Swimming his cattle and horses, he crossed over to the Ohio side. On a triangular point of land at the mouth of the Hocking he built Fort Gower, named in honor of his friend Earl Gower, a member of the House of Lords.

From Winchester Dunmore had sent Lewis a letter requesting him to raise "a respectable Boddy of men and join me at the mouth of the grate Kanaway [Great Kanawha] or Wailen [Wheeling] as the most Convenient for you." The colonel accordingly summoned the officers of the southern counties of Virginia to a council at which he requested them to enlist troops and to meet him at "Camp Union," so designated because they were all to unite there on the Big Levels of the Greenbrier, at present Lewisburg, West Virginia. Within a few weeks large groups of men were gathering on the ground. Clad in hunting shirts, leather leggings, homemade breeches and caps either made from skins of wild animals or knit from wool, they came from stockaded villages, from lonely clearings, from smoky camps.

Each man was armed with a long flintlock or an English musket and was equipped with bullet pouches, a powder horn, a tomahawk and a long butcher knife which prompted the Indians to refer to Virginians in general as the Big Knife. Many of them were experts in Indian fighting. Some had been with Washington at Fort Necessity; others had fought with Forbes at the capture of Fort Duquesne; still others had been with Bouquet at Bushy Run. All of them had seen service in some border warfare.

By the first week of September 1774 Colonel Lewis had assembled his men and was ready to march to the junction of the Elk and Great Kanawha rivers—at the present site of Charleston, West Virginia—where he planned to make dugout canoes in which to transport his supplies up to the Ohio. His force consisted of four commands: the Augusta County Regiment under his brother, Colonel Charles Lewis; the Botetourt County Regiment under Colonel William Fleming; the Fincastle County Battalion composed largely of backwoodsmen from the Watauga region under Colonel William Christian; and several independent companies under Colonel John Field.

One of Christian's captains was Evan Shelby, in whose company were his intrepid son, Isaac, and John Sevier's brother, Valentine. Some of Christian's men had not yet arrived. His battalion, therefore, would not be ready in time to march with the others. The future conqueror of the Cherokee burned to distinguish himself. He asked for permission to go along with what men he had, but Lewis permitted only two of the best companies to march. He ordered Christian to remain at Camp Union with the rest of the battalion until he could gather 300 men. Christian feared his men would be as disappointed as he. "What to do I dont know," he wrote Colonel Preston, "when our men hears they are to stay behind."

Lewis tried to restore Christian's pride by assuring him that he and his men could get down in time to cross the Ohio with the rest of the force. Lewis' efforts at persuasion were in vain— Christian did not relish remaining behind with the worst troops who had been assigned to garrison duty in the surrounding small forts. On September 5 Lewis received from Dunmore a message requesting him to march with all his men to the mouth of the Little Kanawha. He replied that time did not permit him to change his plans and that he must proceed to the mouth of the Great Kanawha.

Dawn on the following day found Camp Union a swarm of busy and noisy men. All morning long commands and shouts and mutterings mingled with the lowing of cattle and the neighing of horses that were being corralled and laden with supplies. In the afternoon the Augusta Regiment, joined by a company of the Botetourt Regiment, fell in line, passed to the playing of drums and fifes over the high hill west of the encampment and disappeared into the wilderness.

The rest of the Botetourt Regiment, the Fincastle Battalion and the independent units followed within six days. Field's Culpeper Minute Men, forty strong, moved so rapidly that they soon caught up with the Augusta Regiment. At the head of the expedition were several hundred axmen, clearing the way and tracing a road, and behind them followed the caravan of pack horses, wagons and cannon.

Fleming kept a careful journal of his itinerary. In sun and rain the long column wound like a serpent of prismatic colors across the lofty summits of the Alleghenies, among dangerous cliffs, and over creeks and rivers, until two weeks later it left behind the rocky masses of the hills. Autumn had already begun to transform the forest into a huge canvas of glowing colors. The glistening green laurel and the somber hemlock contrasted magnificently with the golden linden and sugar tree and the crimson sumac.

At last on September 22 the Botetourt Regiment entered a broad valley covered with buffalo grass and studded with maples and pawpaws. To the east meandered the Great Kanawha. Marching up its northern bank, the troops arrived at the mouth of the Elk where they joined the Augusta Regiment. The soldiers of both units were soon busy felling trees and reducing them to canoes.

Colonel Fleming's thoughts often dwelled on his wife and small son back home. While the canoes, twenty-seven in number, were being completed, he took time from his many duties to write his family a letter. This expressed the general pioneer belief that any campaign against the Indians was a crusade in defense of property, country and home and that, therefore, it enjoyed Divine blessing:

My D^r. Nancy, that You & Lenny are daily in my thoughts, you need not doubt, but as much as I love & Regard you both, I can not Allow myself to wish me with you, till the expedition is finished knowing that it would Sink me in your esteem, & that you would dispise a wretch that could desert an honourable Cause, a Cause undertaken for the good of his Country in general and more immediately for the Protection of his Family, as included amongst the Frontier settlers let thoughts like these Animate you and support your Spirits, and remember my Dr Girl that the Divine Being is Omnipresent as well as Omnipotent, that He who rides on the Wings of the Tempest, and directs the Artillery of Heaven, beholds with serenity, the Rage of a Battle & directs each deadly Shaft where to strike—for a Sparrow falls not to the Ground without his knowledge. His Mercy is more conspicuously displayed, in instances of Preservation & Protection in the fiersest Battles and greatest daingers, than in a calm undisturbed Rotation of time in a quiet peaceble life. thefor My D^r think me as safe on this Expedition, tho we should have a Skirmish or two with the Indians, as if at home. And should it be the Will of God, that I should fall, I must & can not otherwise think, but that he who dies in the Service of & in the defense of his Country, dies in an Act of Religion.

On September 30 Lewis resumed his march toward his destination. After sending his supplies ahead in the canoes, he led his army along the northern bank of the Great Kanawha, crossed several small streams and on October 6 arrived at the mouth of the river where he encamped on a cape of land which his soldiers called Point Pleasant. There three messengers, one of whom was Simon Girty, brought him a letter in which Dunmore requested him to march with all his men to the Indian towns near Pickaway Plains. Though annoyed by this last-minute change of plans, Lewis prepared to set out in the morning. But destiny, having other designs, forestalled him.

From the peaks of the Alleghenies, from the highlands along the Great Kanawha, Cornstalk's spies had seen the progress of Lewis' army all the way from Camp Union to Point Pleasant and had reported it to the chief in his capital on Pickaway Plains. Cornstalk and his headmen had immediately resolved on war and had summoned the warriors to arms. They came by the hundreds, eager for battle.

Cornstalk planned to frustrate the two divisions of white troops by attacking them before they could unite. If Lewis could be beaten, he reasoned, Dunmore could be shot down in the narrow defiles of Hocking Valley. In accordance with his scheme, on October 9 Cornstalk approached the Ohio with his braves and halted in a dense forest in the valley of Campaign Creek near the present village of Addison in Gallia County, Ohio, three miles above the mouth of the Great Kanawha. Soon after dark he began to send his warriors across the river on rafts, until between eight and eleven hundred of them were on the southern side about three miles from Point Pleasant.

The warriors found themselves in a wilderness so dense that they could not see the moon and stars. In the darkness they tramped across decayed trunks of trees strewn in all directions and through weeds interspersed with spicewood until, just before dawn, they approached the camp of the whites. In the dim gray light they made out the forms of two men hunting deer along the bank of the river. They fired, killing one of them. The other ran into camp, giving the alarm.

Instantly drums beat to arms. Sleepy soldiers rolled out of their blankets and primed their flintlocks or rifles. Lewis, believing that the Indians constituted only a scouting party, ordered his brother and Colonel Fleming, each with 150 men, to march up the river. They had not advanced more than a mile when the Indians fired on them, killing the scouts in front.

The report of the rifles, resounding in camp like the clap of thin thunder, convinced Lewis for the first time that the attack was a serious one. He immediately dispatched Colonel Field with 200 men, who arrived to find that the men under Charles Lewis were bearing the full fury of the attack. Lewis, fighting in the open instead of "taking a tree," had been mortally wounded.

"I am wounded," Lewis said calmly, "but go you on and be brave." With these words he handed his gun to a man near him and, assisted by a few others, returned to camp where a few hours later he died.

Fleming, attempting to rally his men, was also wounded. Two bullets entered his left arm below the elbow and broke the bones and another pierced his chest "about three Inches below my left Nipple." Declaring himself "effectually disabled," he walked back to camp where he found that a part of his lung, "as long as one of my fingars," had come through the wound in his chest. When it was restored by one of his attendants he felt a "surprising state of ease." He was destined to survive his wound by many years.

Colonel Field meanwhile had restored the battle and had soon forced the Indians to retreat. Standing behind a large tree, he saw an Indian approaching and jeering at him. He aimed, but too late: two Indians, coming from the opposite direction, shot him dead. Evan Shelby immediately turned his company over to his son Isaac and assumed command of the force. For an hour victory flitted from side to side before finally resting with the whites.

As the frontiersmen advanced their foes turned to engage them in hand-to-hand combat. Groans and cheers and jeers and yells mingled with war whoops and rifle shot.

"Be strong, be strong," thundered Cornstalk, running hither and thither among his braves. "Lie close; shoot well; drive the white dogs in!"

The braves, fighting desperately, taunted their foes for being now too close to death to think of playing their fifes. "You white sons of bitches," they jeered as they fired or swung their tomahawks, "where are your whistles now?"

The whites, receiving reinforcements, gradually forced their foes to give ground. While the best warriors covered the retreat others carried off the wounded and threw as many of the dead as they could into the river for, like all other Indians, they were averse to allowing their comrades, whether dead or alive, to fall into the hands of their enemies. As the Shawnee fell back they reached a strong position provided by underbrush, stumps and steep banks behind which they entrenched themselves.

The whites, realizing the folly of attempting to dislodge them, strung out their line for a mile and a half and continued the fight in a crouching position. The engagement gradually wore down to a series of skirmishes until, toward sunset, Isaac Shelby directed a flank movement by a march along the east bank of Crooked Creek.

The Indians, mistaking this for the expected reinforcements under Colonel Christian, grew discouraged. As the sun sank they began to take to their canoes and to make for the opposite shore. Some of them called back that they, as well as the whites, had 1,100 men and that tomorrow they would return and resume the fight. This was mere bravado; they had suffered too heavily to make good their threat; they abandoned some of their dead together with a number of guns, blankets, tomahawks, powder horns and war clubs.

Darkness came, shrouding the forest with a terrible silence. The whites buried their dead, left the bodies of their enemies to the wolves and vultures, picked up the articles left on the field and dragged themselves back to camp. Forty-six of their comrades had been killed and eighty wounded. Of their officers, seventeen had been killed or wounded, including their second, third and fourth in command. The fifth in command, Colonel William Christian, reached Point Pleasant when the battle was over.

On September 27 Christian had left Camp Union with his battalion and had arrived eight days later at the mouth of the Elk. After dispatching a letter to Lewis informing him of his whereabouts, Christian marched up the northern side of the Great Kanawha. On the day of the battle Lewis had sent messengers to inform the colonel that he was hotly engaged and to request him to hasten his assistance. Christian quickened his march, but he arrived on the battlefield only to learn to his great disappointment that the battle was over.

The Indians meanwhile marched wearily through the wilderness to their villages on the Pickaway Plains. There Cornstalk called a council of his tribe to discuss what should be done. He upbraided the other chiefs for not permitting him to make peace with the whites before the battle.

"What," Cornstalk asked, "will you do now? The Big Knife is coming on us, and we shall all be killed. Now you must fight or we are undone." Silence greeted his words. Cornstalk continued: "Let us kill all our women and children and go and fight until we die." Silence again. Then Cornstalk rose and struck his tomahawk in a post in the center of his council house. "I'll go," he said, "and make peace."

The warriors chorused assent. Instantly Cornstalk sent Matthew Eliott, a white man with the Indian army, and several chiefs to solicit peace from Lord Dunmore.

The governor as yet had no knowledge of the recent battle. He had heard rumors that Lewis had been attacked, but since that officer had 1,100 men and would soon be joined by Christian with 300 more, he was confident that the southern wing could cope with the Indians. On October 11, leaving a garrison of a hundred men at Fort Gower, Dunmore led the bulk of his force toward the Indian villages and sent Lewis word to meet him there. When Dunmore was within fifteen miles of the principal village he met Eliott and the chiefs, who informed him of the recent battle and requested peace. The governor immediately sent Captain John Gibson to tell them in their own language that he would listen to their proposals but that he would not withdraw from their country until satisfactory terms were made. The next day he advanced to within six miles of the village where he halted and formed an encampment which he called Camp Charlotte in honor of the Queen. Here on October 18 he opened negotiations with the chiefs.

Cornstalk appeared at the council meeting wearing a topknot of red feathers, a beaded ornament on his forehead, bone and silver rings in his ears and painted half-moons across his cheeks. He bitterly denounced the white men seated around him for murdering his people and stealing their land. Having thus restored his wounded ego, he surrendered.

On the same day Lewis, having placed Fleming with about one hundred men in command at Point Pleasant with instructions to build a small stockaded fort there, crossed the Ohio and started for the Indian villages. His men, flushed with success and burning to avenge their losses, pushed on rapidly, hoping to strike at the Indians in the first villages they reached. Imagine their chagrin when Dunmore sent word informing them that he had almost concluded a treaty and requesting them, therefore, to return to Point Pleasant.

Instead of obeying the orders, Lewis' men advanced, causing the worried Indians to leave Camp Charlotte to protect their villages from impending attack. Dunmore, fearing that his work of peace would be undone, took Gibson and fifty men and marched to Lewis' headquarters. The next day he gathered the officers, told them what he had done and once more requested them to return to Point Pleasant. This time they reluctantly obeyed. Soon after they recrossed the river they scattered and departed for their homes.

The peace which Dunmore concluded with the Shawnee and their associates was only a preliminary understanding pending final negotiations. Temporarily, the Indians agreed to give up without reserve the prisoners they had taken in wars with the whites, to surrender stolen Negroes, horses and other valuables, and to cease hunting or visiting on the side south of the Ohio. As a guarantee for the faithful compliance of these terms, the Indians agreed to deliver up hostages. In the following year the chiefs were to meet in Pittsburgh to enter into a supplemental treaty by which the terms were to be ratified and fully confirmed.

Most historians have greatly exaggerated the importance of the single-battle conflict known as Lord Dunmore's War. In his celebrated work on the frontier Theodore Roosevelt wrote that the battle of Point Pleasant "rendered possible the settlement of Kentucky, and therefore the winning of the West. Had it not been for Lord Dunmore's War, it is more than likely that when the colonies achieved their freedom they would have found their western boundary fixed at the Allegheny Mountains."

Virgil A. Lewis of West Virginia, perhaps from an understandable desire to glorify the early history of his state, agreed with Roosevelt that the battle at Point Pleasant made possible the settlement of Kentucky and added that this in turn provided George Rogers Clark with the springboard from which he launched his conquest of the Illinois Country. He continued as follows:

In the treaty Convention of Paris in 1783, whereby the independence of the United States was being recognized, and the western boundary of the new Nation determined, the British representatives voted to place this at the crest of the Alleghenies, and the Spanish representative in that body voted with them.

But the Americans stoutly asserted that, not only had they conquered the vast Illinois region, but that Virginia had established civil government therein. So the Mississippi river, and not the Alleghenies, became the western boundary of the United States. Verily, the men who fought the battle of Point Pleasant, were Empire Builders, and the victory achieved by them on that field changed the course of American history.

None of the quoted opinion is substantiated by documentary evidence. On the contrary, it controverts accurate historical information. The Shawnee never kept their promise to stay out of Kentucky. We shall presently see that they attacked Boone and his party in that region just six months after they had agreed to the treaty of Camp Charlotte and that they continued to wage war against the whites throughout the American Revolution.

Kentucky, like other frontier regions, was settled despite the presence of the Indian menace. To believe otherwise is to admit ignorance of the impelling character of the American frontiersmen. Virgil Lewis' other assumptions are also unfounded. Samuel Flagg Bemis, one of the keenest authorities in the history of American diplomacy, states that Rayneval—private secretary to Vergennes, French minister of foreign affairs—asserted in a memorandum that Clark's excursions in the Illinois Country could not seriously be advanced as an American claim. Bemis also points out that Clark had withdrawn his garrisons to the Falls of the Ohio by 1783 and that the Illinois Country was, therefore, a "no man's land." At that time most of the territory was controlled not by Clark's garrison at Fort Nelson but by the British garrisons at Detroit and Michilimackinac.

Thus Lord Dunmore's War had none of the significant results most historians impute to it. Yet it was not without importance in frontier history. It was distinctly an American victory. The soldiers and officers who fought in it were not regulars but colonials, and the training and experience they derived from it redounded to the advantage of American forces from the Southern provinces during the Revolution.

Most of the officers and men who served at Point Pleasant

fought again for the independence of their country. Lewis himself, at the head of an American force, was responsible for driving Dunmore from Virginia. At least ten of his former officers won fame in the Revolution and many of his former soldiers took part in Clark's conquest of the Illinois Country. Among the officers in Dunmore's division was Daniel Morgan, hero of Quebec in 1775 and of Cowpens in 1781. At the beginning of the Revolution Morgan had led his rifle corps, composed of many of the same expert sharpshooters who had served under his command in 1774, into Washington's camp at Cambridge. General William Campbell and General Isaac Shelby, both of whom were captains under Lewis, became the commanding officers in 1780 at King's Mountain where the frontiersmen won an important victory against a British force under Major Patrick Ferguson.

We have seen elsewhere how Colonel William Christian, one of Lewis' regimental commanders, defeated the Cherokee in 1776 at the head of an expedition whose officers and men had also fought under Lewis. Of the officers who had been with Dunmore in 1774, four served in 1788 as members of the Virginia convention that ratified the Constitution of the United States. Several more were destined to become United States senators and governors of Western states. Thus Lord Dunmore's War may be considered a focal point in frontier history.

On their way homeward from Camp Charlotte Dunmore's officers uttered one of the earliest expressions of American patriotism. Sojourning for a few days at Fort Gower, they held a meeting on November 5 to express their true sentiments in regard to the impending contest between Great Britain and her rebellious American colonies. As loyal subjects of George III they had faithfully followed the King's representative in war, but as Americans they sympathized warmly with the Continental Congress.

To assure their countrymen that they would stand with them in the conflict, the assembly at Fort Gower passed resolutions and directed that these be published in the *Virginia Gazette*. Their speaker recalled that they had lived in the woods three months without any word either from the delegates at Philadelphia or from Boston where hostilities were likely to begin. They were the officers, he said, of a considerable body of men; they had lived weeks without bread or salt and had slept "in the open air without any covering but that of the canopy of Heaven"; they could march and shoot with any army in the known world. In view of their prowess they were disturbed by the possibility that they might be falsely accused of being hostile or indifferent to the American cause. They wished to dispel such fears in their countrymen by assuring them that they would not fight save "for the honour and advantage of America in general, and of Virginia in particular." They would remain faithful subjects of George III as long as he ruled over a free people, and they would defend the honor of the Crown and the dignity of the British Empire

... at the expense of life, and everything dear and valuable. But as the love of liberty, and attachment of the real interests and just rights of America outweighs every other consideration, we resolve that we will exert every power within us for the defense of American liberty, and for the support of her just rights and privileges; not in any precipitate, riotous, or tumultuous manner, but when regularly called forth by the unanimous voice of our countrymen.

With this dedication to the freedom of their native land, the victorious officers of Lord Dunmore crossed the Ohio and returned to their homes.

One Indian had refused to bow before triumphant white arms. That Indian was Chief Logan. During the negotiations that led to the Treaty of Camp Charlotte, Dunmore had sent Gibson to invite Logan to attend the conference. The chief replied, "I am a warrior, not a councilor; I shall not go."

So saying, Logan took Gibson aside and suddenly addressed him in a speech which in its simple eloquence has few equals of its kind in primitive oratory. It soon became popular. It was recited in schools and churches, and in time it found its way into the leading newspapers of America and England. Thomas Jefferson, that admirer of literary beauty, praised it highly and subsequently tried to prove the truthfulness of the reference to

Cresap in it. The result was that some of Cresap's relatives and friends attacked the speech as fictitious and attributed its authorship to John Gibson, to Simon Girty and even to the "fertile brain of Thomas Jefferson," though Cresap's defenders failed to provide a reasonable and convincing motive for the deception.

Gibson and George Rogers Clark, who were present when the speech was read, attested to its genuineness. Gibson simply wrote it down, translating it literally and returning with it to Dunmore. When the governor read it solemnly to his soldiers and officers, they understood that Greathouse, not Cresap, had been instrumental in the murder of Logan's family. Clark, turning to Cresap, teased him for being so great a man that the Indians blamed him for everything. Cresap swore "he had a good mind to tomahawk Greathouse for the murder." The chief's speech was no acknowledgment of defeat. It was a direct recital of the wrongs done him, "a fierce and exulting justification of the vengeance he had taken on white men." Said Logan:

I appeal to any white man to say if he ever entered Logan's cabin hungry, and he gave him not meat; if ever he came cold and naked, and he clothed him not. During the last and bloody war, Logan remained quiet in his cabin, an advocate of peace. Such was my love for the whites that my countrymen pointed as they passed and said, "Logan is the friend of white men." I had ever thought to have lived with you, but for the injuries of one man, Colonel Cresap, who the last spring, in cold blood, and unprovoked, murdered all the relatives of Logan, not even sparing my women and children. There runs not a drop of my blood in the veins of any living creature. This called upon me for revenge. I have sought it; I have killed many; I have fully glutted my revenge. For my country, I rejoice at the beams of peace. But do not harbor the thought that mine is the joy of fear. Logan never felt fear. He will never turn on his heel to save his life. Who is there to mourn for Logan? Not one.

8

The

Wilderness Trail

WHEN HIS JUDGESHIP EXPIRED LATE IN 1773 RICHARD HENDERson turned his full attention to Kentucky. On what ground could he justify the planting of a colony in that forbidden region? He knew that the Proclamation of 1763 forbade treaties between private individuals and the Indians. This injunction he decided to disregard. In his single-minded planning Henderson overlooked also the laws of North Carolina and Virginia and, what is more important, obviated the necessity to obtain a royal grant.

Aware that his scheme would meet with stern, perhaps bitter, opposition, Henderson set about to secure for it some show of legality. Assiduous study rewarded him with the discovery that Lord Chancellors had, on two successive decisions, asserted no royal letters patent were required in "respect to such places as have or shall be acquired by treaty or Grant from any of the Indian princes or Governments." The decisions also assured the King that property rights were vested "in the Grantee by the Indian grants, subject only to your Majesty's right of sovereignty."

Now the Indian princes alluded to in the previous quotation were those residing in India, but could not the principle be used in the case of those in North America? Henderson certainly thought so. Thus he found the ground, however questionable, on which to support his ambitious scheme. He and his associates proposed to buy some twenty million acres from the Indians, establish a new colony, retain large tracts of it for themselves and sell the rest to the settlers who were to be charged a perpetual quitrent for every acre they bought.

Henderson's associates were William Johnston, Colonel John

143

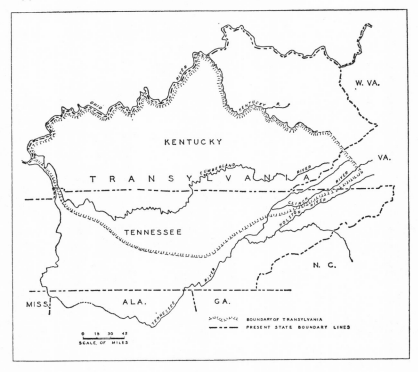

Luttrell, Thomas and Nathaniel Hart and John Williams. These men formed the Louisa Company, named in honor of the Louisa —now called the Kentucky—River in Kentucky. The company's articles of agreement, drawn up in Hillsboro, specified that they rent or purchase for themselves "& our heirs for ever ... a certain Territory or Tract of Land lying on the west side of the Mountains on the waters of the Mississippi River, from the Indian Tribes now in possession thereof." Each associate bound himself "to furnish his Quota of Expenses necessary toward procuring a grant & settling the Country," to share the property equally, to "support each other with our lives & fortunes," and, at a propitious time, to "make & sign such rules and regulations as may be expedient for the security, safety & advantages of ourselves and posterity."

Henderson wasted no time in proceeding to negotiate with the Indians. Accompanied by Nathaniel Hart and guided by the veteran explorer and "linguist," Thomas Price, he visited the Cherokee chiefs at the Otari towns. After holding several lengthy conferences with the white men the chiefs delegated their venerable leader Little Carpenter and his squaw to go to Cross Creek —now Fayetteville, North Carolina—where Henderson had assembled the goods and merchandise he would offer for the tract. The goods, which included sacks of corn, flour, casks of rum, blankets, trinkets, guns and powder and lead, were valued at £10,000 and had been obtained from the Scotch merchants at Cross Creek through the influence of a member of the Louisa Company, William Johnston, who had carried on big business deals with them. Little Carpenter was delighted with the articles, and his squaw thought the women of the tribe would be pleased with the quantity of brilliant trinkets.

With characteristic vigor Henderson everywhere encouraged settlement on the land he was soon to purchase by treaty. On Christmas Day 1774 he issued an advertisement containing a number of inducements, promises, stipulations and regulations for all those who wished to avail themselves of what he presented as a golden opportunity. Fifty soldiers were to be raised for the "protection of the Settlers of the Country," and each was to be rewarded with a plot of 500 acres and three pounds sterling.

Every settler who agreed to employ himself in raising a crop of corn, in bettering the community and in protecting it against Indian attacks was to receive 500 acres and 250 acres in addition for every "tithable person whom he shall take with him." Inducements in the form of land were made to those who should establish iron works, salt factories, "a Great Mill, and saw Mill." The settler who raised the largest crop of corn was to receive 500 acres "in proportion to the number of hands he may have under him the ensuing season." A similar provision was made for the settlers who would take the largest number of sheep to the colony.

The enterprise soon outgrew the articles of the Louisa Company, necessitating a reorganization. The result was the Transylvania Company. Three new names appeared among the partners: David Hart—a brother of Nathaniel and Thomas—Leonard

Henry Bullock and James Hogg, a prominent Scotch planter and landowner from Hillsboro. The plan of the reorganized company, a verbose document covering several large pages, declared that each member was to own an eighth of the interest save David Hart and Bullock, each of whom was to possess one sixteenth.

Henderson made no attempt to obtain the approval of the Crown. Colonel William Preston, surveyor for Fincastle County, Virginia, learned that the judge did "not propose paying Quitrents unless his majesty will recognize his Title." In that case, however, Henderson was prepared not

only [to] give up the sovereignty and pay the usual Quit-rents; but will reserve the granting the land to the Company.

He declares that no Land shall be surveyed with [in] his bounds but such as shall be purchased from him; nor will he suffer those to be Settled which have been Surveyed from the Officers and Soldiers unless the owners Compound with him and behave themselves well.

To George Washington, Preston wrote that "Henderson talks with great Freedom & Indecency of the Governor of Virginia, sets the Government at Defiance & says if he once had five hundred good Fellows settled in that Country he would not value Virginia."

Word of the plans of the Transylvania Company soon reached Governor Josiah Martin of North Carolina. Directly he issued in the *North Carolina Gazette* a proclamation against Henderson and his confederates. In this he quoted somewhat at length from that portion of the Proclamation of 1763 relating to the purchase of lands by private persons in the domain reserved for the Indians. Then he quoted from an act of the North Carolina assembly which forbade

white men . . . for any consideration whatsoever, [to] purchase or buy any Tract or Parcel of Land claimed or actually in possession of any Indian without Liberty for so doing from the

Governor and Council first had and obtained under the Penalty of Twenty Pounds for every hundred acres of Land so bargained for and purchased.

Martin went on to say that Henderson's violation of the Proclamation had caused an "alarming and dangerous Tendency to the Peace and Welfare of this and the neighboring [Virginia] Colony." Henderson and his confederates had agreed "to pay the Indians . . . a considerable quantity of Gunpowder, whereby they will be furnished with the means of annoying his Majesty's subjects in this and neighboring colonies." In addition, Henderson "hath invited many Debtors, and other persons in desperate circumstances to desert this Province and become Settlers on the said Lands, to the great injury of creditors." Martin therefore "thought proper to . . . strictly . . . forbid . . . Henderson and his Confederates, on pain of his Majesty's highest displeasure, and suffering the most rigorous Penalties of the Law, to prosecute so unlawful an Undertaking."

This official threat Henderson ignored. Late in January 1775 he quietly had the goods loaded on six wagons and taken to Sycamore Shoals where they were stored in huts built for the purpose. In the following month Henderson and his associates repaired to the treaty ground while Little Carpenter with his squaw returned to his home on the Little Tennessee to summon his people and send them to Sycamore Shoals for a big talk with the white men.

The Cherokee soon began to cover the little valley. Within a month they numbered about twelve hundred, "lolling about on the grass and under the sycamores, listening to the river as it broke and chattered over the shoals. Occasionally they crowded around the cabins for a peak at the precious goods."

Among the chiefs were Little Carpenter, Raven, Oconostota and Dragging Canoe. The last two were opposed to selling Henderson any land; the white men, said Oconostota, had already taken much of their hunting grounds. Regardless of this hostile attitude, Henderson opened the negotiations in the presence of John Williams, Thomas and Nathaniel Hart, James Robertson,

John Sevier, Isaac Shelby, William Bailey Smith and Daniel Boone.

The assembled chiefs reminded the white men that, by the Treaty of Fort Stanwix in 1768, the Iroquois had surrendered the land to the Cherokee whose ownership had been acknowledged by the British government in the Treaty of Lochaber two years later. Still Oconostota and Dragging Canoe opposed a purchase. The former, leaping in anger into the circle of his seated friends, began an impassioned speech. Before white men began their encroachments, he said, his people had flourished. At first he had believed that white men would not travel beyond the mountains, but now he realized that they would not be satisfied until they occupied all the Cherokee lands.

"This is but the beginning," the angry chief thundered, rising gradually in oratorical power. "The invader has crossed the great sea in ships; he has not been stayed by broad rivers, and now he has penetrated the wilderness and overcome the ruggedness of the mountains. Neither will he stop there. He will force the Indian steadily before him across the Mississippi ever toward the west . . . till the redman be no longer a roamer of the forests and a pursuer of wild game." By now Oconostota's emotion had leaped like a great wave over his eloquence. Reaching for the sky, he fiercely exhorted his people to resist further encroachment. A hubbub of voices brought the conference to a startling end.

But on the following day Oconostota's temper cooled and he grew more tractable. The Indians, resuming their negotiations with the whites, agreed to sell them the land as far north as the Cumberland River. "We give you from this place," said Dragging Canoe, stamping on the ground and circling the spot with his hands. But he felt that the purchase would lead to no good. "Brother," he said, taking Boone by the hand, "we have given you a fine land, but I believe that you will have much trouble in settling it." And pointing dramatically toward the west he declared that a dark cloud hung over the land which would be known as the Bloody Ground. His words proved prophetic.

On March 17, amid feasting and merrymaking, the treaty was

signed. The purchase included almost all the present state of Kentucky and an immense tract of Tennessee, comprising all the territory watered by the Cumberland River and its tributaries. The Cherokee chose John Martin and John Farrar as their lawyers to represent them in the conveyance of the purchase.

The Treaty of Sycamore Shoals, sometimes known also as the Treaty of Watauga, dealt a hard blow to such aspirants to western lands as Washington, Josiah Martin and Dunmore. "There is something in that affair," wrote Washington to Preston, "Which I neither understand, nor like, and I wish I may not have cause to dislike it worse as the mystery unfolds."

Governor Martin hurried to inform Lord Dartmouth, who was Colonial Secretary in London, that Henderson had violated the Proclamation of 1763, and Dunmore, stirred by Preston's letter of March 10, issued a proclamation in which he tried to dissuade Henderson's followers from their purpose. The Virginia governor charged "all Justices of the Peace, Sheriffs, and other Officers, civil and military, to use their utmost Endeavours to prevent the unwarrantable and illegal Designs of the said Henderson and his Abettors."

If Henderson refused to leave the land, he was to be "fined & imprisoned in the Manner the Laws in such Cases direct." At the same time Dunmore wrote to the Indians charging them with "inconsiderately (not to say worse)" listening "to the dangerous proposals of a Certain evill disposed Person named Henderson, and, allured by little present gain, have entered into a bargain for Lands, which they either have Sold or intend to sell." The King, Lord Dunmore warned, would not permit the Indians to sell land to private persons, and therefore, he urged, they should rescind any contract they had made with Henderson.

Dunmore and Martin were justified in issuing their proclamations. While Henderson and his associates deserved none of the epithets hurled against them, in the light of the Proclamation of 1763 their collective action must be considered presumptuous. Despite the widespread dissatisfaction which the colonists expressed toward British rule and which was soon to develop into revolution, no group of citizens had a right to take possession of

Crown lands without a charter and purely for personal profit and aggrandizement. The measures England had taken to control the region west of the Alleghenies cannot be considered unjust or arbitrary.

Daniel Boone was not present when the Treaty of Sycamore Shoals was signed. At Henderson's request he and thirty armed and mounted men from Long Island on the Holston had started a week before to explore the region of the Kentucky River where the capital of the colony was to be established. With him were his brother Squire and a number of old friends and neighbors, among them Michael Stoner and Richard Callaway. Seven of the men were from Rutherford County, North Carolina, including Captain Twitty, a veteran woodsman of great strength, and Felix Walker, a romantic young man who sought adventure.

Boone was the logical man for the task Henderson had assigned him. The territory was as familiar to him as his own flintlock. Yet the journey was a difficult undertaking. The party traveled on a bridle path broken in many places for long stretches. Innumerable thickets of bushes and cane stood in their way and streams, mountains and Indians posed constant threats. Only by choosing the most accessible route could Boone hope to succeed in his task. In so doing he showed the patience of an experienced surveyor and the skill of a seasoned engineer.

Along creeks and rivers, over the lowest mountain passes and across the best fords, he and his companions made their way for more than two hundred miles, blazing the Wilderness Trail which remained a main artery of transportation for over a century. Over it came countless pioneers with their pans and bobbins, their dogs and horses and sheep, their books and even their printing press. Over that trail Kentucky traveled to statehood. Over it Boone left milestones which have made his name immortal in the epic of the pioneers.

From Long Island Boone and his men went northward to Moccasin Gap, turned westward and crossed the Clinch River, Powell Mountain and the Powell River. Entering the narrow valley of this stream, with the Cumberland Mountains rising before them like an endless white wall, they ranged for twenty miles to Martin's Station where Captain Joseph Martin received them warmly and where they augmented their supplies. Then the explorers pushed down the valley for twenty-five miles to Cumberland Gap, filed through it, and picked up and pursued the Warriors' Path to the Cumberland River, which they forded to its northern side.

Soon they abandoned the trail for a buffalo trace Boone had followed during his hunting expedition five years before. Their axes and hatchets now saw rough service. Toiling through scrubby trees, bramble, rhododendron and laurel, they inched to the Laurel River and then to a wide patch of hazel bushes which took them to a ford of the Rockcastle River. For thirty more miles they chopped and slashed through thick cane and bramble and reed, until they came to a wide gap in the mountains in present Madison County. Before them stretched the beautiful plains of Kentucky.

Young Felix Walker kept a journal which, though replete with quaint spelling and quainter sentence structure, is reliable and interesting and sometimes shows a rude literary power. Here, for example, is how he now expressed his feelings and those of his comrades:

Perhaps no Adventureor Since the days of donquicksotte or before ever felt So Cheerful & Ilated in prospect, every heart abounded with Joy & excitement . . . & exclusive of the Novelties of the Journey the advantages & accumalations arising on the Settlement of a new Country was a dazzling object with many of our Company. . . . As the Cain ceased, we began to discover the pleasing & Rapturous appearance of the plains of Kentucky, a New Sky & Strange Earth to be presented to our view. . . . So Rich a Soil we had never Saw before, Covered with Clover in full Bloom, the Woods alive abounding with wild Game, turkeys so numerous that it might be said there appeared but one flock Universally Scattered in the woods . . . it appeared that Nature in the profession of her Bounties, had Spread a feast for all that lives, both for the Animal & Rational World, a Sight so delightful to our view and grateful to our feelings almost Induced us, in

Immitation of Columbus in Transport to Kiss the Soil of Kentucky, as he haild & Saluted the sand on his first setting his foot on the Shores of America.

So far Boone and his party had seen no Indians. They attributed this to Henderson's agreement with the Cherokee and to the treaty Dunmore had made with the Shawnee and their associates in the previous year. Confident that they would not be attacked, they relaxed their vigilance and apparently slept without posting a guard. Great was their bewilderment, therefore, when on the night of March 24 while Boone was lying on the gently rolling ground just outside the present town of Richmond in Madison County, they heard a volley from the woods and saw a small group of Shawnee rushing toward them and swinging their tomahawks.

The scared and sleepy white men grabbed their rifles and scampered like rabbits from the campfire to the protection of darkness and the forest where Squire Boone discovered that he had seized his jacket instead of his powder horn and shot pouch. Crawling around in the darkness, he found his brother from whom he borrowed ammunition. Captain Twitty, shot through both knees, could not move. When the Indians rushed into his tent to scalp him, his bulldog leaped at one of them and threw him to the ground. Another Indian tomahawked the dog and then ran with a comrade. Twitty's wounded Negro, Sam, leaped to his feet, only to fall dead into the campfire. Felix Walker, despite his bad wound, ran with the others into the underbrush. While the unhurt men built a log cabin which they called Twitty's Fort, Boone made medicines from wood plants and nursed the wounded men with "paternal affection." Twitty soon died and was buried beside Sam.

These experiences prompted Boone to urge Henderson to come to his assistance as quickly as possible. "My advise [*sic*] to you, sir," he wrote, "is to come or send as soon as possible. Your company is desired greatly, for the people are very uneasy, but are willing to stay and venture their lives with you, and now is the time to flustrate their intentions and keep the country, whilst we are in it. If we give way to them now it will ever be the case."

Boone concluded his letter by informing Henderson that he intended to lead his men "from the battle ground, for the mouth of the Otter Creek, where we shall immediately erect a fort, which will be done before you can come or send—then we can send men to meet you, if you send for them."

Boone was as good as his word. In a valley surrounded by precipitous hills about a mile from the junction of Otter Creek and the Kentucky River he began to build Boonesboro. The settlement had two springs, one fresh, the other containing sulphur and salt. Stately trees rose profusely over the valley, but the underbrush had been kept down by buffalo and other wild animals which came there to lick. On entering the valley Walker, who was slowly recovering from his wound, saw a sight that gladdened his poetic soul: "A number of buffaloes of all sizes, supposed to be between two and three hundred, made off from the lick in every direction; carelessly, with young calves playing, skipping, and bounding through the plain."

Boone was enchanted with the large sycamores that grew near the rising fort. He joyously christened the place Sycamore Hollow.

Meanwhile Henderson had started out with a number of settlers to meet Boone. In his caravan were also his brother Samuel, two of his associates, Nathaniel Hart and John Luttrell, and William Cocke who was in charge of a group of laborers employed in making the road passable for wagons to Martin's Station, which they reached on March 30. Since the wagons could go no farther Henderson unloaded them and began storing the goods in cabins. He also appointed Captain Joseph Martin agent for the Powell Valley, but restricted him to selling land only to those who proved industrious and who could raise a crop of corn within a year.

On April 4 while Henderson was waiting for the last wagons to arrive and was still storing the goods he could not carry on his pack horse, he was joined by William Calk and four companions—Abraham Hanks, Philip Drake, Enoch Smith and Robert Whitledge. Calk, who—like his comrades—came from Prince William County, Virginia, kept a journal which vividly depicts the hardships endured by these Transylvania pioneers and the methods of travel they were obliged to adopt. Its veracity, its naïveté and its frankness, however commonplace, give to the daily occurrences it records an attraction sometimes absent in more learned journals. Here are the events of April 5 when Henderson resumed his journey:

Wednesday. . . . Breaks away fair & we go on down the valey & camp on indian Creek we had this Creek to cross maney times & very Bad Banks Abrams [Hanks] Saddel turned & the load all fell in we got out this Eavening and kill two Deer.

Two days later Henderson got word that five people headed for Kentucky had been killed by Indians. Nathaniel Hart was so disheartened that he retreated with his companions to Powell Valley, content for the present "to make corn for the Cantuckey people." That same evening came Boone's letter describing his trouble with the Indians. It depressed Henderson and his party. Nevertheless, Henderson wrote to his associates in North Carolina assuring them that the information had not cooled his ardor for the great undertaking and that, indeed, he and his men were "on thorns to fly to Boone's assistance, and join him in defense of so fine and valuable country." He explained that he had been obliged to lay his wagons "aside at Captain Martin's in the valley," and that most of his saltpeter and brimstone had been left behind. His associates replied by sending him powder, lead and salt.

When on April 8 Henderson crossed Cumberland Gap, he saw discouraging signs everywhere. Boone's men, frightened by the Indian attack, were deserting in considerable numbers. At one place, says Calk, they met "a great maney peopel turning Back for fear of the Indians," though, he added proudly, "Our Companey goes on Still with good courage." Henderson, growing anxious and eager to stop the desertions, decided to send a message to Boone's camp on the Kentucky River to assure him of forthcoming assistance.

But who would undertake the dangerous mission? Who would volunteer to ride through the dreaded wilderness? Boone must be assured that he was not being deserted and that support would reach him as quickly as possible. William Cocke agreed to go if Henderson would promise to give him 10,000 acres of choice land and provide him with at least one companion. Henderson assented and then, turning to his followers, offered a second 10,000 acres to anyone who would accompany Cocke. Silence fell on this request. Then with tears in his eyes Henderson appealed again, saying that he and his associates would be ruined if they were obliged to abandon the Transylvania project. Silence again. Finally Cocke reluctantly agreed to undertake the mission alone.

In the next several days Henderson and his party, hampered by their packs and equipage, made slow progress. The hardships they encountered until they reached Boone are best described by Calk:

tuesday 11th this is avery loury morning & like for Rain But we all agree to Start Early we cross Cumberland River & travel Down it about 10 miles through Some turrabel Cainbrakes as we went down abrams [Hanks] mair Ran into the River with Her load & Swam over he foloed her & got on her & made her Swim back agin it is avery Raney Eavening we take up camp near Richland creek they kill a Beef Wm Drake Bakes Bread with out Washing his hands we Keep Sentry this Night for fear of the indians——

Wednesday 12th this is a Raney morning But we pack up & go on we come to Richland creek it is high we toat our packs over on atree & swim our horses over & there We meet another Companey going Back they tell such News Abram & Drake is afraid to go on aney further there we camp this night——

Thursday 13th this morning the weather Seems to Breake & Be fair Abram & Drake turn Back we go on & git to loral River we come to a creek Before where we are obliged to unload & to toate our packs over alog this day we meet about 20 more turning Back we are obliged to toat our packs over loral River & Swim our Horses one hors Ran in with his pack & lost it in the River & got in it——

fryday 14th this is a clear morning with a Smart frost we go on & have avery miray Road and camp this night on a creek of loral River & we are Surprised at camp by awolf

Satterday 15th clear with a Small frost we Start Early we meet
Some men that turns & goes with us we travel this Day through
the plais Caled the Breesh [Brush] and Cross Rockcast[le] River
& camp ther this Night & have fine food for our horses

Sunday 16th cloudy & warm we Start Early & go on about 2
mile down the River and then turn up a creek that we crost about
50 times Some very Bad foards with a great Deal of very good
land on it in the Eavening we git over to the waters of Caintuck
& go alittel Down the creek & there we camp keep Sentry the
fore part of the night it Rains very har[d] all night——

monday 17th this is avery Rany morning But Breaks about 11
oclock & we go on and Camp this Night in Several Companys
on Some of the creeks of caintuck

tuesday 18th fair & cool and we go about 11 oclock we meet
men from Boons camp that came to cunduck us on we camp
this night Just on the Begining of the good land near the Blue
Lick they kill 2 bofelos this Eavening——

Passing by Twitty's Fort where the Indians had attacked Boone
and his party, Henderson's group arrived on April 20 at Boonesboro. Boone had his men salute them with a running fire of all of
the twenty-five guns in the fort. The men's tired and dispirited
faces quickly lighted up, like the sun breaking through a grim
sky. Henderson, who had been gravely concerned about Cocke's
fate, was happy to find his scout in camp safe and sound.

The privations the settlers had endured, the "hilly, stony, slippery, miry, or bushy" road on which they had traveled for a
month, faded from their thoughts as they and Boone's men decreed a day of festivity. Henderson recaptured his joy of that
memorable occasion in a letter to his associates in North Carolina:

To get clear of [our suffering] at once, was as much as we could
bear; and though we had nothing here to refresh ourselves with
but cold water and lean buffalo meat, without bread, it certainly
was the most joyful banquet I ever saw.

The judge's bright spirits were soon dimmed. Though
Boone's men had been on the ground for a month, they had succeeded in raising only a few rude and defenseless cabins. No

doubt they had neglected everything in their mad scramble for land. And Henderson was not pleased with the size and location of the fort Boone had begun to build. It was too small to house everybody. Besides, it rested on low ground which sooner or later was likely to be attacked successfully from the surrounding hills. Henderson decided to build another fort a little farther up the river but still close enough to the older fort that each could assist the other in case of need. There he and his followers moved their tents and began to clear the ground.

But work on the second fort progressed very slowly. Because they had been on the ground first, Boone's men thought they were entitled to the best lands. Each of them grabbed for himself two acres and sometimes wasted much time fussing with his neighbor about this and that trifle. Henderson's men were soon doing the same thing. The judge, indeed, was disturbed to note that one of his own associates, Nathaniel Hart, behaved toward him "in a very cold indifferent manner" regarding the location of the fort. Then Nate chose for himself a piece of ground just outside the town and refused to help the men build the new fort.

Henderson was at a loss to understand Nate's discontent. Was he jealous? Their dissension perhaps grew out of the fact that their personalities were so much unlike. Hart, a practical man of business, saw things as they really were. Henderson appeared to him a pompous and ridiculously ambitious dreamer. In Hart's opinion, the judge was decidedly the wrong man to lead and shape a settlement in the wilderness.

At last necessity compelled the men to straighten out their differences and get down to clearing their land for small patches of corn and vegetables. This done, they began to build cabins. Calk recorded their deeds as he labored with them. On April 25 "in the Eavening we git us a plaise at the mouth of the creek & Begin clearing. . . . Wednesday 26th We Begin Building us ahouse & plaise of Defense to keep the indians off. . . . Satterday 29th We git our house kivered with Bark & move our things into it at Night and Begin housekeeping." Like good neighbors and true pioneers, they had learned to work in unison for the general comfort and improvement of all.

Transylvania

Two important duties faced Richard Henderson: he must provide valid land titles for his men, and he must form a government that would gain their allegiance. He might easily have accomplished both had he had to consider only his own men, but he had also to deal with the land claims of James Harrod and John Floyd, both of whom had preceded him to Transylvania.

In the previous year Harrod with thirty-one Pennsylvanians and Virginians had floated from Pittsburgh down the Ohio to the Kentucky and thence to the headwaters of Salt River where he laid off a settlement which he called first Harrod's Town and later Harrodsburg, the oldest settlement in present Kentucky. Unsatisfied with this acquisition, Harrod soon started another settlement at Boiling Springs, six miles from Harrodsburg, where he raised corn and made his home. He was a large man with rough manners, a hot temper and menacing black eyes. Henderson feared Harrod and wanted no trouble with him.

Floyd he liked better. This young man, only twenty-five years old, had come to Kentucky with thirty Virginians just two weeks before Henderson. Now early in May 1775 he appeared in Boonesboro and asked the judge for a grant of land on reasonable terms. If his request was denied, Floyd said, he and his men would settle north of the Kentucky River outside the limits of Transylvania. Henderson decided to grant the tract, even though Floyd had served as deputy surveyor for Colonel Preston, who had brought his efforts to bear against the Transylvania colony. For the judge thought that the young Virginian had "a great share of modesty, an honest, open countenance, and no small share of good sense." Men of Floyd's caliber were greatly needed in the wilderness; he would restrain his men should they attempt any mischief.

Henderson advised Floyd to settle with his company in a compact body anywhere in the colony save on lands already marked or on those settled by Harrod. Highly pleased with his success, Floyd pledged Henderson his undivided allegiance. But Henderson felt the need of holding the younger man by a bond more powerful than his word. He told Floyd that he proposed to secure harmony in the colony by providing it with an independent government. When Floyd expressed great interest in such a project, Henderson disclosed plans to summon a general convention to which each of the four settlements in the colony should send delegates. Floyd proudly embraced this scheme.

Would Harrod agree to it? Would that ruffian and his "Lawless men," as Henderson called them, recognize him and his associates as sole proprietors of Transylvania? Would they accept the North Carolinians' titles to the land on which they had settled? Would they respect Transylvania's laws? Time fortunately answered all these questions, in the affirmative.

On May 7 Harrod and Colonel Thomas Slaughter came to Boonesboro to ask Henderson to settle a controversy which had arisen between them. Slaughter, with thirty men, also had preceded Henderson to Transylvania and had settled around Harrodsburg. Harrod and his men had claimed priority to the region and had substantiated their claims by marking every piece of valuable ground, building hog pens and seizing every spring within twenty miles of Harrodsburg. On the contrary, Slaughter and his company had, in conformity with Henderson's written instructions regarding settlement in Translyvania, industriously employed themselves in clearing land and had taken steps to plant a large crop of corn.

Henderson naturally favored Slaughter in the dispute but, fearing Harrod's wrath, refrained from voicing this conviction. Instead he decided to reconcile the two men and win them to his side by a stroke of verbal strategy. Dodging the issue at hand, he talked of the existing lawlessness and of the need for a government to guarantee land titles and to adjust differences over land acquisitions. Henderson then brought up the proposed plan of government which he had discussed with Floyd. Harrod and Slaughter, convinced that solutions to these problems could only

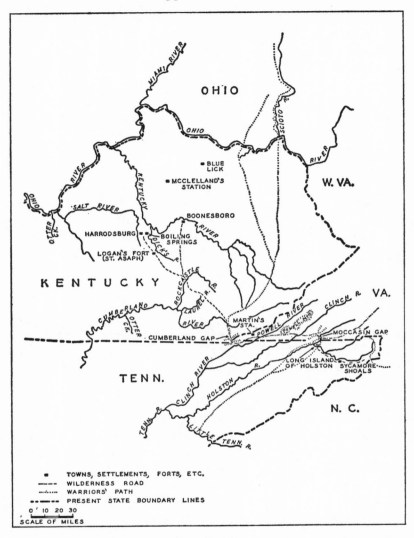

favor their own ends, forgot their differences, shook hands and
departed from Harrodsburg "in great good humor," promising
Henderson their entire support.

Henderson then requested the four settlements to hold elections on May 20 for delegates to the convention. Boonesboro
sent six, and Harrodsburg, Boiling Springs and St. Asaph—re-

cently established by Captain Benjamin Logan—sent four each. Among the eighteen delegates were Daniel Boone, Squire Boone, Richard Callaway, Thomas Slaughter, James Harrod and John Floyd, all of whom Henderson praised as men disposed to serve their constituents faithfully.

In a beautiful valley perfumed by wide patches of clover stood a huge elm. Its branches spread over a hundred feet. On a sunny day it threw a shadow four times that length. In the shade of this magnificent tree gathered the delegates of Transylvania. The convention, under the presidency of Thomas Slaughter, got under way with a great deal of flowery oratory. The clerk of the convention read a speech written by Henderson in his grandiloquent style:

You are called and assembled at this time for a noble and honourable purpose—a purpose, however ridiculous or idle it may appear at first view, to superficial minds, yet it is of most solid consequence; and if prudence and wisdom are permitted to influence your councils and direct your conduct, the peace and harmony of thousands may be expected to result from your deliberations; in short, you are about a work of the utmost importance to the well-being of this country in general, in which the interest and security of each and every individual is inseparably connected. . . .

You, perhaps, are fixing the palladium, or placing the first corner-stone of an edifice, the height and magnificence of whose superstructure is now in the womb of futurity, and can become great and glorious in proportion of the excellence of its foundation. These considerations, gentlemen, will, no doubt, animate and inspire you with sentiments worthy the grandeur of the subject. . . . If any doubts remain amongst you with respect to the force or efficacy of whatever laws you now, or hereafter, make, be pleased to consider that all power is originally in the people; therefore make it their interest, by impartial and beneficial laws, and you may be sure of their inclination to see them enforced. . . .

As it is indispensably necessary that laws should be composed for the regulation of our conduct, as we have the right to make such laws without giving offense to Great Britain, or any of the American colonies, without disturbing the repose of any society or community under heaven; as it is probable, nay, certain, that the laws may derive force and efficacy from our mutual consent, and that consent resulting from our own virtue, interest, and convenience, nothing remains but to set about the business immediately, and let the event determine the wisdom of our undertaking. . . .

Henderson went on to suggest that the convention establish courts, organize a militia and pass legislation to preserve game and to punish errant hunters. He also declared himself against "vice and immorality."

The settlers replied through one of their delegates, perhaps William Cocke, by thanking Henderson "for the care and attention" he had manifested toward their "infant country." Well aware that the lack of government might mean confusion and anarchy, they pledged their vigorous support in providing for one "not doubting but unanimity will insure our success." The style and sentiment of the speech was so similar to Henderson's that historians suspect the judge of having written it also:

That we have an absolute right, as a political body, without giving umbrage to Great Britain, or any of the colonies, to frame rules for the government of our little society, can not be doubted by any sensible, unbiased mind—and being without the jurisdiction of, and not answerable to any of his Majesty's courts, the constituting tribunals of justice shall be a matter of our first contemplation.

The expression of loyalty to the British government indicates that the Transylvanians were unaware of Lexington and Concord and of General Gage's defeat in Boston. Politically they still considered themselves subjects of George III, though spiritually they were Americans who had found his tyranny hard to bear long before they left for the wilderness.

The convention lasted several days and ended with an incident that disclosed Henderson's love of color and ceremony. Standing under the big elm in the presence of the delegates, Henderson and John Farrar, one of the lawyers representing the Indians, performed the feudal ceremony of "Livery of Seizin." Farrar handed Henderson a piece of turf dug from the ground on which they stood. While both men held it Farrar formally declared delivery of seizin and proclaimed Henderson in full possession of Transylvania. The applause was loud and long.

The convention adopted a constitution which, despite Henderson's assurances, showed little respect for democratic principles. Though it granted "perfect religious freedom and general toleration," it placed most of the power of government in the hands of the proprietors. It empowered them to appoint the justices of the supreme courts, the sheriff and "all other civil and military officers." It placed the executive power solely in the proprietors' hands. In addition it gave them the right to collect an annual quit-rent of two shillings for every 100 acres of their claim. Indeed, they expected that they and their heirs should collect forever at that rate on 20,000,000 acres.

The legislative authority was to consist of three branches—"the delegates or representatives of the people; a council not exceeding twelve men, possessed of landed estate, who shall reside in the colony; and the proprietors." The delegates were empowered to elect a treasurer for the colony and to raise "all moneys." The document failed to state the manner in which the councilors were to be selected and the nature and extent of their duties. It was equally indefinite regarding the power of the proprietors. Presumably they were to hold absolute power of veto over all the acts passed by the councilors and the delegates save those relating to revenue and appropriations.

The delegates adopted nearly all of Henderson's suggestions. Daniel Boone introduced a bill aimed at preserving game. Too many men, he said, were wasting meat; from the three, four or five buffaloes they killed each week some of them took home scarcely a horseload. Of the two or three hundred buffaloes seen near Boonesboro when the settlers had arrived six weeks ago none was left. In consequence hunters often were obliged to travel as much as twenty or thirty miles from home once or twice a week to procure meat. Boone's bill passed without dissent. Encouraged by his success, Boone presented another bill, this one concerned with improving the breed of horses. This bill also passed without dissent. Confident that the settlement could defend itself without him, he set out for the East to fetch his family to Kentucky.

The convention produced, if not complete peace of mind, at least a calming effect. The settlers temporarily gained confidence in the validity of their titles and in their security against outlawry and Indian attacks. Floyd assured Preston that the settlers had accepted Henderson as their leader. The judge himself happily informed those of his associates who remained in North Carolina that his wishes with respect to titles had succeeded remarkably well. Apparently nothing now could shake Henderson's confidence. When Governor Martin warned him that Colonel Byrd disparaged him and that Dunmore and Preston had sent to the Cherokee letters requesting them to repudiate him or run the risk of displeasing the King, Henderson made this spirited reply:

Whether Lord Dunmore & Col Byrd have interfered with the Indians or not, Richard Henderson is equally ignorant & indifferent. The utmost result of their efforts can only serve to convince them of the futility of their scheme, and possibly frighten some faint-hearted persons.

But things were not going so well as Henderson led others to believe. How was he to maintain the food supply? The settlers, finding themselves hundreds of miles from any trading post, had little food save the meat of wild animals and corn in the summer. Henderson wrote in his journal that they had to eat meat without bread, that they almost starved and that they placed their hopes on the growing vegetables. Calk complained that, lacking bread on certain days, he was obliged to kill "a turkey and came in & got Some of my breakfast & then went to sot [set] in to clearing for corn."

Food, however, was not Henderson's chief problem. Land was uppermost in his mind and in the minds of his followers. They thought of land by day; they dreamed of land by night.

Land was the most important word in their writing. It appeared more than any other word, and it was capitalized and italicized on nearly every occasion. The settlers' passion for land caused all their disputes—disputes so numerous and vehement that the advice and admonition of their leader fell on deaf ears. They wanted to own not mere ground but choice, fertile land provided with salt springs. Their scrambling for the best land resulted in over-lapping claims, in countless feuds and suits, in needless bloodshed —and in fattening the lawyers' purses. Henderson had tried to appease the Transylvanians by promising them the semblance of a democratic government, but they would have none of it until the titles to their lands should be cleared.

The desire for choice land was an American characteristic found in leaders and followers alike. When Daniel Boone received 1,000 acres, Henderson took a similar amount at the mouth of Salt Lick. Encouraged by this coup, Nathaniel Hart grabbed 1,000 acres near by. Another man then demanded a similar amount, but Henderson turned him down.

The settlers' land hunger cannot be regarded as an expression of greed. They had staked out claims, had made surveys, had built cabins and had cleared the land and planted corn long before Boonesboro became a town. Most of them were backwoodsmen from Virginia, Pennsylvania and North Carolina who had developed a spirit of independence which they regarded as vital as breathing. These typical Americans were not used to accepting restrictions—certainly not from a small group of men whose claims to Transylvania they knew to be shaky and who were considered outlaws by the governors of Virginia and North Carolina. The settlers had accepted Henderson's proprietary government before they realized what it entailed. Now they began to resent it as smacking strongly of the English system and as engendering more of the tyranny against which the thirteen colonies were revolting. Henderson could count on the people's allegiance only as long as they were willing to give it.

Henderson regarded the frontiersmen as nomadic as gypsies. No sooner did one stream of pioneers flow into Kentucky than another flowed out. Before the second group settled, the first unsettled. Under various pretenses they deserted their leader, until their number dwindled from about eighty to fifty, from fifty to thirty.

At last Henderson gave way to despair. In a letter to one of his associates he said he was sorry he could not give him

. . . a more favorable account; but you must take it as it is and make the best of it. . . . Our enterprise has now come to a crisis, and in a few weeks will determine the matter. Harrodsburg and the Boiling Spring settlements, which, some time ago, could have raised and turned out seventy or eighty men, at a short warning, are almost abandoned—on the most emergent occasion, they could not rally twenty men—the better half of them in the woods on the north side of the Kentucky, and perhaps could not be summoned to our assistance, in less than a fortnight.

Something had to be done and done quickly if Henderson wished to save his project from the possibility of collapse. To this end he returned with Luttrell to North Carolina and in the early fall of 1775 called his associates to a meeting at Oxford. All attended save the disgruntled Harts. The attending proprietors chose John Williams as general agent for the colony, with full power to transact business until April 1776. They also made many changes relative to the purchase and disposal of land.

The new regulations permitted each settler to buy 640 acres and 320 acres in addition for each taxable person whom he brought with him, instead of 500 and 250 acres respectively under the original terms. But the price for 100 acres was increased from twenty to fifty shillings with fees of four dollars for surveying, two dollars for entry and warrant of survey and two dollars for a deed. Quitrents, however, were deferred until January 1, 1780. The proprietors voted themselves 2,000 acres in equal shares. To Daniel Boone they voted 2,000 acres for his "signal services," and to Callaway the thanks of the company "for the spirited and manly behavior in behalf of the Said Colony." No grant was made to him directly, but his younger son received 640 acres.

For some time Henderson had entertained the idea of petitioning the Continental Congress to admit Transylvania into the colonies. His motivation is unknown. His "stiched brown books," in which he may have written his reasons, were unfortunately lost. But from his disappointment over his inability to solve the land-title question, from the unstable conduct of his followers and from the possible enmity of Virginia, he undoubtedly deduced that his project would have little chance of survival should he continue his policy of defying the Crown and ignoring the claims of Virginia and North Carolina. He and his associates decided, therefore, to change their stand and play the support of the Crown against that of the colonies. In a revolutionary era when either the King or the colonies might be the victor, what policy would be wiser than that of duplicity?

The judge had first mentioned his plan to his associates at their Oxford meeting when he requested them to draft the necessary memorial to the Continental Congress. The document, quickly written, enumerated the difficulties and dangers which the proprietors of Transylvania had incurred in settling the colony and asserted they had acquired it without violating either British or American laws. Yet the proprietors, though "far removed from the reach of Ministerial usurpation . . . cannot look with indifference on the late arbitrary proceedings of the British Parliament. If the united Colonies are reduced, or tamely submit to be slaves, Transylvania will have reason to fear."

Having thus implied their sympathy for the colonists, the proprietors, despite the fact that they had defied the Proclamation of 1763, declared their allegiance "to their Sovereign, whose constitutional rights and preeminences they will support at the risk of their lives."

But

. . . having their hearts warmed with the same noble spirit that animates the united Colonies, and moved with indignation at the late Ministerial and Parliamentary usurpations, it is the earnest wish of the proprietors of Transylvania to be considered by the Colonies as brethren, engaged in the same great cause of liberty and mankind. And, as by reason of several circumstances, needless to be here mentioned, it is impossible for the proprietors to call a convention of the settlers in such time to have their concurrence laid before this Congress, they here pledge themselves for them, that they will concur in the measures now adopted by the proprietors.

From the generous plan of liberty adopted by the Congress, and that noble love of mankind which appears in all their proceedings, the memorialists please themselves that the united Colonies will take the infant Colony of Transylvania into their protection; and they, in return, will do everything in their power, and give such assistance in the general cause of America as the Congress shall judge to be suitable to their abilities.

As their representative to Congress the proprietors, of course, chose one of themselves, James Hogg, who had long aspired to a seat in that body. Arriving in Philadelphia on October 22, 1775, Hogg became acquainted with Samuel Adams and John Adams. Both the Adamses gave him courteous consideration but warned him that, since Congress was then trying to reconcile the colonies with the mother country, "the taking under our protection a body of people who have acted in defiance of the king's proclamation, will be looked on as a confirmation of that independent spirit with which we are daily reproached."

In his diary John Adams confided that Hogg was one of the proprietors of Transylvania who "have no grant from the Crown, nor from any Colony; are within the limits of Virginia and North Carolina, by their charters . . . They are charged with republican notions and Utopian schemes."

Thus John Adams had detected flaws in Henderson's bold plans. The claims of Virginia over that part of Transylvania which lay north of 36° 30′ proved a serious snag to Hogg's success. When he displayed a map of the colony before the two Adamses they quickly pointed out that it lay partly on territory claimed by Virginia and therefore refused to do anything without the consent of the Virginia delegates. Hogg agreed to confer with them but was unable to see them for several days. Meanwhile he learned that Virginia's representatives were unwilling to admit Transylvania without the approval of their constituents.

Undaunted, Hogg assured Thomas Jefferson and several other

delegates from Virginia that the proprietors were sympathetic toward the American cause, but he refrained from mentioning the memorial or his desire to obtain a seat in Congress. The delegates, too, were discreet, though they asked many questions and insisted that much of Transylvania lay within the Virginia charter and that, if they wished, they could claim the entire colony. Hogg countered by stating that Great Britain and Virginia had recognized by the Treaty of Lochaber the rightful claim of the Cherokee to the region. He also made a bid for Jefferson's support by arguing that Transylvania would serve Virginia as a barrier against Indian depredations. To which Jefferson replied that, though he favored the establishment of a free government in the back country, he would not consent to Transylvania's being recognized by Congress without the approval of Virginia. Jefferson therefore recommended that Hogg request the proprietors to send a delegate to the next Virginia assembly.

Hogg failed to press the matter further; during the remainder of his sojourn in Philadelphia he remained inactive. Despite his failure, he wrote Henderson in January 1776, stating that some members of Congress favored the Transylvania project and that they were convinced of its validity. The truth was that in assembly they denounced the company's quitrents and that some of the delegates advised a law against the employment of Negroes in the colony.

Hogg eventually had to admit to Henderson that most of the delegates had threatened to oppose the project "if we do not act upon liberal principles when we have it so much in our power to make ourselves immortal." In thus denouncing quitrents and objecting to slavery on the frontier, the Continental Congress at this early date expressed the western principle of social equality which forms the foundation of American life.

Soon after returning to Boonesboro late in November 1775 John Williams, as agent of the Transylvania Company, issued an advertisement disclosing the new regulations for the purchase of land. At the same time he requested the four settlements to elect delegates to a new convention at Boonesboro on December 21 "for the purpose of making and ordering such Laws Rules and Regulations as may be thought Expedient and applicable to our present circumstances."

The delegates were duly elected, but bad weather and their resentment over the increase in the price of land kept most of them away. Nevertheless, Williams, hoping to realize his aims, asked the attending delegates for advice. They unanimously recommended that John Floyd be made surveyor and Nathaniel Hart entry taker of the colony. Williams promptly appointed the two men.

This availed nothing. Harrodsburg and Boiling Springs were already seething with discontent. James Harrod, who until now had supported Henderson in the hope of securing political privileges and large tracts of land for himself and his friends, flew into one of his customary rages and induced his supporters to send Williams a letter of protest. This letter bitterly assailed the proprietors for increasing the price of land and for engrossing for themselves and their friends the choice lands at and near the Falls of the Ohio. Williams replied that the proprietors were selling land as cheaply and on terms as generous as they could afford and that dissension in the colony should be eliminated in favor of a united front against the Indians who were threatening to go on the warpath. At the same time he endeavored to appease the grumblers by assuring them that he had orders to grant no more large tracts of land which lay contiguous to the Falls.

Williams' efforts at conciliation proved vain. Harrodsburg and Boiling Springs passed from discontent to open revolt. Harrod and his friend, Abraham Hite, obtained the services of a skilled lawyer, Peter Hogg, to draft a petition to the Virginia assembly. James Harrod signed it first, producing a large scrawl in an audacious hand which recalls that of John Hancock on the Declaration of Independence published a few months later. The names of Hite and eighty-six others followed.

The petitioners stated that they had settled in Transylvania "at great expense and many hardships . . . under the faith of holding the lands by indefeasible title, which [the proprietors] assured them they were capable of making." But the proprietors had "alarmed" them greatly: they had advanced the price of purchase from twenty to fifty shillings for 100 acres; they had "increased the fees of entry and surveying to a most exorbitant rate"; and, by fixing short periods for taking up the land, they had indicated that they intended to stiffen their "demands" as the number of settlers increased.

These offenses troubled the settlers enough, but they only began the list of grievances. The petitioners asserted that they had discovered that the land which Henderson and his associates were selling them had been granted to the Crown as far as the Tennessee River by the Treaty of Fort Stanwix and that, therefore, the proprietors had no valid claim to it. In view of these discoveries the settlers requested that they be taken under the jurisdiction and protection of Virginia "of which we cannot help thinking ourselves still a part." They therefore begged

. . . your kind interposition in our behalf, that we may not suffer under the rigorous demands and imposition of the gentlemen stiling themselves proprietors, who, the better to effect their oppressive designs, have given them the colour of a law, enacted by a score of men, artfully picked from the few adventurers who went to see the country last summer, overawed by the presence of Mr. Henderson.

And that you would take such measures as your honours in your wisdom shall judge most expedient for the restoring peace and harmony to our divided settlement; or, if your honours apprehend that our case comes more properly before the honourable the General Congress, that you would in your goodness recommend the same to your worthy delegates, to espouse it as the cause of the Colony.

The general spirit of revolt soon spread to Boonesboro where some of the settlers had reasons of their own for resenting the proprietors. They, too, addressed a petition to the Virginia assembly:

. . . sd Colo. Richard Henderson had the fence that was made by the people broke and took the rails and fenced in betwixt twenty and thirty acres of the most convenient ground next to the fort which has been held under sd Henderson ever since except the value of one or two acres was taken for gardens for people in sd fort, we your petitioners think it a grand Imposition that sd Henderson should hold a quantity of Ground whilst some of your petitioners have been under the necessity of clearing ground at the risk of our lives and tending our crops around sd Henderson's slaves. In the second place John Luttrell one of the Gent. proprietors entered on S.W. side of sd Township and improved on the Land first allowed by sd proprietors for a Town. In the third place Nathaniel Heart [*sic*] another of the sd proprietors entered the upper half of the Town Land which was cleared and fenced by the people who tended corn the first year. . . .

Such was the general mood of many Transylvanians when in the spring of 1776 they found a new and vigorous champion in young George Rogers Clark. While in Kentucky during the previous year Clark had made himself thoroughly acquainted with the extent and nature of the discord and had given considerable thought to what he should do to remove it. Going to Virginia in the fall, he had found that her leading citizens, including Thomas Jefferson and Patrick Henry, were divided in their opinions of Henderson's claim. Some had thought it good, others had doubted its validity. This incertitude sufficed to convince Clark that Henderson and his associates had worked their own ruin by increasing the price of land and by engrossing choice and large tracts for themselves. The time was therefore ripe to oust them from the colony.

Returning to Kentucky in the spring of 1776, Clark formulated plans which called for a meeting of the settlers on June 6 to elect deputies who should attempt to effect a more definite connection with Virginia. If they failed in this endeavor, he planned to advocate the establishment of an independent state. He reasoned that by giving away a great part of the land and selling what remained he would not only attract a large number of people to the colony but would also command a position to persuade Virginia to supply the means to protect them. Clark naturally chose Harrodsburg as the place for his meeting. To prevent the settlers from splitting into factions, he refrained from divulging his plans in his printed summons. Instead, he endeavored to arouse their curiosity to attend the meeting by simply stating that he wished to discuss with them a matter in which they were vitally interested.

This bit of psychology was needless; his summons sufficed. During his sojourn in Kentucky, Clark had endeared himself to the settlers by his attractive manners, his ready wit, his wealth of information and his lively intelligence. On the day of the meeting, therefore, they responded with enthusiasm. Indeed, they did not wait for Clark to arrive in Harrodsburg with instructions. Surmising his wishes, they began to vote for two delegates to the Virginia assembly. Instead, Clark wanted them to elect deputies who, as diplomatic agents of the people, would be empowered to negotiate with Virginia for satisfactory terms before they acknowledged her jurisdiction over the region. But when he arrived late in the evening, the people had already decided on their delegates, and, not wishing to embarrass or disparage them, he made little effort to change their principle. At the end of the week they elected Clark and a lawyer named John Gabriel Jones.

On June 15 the settlers in and around Harrodsburg drafted a petition which Clark and Jones were to carry to the Virginia assembly. The petitioners charged that Henderson and his associates sold land at exorbitant prices and that the proprietors had introduced a system of policy which "does not at all harmonize with that lately adopted by the United Colonies; but on the contrary, for aught yet appears, this fertile country will afford a safe asylum to those whose principles are inimical to American freedom."

The petitioners further stated that, since the Cherokee had never claimed the land north of the Cumberland River and since it had been ceded by the Six Nations to the Crown, they doubted the validity of Henderson's purchase. They were therefore unwilling to acknowledge the authority of the proprietors, who had little or no power to protect them against the Indians in a region so remote from the colonies. For this reason they prayed for union with Virginia, which held the region by right of charter and of conquest and which had the power to protect, nourish and guide them until they should flourish in trade, navigation, population and wealth.

The Transylvanians assured the assembly that they, as sympathizers with its work and that of the Continental Congress, could be expected to support the revolution with men and money. And they informed the assembly that in order to bring harmony to the region and to justify their position before the world they had established a Committee of Twenty-One which would function as a provisional government until Virginia should constitute adequate government for them. They ended the petition by placing themselves under the authority and jurisdiction of the assembly and by expressing confidence that it would give them such advice as should redound to their best interests.

Five days later the Committee of Twenty-One, with John Gabriel Jones as chairman, addressed to the assembly another petition expressing the desire of the settlers to support the revolution and their contempt for the British Ministry for passing laws forbidding the settling of western lands and the formation of new western counties. The Committee complained that Virginia's westernmost county, Fincastle, which had been declared to extend to the utmost limits of the colony and therefore to embrace Kentucky, was so large—300 miles in length—that the two delegates could not adequately represent the region from which they had been sent. As crack riflemen they proudly offered their military services to Virginia.

In regard to the proprietors, the Committee repeated what had been said in the general petition, adding that the proprietors' action had disturbed those settlers who were sympathetic toward Virginia and had created factions and divisions among them. The Committee reminded the assembly of their defenselessness in case of an Indian attack. The Delawares had notified the settlers of an impending treaty between the English and the Kickapoo and had asked the whites to send representatives to their tribe for further information about that treaty. The Committee reported that James Harrod and Garret Pendergras had been chosen for this mission. The Committee also announced that it had selected a number of desirable men to act as civil magistrates and listed their names. The petition ended by requesting the assembly again to extend its jurisdiction over the Kentucky settlements.

A few days after the petition was written Clark and Jones departed for Williamsburg.

Henderson, who had returned to Boonesboro perhaps early in 1776, was distressed but not discouraged by the Harrodsburg revolt. When he learned that Clark had summoned the people of that settlement to a meeting, he readily understood its significance and resolved to meet the challenge with all the strength of his character. Early in May he journeyed with John Williams to Williamsburg, intending to present his case before the Virginia assembly. He arrived in Williamsburg to learn that on May 18 the assembly had presented the petitions drafted the preceding December in Harrodsburg.

Henderson countered the petitions with a memorial. Presented on June 15, Henderson's response conceived that the right of disposal was incident to property. Henderson and his associates claimed that no existing laws prohibited them from purchasing the land, and that, therefore, they considered themselves sole owners and proprietors of Transylvania, "without incurring any penalty or forfeiture whatsoever." Their sole intention, the memorial declared, was to give "every well-disposed person" an opportunity to settle in the region. In so doing they had incurred considerable expense and had seen several of their friends killed. Further, with many hardships, difficulties and dangers, they had remained actual possessors and, they believed, rightful claimants of the land, never "doubting the equity or legality of their title."

The proprietors averred that the numerous persons who had come to settle in Transylvania had been perfectly satisfied until "artful and designing persons, by cunning, specious and false suggestions, with intent to injure and oppress them, have raised doubts in the minds of some few with respect to the justice and validity of the title, and consequently of the propriety of making payment, according to their original contract and agreement, until some objections be removed, or themselves better satisfied." They declared "with great deference" that matters or disputes pertaining to private property did not concern the Virginia as-

sembly or any other assembly or even Congress. After hurling
this defiance the Transylvania proprietors denied that they had
taken any arbitrary or exorbitant measures against the settlers.
Indeed, they had not even entertained such thoughts. The laws
and regulations passed by the Transylvania convention were
merely temporary; necessity had justified them. The proprietors
concluded by claiming that they always tried to make the benefits of their lands as widespread as possible and that they were
ready now and at all times to submit to the authority of Virginia
or to that of the United States.

In reviewing these arguments William Lester, one of the best
authorities on Transylvania, found that the proprietors sometimes
fell into false assumption and specious reasoning. Never in English law, he explained, had the disposal of property been incident
to its possession. As for the statement that no decrees and laws
existed to prohibit the purchase of Transylvania from the Cherokee, it is easily controverted. In taking possession of the colony
the proprietors had defied the Proclamation of 1763. And even
if this had not existed, they still had broken an earlier law which
forbade the purchase of land already claimed or possessed by
"any Indian or Indians whatsoever."

No less untenable was the assurance of the proprietors that
they were ready to submit to Virginia or to the United States.
They had formed a constitution for Transylvania, and Henderson in his opening speech before the Boonesboro convention had
asserted "the right to make such laws without giving offense to
Great Britain, or any of the American colonies, without disturbing the repose of any society or community under heaven."
Henderson had boasted of the sovereignty of Transylvania, had
denied surveys conducted by officers of Virginia, had spoken of
himself and his associates as "true and absolute proprietors," and
had conducted elections, called a legislature, made a treaty and
appointed officers.

No doubt the assembly detected these inconsistencies in Henderson's arguments, for it soon took favorable action on the Harrodsburg petitions. On June 24 the assembly passed a resolution
permitting all persons who held lands in Transylvania to retain
them "without paying any pecuniary or other consideration

whatever to any private person or persons" until it should reach a decision regarding the validity of the titles granted by Henderson and his associates. The resolution also forbade the purchase of any land within the chartered limits of Virginia "under any pretense whatever, from any Indian tribe or nation, without the approbation of the Virginia Legislature." A few days later the assembly appointed sixteen commissioners to study the claims of the proprietors. After conducting other business it adjourned until October.

Clark and Jones had not yet arrived to throw their support to the side of Virginia in the hope of swaying that colony to take in the Kentucky region. When after experiencing many inconveniences of travel they arrived in Williamsburg to find that the assembly had adjourned, they decided to wait until the fall session. They separated, however, with Jones going to Holston while Clark went to interview Governor Patrick Henry. The governor was ill but he welcomed Clark and expressed sympathy for his party in Kentucky. Henry sent Clark to the Council with a favorable letter of introduction. Clark forthwith requested 500 pounds of powder which, he explained, was sorely needed for the defense of Kentucky.

Clark knew that if he could get the government to commit itself by granting the supply, it would soon have to assert control over the region. After some hesitation the Council agreed to furnish the ammunition but explained that since Kentucky was not as yet a part of Virginia they would lend it only as to friends in distress, and that Clark must assume responsibility for it in case the assembly did not receive the settlers as citizens of the state. Clark replied that he did not have the money to pay for the cost of transporting the powder and the guards necessary to protect it. The Council, feeling they had already stretched their power, would go no further without the consent of the assembly and issued an order to the keeper of the magazine to deliver the ammunition to Clark.

The young Virginian took his leave with some disappointment, but increased determination to succeed in his mission. Concluding after some reflection that Virginia would be reluctant to lose the coveted region of Kentucky and with it perhaps all the chartered territory in the west, he resolved on a bold stroke of psychology. He returned the order for the ammunition and writing to the Council, reiterated his inability to meet the cost of transporting it. He was sorry, he said, that the settlers of Kentucky would have to obtain protection elsewhere; then he added, "if a country is not worth protecting it is not worth claiming." This statement had the desired result; the Council, fearing that the Kentuckians would do as Clark threatened, sent for Clark and placed the powder at his disposal.

The contest, which began with the opening of the assembly on October 8, proved long and bitter. Henderson and Williams were there with the best legal advisers of North Carolina. Clark and Jones were there with such friends as George Mason, Thomas Jefferson and other delegates likely to influence the assembly in reaching its final verdict. Clark had an enemy in Colonel Arthur Campbell, known as Long Jaw because of his irascible garrulity. As a delegate from Fincastle and county lieutenant, Campbell was bitterly opposed to the creation of a new county, for such action would deprive him of authority over the rich region of Kentucky and limit his power to a comparatively small mountain county.

Clark and Jones presented themselves as delegates from the "Western Part of Fincastle County." Despite the petitions they had brought with them they were denied seats on legal grounds while Henderson and Campbell, by a display of their best eloquence and persuasive powers, gave them much trouble. But a petition which was presented to the House by Thomas Slaughter saved the day. Slaughter, on behalf of himself and other settlers of Kentucky, stated that they were exposed to the incursions and depredations of Indians and were incapable of protecting themselves with their small numbers. He therefore prayed that Virginia would extend them the benefit of defending themselves by permitting them to organize themselves into a militia.

The House responded by resolving itself into a committee of the whole to consider the new petition as well as those presented by Clark and Jones. It soon brought in a report stating that "the settlers ought to be formed into a distinct county, in order to entitle them to such representation, and other benefits of government." The bill calling for a division of Fincastle County into two distinct counties made headway for several days. Jefferson, admirably envisioning the future of Kentucky, did everything he could to help Clark. He championed the bill and it passed two readings. But Henderson and Williams and Campbell were equally determined; with legal knowledge, eloquence and force of character, they succeeded in persuading the House to postpone the measure for a week, an action practically foreshadowing its ultimate defeat.

Clark, however, never knew defeat; he merely saw that the time had come for him to make another psychological move such as that which a few months before had won him the ammunition from the Council. He took up his unpracticed but nonetheless persuasive pen to address a short petition to the assembly. Pretending that he and Jones were preparing to return to Kentucky, he reminded the assembly of the distressed and defenseless state of the Kentucky settlers and implored it to send forces for their relief and protection. He added that the interest of Virginia demanded that it prevent the "Inhabitants from abandoning" Kentucky which he pictured as necessary and advantageous to the United States "in Case of an Indian War, an event much to be feared." He concluded by saying that the services of the settlers would save the United States "at least one-half of what an Army must Cost to be levied anywhere else on the Frontier Counties, or any part of America."

With these arguments Clark succeeded in having himself and his colleague presented again to the House, but Henderson and his friends were prepared for them and repulsed the bill. A third reading, which was necessary to secure a vote, was denied. The bill was taken from its place on the calendar and "directed to be read in the usual course of proceedings." Once more Jefferson rushed to the bill's defense, rescued it from possible oblivion, and had it referred to a special committee with himself as chairman. Thenceforth the bill marched to victory.

By this time Virginia had declared herself a free and independent state, both alone and in conjunction with the other colonies; she had published a constitution which had declared her complete independence from Great Britain. Her sovereignty gave her the right to assume full ownership of all lands that she had held and claimed as a dependent colony. Nothing in her original charter could now stop her at the Alleghenies. Nothing in the Proclamation of 1763 could now prohibit her from exercising the sovereignty over the western country. The rights she had enjoyed over it as a colony she now enjoyed as a commonwealth. Her claim over Transylvania was perfectly clear and she resolved to assert it.

Henderson's further efforts were, therefore, useless. On November 25 the House passed the bill and resolved that Fincastle County be divided into Washington, Montgomery and Kentucky counties. The Senate eventually concurred, and on December 7, 1776, most of Transylvania became Kentucky County, Virginia, with an area about the same as the present state of Kentucky.

So ended the revolt against the proprietors of Transylvania, first under the leadership of James Harrod and Abraham Hite and then under that of George Rogers Clark and John Gabriel Jones. Clark returned to Kentucky with the ammunition he had secured from the Council and was hailed as a hero. Henderson's fantastic dream of "true and absolute proprietors" faded, but it did not mean the end of his career. His greatest achievement still lay before him. That is another story and is told elsewhere.

Siege of

Boonesboro

Early in September 1775 Daniel Boone returned to Boonesboro with his wife and their unmarried daughter, Jemima. With them had traveled a group of settlers and twenty young North Carolinians in search of adventure. Supplied with salt, ammunition, a number of dogs and a herd of cattle, they had stayed together until they reached Dick's River, south of the Kentucky, where they separated, some heading toward Harrodsburg and the rest, thirty in number under Daniel Boone, going to Boonesboro. The population of that fort was soon further increased by the return of Squire Boone with Rebecca's kinfolk, the Bryans, and Colonel Richard Callaway with his family.

Before long the settlers discovered that stray bands of Shawnee were lurking around the fort. During their hunting trips these Indians learned that the white men intended to settle permanently in Kentucky. The news soon spread to the Shawnee villages north of the Ohio. Far from intending to keep their pledge to Lord Dunmore to stay on the northern side of the river, the Shawnee now determined to destroy the settlers or to drive them out of what they still considered their favorite hunting grounds.

Some months passed, however, before the Indians were prepared to attack. Just two days before Christmas Colonel Arthur Campbell with two boys named Sanders and McQuinney went searching for rich bottom lands across the river from the fort. Unarmed, the boys climbed a hill while Campbell wandered 200 yards upstream. Soon meeting with "a couple of Indians," he ran toward the fort, losing a shoe. When nothing more was heard from the boys Boone gathered a rescue party and led it into the surrounding forest. After four days of searching the party found McQuinney's scalped body in a cornfield three miles from the fort. The fate of the other boy remains a mystery.

The Shawnee took the precaution of making haste slowly. Having tasted defeat at Point Pleasant, they thirsted for victory. They persuaded some Cherokee bands to aid them in expelling the whites from Boonesboro. The Cherokee chief, Hanging Maw, though usually friendly with the Americans, consented to attack the fort but not before he took full council with other tribal leaders. Hanging Maw had a profound respect for the courage and military sagacity of the settlers. In Watauga he had known Boone whom he and other chiefs called Wide Mouth, and he recognized no brave as this white man's equal. He resolved, therefore, on elaborate preliminaries, one of which called for a thorough scouting of the fort. To this task he assigned five of his most trusted warriors.

On a Sunday in July 1776 Elizabeth and Frances Callaway and Jemima Boone decided to go canoeing on the river just below Boonesboro. Elizabeth was not yet fifteen; the other girls, about fourteen. They paddled toward some flowers that grew at the foot of a high cliff surrounded by forest and cane. As they drew near the shore one of Hanging Maw's scouts sprang from the canebrake. Betsy Callaway tried to jump into the water while Fanny whacked at the Indian with her paddle until it broke. Hanging Maw and three other Indians now appeared, took the girls ashore and set the canoe adrift. They hushed the cries and shrieks of their captives by brandishing their knives and tomahawks. Jemima, having cut her foot, refused to go forward. The Cherokee threatened to kill her. She remained still until they provided her with moccasins. Then the Indians cut the girls' dresses at the knees to facilitate their progress through the forest.

As they marched the girls availed themselves of every means to mark their trail for the benefit of possible rescuers. One of them cut twigs with her penknife and strewed them on the way. They also shredded a white handkerchief and scattered it along their path. Jemima tumbled down as often as she could. The

Indians discouraged these stratagems by shaking their tomahawks, pulling the girls' hair and threatening to scalp them.

To deceive possible pursuers the kidnapers followed ridges where footprints would be dim, walked through the thickest canebrake they could find and, when they were obliged to lead the girls over soft ground, cut off Betsy's high wooden heels. At nightfall they encamped within three miles of the present town of Winchester. They prevented each girl from using her hands by tying her elbows together securely. At night when the Cherokee sprawled on the ground around their prisoners, they placed each girl beyond the reach of another, tying one end of the tug with which she was fastened to a tree and keeping the other for one or more of themselves. Jemima tried in vain to reach her penknife to cut herself and her companions free.

On the following day the Indians came on a pony they had perhaps left behind. They wanted the girls to ride, particularly Jemima because of her injured foot. As the girls reluctantly mounted the pony they tickled it in the flanks with their feet. The pony reeled; the girls tumbled off, thereby gaining a little time. Their captors forced the girls to remount. The pony, becoming spiteful, bit Betsy on the arm. One of the Indians then mounted the pony to show how easily it could be ridden. He was badly bitten; the girls and the other Indians laughed. Again on the pony, the girls began climbing the hills; they suddenly slid off. The Indians then abandoned the pony as a hindrance to their progress.

The girls were not missed until milking time. Then a hunter, probably one of their suitors who had gone out to meet them, gave the alarm. Boone leaped from his bed, grabbed a rifle and ran barefoot down to the river. Samuel Henderson, who was Betsy's sweetheart, threw down his razor though he was only half shaved. Other men followed them.

John Guess—or Gass, as his name is sometimes spelled—jumped into the river and secured the canoe which the Indians had set adrift. In this Boone and five other men crossed the stream while a mounted party which included Callaway, Nathaniel Hart, Samuel Henderson and John Floyd forded it a mile down. Shortly the two parties joined and found the kidnapers' trail. While

Boone and his men followed it, Callaway and his group rode to the Lower Blue Licks to cut off the abductors from possible retreat.

After following the trail for five miles Boone and his men came to a place where nine men were building a cabin. Enlisting the services of three of these men, they pressed on until morning when they arrived at the place where the Indians and the girls had camped the night before. Though they found broken twigs and torn clothing and footprints, they had some difficulty in detecting the trail. Boone then decided to change his method of pursuit. To gain speed and prevent the possibility of being seen by the Indians' rear guard who might kill the girls rather than run the risk of having them rescued, he told his men they would pursue a straight course toward the Scioto River. This wise decision soon rewarded them with success; they found fresh tracks and a stream that was still muddy. Boone observed that the Indians were being less cautious. He therefore ordered his men to follow the old trail again.

Meanwhile the girls shifted between hope and despair. Sometimes Jemima and Fanny cried. Often Betsy reassured them with the certainty of rescue. The Indians, fearing that a fire might reveal them to their pursuers, cooked no food. They ate and offered the girls only unsalted and dry buffalo tongue. The girls would scarcely touch it, and the Indians themselves soon decided on more palatable food. They killed a buffalo and cut from it a choice portion which they prepared to cook. The girls, securely tied, sat watching them. Jemima and Fanny rested their heads on Betsy's lap.

Boone and his men soon came on the remnants of the slaughtered buffalo. Eagerly they followed the tracks to a small stream. Boone guessed that the Indians had waded in the water for some distance to deceive their pursuers and that they were engaged in cooking the meat. And sure enough the group soon came on a patch of thick cane in which all the Indians, save one who stood guard, had secluded themselves. The braves were busy—one was gathering wood, another was forcing a spit through the meat, still another was lighting his pipe at the fire. Hanging Maw had gone without his rifle to the river to fill a kettle. Two of the white men inched to within thirty yards of the Indians and then fired on them. They missed, but Boone and Floyd, instantly coming up, fired on the Indian with the spit, sending him howling into the blaze. His companions fled, leaving everything except a gun. One of the Cherokee, turning as he ran, flung his tomahawk at Betsy. It barely missed her head. The rifles sputtered.

"That's daddy!" cried Jemima.

"Run, gals, run!" yelled the rescuers.

One of Boone's men saw Betsy, a very dark brunette wearing a red bandanna, short skirts and leggings, rise from the ground, and mistook her for one of the Indians.

The man was about to bring the butt of his rifle down on her head when Boone caught his arm. "For God's sake, don't kill her—" he panted—"when we have traveled so far to save her from death!"

The whites were too elated to pursue the kidnapers. They marched with the Indian plunder toward Boonesboro. Just before they reached the river they met Callaway and his horsemen who, having crossed the trail of the retreating Indians, had concluded that the girls were rescued.

The whole fort celebrated the girls' safe return, but a feeling of insecurity swept the Kentucky settlements. Some of the men deserted Boonesboro for Harrodsburg while scattered settlers, fearing Indian attacks even more intensely, abandoned their cabins and went to Boonesboro, Harrodsburg and a newer settlement called McCelland's. The settlers at the latter place soon had an opportunity to use what little ammunition they had. On December 29 the Mohawk chief, Pluggy, attacked them, but they killed him and defeated his men. Realizing, however, that they could not hope to survive another attack which might come at any unguarded moment, the settlers took refuge in Boonesboro.

Depression spread over all the Kentucky settlements. The settlers in seven of them packed their meager belongings and fled to the safety of the East. At the beginning of the year of the "three sevens"—1777—only three settlements remained inhabited. They were Boonesboro, Harrodsburg and St. Asaph, and together they counted no more than two or three hundred people.

Asserting their right as lying within the jurisdiction of Virginia these settlements decided to organize a militia. In this body John Bowman held the commission of colonel, George Rogers Clark that of major. Daniel Boone was one of the captains. These officers inaugurated compulsory military training, requiring every man, whether a permanent resident or not, to join one of the companies for an allotted time. They also began a fairly large fort in Boonesboro and another in Harrodsburg.

These places of defense were still incomplete when on March 6, 1777, the Indians attacked. On that day James Ray invited several of his friends to drink sap at his brother William's sugar camp four or five miles below Harrodsburg. Suddenly forty or fifty Shawnee under Chief Blackfish descended on the place like a cyclone, driving the white men, some of whom were unarmed, in all directions. The Ray brothers stayed together as they ran until William was exhausted. Turning then to fight his pursuers, he was captured, killed and scalped.

James, finding a tree, slipped behind it while a dozen Indians dashed past him, firing into the top of another tree where they supposed he might have hidden. He emerged and, chased by Indians, ran like a deer into the fort. His story naturally spread terror and confusion among the settlers. Hugh McGary took the occasion to express his dislike for James Harrod, whom he accused of neglect and cowardice in connection with the defense of the fort. The dispute grew more and more bitter until the two men leveled their rifles at each other. At this juncture McGary's wife rushed to the scene and pushed his rifle to one side. Harrod then withdrew and the difficulty was adjusted for the moment.

Leading thirty mounted men to the sugar camp, McGary soon found William Ray's mangled body which the men buried. After returning to Harrodsburg, none of them slept that night. Instead they worked at strengthening "some of the open places around the fort." Just as the settlers expected them to do, at sunrise the Indians set fire to some of the cabins and to Ben Van Cleve's turner shop at the outskirts of the fort, apparently hoping to decoy the settlers. A few of the white men, hurrying to put out the fire, ran into some Indians who were hiding in piles of brush which lay between the cabins and the fort. The settlers lost four men; the Indians, one. The settlers brought the dead Indian to the fort, showed him to the women and children, then dragged him to a hole and buried him without ceremony. The marauding Indians withdrew, taking many horses and cattle.

In view of these circumstances the settlers decided to provision the fort for a possible long siege. Fortunately the preceding year had produced a bumper crop of corn, most of which was cribbed in the fields where it was harvested. The settlers wasted no time in bringing the corn in from the various storing places. This proved a wise move, for the Indians lurked around the fort during the rest of the year, not only to prevent the settlers from bringing food into it but also to hinder the production of corn and other foods. The whites could venture out only at the peril of their lives. Preservation demanded eternal vigilance. Ten sentinels guarded the fort during the day and twenty at night. Nevertheless, several of the settlers were killed or scalped.

At Boonesboro the settlers, working under Boone's constant vigilance and persuasion, completed the fort in March 1777 just as Blackfish renewed his attacks. Once the Shawnee succeeded in decoying the settlers outside the stockade where one of them was overtaken, tomahawked and scalped. Boone almost met the same fate. An Indian, seeing him among a group of men who were charging in an attempt to rescue the slain man, wounded him severely in the left ankle and then approached with raised tomahawk. Fortunately Simon Kenton was on hand; he clubbed the Indian with his rifle and took Boone back to the stockade.

"Well, Simon," said the wounded man, "you have behaved like a man today; indeed, you are a fine fellow." Boone never bestowed a greater compliment on any man.

As the year advanced Blackfish hung around more than before, destroying as much of the corn, potatoes and turnips as he could. His men also stole about two hundred horses, forcing the settlers to carry on their backs what meat they could find. Salt became very scarce. The settlers asked Virginia for supplies and men, but that commonwealth, engaged in defending herself against the British, could promise little assistance. Henderson, though no longer claiming ownership of Transylvania for his company, begged North Carolina to send soldiers to rescue the settlers; she turned down his request. Eventually a few trained soldiers arrived from Virginia, but what salutary effect their presence might have had was nullified when they, having completed their term of service, returned home.

At the beginning of 1778 the salt supply, never ample, began to run short. Needless to say, this commodity was a very important one to the settlers. It was needed not only to cure meat and hides but also to add flavor to an otherwise unsavory diet. Few calamities in the forest could be as difficult to endure as the lack of bread or salt. The dwindling of the stores caused more lamentation than Blackfish's depredations and scalpings. Boone, observing that the complaints increased as the salt supply lessened, realized that something must be done to relieve the situation before it lowered the morale of the settlers. Taking a party of thirty men, he packed salt kettles on horses and set out for the Blue Licks whose salt springs were the most important in that area.

At first everything went smoothly. For a few weeks the salt kettles "bubbled merrily"; several horse loads of salt were carried to Boonesboro, and the complaints of the settlers lessened and lessened. Indeed, a feeling of security was beginning to return to the fort for the Indians apparently had gone back to their villages in Ohio, and the settlers dared to hope they might remain there.

One day in February Boone, in carefree mood, went on a hunt. That evening in a blinding snowstorm he loaded his pack horse with buffalo meat and led it slowly along the riverbank toward camp. Suddenly, just as he was passing a fallen tree whose upturned roots left barely enough room to squeeze through, he discovered four Indians close behind him. Boone thought of riding for his life, but, realizing the futility of such action, he dropped his bridle and ran. Too late—the Indians covered him from every direction and drew closer and closer until he realized he must surrender. Slipping behind a tree, he placed his rifle in front of it to indicate that he would offer no resistance. The four

Indians laughed, shook his hands warmly and took him to an Indian encampment near by.

There Boone stared in amazement at what he saw. Around a huge fire blazing in a sheltered part of the valley sat more than a hundred Shawnee, painted for war and fully armed. Among them were Blackfish, Munseeka and Captain Will, Boone's captor of nine years before. But the Indians' number was not all that amazed and chagrined Daniel Boone: advising the Indians were Charles Beaubien, a French-Canadian agent of the British; Louis Lorimier, a French-Canadian trader who commanded great influence among the Shawnee; and "the white Indians," George and James, brothers of Simon Girty, that scourge of American frontiersmen.

What was the meaning of this strange gathering? Boone soon learned the answer. Impetuous American soldiers had three months before murdered Chief Cornstalk, beloved leader of the Shawnee. Cornstalk's tribe had vowed to avenge his death by wiping out the nearest and weakest of the white settlements. Spurred on by the British through their agents, the Shawnee had abandoned their usual custom and had gone to war in the dead of winter.

Yet the Indians greeted Boone in the usual friendly manner. "How d'ye," they said, laughing, as though they had made him the victim of a practical joke in capturing him.

Boone saw Captain Will approaching. "How d'ye," the frontiersman said. He and Captain Will shook hands, and the other Indians enthusiastically repeated the ceremony. They made no secret of the esteem in which they held him. Never, they knew, had he scalped any of their people; never had he shown any cruelty. And he was as good a woodsman as any of them and a far better hunter.

Blackfish now approached. Speaking through Pompey, a runaway Negro, he explained that his braves were prepared to attack Boonesboro. Then he requested the identity of the men at the salt springs. After giving him an evasive answer which he saw was not believed, Boone told him who they were. The chief said he would have them killed.

Boone reasoned that the men at the salt springs were some

distance away. But Blackfish's scouts had seen them; the chief might at any moment send a group of his men to surprise them, as he had said he would. The settlers could not be saved but Boonesboro could be spared, thought Boone; and he proceeded to do so with verbal strategy. He told Blackfish that the fort was strong and could not be taken, that only women and children with some old men and a few warriors remained in it, and that these people would perish if they were forcibly moved. As a solution to this problem he offered to surrender the men at the salt springs as prisoners of war on condition that they were well treated. He also suggested that the women and children in the fort be taken to Detroit in the spring. There the British lieutenant governor, Henry Hamilton—"the hair-buying general" as he was dubbed by the Indians—had promised to pay Blackfish £20 for every well and sound prisoner he delivered.

Blackfish accepted Boone's proposals. At his command a group of braves silently surrounded the saltmakers while they rested under blankets in their camp. Then the Indians sent Boone under guard toward his men through the snow. The saltmakers, seeing the Indians approach, leaped for their rifles. Just then they heard Boone yelling, "Don't fire! If you do, all will be massacred!" In a hurried voice he added, "You are surrounded with Indians and I have agreed with these Indians that you are to be used well and you are to be prisoners of war and will be given up to the British officers at Detroit where you will be treated well." Twenty-six of the thirty men in the party were present, two were in the woods, and two had gone to Boonesboro with salt. The men stacked their rifles and surrendered.

But the young Shawnee warriors were not satisfied. They clamored for the death of all the prisoners save Boone who, they thought, should be compelled to induce the settlers in Boonesboro to move to the Shawnee towns or at least to persuade them to surrender the fort. In the face of this demonstration Blackfish, despite his promises, felt obliged to appease the young men by holding a council of his party. The council proceeded in solemn debate for two hours while each warrior spoke for mercy or for death. Pompey sat beside Boone and translated for him. The saltmakers, understanding no Shawnee, were unaware of what was going on. The Frenchmen and the renegade whites took no part in the council. As it drew to a close Boone was asked to rise and speak. Pompey translated into Shawnee:

Brothers! What I have promised you, I can much better fulfill in the spring than now. Then the weather will be warm, and the women and children can travel from Boonesboro to the Indian towns, and all live with you as one people. You have got all my young men; to kill them, as has been suggested, would displease the Great Spirit, and you could not then expect future success in hunting nor war. If you spare them, they will make you fine warriors, and excellent hunters to kill game for your squaws and children. These young men have done you no harm, they are engaged in a peaceful occupation, and unresistingly surrendered upon my assurance that such a course was the only safe one for them; and I consented to their capitulation on the express condition that they should be made prisoners of war and treated well. I now appeal both to your honor and your humanity; spare them, and the Great Spirit will smile upon you.

For the first time the prisoners realized that they were in danger. They saw the war club pass from brave to brave; they saw fifty-nine of them dash it to the ground; they saw sixty-one let it pass. Blackfish had won. The white men were saved.

The Indians scattered all the salt in the camp on the snow, gathered what other supplies they wanted, and filed off with their prisoners through the bleak white forest toward Little Chillicothe, their town on the Miami. At dusk when they encamped Boone saw braves clearing a path in the snow. He guessed, and guessed correctly, that they were going to run him through the gantlet. This was a combination of test and game to separate the cowardly from the brave while it provided the Indians with sadistic merriment.

Usually every captive was obliged to run through the ordeal even though the tribe intended to spare his life. On approaching an Indian village a captive was usually obliged to sing at the top of his voice, a signal for the entire population—women, children, old men, and what warriors remained in the place—to attack him with clubs, sticks, stones, hatchets and deer antlers. But Boone was let off easy; he had to perform only for the benefit of the party. He was ready for anything they had to offer. By zigzagging from side to side he managed to escape most of the blows. Indeed, he gave more than he took, and after he butted one of the Indians in the chest with his head, sending him sprawling to the ground, the ordeal came to an end. The red men, shaking with laughter, crowded around the hero with profuse congratulations. Blackfish eyed him with admiration.

In ten days they arrived at Little Chillicothe where, during a lengthy war dance, sixteen of the prisoners were adopted into the tribe. Then Blackfish took Boone and ten of his companions to Detroit. Hamilton received the hunter with a show of kindness and offered Blackfish a hundred pounds for him. The chief refused to hand Boone over, either because he had already become attached to him, or because he wanted him to assist in the capture of Boonesboro which he hoped to attack when summer arrived. Blackfish did, however, allow Hamilton to question Boone. And Boone derived malicious satisfaction from informing Hamilton of Burgoyne's surrender at Saratoga, of which until now the lieutenant governor had heard only rumor.

Hamilton requested Boone to refrain from mentioning Burgoyne's surrender to the Indians.

"You are too late, Governor," replied Boone, "I have already told them of it."

Hamilton admired Boone's frankness; he gave the rough frontiersman a horse, a saddle, a bridle and a blanket which the Indians permitted Boone to keep and use as long as he remained with them.

Boonesboro soon learned of Boone's capture. Two of the saltmakers who had been absent from the camp returned, found it empty, thought their companions had tired of waiting to be relieved and had gone back to Boonesboro. But soon the two found an Indian bow, some arrows, moccasin tracks and the salt scattered on the snow. They then hurried to camp to warn the relief party, which rode to the fort at full speed. Simon Kenton with a few companions went in hot pursuit of the Indians through snow six inches deep, but when he reached the Ohio he realized he could not hope to attack so large a force with success and turned back.

Two weeks passed without word of the prisoners. Rebecca Boone, thinking her husband was dead, returned with the families of the other missing men to North Carolina. Jemima, now married to Flanders Callaway, stayed in Boonesboro and was to have the happiness of seeing her father safe and sound.

In Little Chillicothe, Blackfish gave his attention to the ceremony that was to transform Boone into Sheltowee, or Big Turtle. The ceremony was long and cruel. Boone's hair was plucked out until only a narrow tuft remained. This was cut across in several places and each part adorned with ribbons and feathers. Then he was stripped of his clothes and taken into the river where several women washed him and performed the ritual of rubbing all the white blood out of him. He was then taken to the council house where Blackfish delivered a fiery speech, expatiating on the high honors conferred on Boone and detailing the demeanor expected of him. Then Boone's head and face were painted while everybody feasted and smoked.

Boone was now Big Turtle, son of Blackfish, mighty chief of the Shawnee. Though his Indian father and mother assured him that they loved him as much as their own children, he perceived that they did not trust him. While Blackfish permitted Boone to graze his horse, armed Indians were posted behind trees to watch him. He could hunt whenever he liked so long as Blackfish's little daughters could report his whereabouts. Learning that his movements were closely watched, Boone was careful to show every sign of contentment, but he planned to make his escape at the first opportunity. Though he was given only limited quantities of ammunition, he was able to store a supply of lead and powder. He cut bullets in two and used only the halves when he hunted small game. He also managed to hide some jerked venison and one of the rifles which the Indians had requested him to repair.

About the first of June 1778 Boone was taken to near-by salt springs to help make salt. There he learned that the Shawnee planned to attack Boonesboro with a large number of warriors which included Wyandots and Mingo. Boone knew then that he must make his escape as soon as possible. The opportunity came on June 16 when the saltmakers prepared to return to Little Chillicothe.

Boone, who by now was thoroughly trusted, was put in charge of the salt kettles which he lashed on his horse. As the party drew near the Indian town the men began to scatter in all directions to hunt a flock of wild turkeys which had been scared up, leaving Boone alone with the squaws and children. He waited until he knew by the reports of the rifles that the men were occupied, then he cut the lashings of his horse and threw off the kettles. Noticing this, his Shawnee mother asked him what he was doing.

"Well, Mother," replied Boone calmly, "I am going home to see my squaw and children and in a moon and a half I shall bring them out here to live with you."

"You must not go; Blackfish will be angry."

Boone smiled, mounted his horse and, waving his hand, rode off, leaving the squaws screaming the alarm.

Covering his tracks in running streams, Boone rode all night and into next morning until his horse gave out. He turned the exhausted animal loose and went on foot, breaking his trail now and then by running along fallen trees. On the second day he reached the Ohio River which he probably crossed on a raft improvised with three pieces of wood and grapevine. He ate nothing until he had passed the Blue Licks, when he killed a buffalo and cooked a portion of it. Two days later he arrived in Boonesboro. He had traveled over a hundred and sixty miles in four days.

The townsfolk welcomed him with joyous shouts while they gripped his hand and slapped his shoulder. He smiled sadly. He had entered his cabin to find it devoid of everything that constituted his happiness. Of all the members of his family, only Jemima was on hand to greet him. His wife, his other children, his furniture were already somewhere on the Yadkin. He had brought home a buffalo tongue for his little son, but his son was many miles away.

Rough logs, a cold, blackened fireplace and empty pegs greeted his happy expectancy when he opened the door to his cabin. What is so desolate as a house from which home has been taken? After months of captivity, after suffering hunger, cold, thirst and danger he had returned to the poignant despair of an abandoned home. Suddenly Boone felt something soft pressing against his leather leggings. He looked down. It was the cat—Rebecca had left the cat behind. Living as a stray among the other cabins, it had seen Boone, had recognized him, had come home. It purred a long welcome. Boone sat down. The cat jumped into his lap.

The townsfolk crowded around him with consolation and brought him food, but one of his friends feared he would gorge himself and had the solids taken away. Instead he fed the exhausted man nothing but broth until, within a week, Boone was fully recovered.

Boone found that the settlers had completely neglected defenses during his absence and that they could not have withstood the slightest Indian raid. The wooden palisades had crumbled; the gates of the two blockhouses needed repair; the water supply within the stockade was inadequate. Not that the settlers were indifferent or lazy. On the contrary, they had more duties than they had time to perform: they had to clear the land, cut trees, build cabins, hunt, and dry and store away enough firewood to pull them through the winter. Since the Indians were giving them no trouble for the present, they thought these chores were more important than defenses.

But Boone knew trouble was ahead and might come before the settlement was fully prepared for it. Without delay he sent to the neighboring settlements for help. Logan's Station obliged with fifteen men and Harrodsburg with another small force. With the assistance of these settlers Boone repaired the palisades and strengthened the two blockhouses and built two new ones which rose to two stories and were equipped on the second story with defenses as high as a man's head. He had, however, no time to roof them.

For several more weeks the settlers saw no Indians. Yet the fort had plenty of excitement. On July 17, 1778, Stephen Hancock, who had been one of Blackfish's prisoners, appeared at the fort almost naked, badly bruised and so weak from hunger that he could hardly whisper. Hancock said he had been nine days coming. He had lost his way, had become discouraged, had lain down to die. But the Lord scouted his misery and directed his rescue. Looking up, he saw his brother's name carved on a tree and, recalling the place as a camping ground they had once shared, realized he was only four miles from Boonesboro and staggered on.

Hancock said he had been with Blackfish at Old Chillicothe where the chief had held a council at which he had postponed an attack on Boonesboro for several weeks. Hancock had talked with British officers who had brought Blackfish presents from Detroit. He had heard the Indians say they were going to attack with 400 men and four field guns. And he had learned something more of their plans; the settlers were to be asked to join the British, and, if they refused to do so, Boonesboro was to be battered down or starved into submission by siege warfare.

In the light of this information the settlers became more and more apprehensive of Blackfish's plans. Boone petitioned the Virginia military authorities for assistance. "If men can be sent to us in five or Six Weeks," he wrote, "it would be infinite Service, as we shall lay up provisions for a Seige [sic]. We are all in fine Spirits, and have good Crops growing, and . . . intend to fight . . . hard in order to secure them."

Doubting that aid would come in time despite his plea, Boone resolved to save Boonesboro from possible attack by striking at the Indian town of Paint Creek. He started out with thirty men, but beyond the Blue Licks ten of them became discouraged and returned home. With the remaining men Boone advanced to within four miles of Paint Creek. There the party encountered and successfully attacked forty Indians who were on their way to join others in an attack on Boonesboro. Knowledge of their intention prompted Boone to return home.

Soon Blackfish and his men appeared. Befeathered and painted in rose and vermilion obtained in Detroit, the warriors straggled over the hill that overlooked the fort, some hoisting French and English flags, others leading pack horses burdened with provisions and extra ammunition. Among them were three white men: Antoine Dogneaux de Quindre, Blackfish's French-Canadian aide; Isadore Chene, interpreter of the Wyandots and Ottawas; and Peter Drouillard, a French-Canadian trader. Blackfish also enjoyed the services of Blackbird, a Chippewa chief who later deserted the British for the Americans; Moluntha, a formidable raider of the Dark and Bloody Ground; and Black Hoof, who had witnessed Braddock's defeat twenty-three years before.

Presently Blackfish sent Pompey into the clearing. The Negro climbed the cornfield fence and, waving a white flag, yelled for Boone, who answered, "Yes," and went out to meet him. Pompey told Boone he had letters addressed to him from Hamilton, requesting him to surrender the fort peacefully. The wary settlers decided to stay in the fort and ask Pompey to bring the letters to them. When they yelled this decision across the stockade, Blackfish, calling to Boone by his Indian name, asked him to come out. Boone agreed; Pompey met him at a specified stump and escorted him to Blackfish who spread a blanket out for him.

"Well, Boone, how d'ye?"

"How d'ye, Blackfish?"

"Well, Boone, what make you run away from me?"

"Why, I wanted to see my wife and children."

"Well, why you run away? If you ask, I let you go."

So saying the chief gave Boone a letter and proclamation from Hamilton urging him to surrender and warning him against the folly of resistance. Boone explained that he had been so long absent from the fort that he was no longer in command of it and that the great Virginia father had sent an unconquerable captain in his stead. Whereupon he went to the fort and soon returned with Major William Bailey Smith, who in the previous July had come to the aid of the fort with some forty North Carolinians most of whom were friends and neighbors of the Boones. Elaborately dressed in a scarlet uniform and a hat adorned with ostrich feathers, Smith impressed the Indians as a man of superior authority.

The parley broke up without any agreement on the part of Boone to surrender the fort. Yet Boone knew that the Indians were growing hostile and that negotiations could not be much longer delayed. What policy should the settlers pursue? Should

they permit Blackfish to take them to Detroit as he had promised?
That meant surrender. Should they offer resistance? That seemed
a more honorable course. They all agreed to fight to the last.
"I'll die with the rest," Boone said gravely.

Yet the Kentuckians felt confident that Virginia would eventually send them relief. Boone therefore adopted the policy of
dragging out negotiations with Blackfish as long as he could. Accompanied by Callaway and Smith, he went to see Blackfish
again. The chief received them courteously, spreading a panther
skin for them to sit on.

Displaying a wampum belt in three colors—black for warning,
white for peace and red for war—Blackfish made a speech which
ended with these words: "I am come to take you easy."

Smith reminded the chief of the difficulty of removing so many
women and children. "I have brought forty horses," replied
Blackfish, "on purpose for the old people, women, and children
to ride." Boone then asked for two days to consider the matter.
Blackfish agreed and escorted the white men back to the fort.

The settlers took council. If Blackfish really had brought
forty horses with him, reasoned Boone, he must have exaggerated
the number of men in the fort. He quickly saw the advantage of
encouraging this delusion. At his suggestion Callaway dressed
up the children, women and slaves and kept them moving back
and forth in the fort. He also had hats put on sticks and bobbed
over the stockade, and had dummies paraded before the open gate
of the fort. When Pompey, full of curiosity, stole close to the
building he was detected and warned to stay away.

The masquerade enabled the settlers to make hasty preparations
for defense. They passed the powder; they picked the flints; they
cleaned the rifles; they molded the bullets. And they carried
countless buckets of water from a spring into the fort, drove in
all the cattle and horses they possessed, and gathered the potatoes
and corn they had raised just outside the fort.

Every night Boone posted sentinels in the blockhouses to alert
the settlers in case the Indians attacked. At last Boone informed
Blackfish that the settlers were determined to fight. Whereupon
the dissembling chief, talking through his interpreter, De Quindre, assured Boone that the Indians had come to talk of peace,

not of war; that Hamilton had given orders to avoid bloodshed; and that if the white men refused to go to Detroit they might still live quietly with their Indian brothers. Why not hold another council to draft a treaty? If nine representative men from the garrison would sign it, said Blackfish, the Indians would go home. The settlers naturally consented to the proposition.

The council was held on the following day in a friendly atmosphere. The settlers and the Indians, while they ate and drank, reached an agreement. Blackfish stipulated that the white men abandon Boonesboro within six weeks and submit to the authority of Governor Hamilton at Detroit. When the settlers spurned these terms Blackfish inquired: "Brothers, by what right did you come and settle here?"

Someone reminded the chief of the Treaty of Sycamore Shoals between Henderson and the Cherokee. Blackfish pretended he had never heard of the treaty and inquired of a Cherokee in his party if the settlers' story were true.

Assured that it was, Blackfish expressed great surprise. "Friends and brothers," he said, "as you have purchased this land from the Cherokee and paid for it, that entirely alters the case; you must keep it and live on it in peace."

With these words he ordered the "pipe-tomahawk"—half hatchet, half pipe—to be passed around to each Indian negotiator who took a puff or two as he passed it to his neighbors. Boone noticed that it was offered only to Indians. Acquainted with their customs, he burned with suspicion, but he remained silent while one of his men drew up the agreement. When this was completed, Blackfish said one thing must be added—he must give a big talk to his young men in order that they might fully understand what a firm peace had been made. And he began to address the braves in Shawnee—an eloquent and vigorous speech which few understood and everybody applauded.

Then, turning to the white men, Blackfish made them an extraordinary proposal: in becoming friends, he said, men usually shake hands; but in making a sincere and lasting peace, something more must be added; they must shake *long hands*; two Indians must embrace one white man, bringing their hearts together. With these words he and another Indian quickly seized Boone by his arms while other pairs of Indians grappled with each white man. The settlers quickly sensed the red men's strategy.

Neither side had taken the treaty seriously; the Indians had simply been waiting for an opportunity to try their trick while the white men had been abiding their time in the hope of receiving aid from Virginia. Just as the grappling began an Indian concealed near by fired his gun—the signal for each pair of Indians to drag their particular "brother" over the high, steep banks of the Kentucky River where, outside the range of musketry from the fort, they could the more easily be subdued. This endeavor failed. Callaway broke loose; a bullet from the fort killed one of the Indians grappling with Smith. Boone sent Blackfish sprawling and loosed himself from the grip of the other Indian. The rest of the Indians, thinking their chief had been killed, became demoralized. Making the most of the situation, the whites ran toward the fort, bounding like rabbits from behind each tree and stump on the way. While women screamed and children cried and dogs howled and cattle stampeded, the men reached the building in safety.

The Indians, seeing that their fire produced no results, scattered flax along a fence leading to the stockade and set fire to it. The settlers met this threat by running a trench under the well and out to the fence. Sheltered by this device, they crawled out and pulled down a part of the fence connecting with the stockade. During the night Nathaniel Henderson's Negro, London, saw an Indian creep up to within fifteen paces of the fort. London crawled out into the ditch and fired at the flash of the Indian's rifle. His bullet missed, and the Indian killed him.

Failing in his endeavor to capture the leaders of Boonesboro, Blackfish tried another trick. He ordered his followers to catch, saddle and load the horses and while so occupied to make as much noise as possible. This done, he had a few men bawl out orders of retreat from the thickets while he ordered as many of his braves as could find hiding places to creep up close to the fort. Then just before daylight all the Indians save those in hiding made off, tooting a bugle and making a great deal of noise.

This stratagem deceived nobody. The settlers knew that the redskins, if they really intended to retreat, could creep through the forest as silently as a snake slithers into the underbrush. Before long the warriors returned and hid themselves near a buffalo road just across the river. The settlers kept the gates of the fort closed and made no sign of coming out. The concealed Indians, soon realizing that the trick had failed, rejoined their comrades.

Now Blackfish resolved to try to reduce the fort by siege. He ordered some of his men to continue to fire on the fort, while he used the rest to fell trees. Then a broadening muddy streak began to appear on the river downstream while upstream remained clear. What were the Indians doing now? One of the settlers soon noticed a cedar pole waving back and forth on the edge of the riverbank; apparently somebody was loosening dirt.

Yes, the Indians were digging. De Quindre, perhaps, had persuaded them to run a mine from the river to the stockade. But what did they intend to do when the mine reached the fort? Bring in powder to blow it up or set fire to it? To determine Blackfish's intention, the settlers built a makeshift wooden watchtower and lifted it to the roof of a cabin which Richard Henderson had used as a kitchen. From the watchtower sharpshooters could look over the edge of the steep banks and see the Indians dumping fresh earth into the river.

The settlers promptly resolved to frustrate the scheme by digging a trench across the mine. The trench, four feet deep and three feet wide, began under the watchtower and ran through four other cabins to the blockhouse which the mine would eventually reach. Under the blockhouse they dug out the whole floor to the depth of four feet, so that they would have plenty of room to shoot the Indians as they emerged one by one from the mine.

An irascible settler named John Holder gathered the largest stones that were dug up and hurled them with all his might at the Indians behind the riverbank. Cries of pain mingled with volleys of profanity as the redskins bade the settlers "fight like men, and not try to kill them with stones like children." One of the women adjured Holder to stop throwing the stones because, she said, they might injure the Indians and make them want to take revenge.

Pompey climbed a tree and did his level best to pick off as many of the whites within the stockade as he could. He did not know that William Collins had discovered him and was waiting for him with cocked gun. When the Negro stuck out his head from the trunk of the tree, Collins fired, and Pompey's terrestial hopes came to an end.

As Virginia militiamen the settlers had tacked the new American flag to a long pole and hoisted it in the stockade. The Indians soon shot the pole to pieces and yelled triumphantly when the flag toppled to the ground. But in a few minutes the flag went up again amid rousing cheers.

One night the Indians decided to try to force the settlers to surrender by setting fire to the fort. Stealing up close, they hurled torches over the stockade and cabins while they shot blazing arrows which had been either wrapped in oily fibres of shellbark hickory or filled with powder lighted by a piece of punk. Most of the arrows and the torches fell harmlessly in the open square of the fort, lighting up the interior to the extent that the settlers could see to pick up a pin. When an arrow or a torch chanced to fall on a roof a few settlers would climb up and sweep it off with a broom or kick off the blazing shingles or punch them off from inside the cabin.

But the torches that fell on the stockade could be put out only from the outside. This was a dangerous venture, but the peril did not deter John Holder. Seeing a torch falling on the door of a cabin which was already ablaze, he dashed out along the stockade and, swearing soundly, doused it with a bucket of water. He escaped injury or death—but not Mrs. Richard Callaway's indignation: instead of swearing, she cackled, they should all be praying! Holder consigned prayer to perdition and returned coolly to his duties. Next afternoon a light rain made the wood so damp that the fires flickered out.

Meanwhile the Indians kept digging. Now and then the sharpshooters in the watchtower and the Indians under the riverbank would indulge in friendly banter.

"What are you red rascals doing down there?" yelled an old hunter in Shawnee.

"Digging; blow you all to devil soon; what you do?"

"Digging to meet you and make a hole to bury 500 of your yellow sons of bitches."

One night a few Indians killed a stallion which the settlers had brought into the stable outside the fort to improve the breed of horses. This exploit inspired a gem of Shawnee humor:

"White man keep a horse in the house!"

"Go and feed the horse!"

"The horse wants water."

"Go take him to the river."

The settlers sometimes flung back taunts of their own. Though they all knew that Pompey was dead they often inquired of his whereabouts. The Indians were ready with a sheaf of answers: Pompey had gone to Chillicothe to fetch more Indians; Pompey had gone to hunt in the woods for some of the white men's roaming pigs. Then one brave yelled: "Pompey ne-pan." (Pompey is asleep.) Another corrected him: "Pompey nee-poo." (Pompey is dead.) Redskins and settlers chuckled at the play on words.

The siege dragged on. For eight days the settlers had worked unremittingly with too little food to strengthen their bodies and with too little sleep to lift their spirits. The Indians were still digging steadily underground. Anxiety and the strain of constant vigilance were beginning to instill distrust and suspicion in the leaders. And the weather did everything to worsen the general feeling of insecurity. A heavy rain during the night drowned all sounds of warning. The guards could see the soggy clearing only during flashes of lightning. Could not the Indians easily creep up undetected in the impenetrable darkness? Might they not blow up the gate of the fort? Might they not break into the fort through the mine? Or was their mining a mere trick to conceal a deeper and deadlier plan? These and a hundred other macabre thoughts surged through the minds of the besieged as they nervously awaited daylight.

At last the sun rose and the rain ceased. Everything was changed. A deep silence pervaded the countryside. Not a sound was heard in the mine. Not an Indian lurked around the fort. Not an arrow whizzed through the air. What had happened? What were the Indians doing now? Were they about to try another ruse?

Gradually the beleaguered fort learned that the rain had come as a conquering ally. It had soaked the earth, causing the mine to sink in many places. This had crushed Blackfish's spirit. He gave up the siege, collected his braves and withdrew in disgust toward his capital in Chillicothe. At noon the settlers coolly opened the gates of the fort, strolled into the clearing, stretched their weary legs and sent their starving cattle out to pasture. Then, rejoicing, they lay down to the luxury of long-desired rest.

No sooner was the siege ended than Colonel Richard Callaway and Captain Benjamin Logan, founder of St. Asaph, accused Daniel Boone of treason. Not that Boone was guilty of the charge. Jealous of him, the two officers simply saw in his popularity the shadow of their own. Boone and Callaway had shared experiences on which they might have built a lifelong friendship. For many years they had been neighbors in North Carolina. They had been among the first settlers in Kentucky, had worked together for Henderson and had joined in directing the rescue of their daughters from the Indians. Callaway's nephew, Flanders, had married Jemima Boone. Even this tie failed to dissipate Callaway's envy of Boone. He had strongly opposed the expedition to Paint Creek town and had scorned what he considered Boone's foolhardiness in leaving the fort to parley with Blackfish. He needed no coaxing to ignore the fact that the parley had gained invaluable time for the settlers. This point in Boone's favor doubtless increased Callaway's resentment.

He began to cast aspersions on Boone's loyalty. Had not Boone permitted himself to be captured? Even worse, had he not guided the Indians to the salt camp and urged the saltmakers to surrender without offering resistance? Callaway could marshal other evidence in support of his charges against Boone. One of the escaped saltmakers, Stephen Hancock, an inveterate gossip, had spread and stretched tales of how Hamilton received Boone with a marked show of friendship. Hancock had also said that Boone agreed to surrender the fort to the British officers and to take the settlers to Detroit where they would live under the jurisdiction of the British government. And when the Indians arrived at Boonesboro just before the siege, was not Boone the first man they requested to see? When Callaway objected to a parley with them, had not Boone overruled him?

A suspicious man construes his suspicions as truths and soon finds justification for them. Callaway believed that Boone had lived with Blackfish for four months as his adopted son because he was secretly a lover of Indians and a Tory to boot. The colonel could show that Rebecca Boone's kin were mostly Tories, some as armchair sympathizers, others as soldiers in the British army. One of them, Samuel Bryan, had recently been killed fighting in North Carolina. From these facts Callaway deduced that Boone had never desired to fight for the American cause and that he had gone to Kentucky in 1775 to avoid service in the impending Revolution. He found justification for these notions by recalling that Boone had boasted during his captivity that he maintained constant contact with Boonesboro. Boone probably meant that his scouts had been able to keep a constant watch on the fort from the hills across the river, but Callaway interpreted his statement as evidence of treachery within the fort itself.

Armed with these suspicions, Colonel Callaway and his friend Benjamin Logan served notice on Boone to stand trial before a military court composed of his fellow officers in the Virginia militia. At the trial Callaway and Logan preferred four specific charges: Boone had voluntarily surrendered the saltmakers to the Indians at Blue Licks; he had made an agreement with Hamilton to surrender the fort and take the settlers to Detroit; he had influenced his men to undertake the expedition to Paint Creek town; and he had, on the pretext of making peace, taken the white officers of the fort to the Indian camp beyond the protection of the garrison's guns. On these grave charges Callaway and Logan pronounced Boone a traitor and recommended that he be "broak of his commyssion."

Boone denied the charges categorically with a firm but quiet dignity. True, he had induced the saltmakers to surrender, but only to avert an attack on the fort which, he believed, it was too weak to resist. He had used duplicity to stall off the Indians by telling them that the fort was too strong to be taken with their small numbers and by recommending that they return in the spring with a greater force. The Paint Creek town expedition, Boone explained, had done no harm; indeed, it had turned out very well. As for the negotiations before the fort, he simply had been "playing" the Indians in order to gain time for the reinforcements he expected from Virginia. He might have added that the Indians enjoyed superior numbers and that they were sure to find the Blue Licks, which were located on a much-traveled warpath.

Boone's adroitness had actually saved Boonesboro from capture. This also meant that he had possibly saved the lives of the saltmakers, of the relief party about to leave Boonesboro, and of the men, women and children in the fort, including the two men who had brought him to trial. When Boonesboro was finally attacked it was no longer weak; it had been repaired and had been warned repeatedly of imminent onslaught.

The court-martial found Boone not guilty. The verdict was, moreover, no ordinary one of not guilty, but a complete exoneration by his friends and neighbors, for immediately after the trial he was promoted to the rank of major. While Callaway and Logan were "not pleased" with the verdict, they accepted it quietly and raised no further protest. Once cleared of the charges Boone hurried off to the eastern settlements to find his wife and family. He found Rebecca and their children living comfortably in a small cabin near that of her brother, William Bryan, who had married Boone's sister. Soon they all returned to the East where they remained throughout the winter of 1778-1779 and all of the succeeding summer.

Pattern of

Life

THE PIONEER OF THE POPULAR MIND IS DOUBTLESS ONE OF THE most familiar characters in American folklore. Who has not admired his unpolished figure? Who has not thrilled to his intense love of freedom, his frank manner and his exuberant courage? He has become a tradition, a cherished generalization, a Lochinvar in buckskin. He is a makeshift personality in the old, old world. He belongs to no particular frontier—yet he belongs to many. No matter to what period of frontier history he is assigned, his costume is usually an anachronism; no matter on what frontier he lives, he seldom adheres to his environment. He is one man—and any man.

This idealized figure has been depicted by many writers as perhaps the happiest of mankind. Exercise and excitement give him health. Brilliant hopes of future wealth intensify his efforts. And common danger makes him interdependent with his fellows and yet unflinchingly courageous. Moving in a limitless world, he feels for his neighbor little of the envy which engendered so much misery in older societies. He sits around a log fire or on a puncheon stool, giving the world some of its heartiest laughter. His fiddle is heard with more delight than was Apollo's lyre.

Some historians have with more sentiment than truth also thus exalted the life of the pioneer woman. An old chronicler of Tennessee, reminiscing on the good old days when his state was still a frontier, wrote that the polished eastern belle dancing to the music of a full band in an ornamented ballroom never enjoyed herself half so much as the settler's daughter keeping time to a

self-taught fiddle on the bare earthen floor of a log cabin. He
elaborated this opinion with aqueous metaphors:

The smile of a polished beauty, is the wave of the lake, where
the wave plays gently over it, and her movement, is the gentle
stream which drains it; but the laugh of the log cabin, is the gush
of nature's fountain, and its movements, its leaping waters.

Thus man sublimates the hardships of youth and bygone days
by interpreting them as elements which build character, morals
and culture. But the real pioneer, in whatever frontier he lived,
had to face hard reality. He had to adjust himself to his environment, had to solve his social and economic problems in his own
way in order to survive. He was, therefore, purely a regional
character. An authentic re-creation of his daily life is possible
only by using the materials of his particular region. General
information on pioneering life would result in a composite picture which would be essentially inaccurate. The pioneer of the
Appalachian Frontier had entirely different problems from those
of the pioneer of another region.

He adhered strictly to a code fashioned largely by his own
environment. Living in a primitive stage of society, he gave
little consideration to wealth, position and family tradition. His
only passport to esteem was his own personal merit. His moral
and physical courage, his capacity to amuse and instruct, his in-
nate civility—these were the qualities that decided his standing as
a desirable neighbor. Without them he was friendless, unwanted.

To say of a man that he was "not true" was tantamount to
branding him an outlaw. Such a man was usually nicknamed
"Lawrence" or given some other name which the pioneers regarded as opprobrious. Sometimes if he failed to perform military
service he was "hated out" as a coward. If he lacked any of the
war implements, such as ammunition, a sharp flint, a scalping
knife or a tomahawk, he was regarded with contempt or ridicule,
and when the time came for him to take his turn in a scouting
party or military campaign he met expressions of indignation in
the faces of the neighbors who fastened on him merciless epithets
concerning his honor.

A thief was detested like the plague. The man who stole bread while it was baking in the ashes was nicknamed "Bread Rounds," a cognomen that spread rapidly over the entire community. When the thief would approach a group of his fellow villagers one of them would call, "Who comes there?"

Another would answer, "Bread Rounds."

The first would then ask, "Who stole the bread out of the ashes?"

The other would give the thief's name in full.

A third would give confirmation by exclaiming, "That's true and no lie."

This form of tongue-lashing would punish the thief for the rest of his days. Sometimes a thief would be sentenced by a jury of citizens to be whipped. After receiving thirteen stripes he was doomed to carry the flag of the United States on his back as a symbol of his punishment. In the case of a larger theft, the offender was usually condemned to Moses' Law, that is, forty stripes less one. The punishment was followed by a sentence of exile. The culprit was told he must decamp in so many days or suffer the penalty of having the number of stripes doubled.

To say of a man that he had "no neighbors" was, in those times of mutual want and mutual benefactions, enough to make him despicable. His failure to help a neighbor raise a cabin or clear a field or "chop frolic" amounted to worthlessness. The "good neighbor" wanted to contribute his share to the general comfort and public improvement. He felt aggrieved and insulted if an opportunity to do so was not given him. The settler whose neighbors permitted him to remain at home during "cabin raising" was usually anathematized with the expression: "A poor dog is not worth whistling for."

The ever-present Indian menace made rapid building necessary and group building imperative. On foot and by horseback neighbors would come to the newcomer's holding and help him raise a cabin. They kept their rifles with their axes, ready to meet any Indian attack on themselves and their families, who usually came along with their pots and kettles.

The average cabin was composed of a single room usually measuring sixteen by twenty feet. Its foundation consisted of four logs of hickory, oak, young pine, walnut or persimmon, firmly notched and grooved. Upon this base were laid, and notched into one another, logs in the round, usually to the height of seven feet. On these walls were mounted parallel timbers and puncheons to make the roof which was usually composed of logs and wooden slabs. The chinks between the logs were daubed with red clay and moss. When the structure was completed spaces for a door and windows were cut. The door was usually thick and heavy; the windowpanes were made of paper treated either with hog fat or with bear grease.

Every object of the interior furnishings was made by hand on the spot. Some of the chairs were constructed from hickory blocks, others from slabs resting on three logs. The movable table was a slab or two with four legs; the permanent table, built against the wall, was supported at its outer edge by two sticks. Built in the same way was a low bed softened by a mattress of pine needles, chaff or dried moss. In the best light that the greased windowpanes could provide stood the spinning wheel and loom on which the yarn for the family garments was spun and the cloth woven.

Over the fireplace which was made of large flat stones with a mud-plastered chimney hung the firearms, knives and powder horns carved in Indian fashion with scenes depicting war or the hunt. Wooden spoons, plates, bowls and noggins could be seen on a shelf or on pegs. At the hearth in the spring the men would tan and dress the deerskins that were to be sent out with the trade caravan while the womenfolk sewed or made moccasins or mended them in the light coming through the knotholes or provided by candles of bear's grease.

The household utensils, usually known as "cooking irons," consisted of a bulbous pot with a flare at the top to hold the lid; a heavy frying pan with three legs, generally called a "spider"; and another, deeper pan or oven, often with a rounded bottom and a lid with edges curled up to hold the hot coals on top. The gourd, in many sizes and shapes, played an important part in domestic life. It was used as a dipper at the well, at the cider barrel, at the whisky jug, for the "soup, soap, and sap." Another indispensable household article was the hickory broom. This was made from a sapling several inches in diameter. The lower end was carefully slivered until the heart was reached and removed. The slivers were then fluffed out, sometimes spread over a center-piece, and bound into place and the handle cut to size.

The most prized possession of every frontiersman was his Kentucky rifle. By it he fed, clothed and protected himself and his family while he conquered an empire and built on it a new nation dedicated to his concept of life. Developed from 1728 to about 1760 by skilled German gunsmiths living around Lancaster, Pennsylvania, the Kentucky rifle well fitted the needs of the frontier where powder and lead were scarce and loud reports of .50 and .75 caliber muskets were often dangerous.

The rifles that the pioneers used against the Indians or big game were usually of .45 caliber, while "turkey" rifles were about .30. The Kentucky rifle weighed from eight to twelve pounds, and the bullets used in them ran from approximately thirty-seven to a pound for a .50 caliber gun to one hundred seventy-five for a .30 caliber. For accurate shooting the rifle ball was loaded with a greased patch of cloth. The flintlock and the single trigger were the fashion. Many of the gun barrels were made by blacksmiths who hammered out the barrel from bar iron, bored and rifled it, tempered it, made the flintlocks and double triggers, set a segment of a slick quarter for front sight and rounded out the set and the hindsight, made the bullet molds, stocked the gun with curly maple or black walnut, and tested it on their own ground.

The Appalachian pioneers fashioned most of their clothing from products of their own environment. The spinning wheel spun the cloth for nearly all the family apparel, including dresses, socks, shirts, trousers and underwear. William Poague introduced the spinning wheel in Kentucky in 1776; it spun coarse yarns from buffalo wool. Soon thereafter settlers improvised a few rude looms which wove "a rough cloth suitable for men's winter wear."

Before the introduction of the spinning wheel the migrating farmers had brought their clothing with them. **Many** women

spent the last few months in their old homes making enough garments to last them and members of their families for several
seasons. Just before the McAfee families moved to Kentucky in
1776 their wives and daughters busied themselves day and night
weaving blankets, bed clothing and articles of linen and flannel.

Now the presence of the spinning wheel made such toil unnecessary. In winter the women wore linsey; in summer they
preferred linen. Instead of wearing hats or bonnets, they tied
handkerchiefs around their heads. As yet their wardrobes lacked
such luxuries as broadcloth, gingham and calico. In place of
overcoats and cloaks they threw blankets over their shoulders.
The women, anxious to supplement the cotton and woolen goods
brought from the east, made yarns and cloth from what material
they could come by. Before the production of flax and wool
they made cloth from fiber obtained from nettles which were
gathered in late winter or early spring when the wet weather
had rotted the stalks. The fibers made a very strong thread
which, combined with buffalo-wool yarn, formed the warp in a
very serviceable cloth.

The Indian influence was evident in the pioneer's hunting
apparel. Only the 'coonskin cap with tail was his own design.
The moccasins, cut from a single piece of deer or buffalo skin;
the leggings, laced well up the thigh; and the long, fringed hunting shirt of leather—all these were borrowed from the Indians.
About the loins the pioneer wore, in Indian fashion, a textile
breechcloth and sometimes an undershirt of soft deerskin. Not
until the beginning of the nineteenth century did he discard
leather for textile clothing.

The early Tennessee settlers were acquainted with knee
breeches and cocked hat, but only the leaders cared to wear them.
When Casper Mansker was elected lieutenant colonel of militia
in the Cumberland settlements he wore "a neat fitting suit of
regimentals." John Sevier wore "civilized clothing" at home and
Indian dress when he was fighting the Cherokee. The newcomer
to the back country discarded his ruffles, broadcloth and queue
rather than risk the ridicule of his neighbors.

Joseph Doddridge, one of the best authorities on pioneer life in western Virginia, described the costume of the region in characteristically vivid detail. It was a kind

. . . of a loose frock, reaching half way down the thighs, with large sleeves, open before, and so wide as to lap over a foot or more when belted. The cape was large, and sometimes handsomely fringed with a ravelled piece of cloth of a different color from that of the hunting shirt itself. The bosom of this dress served as a wallet to hold a chunk of bread, cakes, jirk, tow for wiping the barrel of the rifle, or any other necessity for the hunter or warrior. The belt, which was always tied behind, answered several purposes, besides that of holding the dress together. In cold weather the mittens and sometimes the bullet bag occupied the front part of it. To the right was suspended the tomahawk and to the left the scalping knife in its leathern sheath. The hunting shirt was generally made of linsey, sometimes of coarse linen, and a few dressed with deerskins. . . .

A pair of drawers or breeches and leggins were the dress of the thighs and legs. A pair of moccasins answered for the feet much better than shoes. These were made of dressed deer skin. They were mostly made of a single piece with a gathering seam along the top of the foot, and another from the bottom of the heel, without gathers as high as the ankle joint or a little higher. Flaps were left on each side to reach some distance up the leg. These were nicely adapted to the ankles, and lower part of the leg, by thongs of deerskin, so that no dust, gravel, or snow would get within the moccasin. . . .

In wet weather it was usually said that wearing them was "a decent way of going barefooted."

Most of the food came from the forest. Elk and buffalo disappeared early from the Appalachian Frontier, but deer and bear meat supplanted beef and pork until the beginning of the nineteenth century. J. F. D. Smythe, who toured the region late in the eighteenth century, wrote that game was so plentiful that a man could easily kill six or eight deer every day, "which many do merely for their skins, to the great injury and destruction of their species, and to the prejudice and public loss of the community at large." Wild turkeys, he said, were very large and fat and could be seen in flocks of as many as 5,000. In the fall and early winter the settlers hunted bear and other fur-skinned animals. An early hunter, Daniel Trabue, thought that the most beautiful thing he ever saw was "a parcell of dogs in full chase after a bear and they a yelping every jump, they would soon stop him and the hunters would shoot him."

One of the earliest chroniclers and surveyors of the frontier, Colonel William Byrd, who always wrote with vigor and often with great charm, learned from one of his Indian guides that bear meat contained properties helpful to procreation. On being asked to explain why few or none of his countrywomen were barren, the Indian replied

. . . with a Broad grin upon his Face, they had an infallible SECRET for that. Upon my being importunate to know what the secret might be, he informed me that, if any Indian woman did not prove with child at a decent time after Marriage, the Husband, to save his Reputation with the women, forthwith entered into a Bear-dyet for Six Weeks, which in that time makes him so vigorous that he grows exceedingly impertinent to his poor wife and 'tis great odds but he makes her a Mother in Nine Months.

Time proved to Byrd that his Indian spoke truth. All the "Marryed men of our Company were joyful Fathers within forty weeks after they got Home, and most of the Single men had children sworn to them within the same time." An exception was the chaplain, "who, with much ado, made a shift to cast out that importunate kind of Devil, by Dint of Fasting and Prayer."

The settlers also ate the meat of the domestic animals they had brought with them. Their cows and hogs, turned loose in the woods, fed on white clover and luxuriant grasses. The presence of wolves made sheep raising difficult. Throughout the winter the cattle throve on cane that grew wild everywhere, and the hogs ate nuts and mast. From roaming in the woods these animals became wild, forcing their owners either to put bells on them or to distinguish them as their own by branding them or by cropping their ears in various ways. The settlers took good care of their livestock—particularly of their milch cows—which the Indians made every effort to drive off, more to deprive their owners of food than to obtain it for themselves.

The woods abounded with hickory nuts, walnuts, wild grapes and pawpaws which helped to balance the pioneer diet. The basic crop was corn: it needed the least care and trouble; it stood all winter long upon the stalk without injury from weather or danger of damage by disease. Therefore, in the spring of 1776 the Kentucky settlers planted corn and reaped a good harvest. When the corn matured it was either roasted in hot ashes or made into hominy or ground into meal. In addition to corn the settlers grew potatoes, turnips, pumpkins, watermelons, muskmelons, peppers, cucumbers and other vegetables. Maple sugar furnished them virtually their only dietary luxury; it was sometimes used to sweeten parched corn which had been ground into meal. The first wheat in Transylvania was planted at Harrodsburg in 1776 by Thomas Denton.

The most precious of the primary foods was salt. No pirate ever guarded his treasure chest as carefully as the pioneer guarded his salt gourd. Brought on pack horses from Augusta and Richmond, salt commanded as much as ten dollars a bushel. Small amounts, however, could be secured from salt springs. Five to eight hundred gallons of water boiled in large iron kettles usually left a residue of one bushel of salt, which weighed about eighty-four pounds and equaled the value of a good cow and calf.

In the latter part of 1777, as the result of Indian incursions, Kentuckians found themselves in such desperate need for salt that they were constrained to petition the Virginia assembly for relief. Complaining that many of the salt springs were on properties of persons "who had never been at any Pains or Expense to erect Manufactories at them," they urged the assembly to appropriate them, convert them into public property and undertake the manufacture of salt. This, they explained, would bring relief to the settlers of Kentucky and at the same time provide the mother state with a profitable industry. The assembly ignored the petition.

The typical settler was a small farmer who lived with his wife and a swarm of children on a big tract of wooded land. He rarely cleared more than forty of his large number of acres. Though he seldom possessed a dollar in specie, he was never in want. The extraordinary fertility of the soil in Kentucky and Tennessee early brought him wealth, though he started with a small capital. Save for corn and wild clover, his livestock needed no provender during the greater part of the year. After the second year he could well afford to feed them, for the cleared and quickly cultivated land yielded fifty to sixty bushels of corn in the first year and seventy to one hundred and fifty in the second year.

With a little attention, his garden produced all the vegetables he needed. His domestic animals increased; he had plenty of meat. By the third and fourth years he could build a better home which would cost him little more than the labor of his family and his servants. He could furnish his new home by bartering or selling a part of his farm produce. After the second year of improvement the value of his estate increased nearly thirty per cent. If he desired to move westward to cheaper lands, he could easily sell his farm at a handsome profit to an immigrant who sought a ready supply of animals and corn for his family.

The pioneer usually cleared his land by burning. In early spring he would set fire to the dead grass on the meadows to reveal the young green grass to the cattle and other stock. He would belt or gird trees by chopping a ring around each of them with an ax. After they died he could fell them, cut them into logs, roll them into piles and burn them. He also burned the stumps to the ground and sometimes dug them out. Sometimes the fire would get beyond control and would destroy a large area of forest lands which thereafter became known as barrens.

The farmer chopped the cane with his ax and dug out the roots with his mattock. He cultivated his farm with the plow, the hoe and the harrow. With his crude moldboard plow he broke up the ground which needed no deep digging into the rich, new soil. He gave all his attention to breaking up the difficult virgin soil with his plow while a small boy usually rode the horse to guide it. This was no easy task, for the horse was frequently lean and lazy and the hours long and hot under the summer sun. The plow would repeatedly snag under a root, giving the rider a savage jolt in the stomach. The farmer broke the clods of earth by dragging over them a narrow wooden harrow or a brushy limb of a tree. He planted all his grain by hand.

Teutonic racial pride prevented all but a few of the unmarried pioneers from taking squaws as their wives though they seldom overlooked an opportunity to take them for their pleasure. One of the very few prominent Virginians free of this prejudice was Colonel William Byrd who, writing in 1728, openly advocated union of the two races as the only means of removing the hostile feelings between them. Squaws, he asserted, possessed all the qualities of white women.

The Indian Woman would have made altogether as Honest Wives for the first Planters, as the Damsels they us'd to purchase from aboard the Ships. It is Strange, therefore, that any good Christian Shou'd have refused a wholesome Straight Bed-fellow, when he might have had so fair a Portion with her, as the Merit of saving her Soul.

The English could never hope to win the esteem of the Indians so long as they disdained to intermarry with them. Wrote Byrd:

Had such Affinities been contracted in the Beginning, how much Bloodshed had been prevented, and how populous would the Country have been, and, consequently, how considerable? Nor wou'd the Shade of the Skin have been any reproach at this day; for if a Moor may be washt white in 3 Generations, Surely an Indian might have been blancht in two.

Free of prejudice, the French saw the Indians as they were— attractive, tall and well proportioned.

Their late Grand Monarch thought it not below even the Dignity of a Frenchman to become one flesh with this People, and therefore Ordered 100 Livres for any of his Subjects, Man or Woman, that wou'd intermarry with a Native.

By this wise policy, the French strengthened their interests among the Indians while their religion propagated just as far as

their love. "I heartily wish," concluded Byrd, "this well-con-
certed Scheme don't thereafter give the French an Advantage
over his Majesty's good Subjects on the Northern Continent of
America."

Unlike the squaw, the pioneer woman led a life of hardship.
She did as much work as her husband. She cooked, churned,
fed and milked the cows, hoed corn, dried beans, chopped wood,
carried water, spun clothing and made floating wick lamps from
clay and bear grease. Her unremitting toil, her affection for
her family and her sterling good sense won her the admiration of
several pioneer writers, one of whom idealized her as womanhood
"in her true glory." According to this writer, the frontier woman
was not, as were women elsewhere, "a doll to carry silks and
jewels," a "puppet to be dandled by fops," an "idol of profane
adoration, remembered today and discarded tomorrow." On the
contrary, she ruled by affection, not passion. She imparted to
her man her constancy, not her weakness. She was not, like her
more polished sister in the East, "the source and mirror of vanity." Assuming the cares of the wife, she guided the labors of
her husband and spread cheerfulness by her domestic diligence.
As a wife she placed all her joy in the merited approbation of her
husband. As a mother she was affectionate, ardent in instructing
her children and careful in training them to think, meditate and
pray. This encomiast seasoned his sentimentality with not a few
grains of truth.

The unmarried girl found plenty of time for the pleasures of
courtship. She started "sparking" in her early teens. If she was
still unmarried at twenty she was regarded as unfortunate, out
of circulation, a thing of scorn. Weddings were very festive
affairs. Since the entire neighborhood was present at them, they
were usually held in the bride's front yard where a gay fire and
buckets of whisky put everyone in a romantic mood. The most
popular song of the time was "Old Sister Pheby," which was
sung all night long around the fire.

The first marriage in Kentucky took place at Boonesboro in
the summer of 1776 when Elizabeth Callaway became the bride
of Samuel Henderson. Even for that time and place the bride and
groom wore clothes unsuited for the occasion. Elizabeth wore

a plain Irish linen dress and Samuel was attired in a hunting shirt borrowed from a friend. The only delicacy of the bridal feast was watermelon. In view of the instability of the government founded by the Transylvania proprietors, the bride's father, in consenting to the match, "required a bond of Henderson that the marriage should be again Solemnized, by authority less doubtful, at the earliest opportunity." The pledge was sacredly fulfilled.

If you became ill, your life depended on whether your constitution could overcome not only the disease but also the concoction prescribed to cure it. Doctors were few and far between. "No one who bore the name of doctor," says Doddridge, lived "within a considerable distance of the residence of my father." In these circumstances death was an easy ravager before the puny force of home remedies. The only disease partly understood seems to have been pleurisy. If you had a fever, you were given warm drinks to induce sweating. Of course you were denied cold water and fresh air.

If your child had worms, you usually expelled them by the application of salt. Or perhaps by the scrapings of pewter spoons, usually from twenty to forty grains, commonly given with sugar. If that proved useless, you applied large doses of green copperas or sulphate of iron. A burn was cooled with poultices of Indian meal or of roasted turnips.

The croup, which the pioneers called the "bold hives," was the most common disease of children. Its cure consisted of the juice of roasted onions or garlic or, better still, of "wall-ink." If the stricken child had a fever, he was sweated with a dose of Virginia snake root oil. To this was usually added the physic of half a pint of white walnut bark which had been peeled downward. If the child needed to vomit, it received the same amount of white walnut bark which had been peeled upward.

The bite of a copperhead or of a rattlesnake sent an imposing array of specifics to the rescue. Doddridge gives a vivid account of how a bitten man was treated:

I remember when a small boy to have seen a man bitten by a rattlesnake brought into the fort on a man's back. One of the company dragged the snake after him by a forked stick fastened in its head. The body of the snake was cut into pieces of about two inches in length, split open in succession, and laid on the wound to draw out the poison, as they expressed it. When this was over, a fire was kindled up in the fort yard and the whole of the serpent burned to ashes, by way of revenge for the injury he had done. After this process was over, a large quantity of chestnut leaves was collected and boiled in a pot. The whole of the wounded man's leg and part of his thigh were placed in a piece of chestnut bark, fresh from the tree, and the decoction poured on the leg so as to run down into the pot again; after continuing this process for some time, a quantity of the boiled leaves were bound to the leg. This was repeated several times a day. The man got well; but whether owing to the treatment bestowed on his wound is not so certain.

Sometimes, in the absence of a specific remedy, the pioneers substituted cupping, sucking the wound and filling deep incisions with salt and gunpowder.

A common disease of the time was the itch, which was generally treated with an ointment made of brimstone and lard. Slippery elm bark and flax seed and other such poultices soothed gunshot wounds. Hunters gnawed with that plague of their occupation, rheumatism, got relief by sleeping with their feet in the fire and by applying rattlesnake oil or the grease of wolves, bears, raccoons, ground hogs and polecats on the swelled joints.

Those wracked with coughs or prostrate with pneumonia drank great quantities of a syrup consisting principally of spikenard and elecampane. If honored remedies failed to cure a person of a disease, his or her kinfolk had recourse to choruses and incantations. In his youth Doddridge learned the incantation in German for curing burns, for stopping toothache and for charming away bullets in battle, but he had no faith in its efficacy. Some pioneers believed that only the blood of a black cat could cure erysipelas, which was commonly called St. Anthony's Fire. The result of this superstition was that a black cat with whole ears and tail was as rare on the frontier as money.

Many pioneers laid certain diseases to witchcraft. These were cured by drawing a portrait of the witch on a stump or piece of board and then shooting at it with a bullet that contained a small quantity of silver. The bullet quickly transferred a painful and sometimes a mortal spell on that part of the witch which corresponded with the part of the portrait struck by the bullet. Another method of cure was that of hanging up in a chimney a corked vial containing a child's urine. This cast on the witch a spell which lasted as long as the vial remained in the chimney. She could break the spell only by borrowing some article from the family of the person she had bewitched.

Bewitched cattle and dogs were burned on the forehead with a branding iron. If they were dead, they were burned to ashes. This inflicted on the witch a spell from which she could disengage herself only by borrowing something from the owner of the dead animal or animals. Many settlers blamed witches for draining those of their cows that failed to furnish an adequate or expected quantity of milk. For each cow they intended to milk the witches were said to hang over the door of the barn a new towel on which they had fixed a new pin. They extracted the milk from the fringes of the towel, in the manner of milking a cow, while they uttered certain incantations.

The early German glass blowers in Kentucky believed that witches blew out the fires in their furnaces. They sought to forestall a recurrence of this evil by throwing live puppies into the burning coals.

Surrounded by constant danger and separated from one another by walls of trees and sometimes of mountains, the pioneers of the Appalachian Frontier felt great need for the comforts of religion. And the religions that the majority preferred were those that filled their lonely and hungry souls with all the fervor and zeal they could command and alleviated their feelings of guilt by paroxysms of repentance.

Many Presbyterian settlers found their faith too stiff and formal to satisfy their spiritual needs. Its ministers smacked too strongly of the seminary and stayed too close to their churches. The settlers wanted a religion in which they could personally participate, one which radiated human sympathy and which summoned them like a trumpet call to repentance. Such were

the Methodist and Baptist faiths. With their democratic governments and evangelistic zeal these religions satisfied so well the
needs of the frontiersmen that membership in each of them outnumbered that of any other religion in the Old Southwest.

But the earliest known faith practiced there was Presbyterianism. Its first ministers followed closely behind the first settlers
and shared the rigors of frontier life with them. In fighting the
Indians they

. . . felt they were dispossessing the Canaanites, and were thus
working the Lord's will in preparing the land for a race which
they believed was more truly His chosen people than was that
nation which Joshua led across the Jordan. They exhorted no less
earnestly in the bare meeting-places on Sunday, because their
hands were roughened with guiding the plow and wielding the
axe on week-days; for they did not believe that being called to
preach the word of God absolved them from earning their living
by the sweat of their brows.

Of this ilk was Charles Cummings, the earliest minister in eastern Tennessee, a firebrand born in Ulster and educated in Pennsylvania. Every Sabbath for thirty years he would "put on his
shot pouch, shoulder his rifle, mount his dun stallion, and ride off
to church," where he preached, often for two hours, with his
eyes constantly shifting from Bible to gun.

No less militant was Samuel Doak, whose Mosaic figure and
stentorian voice kept his congregation in rapt attention even
when once he preached for two hours in a graveyard in pouring
rain. This stern, hard Man of God had walked through Maryland and Virginia driving a flea-bitten gray nag loaded with a
sackful of books, had crossed the mountains and had followed
narrow trails down to the Holston settlements where he established Salem Church near Jonesboro. He purchased a farm and
built on it a log school which in 1785 was incorporated as Martin
Academy. Ten years later it became Washington College with
Doak as president.

At first the highly educated Presbyterian ministers easily dominated the religious life of the German and the Scotch-Irish
immigrants. But in the next generation when the population of

the Old Southwest was composed largely of those born and raised on the frontier, the influence of the Presbyterian faith waned while that of the Baptist and the Methodist rose and spread. The uneducated ministers of these religions, belonging economically to the same class as the majority of the settlers and being democratic in their political ideas and in their church government, fitted well into the social pattern of the frontier. The nature of their religious programs, too, appealed strongly to the settlers, many of whom were drinkers, gamblers, blasphemers and libertines whose feelings of guilt moved them to seek repentance through a passionate gospel of hell-fire and salvation.

In the Tidewater the Baptists and Methodists had been subjected to the contempt and persecution which the followers of accepted faiths have always reserved for those of newer ones. Episcopalians and Presbyterians regarded the Baptists as an outlandish group and spread the impious word that most of them were deformed in one way or another. One credulous old Episcopalian lady inquired of a Baptist minister why most people of his faith were hard-lipped, bleary-eyed, bowlegged, humpbacked and clubfooted.

The motto of the Baptist faith was said to be: "Water! Water! Water!" They were accused of "strong plunging" and of "letting their poor children run wild." Even the Methodist minister, Peter Cartwright, saw the Baptists with prejudiced eyes. They "made so much ado about baptism by immersion," he wrote, "that the uninformed would suppose that heaven was an island, and there was no way to get there but by diving and swimming." Thirty or more of the Baptist preachers "were honored with a dungeon"; some of them "were imprisoned as often as four times"; in a single year, five were arrested in Spottsylvania County as disturbers of the peace. One of the charges made against them was that "they cannot meet a man upon the road, but that they must ram a text of scripture down his throat."

Abused and persecuted for their religious ideas and forced to pay taxes for the support of worldly ministers of other faiths, "whose only recommendation was that they had received a university education," the Baptists of Virginia agitated for religious liberty and for separation of church and state. Backed by such champions of western ideals as Thomas Jefferson, James Madison, Patrick Henry and George Mason, the Baptists in 1785 saw their wishes realized. Thus they were the chief promoters of a principle which has been called "the greatest distinctive contribution by America to the sum of Western Christian civilization."

Rejoicing in their triumph, the Baptists resolved to carry their evangelistic faith across the mountains where among the canebrakes and forests of Kentucky and Tennessee they sought an "ampler ether, a diviner air" in which to worship God as they pleased and to increase the fold. They soon won the sympathy of the pioneers by their democratic ideals, their piety and goodness and the patience with which they had suffered persecution. Their ministers, too, came from among their flocks and lived and worked as they did. They dwelled in small cabins with dirt floors, slept on skin-covered pole bunks, cleared the ground, planted corn and vegetables, split rails and raised hogs and cattle.

Because they had been taxed in the Tidewater to support Episcopalian and Presbyterian ministers, some of whom were unworthy of their calling, the Baptist preachers and their people regarded all highly educated ministers with suspicion. They thought ministers should come from the people and should support themselves by pursuing secular occupations. A typical Baptist minister, John Taylor, lived in a cabin sixteen feet square which had no floor, table, bedstead or stool. Depending largely on meat, Taylor often went out with hunters, but, being a poor shot, he seldom bagged anything. The hunters always shared their meat with him. He did a prodigious amount of work. Altogether he cleared nearly four hundred acres in the heaviest forest of Kentucky and made numerous improvements on the land. In one day's work he put up 100 panels of fence six rails high. And he had had to carry the rails which were eleven feet long for a considerable distance. While Taylor thus supported himself and his family in the winter of 1784-1785 he conducted the first Baptist revival in Kentucky.

Under Taylor's ministry, and that of another of his caliber, Lewis Craig, Baptist churches sprang up in considerable numbers along the banks of creeks and rivers where scores of repentant pioneers each year sought salvation in baptism.

The organization and doctrine of the Methodist church were even more congenial to the religious needs of the settlers than those of the Baptist. The democratic nature of the Methodist church government, its fiery evangelism and the emphasis it placed on individual responsibility made it particularly agreeable to the pioneers who, engaged in conquering a continent, prized "individual independence above all earthly possessions." Living remote from human contacts, they also found great comfort in the Methodist doctrine that stressed the close relationship between God and man.

The bearer of this comforting doctrine was the circuit preacher. He lived on his horse; his house was his saddlebags. Wherever he found himself—in a crude cabin, on his horse or under the branches of a cooling beech or maple—he was equally at home. He was so ardent in pursuing his work that he awaited neither manner nor means. He never followed wagon trails; he preceded them. Like the Baptists, he came from the same class as his flock; he had a perfect understanding of the habits, feelings and prejudices of the pioneers.

He harmonized perfectly with the fluid nature of the frontier, sometimes covering a territory of four or five hundred miles. He was the working embodiment of the Biblical passage, "Take no thought for your life, what ye shall eat, or what ye shall drink; nor yet for your body, what ye shall put on." With a salary of only a few dollars a year he placed complete reliance in the Lord. He conquered hardship and danger with zeal and courage. Sometimes he rode twenty or thirty miles without seeing a soul; but his host always received him with joy, fed him and let him rest on a rug before the fireplace. If the rug was full of fleas that disturbed his slumber, he cheerfully found refuge on a clean plank or couched himself in a hollow log.

At dawn, rain or shine, he resumed his circuit. His defiance of wind and rain inspired the proverb that pioneers were wont to utter on an inclement day: "There is nothing out today but crows and Methodist preachers."

The typical Methodist circuit rider was so familiar and lovable a figure on the frontier that even small children and their pets welcomed him. His costume was that of the ordinary minister of his day: short breeches, long stockings and a dingy black double-breasted coat that fell almost to his buckled shoes. He was no Chesterfield in his manners. His hair, parted in the middle and falling to his shoulders, gave him a saintly air, and heightened the paleness of his face, which resulted from insufficient food and frequent exposure.

At the beginning of the service the circuit rider sang a hymn with his congregation. Then he prayed with such sweet pathos that heaven and earth for the time being seemed to join. Then he read a favorite text, such as "the upright shall love thee," upon which he preached a sermon so charged with emotion that, because of its wildness and incoherence, it quailed some of the most hardened listeners. Man, he said, was conceived in sin; but Jesus Christ died to save him—died to save *all*. Man is endowed with free will, he has the power to choose between good and evil; therefore, he must give an account of himself to God. Man can be newly created, can be regenerated, not by a change of purpose but by a change of character. Thus he is converted, is endowed with a "new spirit" that is necessary for admission into the kingdom of heaven. What constitutes conversion? Faithfulness to godly living. But the "backslider"—the Methodist who, having once been converted, fails in faithfulness—is doomed to eternal damnation. Such preachments harmonized with the essential practicality of frontier life.

Yet the combined efforts of the Presbyterian, Baptist and Methodist churches failed to lessen frontier immorality. After the American Revolution countless waves of migration poured into Kentucky and Tennessee from all directions. Some of the settlers gave way to the loose living that inevitably follows war. More were sympathizers of the French Revolution who entertained ideas incompatible with the teachings of conventional faiths. Many were veterans who, enjoying the security of the victorious, gave little or no thought to "the spirit of the gospel." All had left the relatively comfortable life of the East for the barren existence of the frontier.

These factors, and the endless search of the settlers for choice land, their untold hardships and the dangers they daily encountered, engendered a materialistic outlook, a greed that sustained them in their bleak environment. But as they grew in wealth they coarsened and petrified in spirit. While they welcomed Sunday as a day free from labor, they spent most of it in rowdy entertainment. They quarreled, fought, whored, blasphemed and got drunk. A minister who made a trip to Kentucky at this time was so distressed by the "pride and profaneness" of the settlers that he feared a "great decay of true and vital religion."

During a visit to eastern Tennessee Bishop Francis Asbury of the Methodist Church sensed a deplorable lack of religious sentiment in the people. "When I reflect that not one in a hundred came here to get religion; but rather to get plenty of good land," he wrote, "I think it will be well if some or many do not eventually lose their souls."

But the hour of their deliverance from evil was at hand. The spiritual barbarism of many frontiersmen so horrified the Presbyterian minister James McGready that he resolved to bring them back to Christian living by introducing the revivalistic methods which he recently had seen working with such excellent results at Hampden-Sidney College. McGready's teachings deviated considerably from the accepted dogmas of his religion. He was interested not in predestination, but in bringing sinners to walk in the path of God. His sermons, full of fire and brimstone, had a tremendous appeal. His description of hell was so vivid that his congregation trembled and sweated. They saw the lake of fire yawning before them and God's angry hand thrusting them down into its scorching and bottomless incandescence.

McGready talked endlessly of rebirth, repentance, redemption. He demanded that his congregation pray every Saturday night and Sunday morning and all day on the third Saturday of each month for rebirth, repentance, redemption. These practices attracted such large crowds for several days that McGready was obliged to provide them with some accommodation. They accepted his invitation to camp at the meeting ground, thereby initiating the camp meeting which Baptist and especially Methodist ministers promptly adopted in a mighty effort to turn the pioneers away from their sinful pleasures and worldly pursuits.

The pioneers responded with overwhelming enthusiasm. Many

of them suffered from feelings of guilt resulting from a conflict between their stern Christian upbringing and their general worldliness. In the soul-shaking preaching, praying and singing of the camp meetings they found expiation for their sins. The camp meetings also served many as the only social events in their otherwise bleak existence. No man ever longed for the company of his fellow man as ardently as did the American pioneer. Small wonder that, seldom seeing a new face all winter long and sensing his spiritual emptiness, he looked forward to camp meetings as the chief social events of his life.

When in late August or early September the camp meeting season opened, hundreds—sometimes thousands—of settlers with their families thronged on foot, by horseback and in their crude wagons toward the place designated for the "holy fair." For several weeks the settlements were deserted and the fields were left unworked. Some of the settlers had to travel as much as thirty or forty miles, but they considered this a small price to pay for the social uplift that awaited them.

After traveling a few miles one group usually met another; they would join and share experiences the rest of the journey. When they reached the camping ground they called joyfully to acquaintances from a distance and warmly greeted friends they had not seen for months. The early arrivals made bonfires from pine knots to guide those who might come after dark. By evening the camp was in order, the wagons were drawn up in a wide circle, and around each group women busily arranged the provisions and sleeping quarters as they gossiped to one another.

The best picture of a camp meeting is perhaps a composite one drawn from the salient features of several meetings. The minister mounted a stump or wagon and called his audience to attention. With a hard, piercing look he hurled this accusation: "You are a moving mass of putrefaction!" Then in a more subdued voice he "related his trials, experiences, travels, persecutions, sorrows and joys," while the audience now and then gave approval.

"Amen!"

"Tell it, brother!"

"Yes, I know it!"

"Praise God!"

"Come to the Lord!"

Suddenly a woman's laugh—wild, piercing, Mephistophelean—inspired the minister to greater eloquence. His voice, as loud as a priest of Baal, rose to an uproar, then softened to a hissing whisper, then crescendoed again to a mighty fortissimo. The crowd swayed as if participating in a modern swingfest; some rose to their feet and began a wildly rhythmic dance. And the minister, having "got up the 'rousements" and brought "the battle to the gate," continued to pour out his harangue of hell and damnation. The audience groaned and wept, as much from terror inspired by his voice and wild gesticulations as from its own conviction of guilt.

Suddenly the preacher stopped talking and began to sing a hymn. A small group joined him. Another group started a hymn of its own. Still another group followed, until six different hymns echoed through the countryside while here and there persons sobbed and groaned and convulsed in the name of the Lord.

At this point several preachers made their appearance in different parts of the field. Mounting a stump or jumping into a wagon bed, each gathered around him a crowd whose size depended on the intensity of his eloquence. In the midst of a sermon a man or woman gave a joyful shout. Conversion had come, and the repentant sinner, lifted onto the shoulders of a neighbor, was carried through the crowd, which sent up a paean of praise to the goodness of the Lord.

Children were suddenly endowed with the tongues of veteran evangelists. With tears streaming down his cheeks a boy of twelve preached until he was exhausted. Mustering his last bit of strength, he let fall a soggy handkerchief as he cried, "Thus, O Sinner, shall you drop into hell, unless you forsake your sins and turn to the Lord."

Two girls, aged nine and ten, sobbed for mercy. Relieved of her anguish, one of them turned to the other and cried, "O, you little sinner, come to Christ!" She came.

A boy of seven spoke in a "rapturous language" and then fell into a trance. Hours later he awoke into religious ecstasy.

The omnipresent frenzy induced bodily changes in many. One man's arms and legs stiffened as if with arthritis, his heart beat furiously, and he fell with a sharp scream to the ground. He lay for several hours as if dead and then rose shouting: "I am saved! I am saved!" By this hysterical seizure, known as the "falling exercise," he won the kingdom of heaven.

Thenceforth men and women fell all over the field like corn in a windstorm. Three thousand fell at Cabin Creek. Many who came to witness the phenomenon were similarly affected. Realizing their weakness or susceptibility, some tried to run away into the woods, but there they succumbed. In a few days the prostrate bodies were so numerous that they were laid in rows to prevent the gyrating and contorting multitude from trampling them. Moreover, clean straw was spread in different parts of the fields to soften the blow for those who were expected to fall. Bad and good people fell with equal rapidity.

The leader of a group of rowdies bent on breaking up a praying circle mounted his horse and rode furiously toward the crowd. Before he reached it, however, he suddenly wheeled his horse with the intention of scattering the group more effectively. Instantly he fell from his horse as if struck by lightning and lay on the ground rigid and unconscious.

A woman of easy virtue lay senseless for seventy-two hours. Many thought her dead when suddenly she disengaged herself from her trance with the ease of a child waking from sleep, sprang to her feet, and began shouting and singing.

Young men and women became victims of spasmodic convulsions known as the "jerks," which usually started in the forearm and gradually affected every muscle of the body. They were unable to walk but jerked backward and forward in rapid succession and almost touched the ground with their heads. Those with pronounced guilt feelings jerked with such violence that they feared they would tear themselves to pieces. The hair of female jerkers, becoming disheveled, lashed and cracked like whips and could be heard twenty feet away. Sometimes jerkers, holding on to trees, kicked up the earth, like horses stamping flies. The minister doubtless helped to induce the convulsions.

A thoroughgoing exhibitionist, he jerked, danced, chanted and gesticulated madly.

His antics brought many conversions, but few were permanent. Indeed, religious ecstasy often degenerated into adultery. Some persons jerked and fell one night only to indulge in baser passions on the next. Watchmen, appointed by the ministers, made the rounds with torches made of pine knots in search of fornicators. One found six men sleeping with a young woman. Another discovered, doubtless with some pique, a couple fornicating in a cornfield. The months following a camp meeting always brought good harvest of illegitimate children.

One Becca Bell, who had fallen or jerked at several different times, became "as big as all get-out" to "a wicked trifling schoolmaster who says he'll be damned to hell if he ever marries her." Shocked ministers of several faiths recorded in their diaries the names of girls who, at the camp meeting, embraced Christ only to adore Beelzebub.

Small wonder that a number of the more level-headed ministers deplored the emotional excesses of the camp meeting. At first even Francis Asbury doubted its value. Another minister, a Presbyterian, condemned it on the ground that God is a God of order and not of confusion and that "whatever tends to destroy the comely order of his worship is not from him, for he is consistent with himself." Still another, John Lyle, wrote with perhaps more psychological insight than he knew that the paroxysms of the camp meeting were "not the effects of a Divine impulse" but rather "the evidence of human infirmity."

Nevertheless, the camp meetings were responsible for increasing the membership of the Methodist Church threefold within ten years. And Francis Asbury no longer doubted. As he made plans to carry the evangelical work north of the Ohio, he wrote: "Bohemia has a great work—camp meetings have done this, glory to the Great I Am!"

The favorite sports were designed to meet the dangers of frontier life. Nearly every well-grown boy entering his teens was given a rifle which he learned to shoot accurately by using a log or a forked stick as a rest and by placing a moss pad under the barrel to keep it from swerving and spoiling his aim. After practicing on raccoons, squirrels and turkeys he usually proved an expert marksman in shooting Indians.

Constantly jumping over brambles or fallen timber, the boy developed agility in escaping from Indians and in extricating himself from their ruses. In autumn he could walk over the fallen leaves without crushing one or breaking a twig. He developed a remarkable sensitivity to sound. He could tell by the report of a rifle whether it belonged to an Indian or to a white man. He wrestled with his neighbor, knew how to throw him and preferred the scalp hold to the toe hold. He showed consummate skill in throwing the tomahawk. He learned that a tomahawk with a handle of a given length made so many revolutions in a given distance. At five steps it struck with the handle downward; at seven and a half, with the handle upward. The experienced boy could measure distance with his eyes as he walked through the forest and could bury a tomahawk in a tree in any way he wished.

The adroit imitation of the songs of birds and the calling of beasts was a necessary part of the frontier boy's education. The marvelous tales of Cooper pale into insignificance when compared to the wonderful feats and adventures of Edmund Jennings, son of Jonathan Jennings, whom we shall presently see with John Donelson in his amazing voyage up the Tennessee. Young Jennings could imitate the hoot of an owl, the scream of a panther, the bleat of a fawn and the gobble of a turkey so accurately that "the owl would perch above his head, the panther creep from his lair, the fawn run to meet its dam, and the turkey to join its mates."

The forest speech was not only the language of sport; it was also the "settler's secret code of war." Stray Indians put themselves in touch again with the band by turkey calls in the day time and by owl or wolf calls at night. The pioneer used the same means to trick the Indians into betraying their whereabouts or to "lure strays, unwittingly, within reach of the knife." A young pioneer named Benjamin Castleman was so sensitive to sound that he could detect the slightest inaccuracy in the imitation of an animal. Once, in roaming through the forest, he heard the imitation of an owl. Though it was almost perfect, he grew suspicious. The woo-woo call and the woo-woo answer were not well timed and toned; the chatter was a failure; and, moreover, it emanated, not from a tree, but from the ground. "I'll see you," he said to himself, and as he approached he saw something of about the height of a stump standing between the forks of a chestnut tree which divided near the ground. Well, he knew that no stump could be there; he put "Betsy" to his face, and instantly the stump was a live Indian that thumped to the ground near the roots of the forked chestnut.

One of the favorite school games of the frontier shows that children were typically American in their hatred of oppression and their desperate willingness to fight for freedom. The game was that of barring out the master before the Christmas holidays. The master, anticipating the annual revolution a few weeks before it took place, would become as oppressive and stern as a czar. Whereupon his subjects, growing less patient of restraint, would call a convention where one "born to command" would propose a rebellion aimed at overthrowing the "despot."

The plan, meeting the general approval of the student body and supported by "some congenial spirits of the neighborhood," would be put into operation on the Friday morning preceding Christmas when at an early hour, the children would take possession of the school, make a large fire in the fireplace, barricade the doors and greet the master with shouts of defiance. They refuse him admittance; he commands submission; they decline to surrender, except on honorable terms—a treat and a week of holidays.

Conferees of both sides then meet and negotiate; the master finds their terms excessive; he refuses to bow to them. Then the war is resumed. The besieged remove the benches from the barricaded door and capture the recalcitrant master in one swift charge. A prisoner in their hands, he learns that if he persists in his folly he will be ducked in cold water. This threat convinces him; he yields to the demands; he sends a messenger off for apples and cider and perhaps whisky; the cold war is brought to an end.

Merriment fills both victors and vanquished; the holidays are spent in rural sports and manly amusements that obliterate all recollection of past differences between master and mastered. When books are reopened, each one quietly and cheerfully resumes his proper position in school. The master becomes master again and the late rebels return to their allegiance. After a pleasant relaxation from their duties they are anxious to return to them with profit and diligence.

King's

Mountain

DURING THE FIRST HALF OF THE CONFLICT FEW PIONEERS OF the Appalachian Frontier took part in the American Revolution. Indeed, the struggle of the thirteen colonies for independence was almost as remote to the frontiersmen as if it were taking place on another planet. Yet in conquering the wilderness they were unconsciously helping to build that political edifice for which their warring brothers to the east were laying the foundation.

The conquests of the pioneers resulted in the establishment of new commonwealths which, united to the thirteen original colonies, were to advance the borders of the United States to the Mississippi River and eventually even beyond it. While the settlers were jealous of their local independence, as Americans they felt drawn to a larger commonality for whose cause they were always ready to fight. And now they were about to be given an opportunity to come to the relief of their brothers on the seaboard and, in so doing, to strike a telling blow in the advance of American nationality.

In 1779 the theater of operations shifted from the North to the South. By the end of that year the British had conquered Georgia. In the following spring they captured Charleston, reduced all of South Carolina and marched triumphantly northward. Their leader, Charles, Lord Cornwallis, commanded a formidable force of British and Hessians, Irish volunteers and refugees from Florida. Cornwallis could count, too, on the support of numerous Tories who flocked to the royal standard in increasing numbers with each new victory. In addition he had bands of warriors sent him by the half-breed, Alexander McGil-

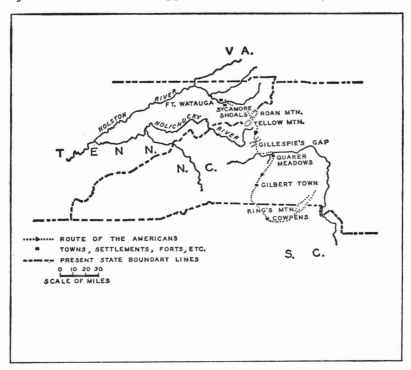

livray, chief of the Creeks, and some Cherokee who, never friends of the Americans, eagerly sought vengeance by aiding the British. In the face of this threatening human avalanche the patriots for the moment lost all hope of victory and retreated westward.

As Cornwallis marched northward he ordered two of his most redoubtable officers, Colonel Banastre Tarleton and Major Patrick Ferguson, to scour the country, raise Tory regiments, scatter patriot troops and crush what opposition remained. The two men were vastly different in character and personality. Tarleton, commander of a cavalry force, was a uniformed brute. His men plundered and ravaged, mistreated prisoners, outraged women and hanged all those whom Tarleton suspected of being in sympathy with the Americans. His victories were nearly always preludes to massacres. Once he attacked over three hundred Virginians under Colonel Abraham Buford. One hundred thirteen of these unfortunates were shot or butchered on the spot while they begged for quarter, a hundred and fifty were wounded, and the rest were taken prisoner.

Ferguson, son of Lord Pitfour of Aberdeen, was a lean, dark man of thirty-six years. Standing scarcely eight inches above five feet, he was short for a Highlander. His hair, straight and black, suggested a Celtic strain in his blood. No pleasant features graced his face, but his solid military gifts, his sincere manner and the calculating intelligence which gleamed in his eyes when he spoke won him the esteem of his officers and men alike. Toward the enemy he showed on several occasions a princely magnanimity.

Once when he was lying with his men in a forest near Brandywine Creek, Pennsylvania, Ferguson saw two mounted American officers approaching, one dressed as a hussar and the other in a dark green and blue uniform with a high cocked hat. He gave and then recalled an order to fire three shots near them. The hussar wheeled his horse away, but his companion came to within a hundred yards of Ferguson, who, advancing from the forest, ordered him to halt. The American looked at Ferguson and then moved on. Ferguson, leveling his pistol at the man, repeated his command in vain. He could have "lodged half a dozen balls in or about him" before he was out of reach, but his principles forbade him to "fire at the back of an unoffending individual, who was acquitting himself very coolly of his duty."

The next day Ferguson was relating the incident to some wounded officers when a surgeon joined the group and told them that George Washington, attended only by a French officer in hussar dress, had been in the vicinity. Ferguson later wrote that he was not sorry he had been unaware of Washington's identity at the time of the encounter.

Toward American women Ferguson showed the same nobility of character. Once when he was taking part in an action commanded by Hessian officers he learned that some American women had been mistreated. He went in a rage to the commander and demanded that the men who had disgraced their uniforms be instantly put to death.

At fifteen Ferguson had received his baptism of fire in Flanders. A few years later, as a captain of infantry, he quelled a revolt of the Caribs on the island of St. Vincent. While studying tactics and strategy at Woolwich he invented a rifle that could be loaded at the breech without ramrod and could fire four aimed shots a minute. Generals and statesmen attended his shooting exhibitions, and once even George III appeared with his guards to watch him use his ingenious weapon.

In 1777 Ferguson with a hundred officers and men, each armed with the new gun, joined Cornwallis in America. Ferguson quickly earned the reputation of being the best shot in the British army. He reputedly could load and reload his rifle quicker than the quickest American pioneer. Sometimes, seeing a bird on a bough or fence, he would drop his reins, draw "a pistol from his holster, toss it aloft, catch it as it fell, aim, and shoot" off the bird's head. At Brandywine he won acclaim as commander of a corps of picked riflemen. In that battle, however, a ball shattered his right arm which hung useless for the rest of his life. On recuperating he took up left-handed swordplay, at which he became very proficient.

As commander in the back country Ferguson was obliged to undertake duties lying outside the scope of a military officer. He was, in the words of Cornwallis, "more . . . of a justice of peace than . . . a soldier." Beside commanding his own independent unit, he organized and regulated all loyalist volunteers, inspected grain and cattle and performed marriage ceremonies. The Tories of the back country of Georgia and the Carolinas responded eagerly to his call. Soon finding himself at the head of nearly a thousand men, he made preparations to invade the back country of North Carolina.

Word of Ferguson's activities had reached a small force of Americans under Colonel Charles McDowell of Burke County, North Carolina. Convinced that he could not dispel the threat with his own meager numbers, McDowell sent a messenger across the mountains to the Watauga and Holston settlements, requesting the assistance of John Sevier and Isaac Shelby. Shelby responded with approximately two hundred mounted riflemen and a part of Sevier's regiment under Major Charles Robertson. Sevier had trained these men to fight according to the Indian motto, "Fight strong and run away fast." They used the red man's tactics of ambuscade, surprise attack at dawn and swift flight.

For a month the forces gave and took. At Musgrove's Mill Shelby and an officer named Elijah Clarke routed a force of Tories and then made preparations to attack the settlement of Ninety-Six, which had fallen into Royalist hands. The defeat of the American army under Horatio Gates at Camden, however, forced Shelby and his men to abandon their plans. Rejoining McDowell, they left their prisoners with him and, forseeing the uselessness of attempting to dislodge Cornwallis from Ninety-Six with their small numbers, returned to their homes on the Watauga and the Holston. McDowell and his men soon followed.

Ferguson pursued them to the gap through which they had passed only a half hour before and then, realizing that his forces were too small and too exhausted to engage McDowell's troops and their frontier friends on their own ground, marched to Gilbert Town in Burke County. There he penned a warning to the pioneers that, if they refused to surrender and return to their rightful allegiance, he would invade their country, destroy their homes and hang their leaders. Ferguson then paroled a prisoner, Samuel Phillips, whom he had taken in the chase, and sent him with the warning to Shelby.

While waiting a reply he pursued the duty of arresting rebels in the district. One of them was a certain Captain Thomas Lytle, whose beautiful and spirited wife, learning that Ferguson was about to appear with his men, availed herself of the occasion to put on her newest gown and beaver hat. When Ferguson arrived, Mrs. Lytle asked him to dismount and come in, but he ignored the invitation. Instead he advised her to persuade her husband to return to the allegiance of the King.

"Colonel Ferguson," she replied, firmly, "I don't know how this war may end; it is not unlikely that my husband may fall in battle; all I positively know is, that he will never prove a traitor to his country."

Ferguson fixed upon her a patronizing gaze. "I admire you as the handsomest woman I have seen in North Carolina—I even *half way* admire your zeal in a bad cause; but, take my word for it, the rebellion has had its day, and is now virtually put down. Give my kind regards to Captain Lytle, and tell him to come in. He will not be asked to compromise his honor; his verbal pledge not again to take up arms against the King, is all that will be asked of him." The British commander bowed and led away his soldiers.

Meanwhile on the Holston Shelby had received Ferguson's warning to the frontiersmen. Leaping onto his horse, he sped to Watauga to confer with Sevier. He found the settlers enjoying a barbecue and a horse race given by Sevier on the banks of the Nolichucky. Stealing away from the crowd, the two men planned to meet Ferguson and defeat him before that officer could carry out his threat.

They sent messengers to ask Colonel William Campbell, who lived in a Virginia settlement on the Clinch, to hurry to their assistance. At first Campbell, preferring to strengthen his position at home and let Ferguson interpose himself between the mountains and Cornwallis, refused; but, on receiving a second plea, he decided to co-operate. The valley soon rang with the call to arms. Pioneers poured into Sycamore Shoals from every direction. McDowell with his troops dashed across the mountains over which they had escaped a few weeks before.

Daybreak on September 26, 1780, found over a thousand soldiers and civilians gathered on the level ground beside the river. Most of them were armed with the Deckard rifle, "a gun of remarkable precision for a long shot, spiral grooved, with a barrel some thirty inches long, and with its stock some three and a half feet, carrying bullets varying from thirty to seventy to the pound of lead."

The Americans were little encumbered with baggage—each carried a blanket, "a cup . . . with which to quench his thirst, a wallet of provisions" which included mixed corn and meal and a skillet to cook his meat. This assemblage was vastly different from that which had gathered on the same spot six years before to buy the Dark and Bloody Ground. Now no Indians were present. No money figured in the Americans' endeavor to secure the limitless frontier. The Indians' local chief, Dragging Canoe, new leader of the Chickamauga, in 1779 had gone on the warpath, had suffered defeat at the hands of Evan Shelby and had fled to the caves of the far Tennessee. No white woman had been present then, only the advancing white men and the retreating red men. But now mothers, sisters, wives, sweethearts and children emerged from the cabins to cheer on the men who were going to secure the liberty of their homes.

The men leaned on their rifles in an attitude of respectful attention while their beloved preacher, Samuel Doak, invoked Divine protection and guidance and closed with the Bible quotation: "The sword of the Lord and of Gideon!" The women took up the words, crying again and again: "The sword of the Lord and of our Gideons!" To these shouts, "as bugles on the wind of dawn, the buckskin-shirted army dashed out upon the mountain trail."

The frontiersmen took along a number of cattle which, however, soon impeded their advance. Abandoning them on the mountainside, they decided to rely for food on wild game and on the mixed corn meal and maple sugar each man carried. Passing between Roan and Yellow mountains to the summit of the range, they halted for drill and rifle practice in ankle-deep snow.

When Sevier reviewed his men he found that two of them were missing. Knowing that the Watauga settlements were infested with Tories, he suspected that the missing men had slipped away to carry warning to Ferguson. If this suspicion was justified, he faced two problems: to accelerate the march of his men to keep Ferguson from getting reinforcements from Cornwallis, and to march by another trail to prevent being captured before they themselves received reinforcements.

Descending the deep side of the mountain, the ragged army crossed the Blue Ridge Mountains at Gillespie's Gap and pushed on to Quaker Meadows where Colonel Benjamin Cleveland, whom we have already met as a hunter in Kentucky, joined them with 350 men. Along their route scores of settlers who had been eager to march at the tap of the drum swung into their column.

The American force now numbered about fifteen hundred men, but they had no commanding officer. During their advance, differences and quarreling among their men had caused them no little trouble. When on October 2 they encamped only about eighteen miles from Gilbert Town where they expected to find Ferguson, they decided that the time had come to remedy the situation. McDowell volunteered to carry a message to General Gates who, after his defeat at Camden, had retreated into North Carolina with some of his staff and was believed to be somewhere in the vicinity of Hillsboro.

While they were writing the letter Sevier and Shelby realized that Gates might, on receiving their request, wonder why the governor of North Carolina, the highest military officer of the state, had not provided them with a commander. The truth was that Sevier had done something of which he thought the governor might strongly disapprove. Unable to borrow sufficient funds on his private responsibility, he had conferred with John Adair, who was in charge of the North Carolina land office, and suggested that the public money in Adair's possession be turned over to Shelby to meet the military exigencies of the hour.

Adair had replied: "I have no authority by law to make that disposition of this money; it belongs to the impoverished treasury of North Carolina, and I dare not appropriate a cent of it to any purpose; but, if the country is over-run by the British, our liberty is gone. Let the money go, too. Take it. If the enemy, by its use, is driven from the country, I can trust that country to justify and vindicate my conduct—so take it."

Thus Sevier had obtained between twelve and thirteen thousand dollars. In these circumstances he felt that an interview with the governor had better be deferred. Hence the request to Gates was worded as follows:

As we have at this time called out our militia without any orders from the Executive of our different States and with the view of expelling the Enemy out of this part of the Country, we think such a body of men worthy of your attention and would request you to send a General Officer immediately to take the command. . . . All our troops being Militia and little acquainted with discipline, we would wish him to be a Gentleman of address and able to keep up a proper discipline *without disgusting the soldiery*.

Gates, perhaps annoyed by the wording of this letter, failed to reply. Shelby then suggested that they appoint Colonel William Campbell, who, being the only Virginian among the officers, would arouse no jealousy by his position. The officers all agreed to this choice. The new commander, a settler of the Holston region, had fought in Lord Dunmore's War and had been one of the officers who at Fort Gower pledged themselves to fight in defense of American liberty.

At the beginning of the American Revolution Campbell had been commissioned captain and had assisted General Andrew Lewis in dislodging Dunmore from Virginia. Repairing to the Holston region, he studied military tactics which were to prove of great value in his subsequent campaign at King's Mountain. In April 1780 he was promoted to the rank of colonel. He served briefly as a member in the house of delegates, and led an expedition against the Chickamauga towns which had declared for the British. He was fighting Tories in the back country of North Carolina when he was called to join the pioneers in the campaign against Ferguson.

Campbell was a ruddy-complexioned man with reddish hair and bright blue eyes. Slightly over six feet tall, raw-boned and muscular, he stood as straight as an Indian. His irascible temper concealed a heart of gold. In church after the sermon ended he would look around to assist all the women of the neighborhood, especially the aged, in mounting their horses. Of Scotch-Irish descent he had acquired the principles and predilections of his persecuted ancestors. His devotion to liberty was deep and fervent.

The two Tories who had deserted Sevier's troops soon reached Ferguson who thereupon left Gilbert Town and marched southward to make contact with Cornwallis. Ferguson's force was much reduced. Some of his men were pursuing Elijah Clarke toward Augusta and a number of others were on furlough. On reaching Denard's Ford, about eight miles from Gilbert Town, Ferguson posted a notice calling on Tories to join him:

Gentlemen:—Unless you wish to be eat up by an inundation of barbarians, who have begun by murdering an unarmed son before the aged father, and afterwards lopped off his arms, and who by their shocking cruelties and irregularities, give the best proof of their cowardice and want of discipline; I say, if you wish to be pinioned, robbed, and murdered, and see your wives and daughters, in four days, abused by the dregs of mankind—in short, if you wish or deserve to live, and bear the name of men, grasp your arms in a moment and run to camp.

The Back Water men have crossed the mountains; McDowell, Hampton, Shelby, and Cleveland are at their head, so that you know what you have to depend upon. If you choose to be degraded forever and ever by a set of mongrels, say so at once, and let your women turn their backs upon you, and look out for real men to protect them.

With this piece of propaganda Ferguson attracted several hundred more men.

On the evening of October 6, 1780, Ferguson and his men—about eight hundred strong—arrived at King's Mountain—a mile or so south of the North Carolina line in present York County, South Carolina. The summit of the mountain, known as the Pinnacle, jutted its isolated rocky spur sixty feet above the surrounding countryside. Saplings and big timber of oak and pine palisaded its steep sides. Its bald top, resembling an Indian paddle varying in width from 120 yards at the blade to 60 yards at the handle, was cropped with rocks and boulders and was so narrow that a man standing on it could be shot from either side. Falsely confident of the strength of the mountain and determined to "distinguish himself on the glorious field of Mars" and win "undying honors and fame from his King and country," Ferguson led his troops resolutely up the rocky eminence. As the sun sank and the tents sprang up he boasted to his officers that he was on

King's Mountain, that he was king of that mountain, and that God Almighty could not drive him from it.

Meanwhile, on the same evening the pioneers arrived at Cowpens, a large estate which they seized from its wealthy Tory master. After supping on his roasted cattle and his corn—they themselves had speedily mowed the corn—they sent out a man named Gilmer, a skillful actor who could cry, laugh or pretend lunacy with conviction, to obtain information of Ferguson's whereabouts. From a Tory to whom he pretended that he wished to join Ferguson, Gilmer learned of the British commander's approximate strength, his route and the manner in which he communicated with Cornwallis.

On receiving Gilmer's information, Campbell held a council of his officers and agreed to attack Ferguson with a detachment of their best men before aid could reach him. The flickering firelight in Cowpens retreated and faded away as the picked men, numbering over nine hundred, thundered toward their destination. The rest, following at their best pace, joined their comrades in time to share the glory of victory.

Rain overtook Campbell's forces as they rode. Though soon drenched to the skin, they managed to keep their weapons and powder dry by wrapping them in knapsacks, blankets and hunting shirts. Some of the horses bogged down in the soggy earth. Their owners pulled them out and whipped them forward. The men halted neither for food nor for rest. Two or three miles from King's Mountain they captured a messenger whom Ferguson had sent to Cornwallis with another appeal for help. They asked him how they would recognize Ferguson. He replied that the British commander had the habit of wearing a checkered shirt or duster over his uniform. Colonel Hambright, native of Germany, told his men to bear this in mind. "Well, poys," he said, "when you see dot man mit a pig shirt on over his clothes, you may know who him is, and mark him mit your rifles."

In the afternoon of October 7 the Americans reached their destination. The rain had ceased; the sun shone brilliantly. The men dismounted and tethered their streaming horses. Then they received the final order: "Fresh prime your guns, and every man go into battle firmly resolving to fight till he dies!" The plan of battle was simple enough: they were to surround the mountain, to hold the enemy on the summit and to keep firing from behind trees and rocks.

Campbell, leading the attack, exclaimed in a stentorian voice: "Here they are, my brave boys; shout like hell and fight the devils!"

Instantly a swelling cacophony of savage yells shook the forest, momentarily filling Ferguson and his men with dread. Captain Abraham De Peyster, remembering that Shelby's men had yelled at Musgrove's Mill, said to Ferguson: "These are the damned yelling boys!"

Cleveland and his men, passing around the left side of the mountain, halted before a swampy piece of ground. Availing himself of the temporary delay, Cleveland went among his men making the following speech by piecemeal:

My brave fellows, we have beaten the Tories, and we can beat them again. They are all cowards: if they had the spirit of men, they would join with their fellow-citizens in supporting the independence of their country. When you are engaged, you are not to wait for the word of command from me. I will show you, by my example, how to fight; I can undertake no more. Every man must consider himself an officer, and act from his own judgment. Fire as quick as you can, and stand your ground as long as you can. When you can do no better, get behind trees, or retreat; but I beg you not to run quite off. If we are repulsed, let us make a point of returning, and renewing the fight; perhaps we may have better luck in the second attempt than the first.

The British outposts, seeing Shelby leading his men across a gap in the forest, sounded the alarm. Instantly Ferguson jumped into the saddle and blew his silver whistle as a command for his men to charge. Some of them, fixing their bayonets, charged down the slope only to be shot by groups of Americans behind them. Most of them fell on Shelby's men who, having no bayonets, recoiled before the onslaught. As the pioneers backed down the slope they heard Campbell's stentorian voice commanding them to return to the fight. They stiffened and aimed at the

soldiers on the summit. They began to climb the hill again, dart-
ing from tree to tree. With a large sword—the claymore of
Argyle—gleaming in his hand and his blue eyes glittering with
determination, Campbell galloped hither and thither until his
horse gave out. Then he led his men on foot, his voice growing
hoarse, his face blackening with powder smoke.

A Tory thrust his bayonet through a hand and into a thigh of
Robert Henry, a boy of sixteen who was aiming at him from
behind a log lying across a hollow. Completely transfixed, Henry
fell on his antagonist. Just then one of his companions, William
Caldwell, pulled the bayonet out of Henry's thigh, and, finding it
still sticking in the boy's hand, Caldwell loosed it from its hold
with a kick. Jumping to his feet, Henry picked up his gun with
his uninjured hand, only to find it empty. When he fell on the
Tory he had discharged his rifle. The Tory's profuse bleeding
indicated that the bullet had severed a main artery.

Meanwhile Shelby and his men still advanced up the slope on
the other side. Some of Ferguson's men drove them down the
hill again; but only for a moment, for they returned with a deadlier fire. The battle raged on every part of the mountain. Now
it flashed along the summit; now, around the base; and now, up
the sides, like the sulphurous blaze of a volcano. The shouts of
the Americans, the reports of hundreds of rifles and muskets, the
loud commands and encouraging words of the officers mingled
with the groans of the wounded all along the line, and every now
and then with the shrill screech of Ferguson's silver whistle high
above the din and confusion of battle.

At this juncture Shelby and Sevier, leading their Wataugans,
reached the summit. The firing circle pressed in. The pioneers,
leaping over the boulders, swung their tomahawks and long
knives. White handkerchiefs fluttered. Captain De Peyster,
realizing that the morale of the troops was gone, begged Ferguson to surrender. "Surrender to those damned banditti?" the
Scotsman growled. "Never!" And turning his horse downhill
he charged into the Wataugans, hacking right and left until his
sword was broken at the hilt.

One of Sevier's men, Gilleland, seeing Ferguson approach,
leveled at him, but his gun snapped. Turning to a companion,

Robert Young, he shouted: "There's Ferguson—shoot him!"

"I'll try and see what Sweet-Lips can do," muttered Young, drawing a sharp sight and discharging his rifle.

Others also fired on the commander. Ferguson slumped on his horse with six or eight wounds, one of which had penetrated his head. Two of the Wataugans seized the bridle of his frenzied horse which had plunged on with its dead master hanging from a stirrup.

The battle had lasted less than an hour. When Ferguson fell De Peyster assumed command and, advancing with a white flag, surrendered his sword to Campbell. Other white flags waved along the hilltop, yet the firing continued because many of the pioneers were ignorant of the meaning of the flags. Sevier's sixteen-year-old son, having heard that his father had fallen, kept on furiously loading and firing, until presently he saw his father ride among his troops, commanding them to cease.

Of the Americans, 28 were killed and 62 were wounded. The British losses were much greater: 225 killed, 163 wounded, and 715 taken prisoner. The Americans captured 17 wagons full of supplies.

Some of the leading officers divided Ferguson's belongings among themselves. Captain Joseph McDowell helped himself to six of the commander's china dinner plates and a small coffee cup and saucer. Shelby took Ferguson's silver whistle. Sevier took his silken sash—his commission of lieutenant colonel—and De Peyster's sword. Campbell took Ferguson's beautiful white horse because his own had been killed and he was too heavy to travel on foot. Another officer took Ferguson's pistol and still another, his large silver watch.

Surrounded by the stench of the dead, the groans of the dying, and the pitiful begging of the wounded for a little water, the victors rested that night on the battlefield.

Two pressing motives impelled them to rise with the sun. They had to hasten homeward for badly needed supplies. And, encumbered as they were with so many prisoners and wounded and wagons, they feared the arrival of Tarleton and a formidable force might catch them unaware and completely undo the recent victory. They hurriedly buried their dead. Feeling that the wagons would retard their march over the rough country, they drew them over their campfires and let them burn. Then toward noon all of them began to leave the field save Campbell who remained with a few of his men and a handful of prisoners chosen to bury their fallen comrades. The rest of the prisoners were permitted to carry their own rifles—with the flints removed from the locks. The wounded were borne away on horse-drawn litters made of tent cloth or blankets.

Ferguson's body was stripped of uniform and boots, wrapped in a cowhide and thrown into one of the ditches. After they had buried as many of the dead Tories as they could find, Campbell and his charges rejoined the marching column. The smell of flesh and blood persisted on King's Mountain for several weeks, attracting wolves from the surrounding hills. The gaunt gray beasts feasted on the corpses that had been overlooked and left unburied, and even scratched out several bodies from the shallow graves. In time they became so bold that they attacked several persons that visited the field. For a long time after the battle King's Mountain was the favorite resort of wolf hunters from both the Carolinas.

Burdened with the wounded, the Americans made slow progress on their march homeward. By the end of a week they got as far as Bickerstaff's, only forty miles from King's Mountain. All along the way settlers complained to the officers of the outrages they and their families had endured at the hands of some of Ferguson's men. Tories had robbed and burned homes, raped wives and daughters, whipped children and even killed some of the settlers.

Swayed by repeated recitations of these enormities, Campbell and his fellow officers halted at Bickerstaff's to investigate the tales. The suspected prisoners were tried and thirty-nine of them—found guilty of theft, arson, rape and murder—were condemned to be hanged. The officers found ample justification for passing these severe sentences. No court of justice, they reasoned, could punish the offenders, and to detain them as prisoners of war was to make them objects of exchange. Should such pests of society be turned loose, probably to renew their crimes? If a captured deserter is not exempt from the gallows, why should a murderer be?

That night, by the light of pine knot torches, the first group were swung up on a huge oak, three at a time, until nine had "gone to their final account." Three others were about to follow suit when suddenly an amazing spectacle unfolded before them all. One of the condemned men was Isaac Baldwin. As leader of a gang in Burke County he had often sacked homes, stripped occupants of food and all their clothing save what they were wearing, and tied them to trees and whipped them severely, leaving them helpless and bloody.

All eyes were turned on Baldwin and the two men who were to die with him. Baldwin's brother, a mere lad, approached to bid him farewell. The boy managed to cut the rope that bound his brother while he threw his arms around him and screamed and lamented. In a flash Baldwin broke through the line of soldiers that surrounded him and under cover of darkness darted away toward the forest. Dumbfounded, the soldiers let him get away; and when they realized that he had eluded more than a thousand marksmen—the best of the frontier—they admired his daring feat so much that not one of them would agree to go after him. And furthermore, the diversion created by Baldwin's daring softened their hearts. They had had enough of the executions. Sevier and Shelby, who were in charge, stopped the hangings then and there. The twenty-nine remaining condemned men were untied and pardoned.

The journey was resumed. Still fearing the arrival of Tarleton, the Americans hastened their march, crossed the Catawba River and sojourned for a few days at McDowell's estate at Quaker Meadows. All along the road small groups of the prisoners managed to escape. When the Americans arrived at the Moravian villages of Salem and Bethabara late in October they had only about two hundred prisoners left in their custody. These eventually were taken to Hillsboro and placed in prison. At the end of the Revolution they were released. Soon after they arrived in Hillsboro the Americans scattered and quietly returned to their homes.

News of the victory of King's Mountain soon spread throughout the embattled colonies. George Washington called the battle "an important object gained" and "a proof of the spirit and resources of the country." Congress praised "the spirited and military conduct" displayed by Colonel Campbell and his officers and men. General Nathanael Greene was convinced that the "militia of the back country are formidable." To General Horatio Gates the victory was "great and glorious." Thomas Jefferson wrote later that King's Mountain "was the joyful annunciation of that turn of the tide of success, which terminated the Revolutionary War with the seal of independence."

Time, however, has sobered these encomiums somewhat. Most historians no longer regard King's Mountain as a major victory. Nevertheless, it certainly had important results. It forced the British forces to withdraw from North Carolina. Cornwallis retreated ninety miles, from Charlotte to Winnesboro, South Carolina. The British commander's withdrawal broke the Tory spirit in the whole back country while it heartened the rebels who, since Gates's defeat at Camden, had been greatly depressed. A few days after King's Mountain Nathanael Greene succeeded Gates and strengthened the American cause by his bold strategy.

By dividing his army, for example, Greene compelled Cornwallis to do likewise, enabling Daniel Morgan to strike at the British under Tarleton at Cowpens and to win a brilliant victory on January 17, 1781.

About two months later Cornwallis defeated Greene at Guilford Court House in the back country of North Carolina, but it was such a costly victory that Tarleton called it "the pledge of ultimate defeat." Three days later Cornwallis retreated toward Wilmington. Since all these movements emanated from King's Mountain, that battle may be considered "the pivot of the war's revolving stage, which swung the British from their succession of victories toward the surrender of Yorktown."

Settlements

on the Cumberland

RICHARD HENDERSON WAS FAR FROM DISCOURAGED BY HIS FAIL-
ure in Transylvania. With characteristic energy and aggressive-
ness he determined to repeat on North Carolina soil the revolutionary experiment which Virginia had denied him. He firmly
believed that he and his associates had purchased millions of acres
from the Cherokee within the limits of North Carolina, for the
grant extended from the "Cumberland River, including all its
waters to the Ohio River." His first consideration, therefore, was
to determine whether the aforementioned territory lay in North
Carolina, which, unlike Virginia, had made no move to nullify
his claims. This could be done by extending the dividing line
between North Carolina and Virginia, which had been surveyed
only as far west as Steep Hill Creek.

Henderson planned to locate the settlement of his new project
at French Lick on the Cumberland—the present site of Nashville. At this place in 1776 George Rogers Clark purchased
3,000 acres from Virginia. But Henderson doubtless intended
to pay Clark the purchase money for "cain rights" should the
planned survey show that his property lay within the chartered
bounds of that colony.

Henderson chose James Robertson and John Donelson as the
leaders of the new enterprise. In this he showed the same prudence and foresight with which he had chosen Boone for the
Boonesboro project. Robertson needs no introduction. Colonel
John Donelson was admired for his marked resourcefulness and
proved stability. Born in Maryland, he had moved to Virginia

where he served as vestryman for two parishes, as surveyor, and three times as a member of the House of Burgesses. A lieutenant colonel of militia he had traveled widely on the frontier, serving successfully as a peacemaker among the Cherokee.

Henderson undoubtedly offered Robertson and Donelson large inducements for their services. Otherwise, Robertson would hardly have relinquished leadership of the Watauga settlements and Donelson would have refused to abandon the ambition to speculate in extensive western lands.

With untiring energy and efficiency Robertson recruited a party for the preliminary exploration of the country. In a letter to the governor of North Carolina he predicted that, by the beginning of March 1779, as many as two hundred men with their families would be ready to leave Long Island on the Holston for the Cumberland region. In order to provide the prospective settlers with bread on their arrival in the fall of that year, Robertson with eight white men and a Negro left for French Lick to plant corn.

The party followed buffalo paths through dense forests and canebrakes, wandering and exploring and hunting, until they arrived at their destination. There they were soon joined by another small group whose leader, Casper Mansker, claimed the land by right of settlement. They cleared the land, built rude fences and planted and cultivated corn. Then all of them, except Robertson and three other men, returned to Watauga. Robertson, believing that the settlement lay within the jurisdiction of Virginia and that, therefore, the property belonged to George Rogers Clark, went to see that officer in Vincennes. Clark agreed to accept "cain rights" should the land prove to lie in Virginia. Robertson returned to Watauga to command the migration.

Meanwhile Virginia and North Carolina had taken steps to complete the surveying of their mutual boundaries to the Mississippi River. As commissioners for this task Virginia appointed Dr. Thomas Walker and Major Daniel Smith, and North Carolina chose Richard Henderson, John Williams and William Bailey Smith. Thus Henderson, in his efforts to place the jurisdiction of the French Lick settlement in North Carolina, had, by some means known only to himself, succeeded in having members of

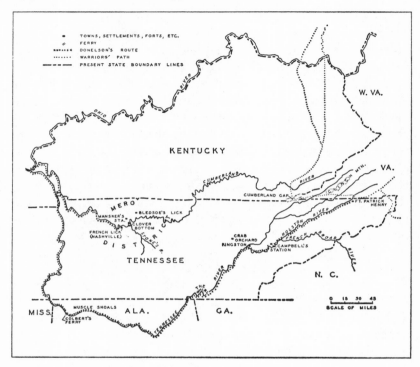

the Transylvania Company appointed as two of the North Carolina commissioners. Furthermore, the third commissioner from North Carolina had been closely associated with Henderson from the very beginning.

The five commissioners from the two colonies met at Steep Hill Creek on September 1, 1779, and began surveying toward the west. They soon disagreed, however, in regard to the observations on which the running of the line should depend. On Cumberland Mountain the North Carolina commissioners abandoned their work, but Henderson, accompanied by his brothers, Pleasant, Nathaniel, and Samuel, advanced with the Virginia commissioners to the Tennessee River. From there they repaired to Boonesboro which they reached on Christmas Day.

Henderson had two reasons for going to the settlement. He had patched up his difference with Nathaniel Hart and wished to induce him to settle on French Lick. He also hoped to persuade Hart to sell him 300 bushels of corn. Henderson succeeded in both undertakings, though extremely cold weather delayed the corn until the middle of March 1780 when it was loaded in pirogues and taken down the Kentucky under the direction of William Bailey Smith. From the falls of the river it was floated down the Ohio to the mouth of the Cumberland and thence to French Lick.

The expedition to the Cumberland country was to be made by two parties, one by land and the other by water. Robertson was to lead the land party of skilled hunters and Indian fighters through Cumberland Gap, while Donelson took their families and some older men and slaves in boats down the Tennessee and up the Ohio and the Cumberland—a veritable modern Odyssey of 985 miles which in its heroic details has few equals in the entire history of the American frontier.

Robertson conferred with Donelson and agreed to explore the country between French Lick and Muscle Shoals if circumstances permitted. Should Robertson discover a practicable overland route from Muscle Shoals to the north, he was to inform Donelson by leaving some message or sign at the head of the Shoals. Donelson was then to disembark, thereby saving himself and his charges the hardships of the rest of the long and tedious journey by water.

Robertson started first. He and his men went through Cumberland Gap, followed the Warriors' Path for some distance and then blazed a trail of their own. As they progressed slowly in deep snow and bitter cold they fell in with some families who had intended going to Kentucky but who quickly joined them. At length the party reached the Cumberland, a curving avenue of solid ice which they crossed on foot with their cattle. On its banks they started a settlement, naming it Nashboro in honor of General Francis Nash of North Carolina revolutionary fame.

On December 22, 1779, Donelson launched his expedition from Fort Patrick Henry on the Holston. It inched like a file of black insects in the heavy snowfall which early in the previous month had precipitated one of the coldest winters on record. Donelson's flagship, appropriately named the *Adventure*, carried his wife and eleven children, several slaves and the household silver engraved "JD^e." About thirty smaller boats joined him as he journeyed down the river.

The *Adventure* was a large flatboat, probably one of those constructed of heavy, squared logs known as "broadhorns." Most of its hull was roofed and its sides bulwarked. Rough bunks provided sleeping quarters for the voyagers, and a stone hearth warmed their bodies as well as their spirits in the desolate surroundings. In calm weather the boat was steered by sweeps; in rough, it was propelled by poles. It floated rapidly downstream but struggled upstream. The boats that accompanied it were of a similar type.

Donelson kept a journal of the expedition. Though written in the stilted and diffuse style of the period, clearly not the work of a practiced literary man, it is one of the most vivid and forceful documents in the pioneer literature of America. Donelson's diary provides stark evidence of the suffering a man is capable of enduring for the sake of realizing an ideal. On the first day of his voyage Donelson floated only three miles, to the mouth of Reedy Creek, where he encamped in the snow.

There the entire party remained, enduring cold and privation until in February 1780 the thawing ice enabled them to sail for Cloud's Creek. Joined by the smaller boats of the expedition, they took their departure and struck Poor Valley Shoal where they lay grounded that afternoon and succeeding night "in much distress." In the morning rising water came to their rescue. They lightened their boats enough to set them free, but in attempting to land on an island they lost some of their baggage.

Icy February melted before a rainy and windy March. Yet the travelers saw no signs of spring. Only the dark cones of cedars on the lower slopes and the pine groves among the hardwood forest relieved the drab gray that spread all around them. Impenetrable clouds hung eternally on the ranges. Patches of sage grass intruded on young trees and on clusters of brier and bramble. Skeletons of sycamore and oak waved in driving sheets of rain.

On March 2 in the continuing downpour Donelson led his fleet past the mouth of the French Broad River where the strong current damaged one of the boats, sending much of its cargo to the bottom and endangering the lives of its crew. To the rescue of the distressed went the whole fleet. The men snatched floating articles, helped dry the shivering passengers and bailed the boat in order to reload her cargo.

That afternoon Reuben Harrison went hunting and failed to return by nightfall. Early in the morning Donelson ordered a four-pounder to be fired and sent out a few men to search the woods for the missing man. Failing to find him, Donelson left Harrison's father in charge of a few boats to continue the search and proceeded downstream. There Donelson found Reuben. That afternoon they passed the Tennessee, and ten miles farther encamped on the southern shore of the river.

Since they were now in Indian country, the sailors took the precaution of posting sentinels. Blinding sheets of rain followed by dense fog had slowed some of the boats to the extent that Donelson was forced to wait until the fleet reassembled. That night one of the Negroes died in camp from frozen feet and legs.

Now the fog vanished before a stinging wind. The *Adventure* advanced steadily on the furious waves, but the smaller boats tossed like chips of wood on a ruffled lake. The wife of Ephraim Peyton was delivered of a child. Ephraim himself did not witness the blessed event for he had "gone through" by land with Robertson, leaving his wife in the care of the Jennings family.

Soon the voyagers saw Indians crowding the southern bank. With cries of "Brothers! Brothers!" the red men invited them by signs to land. At this Donelson's son and John Caffrey boarded a canoe which the colonel had in tow and began crossing the river. In midstream they were met by a canoe full of Indians under the leadership of a half-breed named Archy Coody, who advised them to return to the boat. When the young men turned their canoe Coody and his companions followed them.

Reaching the boat immediately after Caffrey and young Donelson, the half-breed and his companions sprang on board. The Indians appeared friendly. Donelson gave them presents which they accepted with much pleasure. Suddenly the voyagers saw on the shore a group of Indians, armed and painted red and black, embarking in canoes. Coody signaled his companions to return to their canoes while he and a friend remained on board and urged Donelson to move off quickly. The colonel obeyed, and not too soon, for he saw a number of armed and painted Indians running down the riverbank in an attempt to intercept the voyagers. A few miles downstream Coody and his friend left with the assurance that the white men had passed danger.

At another town near an island on the southern bank the voyagers saw Indians shouting for them to disembark. The red men, seeing the boats standing off the opposite bank, assured the travelers in a friendly manner that the south side was better for navigation. This inducement the voyagers ignored and sailed on, but before long a man named Payne was killed from ambush as his boat hugged the northern shore which Donelson presumed to be safer. The boats, however, went by so quickly that the Indians were unable to organize a real attack.

Nevertheless, the savages succeeded in picking off the last boat in the fleet. This belonged to Captain Stuart, and had on board twenty-eight persons, including Stuart, his family and friends. Some days earlier one of his children had contracted smallpox which soon spread. Donelson requested Stuart to keep behind the other boats, assuring him that he would inform him of the place of encampment each night by sounding his horn. The Indians, observing the straggling boat, fell on it and massacred all its passengers. To those ahead the yells of the Indians, the screams of the women and the crack of the guns bespoke the futility of attempting to rescue their unfortunate friends. Perhaps they found lean solace in the grim hope that the smallpox would avenge the tragedy.

The Indians pursued the voyagers along the rocky paths that paralleled the river until Cumberland Mountain removed them from sight. Now the river itself demanded their vigilance. They had arrived at the Whirl where Cumberland Mountain, jutting out on both sides, compresses the river to about half its usual width. The eddies and cross currents of the narrows, intensified by heavy rains, dashed and tossed the fleet while crews, standing on the bows and sides with poles, fended the boats off from rocks and the drifting trees that raced with them in the flood.

Before entering the narrows John Cotton had safeguarded his family by transferring it to a larger boat. To its stern was tied a large, goods-laden canoe which, dashing wildly to and fro, presently overturned. Cotton's friends immediately decided to recover the cargo. Landing at a level spot on the northern shore, Donelson and his men started to walk toward the scene of the wreck when they heard the crack of guns and the whistle of bullets. Standing immediately over them on the overhanging cliffs of the shore were Indians who were firing down on them. Hastily the would-be rescuers retreated to the boats, leaving Cotton and his crew to solve the problem as best they could.

The Indians continued to fire on the boats as they moved off, wounding four men. Young Nancy Gower seized the rudder and steered the boat until the menfolk were reorganized. When the flurry was over, Mrs. Gower noticed that Nancy's skirt was soaked with blood. The girl had suffered a shot through the thigh without uttering a sound.

By now they had passed the narrows. The river widened with a placid and gentle current. All the boats were safe save the one commanded by Jonathan Jennings, which had run into a large, partly hidden rock jutting from the northern shore. Early next morning Donelson was awakened in camp by shouts of distress far in the rear, and he soon saw Jennings and several passengers of his boat emerge from the forest.

The stragglers were cold, hungry, bedraggled. Jennings told an exciting tale. As soon as the Indians discovered his predicament they had turned a galling fire upon the boat. He ordered his wife, his nearly grown son, a friend of his son, and his Negro man and woman to throw the baggage into the river to lighten the boat so that it might be moved off the reef. While the others were thus engaged, Jennings covered them by rifle fire which, since he was an excellent marksman, always found its target. Instead of carrying out Jennings' orders, the younger men and the Negro, seized with panic, jumped from the boat. The Negro was drowned and young Jennings and his friend were wounded and captured by the Indians. Jennings' wife, aided by the Negress, succeeded in unloading the boat and shoving it off the rock; indeed, it started so suddenly that Mrs. Jennings lost her balance and almost drowned. In the confusion, Mrs. Peyton's child was killed, but the mother, though only eighteen hours from childbed, retained her health despite cold, water and exertion.

Two days later the voyagers sighted Muscle Shoals. Here, on the northern shore, they halted to look for the pre-arranged signal from Robertson. They found neither Robertson nor any signs of him. Concluding that they should continue by water, they trimmed their boats in the best manner possible and before nightfall approached the shoals. These presented a fearful spectacle. The high water, swift and broken, surged in waves and roared among piles of driftwood around the points of the islands where the currents ran in all directions. Frequently the boats touched bottom. They tossed as much as in a rough sea, and the passengers lived every moment in deadly fear of being dashed to pieces. But a kind fate protected them and within three hours the dreadful ordeal passed without accident. Humbly grateful to God, they camped for the night on the northern shore. And God rewarded their fortitude by granting them a day's respite from their troubles.

In the morning, however, the Indians fired on two boats near the shore, slightly wounding five of the crewmen. That night the voyagers encamped near the mouth of a creek. Hardly had they built their fires and lain down to rest than the frenzied barking of dogs brought them to their feet. Thinking that they were about to be attacked, they hastily broke camp, took to their boats and fell down the river about a mile where they encamped again. In the morning Donelson persuaded his son John and Caffrey to return to the earlier camp in a canoe and recover the utensils abandoned in their retreat. They found a Negro whom they had left behind still asleep by the ashes of a campfire.

The wayfarers moved peacefully on the now gentle stream to the junction of the Tennessee and the Ohio rivers. The sight gladdened their hearts for they knew that much of their voyage lay behind them. They rejoiced, too, at the passing of cold weather. Spring at last was definitely in the air. Here and there in the sheltered places beyond the canebrakes and gaunt white sycamores on the shores, delicate green began to appear on dogwood and maple and crab apple. But the pioneers rejoiced too soon. Sailing up the Ohio toward the Cumberland they found the river very high. Like chips of wood in water from a broken dam, the lumbering boats were dashed back and forth by the rapid currents. Moreover, the crews were famished and fatigued. Some of them, refusing to ascend the river, floated down the Mississippi to Natchez, and others—among them Donelson's daughter and husband—made for the Illinois country.

Donelson grimly pursued his course, taking more than four days to pole, shove, tow and otherwise work the boats up the Ohio to the Cumberland. His efforts were rewarded. His passengers found the Cumberland gentle, and its banks generously provided them with poke salad, buffalo and wild swan which proved "very delicious."

In better spirits they ascended the river until on the last day of March they met Henderson and rejoiced. Henderson regaled the settlers with an account of his own travels and cheered them by telling them of the corn he had bought from Hart. Worn by the long voyage and the privations they had endured, they yet went on in exultant mood. On April 23 they reached the first settlement on the north side of the river, a mile and a half below the lick called Eaton's Station. Next day they arrived at French Lick and climbed to the cluster of cabins Robertson and his company had built. The long, hard voyage was ended at last. Out of the 167 who had begun the expedition 23 had lost their lives either in the river or at the hands of Indians. Nine bore the marks of bullet wounds. All thought themselves fortunate for having completed the expedition.

In the ensuing days the vast Cumberland Valley clamored with human activity. All around in the deep forest rose cabins, stockades and stockhouses with gardens and yards surrounded by stout palings. Gradually eight separate settlements or "stations" appeared, each named, in typical pioneer fashion, after the original settler or some natural object: a river, a ford or a hill.

On a limestone bluff covered with cedars, which became the center of the community, rose the little stockaded village of Nashboro. The other stations, scattered along both sides of the river, were hidden from one another by stretches of cane that covered the intervening ground.

At Clover Bottom on Stone's River, about seven miles from the village on the bluff, John Donelson encamped with his large family, cleared several acres and planted corn and cotton. Two months later rising water forced the Donelsons to take refuge in Casper Mansker's blockhouse ten miles away where they remained until at the end of the summer the receding river permitted them to return to their clearing. One day Indians attacked Donelson and some of his slaves while they were gathering in the corn and cotton that had survived the flood. Two of the slaves were killed. Perceiving the difficulty of obtaining a clear title to his grant, Donelson soon left the Cumberland region and joined his son in Kentucky. His neighbor, Richard Henderson, remained to sell lands under the deed he and his associates had secured from the Cherokee in the Treaty of Watauga five years before.

More than any other man in the community Henderson realized the numerous problems which confronted the settlers. They must be protected from attack by Indians and by whites as well. They must move under just laws. They must mold their habits to Christian precepts for their own benefit. Henderson had no desire to repeat the mistake he had made in Transylvania by attempting to establish another independent colony. Indeed, he enlisted Robertson's advice in forming a government for the new settlements. Both men sought a government of the settlers, by the settlers and for the settlers, somewhat akin to the one Robertson had formed in the Watauga region.

Henderson requested the settlers of the eight stations to elect delegates to an assembly. On May 1, 1780, this body met at Nashboro and entered into an agreement of government known as the Cumberland Compact. Robertson's influence in the document is seen from the very beginning:

That the well-being of this country entirely depends, under Divine Providence, on unanimity of sentiment and concurrences in measures, and as clashing interests and opinions, without being under some restraint, will most certainly produce confusion, discord, and almost certain ruin, so we think it our duty to associate, and hereby form ourselves into one society for the benefit of present and future settlers, and until the full and proper exercise of the laws of our country can be in use, and the powers of government exerted among us: *we do most solemnly and sacredly declare* and promise each other, that we will faithfully and punctually adhere to, perform, and abide by this our Association, and at all times, if need be, compel, by our united force, a due obedience to these our rules and regulations.

Thirteen days later the male settlers, 256 in number, ratified the work of the delegates and signed the Compact. By so doing, they guaranteed one another their rights to the land, their personal security against wrongdoers and their faith in the integrity of the community.

The Compact provided that the affairs of the community be administered by a committee of twelve judges or triers to be elected by voters over twenty-one years of age. Three of the judges were to come from Nashboro, two from Mansker's, two from Bledsoe's and one from each of the other five stations. If the people should grow dissatisfied with their judges

they may call a new election in any of the said stations, and elect others in their stead, having due respect to the number now agreed to be elected at each station, which persons so to be chosen shall have the same power with those in whose room or place they shall be chosen to act.

The judges were to serve without salaries, but the Clerk of the Court was permitted to accept small fees, "just enough to pay for the pens, ink, and paper, all of them scarce commodities."

The Compact established a land office over which the court had complete jurisdiction in all cases of conflict over land titles. A good part of the Compact was devoted to the rules of the land office. In the case of a land dispute, a majority of the twelve judges could give a binding decision which was to be recorded in the land office by the entry taker, an official appointed by Henderson. All future marked or improved claims and all improvements not registered with the entry taker within twenty days after the Compact had been formed were declared null and void. Any entry taker found guilty of fraud in office was to be removed.

In the absence of any constituted authority of government, the judges were to consider themselves a "proper court" for the recovery of debt or damage. In cases of a controversy involving less than $300, three judges sufficed; but in those involving more than that sum, appeal could be had in a court consisting of as many as nine judges whose decision would be final.

The court, of which Robertson was elected chairman, enjoyed large powers. It levied taxes and performed marriages, passed sentences and awarded contracts, granted letters of administration on estates of deceased persons and punished disturbers of the peace and those who committed capital crimes—provided it refrained from sentencing death or bodily harm. Perpetrators of crimes considered dangerous to the state were to stand trial in the regular courts of North Carolina. Thus the Compact acknowledged the legal jurisdiction of North Carolina over the region and promised obedience to her constitution and laws.

Because of the Indian depredations, the Compact established a militia composed of officers and men from the various settlements. Robertson was chosen colonel. The officers had the power to call out the militia in time of need, to punish shirkers and deserters and to impress horses for warfare. The settlers of the stations were to pay proportionate damages—as determined by the court—for those horses which were injured.

Two weeks later the Compact was amended. The change provided that all males over sixteen years old and able to perform military service could enter lands, a policy which naturally increased sales. The amendment also provided that the entry taker would receive twelve dollars for each entry, and that the entry book would be open to the judges at all times.

Mindful of his disappointment in Virginia, Henderson took pains to incorporate into the Compact provision for a petition addressed to Congress "giving the fullest assurance of fidelity and attachment to the interest of the Country, and obedience to the laws and Constitution thereof." He assured Congress that "we do not desire to be exempt from the rateable share of the public expense of the present War or other contigent charges of government."

The Compact declared that it was designed as a "temporary method of restraining the licentious" and that the Cumberland settlers regarded themselves as citizens of North Carolina. It asked the mother state to extend them immediate protection by making them a separate county. The document admirably met the needs of the backwoodsmen who were too shrewd and too practical to attempt to live by an untried government. Familiar with the county system, they modified it to fit their needs.

Henderson stayed in the settlements only a short time. Learning that the North Carolina assembly disputed his land claim, he went to defend it before that body. Early in 1782 the assembly declared that his claim to the Cherokee cession was illegal. As compensation for his expense, trouble and risks, however, it granted him 200,000 acres in Powell's Valley. This tract proved to be "mountainous barren land, altogether unfit for cultivation," and Henderson never surveyed it. Later he settled on a small grant which Virginia gave him in Kentucky where he established the present city that bears his name.

Leadership of the Cumberland settlements passed to Robertson, who in the next seven years defended them against Indian attacks, preserved law and order and persuaded the settlers to remain until success should crown their perseverance.

The attacks began with alarming suddenness in April 1780, when a group of Chickasaw massacred Jonathan Jennings and one of Robertson's sons, killed pigs and cows and drove off the horses. Thereafter the Chickasaw murdered on farms, by stockades, at licks and in the forests, wherever they could lure their victims by gobbling like turkeys or growling like bears. And the settlers responded pitifully. Gradually they deserted stockade and cabin until by midsummer all the eight settlements save Nashboro and Freeland's stood lifeless.

The exodus shook, but never enfeebled, Robertson's tenacity. The death of his son, the spasmodic Indian attacks and the panic of the settlers only strengthened his resolve to remain in Nashboro and see that settlement pull through its crisis and enjoy the glory it deserved. He was everywhere—encouraging, consoling, sympathizing. And before long the remaining settlers rose to receive the comfort of his heartening words. Abandoning the futility of trying to live by their stock and crops, they took to the woods where their expert marksmanship quickly rewarded them with an abundance of game.

During the winter one party of hunters killed over a hundred bears, seventy-five buffaloes and eighty-seven deer. Such prodigalities soon exhausted their ammunition. To overcome this emergency Robertson announced that he would fetch the needed ammunition from Kentucky. Passing fearlessly across an endless desert of snow and through desolate, Indian-infested country, he purchased the powder and began to retrace his journey. On the evening of January 15, 1781, he reached Freeland's. The settlers received him joyfully, listened around a late supper table to the details of his journey and then went to bed without taking the precaution of posting sentinels.

They all slept soundly except Robertson, who tossed suspiciously. A late moon threw a silvery gloss over stockhouses and stockade. Suddenly Robertson heard the heavy chain of a gate clang, heard figures slipping across the yard, heard them stealing around the heavy timber pickets of the palisades. "Indians!" he shouted, springing from his bed and firing his gun into the darkness. Thus aroused from sleep, his companions flashed their rifles through the merlons, scaring off the enemy. Robertson killed one of the Indians. The Indians killed two settlers and wounded two others.

The next day a formidable number of Indians attacked the fort in Nashboro. For several days they hovered like vultures over the settlement, burning cabins and fences, driving off cattle and picking off those men, women and children who for one reason or another ventured outside the walls. Finally they set fire to the fort and fell back into the forest. While one group of settlers put out the fire, another galloped after the red men, overtook them at a creek and engaged them in a duel of musketry.

Meanwhile a larger group of Indians, concealed in underbrush and behind cedars, prepared for an assault on the fort in the rear of the combatants. The settlers, becoming aware of this maneuver, saw their only chance lay in forcing their way back to the fort through their numerically superior enemies. This was a desperate venture, for the settlers had discharged their guns and had no time to reload them. But fate came to their rescue in the form of a freakish incident. Their bewildered horses, running back to the fort, passed a group of the Indians who pursued them to make them their own.

Meanwhile the settlers in the fort, sensing what was happening, made preparations of defense while the women leveled guns through the merlons or lifted axes at the gate. Even the dogs of the fort had their day. These stout, powerfully built animals—some hounds, some watchdogs and all accustomed to fighting bear and buffalo—saw the line of Indians drawn up between the fort and their masters and instantly sensed their duty. Furiously they attacked the Indians, scattering them in all directions.

Availing themselves of the opportunity this circumstance provided, the settlers ran through the lines and gained the fort. Five of the white men were killed and two were wounded. Another man fell with a broken thigh near the gate; he rose, reloaded his gun and fired as he attempted to run, thereby saving his scalp.

Under the walls an Indian overtook a settler and began to whack him on the shoulder with his gun while he pulled the trigger. The Indian's bullet missed—but the settler's did not. The Indians, seeing that the gates were closed and the settlers ready, abandoned their effort to capture the fort. They had taken five scalps and a number of horses, and the whites had taken two scalps and wounded a number of their enemies.

Thereafter the Indians made only small raids against the fort. These, however, sufficed to prevent planting corn. The settlers' days were spent in endless vigilance. When one drank from a spring, another stood by with rifle ready to protect him against a lurking Indian. When four or five assembled at a place where business required their presence, they held their guns in their hands with their backs turned to one another—one or more facing each direction—ready for the enemy.

Depression seized some of them; they began to talk of deserting the settlements; they dreamed of safer homes in Kentucky or on the Holston. Robertson pertinaciously resisted the settlers' mutinous longing. He pointed out to them the impossibility of reaching Kentucky: how were they to elude the Indians who, in large numbers, held all the roads and passages leading to that region? How were they to reach the Holston? They might, he said, go down on the river to Illinois, but even this route presented insurmountable obstacles. How were they to come by the wood with which to build their boats? Every day Indians lay concealed in shrubs and behind cedars, ready to pick them off the moment they appeared in the forest. Why should they risk danger and death when they were so near to possessing, if they but persisted a little longer, this fine country which God had sent them to settle? Soon veterans would join them from the older settlements; surely they could defend and support themselves until help could arrive.

Robertson's encouraging words prevailed. The settlers' anxieties diminished. They thought less and less of abandoning the settlements. They resolved to remain on the ground which their recollection of past dangers, of enduring toil and of conquered difficulties, had made precious.

A kinder day rewarded their forbearance. At the end of 1781 they learned of Cornwallis' surrender. As Robertson had anticipated, this put an end to the Indian attacks for the present and at the same time brought an inflow of veterans, both officers and men, seeking the bounty lands which the North Carolina assembly reserved for them when in 1782 it converted the Cumberland country into a military district.

In the fall of the following year the assembly provided them with a local government by creating Davidson County, named in honor of the North Carolinian hero General William Lee Davidson, who lost his life at Cowan's Ford while resisting the advance of British troops.

Each veteran claimant was given his preference of the land not already pre-empted by the original settlers of the country. A private received 640 acres; a noncommissioned officer, 1,000; a subaltern, 2,160; a captain, 3,840; a colonel, 7,200; a brigadier, 12,000; a chaplain, 7,200; a surgeon, 4,800; and a surgeon's mate, 2,560.

The three commissioners sent out to apportion the district, Absalom Tatum, Anthony Bledsoe and Isaac Shelby, were accompanied by 100 guardsmen whose presence encouraged the settlers and strengthened the defense of the country. The veterans gradually restored the old stations and established new, and built corn mills and "hominy pounders" on the banks of some of the streams.

Eager for justice between man and man, Robertson meanwhile had reorganized the committee of judges which had not met for two years. At his request the settlements elected ten men, with Robertson as chairman and colonel of the militia. For the next seven months the ten judges, meeting in Nashboro, ruled the settlements with sovereign power. The records of the court have been preserved and provide an illuminating picture of some of the vicissitudes of life in the wilderness.

At its first session, which began on January 7, 1783, the court issued an attachment against the estate of one John Sadler, who had absconded after giving a bad note in "payment of two good cows and heifer with calf." Humphrey Hogan sued one of his neighbors for stealing a kettle. The court awarded the kettle to Humphrey and ordered the defendant and his mother-in-law, who was involved in the theft, to pay the cost of the suit. In another case a settler sought to secure judgment for cattle that he had won "in gaming at cards," but the court judged "the debt illegal" and dismissed the suit.

One of the court's regulations followed an economic principle of doubtful value. Some enterprising settlers, taking advantage of the fact that the community had drunk nothing but water for months, brought in casks of whisky and sold them at an enormous profit. Whereupon the court passed a decree forbidding further profiteering by persons bringing in liquors from "foreign ports" and carrying away the money to the consequent "impoverishment of this infant settlement." The decree required such persons to give bond to charge not more than one silver dollar "for one quart of good, sound, merchantable liquor." Several months later the court set the price at one silver dollar per gallon.

In 1784 the North Carolina assembly gave Nashboro the status of a town and changed its name to Nashville. The assembly also appointed a board of commissioners to act as governors of the town, to survey it and to dispose of the lots on which it stood. Under the commissioners' watchful eyes a public square gradually took shape on the crest of the limestone bluff that faced the river. And on the square rose a courthouse of hewn logs, furnished with "benches, bar, and table for the use of the Court" and a jail "of square hewn logs, a foot square, both with floor and loft, except the same shall be built on a rock."

The old committee of judges was abolished, and the judges of Davidson County, including Robertson, took their oaths of office. The new seat of justice grew rapidly. Before long the stockade of the old fort had to be torn down. But when some stray Cherokee knifed their way into the town, depriving it of several of its solid citizens and members of their families, the residents threw up a stronger and higher stockade around their dwellings. While the town caught its breath it played host to a small group of well-to-do Easterners. They liked Nashville and decided to stay. Soon frame houses sprang up proudly here and there among the thirty original log cabins, presaging the passing of Nashville from a crude frontier town to the elegant city of a later age.

No less auspicious than its physical origin were Nashville's intellectual beginnings. Robertson, perhaps because he had learned his letters and how to spell in mature years, had a profound respect for knowledge. He persuaded the Reverend Thomas B. Craighead, a graduate of Princeton, to settle in the Cumberland country and promote education. Craighead put up at Haysboro, six miles northeast of Nashville, where he built Spring Hill, a rough stone building which served as a church as well as a school.

The North Carolina assembly was so impressed by Craighead's pedagogical zeal that it passed an act in 1786 establishing Davidson Academy for boys in his meeting house, appointing him its president and naming nine other men, including Robertson, as trustees. The academy was exempt from taxation for 99 years and was supported by a grant of 240 acres and the tolls of the local ferry. Tuition was "four pounds per annum, hard money or its equivalent." Because of the scarcity of ready cash the fees were usually paid in corn.

The curriculum of Davidson Academy was designed to furnish the students with the practical knowledge needed to earn a good living without denying them the cultural background required to lead a good life. Grammar, spelling, arithmetic and geography strove with such literary masters as Terence, Sallust, Lucian, Erasmus, Virgil, Xenophon and Aesop. After 1787 the teachers tried to instill in their charges a feeling for the responsibilities of being Americans by requiring them to learn the new Constitution of the United States.

Elected as one of the two representatives from Davidson County, Robertson in 1785 prevailed on the assembly to provide some kind of protection against the almost incessant Indian attacks on the Cumberland settlements. Accordingly, 300 soldiers were assembled at the lower end of Clinch Mountain with instructions to build from that point to Nashville a road wide enough for the passage of wagons and carts. From time to time the soldiers were to be marched to the Cumberland country and stationed at those places in numbers which would induce the Indians to stop their attacks. For this endeavor the commanding officer was invested with the authority to use the soldiers in whatever capacity he saw fit.

By the end of the year the road was completed. It provided a much shorter route to the Cumberland country than the original one through the wilderness of Kentucky. So many "movers" settled in the unclaimed sections that in the fall of 1786 the North Carolina assembly was obliged to provide them with a local government by creating from a portion of Davidson a new county, Sumner, named in honor of another North Carolinian hero, General Jethro Sumner.

The 300 soldiers had been so busy guarding the settlements that they failed to cut a road adequate to serve the vast migration. The assembly, therefore, began a wider and more level road. This, completed in September 1788 and called the Nashville Road, ran from Campbell's Station, a few miles west of Knoxville, to present Kingston, then to Crab Orchard and the upper Cumberland and finally down to Bledsoe's Lick and Nashville.

In the first company to move west on the new road were a young lawyer named Andrew Jackson and his friend, John McNairy, who had recently been appointed judge of the Supreme Court in the Cumberland country. One night an incident occurred which disclosed Jackson's eminent fitness for pioneer life. While he and his party were sleeping by a fire a group of Indians, hooting like owls, surrounded them. Jackson awoke. Having the sensitive ears of an experienced frontier scout, he discerned that this was not the hooting of owls but its imitation. He aroused his companions and advised them to move on quickly and quietly. They did so—just in time to escape the scalping knives that brought down four hunters on the spot. A few days later Jackson, after shooting a panther and tomahawking its cub to prevent their killing a colt, reached Nashville and plunged into the flamboyant career of lawyer, judge, statesman and soldier that eventually took him to the White House.

Nashville now and then talked about a victory that Robertson had won over the Indians in the previous summer. In the past three years the Cherokee and some Creeks had conducted many small raids in the courses of which scores of Cumberland settlers had been killed. Then, in May 1787, a handful of Cherokee tomahawked Robertson's brother, Mark, in broad daylight as he was walking home. Full of grief and anger, James Robertson resolved to avenge his brother's death and, at the same time, attempt to stop the Indian depredations.

Robertson's suspicions fell on some Creek and Cherokee braves living in a town on Coldwater Creek, a tributary of the Tennessee near Muscle Shoals and at the present site of Tuscumbia, Alabama. To this place came French traders from the Illinois or Wabash country, encouraging the Indians in their warfare against the Cumberland settlers and at times even providing them with guns and ammunition. Early in June Robertson gathered 120 men and, guided through the forest by two Chickasaw, one of whom was a chief named Toka, marched toward the town. Another force, under the direction of Captain David Hay, started at the same time by water but fell into an ambush and returned.

Pushing briskly across dense cane country, Robertson and his men soon heard the Tennessee as it roared over the falls. For a day they concealed themselves under the cane, awaiting a favorable time for crossing. In the night Edmond Jennings, the fearless son of the unfortunate Jonathan Jennings, and Joshua Thomas, his inseparable companion, swam across the river and returned with a big canoe that had been tied to a stick driven into the bank. In the morning forty of Robertson's men piled into the canoe and after stopping its leaks with shirts and linn bark crossed the Tennessee, while the remaining troops swam over with the horses.

After drying their clothes and equipment the men marched five or six miles and swooped down into the town which lay in a ravine surrounded by cornfields. The surprised Indians and their French guests fled to their canoes, closely pursued by shooting and yelling white men. Three braves, three French traders and a white woman fell dead on the bank of the river. The principal traders and five or six other Frenchmen, all wounded, surrendered. By now many of the Indians were paddling furiously away from the bank, only to jump into the river to seek safety from the bullets that whizzed all around them. Twenty-six died from wounds or drowning.

Robertson's men quickly occupied the town and in the stores seized taffia, sugar, coffee, cloth, blankets, Indian wares of all sorts, salt, shot, Indian paints, knives, powder, tomahawks, tobacco and other articles suitable to Indian commerce. Then they buried the white men and woman they had killed, destroyed the domestic animals and burned the town to the ground. The two Chickasaw, presented with their portion of the booty, returned home. The remaining goods and the prisoners were put into three or four canoes and taken under guard down the Tennessee, and Robertson with the remainder of his men rode along its bank. At Colbert's Ferry the two parties joined and proceeded to Nashville where the prisoners were released. The booty was sold at Eaton's Station and the proceeds divided among the troops.

The expedition involved Robertson in a difficulty with the nation which had been our stanch ally in the Revolution. He therefore wrote to a French functionary living in the Illinois country, explaining the causes and motives which had led him to undertake the campaign. If innocent people, whether Frenchmen or Indians, had suffered in the attack, he said, they had nobody to blame but themselves. They were judged by the company they kept. His men unfortunately were unable to distinguish between the good and the bad. Robertson concluded his letter by warning the French that their traders would "render themselves very insecure" if they continued to furnish the Cherokee with weapons. At the same time he warned the Cherokee that a war would "compel ous to retaliate, which will be a grate pridegedes [prejudice] to your nation." "He did not spell well," says Roosevelt, "but his meaning was plain, and his hand was known to be heavy."

The Indians paid Robertson's warning no heed. In the fall of 1787 Cherokee and Creeks joined in a piratical attack on some boats from Louisville and the Illinois settlements, killing their crews. Robertson wrote that, in the course of the year, the Creeks also killed forty-one settlers and that their depredations had actually stopped business as well as immigration.

But adversity only strengthened Robertson's resolve to get relief for his people. He realized now that they could hope for effective help from neither their neighbors in Kentucky—whom, in desperation, they had hoped to join politically—nor North Carolina. Congress was their only refuge, but even Congress could do nothing for them in this year of change from confederation to Federal union.

Robertson saw clearly that, ironically, immediate relief could come only from the settlers' enemies—from the Creeks themselves or from Spain, the instigator of the attacks. This realization impelled Robertson to employ, with the consent of leading Cumberland settlers, an artifice, a subterfuge expressive of his realism and political acumen. The stratagem, says Arthur Preston Whitaker, aimed "to serve simultaneously as a threat and as a promise. As a threat to reluctant North Carolina, it would secure a cession of that state's western territory to Congress. As a promise to Spain, it would obtain from the Spanish governor of Louisiana commercial concessions and, above all, relief from Indian attacks."

In pursuance of his scheme Robertson, with the assistance of two other influential Cumberland settlers, Anthony Bledsoe and Brigadier General Daniel Smith, began to correspond with Governor Samuel Johnston of North Carolina, with Governor Estéban Miró of Louisiana and with the unscrupulous and shrewd half-breed chief of the Creeks, Alexander McGillivray, who in 1784 had put his people under the protection of Spain. This correspondence has aroused a great deal of suspicion among some superficial and unimaginative scholars and writers who, more the bane than the boon of history, have seen in it evidence of a design on the part of Robertson and the Cumberland settlers to place the region under the domination of Spain.

A careful study of the so-called Spanish conspiracy and an understanding of the situation and the character of the settlers involved, however, shows that neither Robertson nor any of the Cumberland settlers had any intention of turning traitors. Robertson was a practical man who sought only such practical ends as the protection of life and property. By sending veiled threats to North Carolina he hoped to get that state to cede her western lands to Congress, while by making promises to Spain he simply hoped to find out what she was willing to do for the Cumberland settlers in regard to such vital issues as trade, land and the Indian attacks.

The typically American frontier folk would scarcely have given serious consideration to repudiating their Protestant faiths and their even more sacred individualism in return for the questionable protection of a Catholic and completely foreign nation. And Spain, for her part, wanted only submissive subjects. She looked with intense suspicion on all Americans whom, with their heretical notions of equality and freedom, she regarded as good only to weaken and perhaps to defeat her traditional concepts of government.

Robertson, with the assistance of Bledsoe, initiated his scheme in January 1788 with a letter to Governor Johnston. Obliquely charging Spain with encouraging the Indian attacks, the correspondents urged Johnston to appeal to Congress and especially to make representations to Don Diego de Gardoqui, Spanish diplomatic representative in New York, to exert his influence with McGillivray to stop the Indian depredations.

Johnston, being a loyal son of North Carolina, felt little sympathy for the frontiersmen, but he transmitted the letter along with other correspondence to Dr. James White, Superintendent of Indian Affairs for the Southern Department, with the conciliatory comment: "It is not my opinion that the Court of Madrid or any other officers have the least share in abetting the grievances they (the Gentlemen beyond the Mountains) complain of." Dr. White referred the matter to Gardoqui, who on April 18 replied to Robertson as follows:

The news has caused me great sorrow, but I am extremely surprised to know that there is a suspicion that the good government of Spain is encouraging these acts of barbarity. Very different are the orders of His Majesty, to our way of thinking, and it may be asserted that, just as the King is a friend of the United States in general, so also he takes pleasure in giving every evidence of good will and generosity to the region of the West in particular, whenever occasion is offered.

On receiving this denial that Spain had instigated the Indian attacks, Robertson hastened to appeal to McGillivray himself. In April he sent two trusty messengers to the chief with a letter urging him to establish peace between the Creeks and the Cumberland settlers. McGillivray replied:

Agreeably to your request, I will be Explicit and Candid in my answer to yours, and will not deny that my Nation had waged war against your Country for several years past, but that we had no motives of revenge, nor did it proceed from any sense of Injurys Sustained from your people, but being warmly attached to the British, and being under their Influence, our operations were directed by them against you in common with other Americans.

Despite this serene effrontery, McGillivray generously granted the Cumberland settlers an armistice pending the meeting of the Creek assembly.

At this stage of the intrigue Andrew Jackson in a letter to Brigadier General Daniel Smith provided evidence that the Cumberland people were neither resentful toward the United States nor devoted to Spain but simply anxious to try anything that might bring them relief from Indian attacks. Early in 1789 Jackson met André Fagot, a militia captain in the Spanish service, stationed in the Illinois country, who wanted to trade with the Cumberland region.

Jackson saw in this trade the possibility of securing a lasting peace with the Indians. Writing to Smith, he introduced Fagot and asked him to write to Miró requesting a commerical treaty. Fagot was to deliver the letter and request a permit to trade with the Cumberland people. Fagot, by misrepresenting himself as a close kinsman of Miró, made Jackson feel confident that the permit would be granted without difficulty. "Then," continued Jackson, "he will show the propriety of having peace with the Indians for . . . the benefit . . . of the trade . . . and also show the governor the respect this country honors him with."

Here Jackson was alluding to the fact that in the previous August Robertson had requested and received permission from the North Carolina assembly, of which he was again a member, to change the name of the Cumberland country from Western District to District of Miró. The Cumberland leaders, knowing no Spanish, spelled the name as it sounded to them, "Mero," and it thus appeared in their letters and official documents. The motive for bestowing the honor on Miró is easily surmised. Robertson hoped that the flattered governor would reciprocate by persuading McGillivray to call off the new attacks which the Creek assembly had recently sanctioned. In this he was to be disappointed.

Jackson's proposals were adopted. In writing his letter to Miró, Smith introduced Fagot as a man in whom the Cumberland people "have very great confidence . . . and beg leave to refer your excellency to him for a particular intelligence. We have honored our district with your Excellency's name . . . and I should look upon myself as much honored by a Correspondence from you." The "particular intelligence" to which Smith referred was given verbally: in September the Cumberland settlers were to hold a convention to secure a separation from North Carolina. This done, they were to send delegates to New Orleans to arrange a union with Spain.

To this important information Miró replied as follows: "His Excellency Dan.[1] Smith Brig.[r] gral & Commander of Miro District &ca, &ca, &ca. I have had the greatest satisfaction in the honour I received in being acquainted that the Inhabitants of your District have distinguish[ed] my name . . . for the denomination of that country." This, he continued, impelled him to give any number of good wishes for their prosperity. And, of course, he "anxiously expected the consequences of the operation you are to transact in September."

When, on the first day of the month, the delegates convened, their purpose was simply and clearly expressed in resolutions to urge North Carolina by every possible means to cede her western lands to Congress. No motion whatever was made to choose delegates to negotiate a union with Spain, for no such union was ever contemplated. On September 2 Robertson wrote to Miró, informing him that the convention had been held and that the Cumberland people had agreed to seek a separation from the mother state. He also stated that his people, though "unprotected" and though they desired "a more interesting Connection," would remain "obedient to the new Congress of the United States. . . . The United States afford us no protection. The district of Mero is daily plundered and the inhabitants murdered by the Creeks, and Cherokee, unprovoked."

In one of his letters to Robertson, Miró had extended him an invitation to settle in Spanish territory. To this invitation Robertson now replied: "For my own part, I conceive highly of the advantages of your Government. But my estate, here, is such that I could not flatter myself to equal it by removeing [sic] to anypart; our lands Satisfying my utmost wishes, and being infinitely before anything I have seen elsewhere."

The purport of this letter, if it is read objectively, is unmistakably clear. The Cumberland people, while expressing dissatisfaction with the United States for failing to provide them with effective protection against Indian attacks, still had no intention of repudiating her for Spain. That Spanish and frontier principles were irreconcilable is indicated by Robertson's rejection of Miró's invitation. Neither side had any intention to meet the needs of the other. Robertson and Smith were not surprised, therefore, at Miró's noncommital replies to their letters. He promised them neither to use his influence to stop the Indian attacks nor to grant Fagot the trade permit that Jackson had sought for him in the hope of securing a lasting peace with the Indians.

As for the Cumberland settlers, they knew the Spanish government too well to hope that Miró would extend them the privileges of local government and religious freedom—privileges which they as Americans would have expected had they entertained any notion of joining a foreign power. They remained constant in their objective: to urge North Carolina to cede her western lands to Congress which, after all, remained their ultimate refuge.

The truth of this supposition is borne out in a letter which Robertson addressed to Governor Johnston on the same day that he wrote to Miró. The Indian depredations, he said, were driving many of the people to seek safety under a friendly foreign power.

I wish your Excellency to be informed that there is a Colonel [Robert] Stark who openly confessed a desire to take the inhabitants into the Spanish dominions as subjects to that power, and many people are upon the point of going down, were it not for the representations of people just from there, particularly Dr. White, who had been of general service in dissuading people from that country and government. . . . [I wish] to be informed if there are no legal means to prevent Colonel Stark and others from debauching our citizens to emigrate in so public a manner.

The purpose of this letter is obvious. Robertson is saying that the people of the Cumberland, "being without hope of securing protection from North Carolina, are in a dangerous mood, but a cession of this region to Congress will probably quiet their minds."

The settlers had not long to wait. In December 1789 the North Carolina assembly at last ceded her western country to Congress, which accepted it and converted it into the Southwest Territory.

Franklin,
the Lost State

ON RETURNING HOME FROM KING'S MOUNTAIN IN THE FALL OF
1780, John Sevier found himself a popular hero. The Wataugans
soon began to regard him as their leader now that Robertson
had moved to the Cumberland country. They had pressing
need of Sevier's soldierly gifts and cool courage. In his absence
the Cherokee, learning that the Wataugans lacked necessary
protection, had again invaded the settlements, burning and scalping the citizens and stealing a considerable number of horses.
The triumphant veterans of King's Mountain had returned in
time.

Sevier quickly summoned the militia of Washington County
for an expedition against the Cherokee overhill towns. The settlers responded with alacrity. All the men loved "Chucky
Jack," as they called Sevier, because in 1778 he had settled on
the Nolichucky River. He had qualities which pioneers prized
as highly as they did their property and freedom. He was affable,
gracious and understanding; he carried a cool head on dauntless
shoulders. He "gave his commands as to equals, and, because
these orders appealed to his men as being wise and practical, they
gave unquestioned obedience." In fighting he enjoyed his best
ease, for he was an expert marksman and a skillful horseman:
his shot rarely missed its target and his white race mare, when
she plunged up a steep hill, was as surefooted as a mountain goat.
Roosevelt vividly describes Sevier's tactics in Indian fighting:

Much of his success was due to his adroit use of scouts or spies.
He always chose for these the best woodsmen of the district,
men who could endure as much, see as much, and pass through

the woods as silently, as the red men themselves. By keeping these scouts well ahead of him, he learned accurately where the war parties were. In the attack itself he invariably used mounted riflemen, men skilled in forest warfare, who rode tough little horses, on which they galloped at speed through the forest.

On the battlefield the frontier fighters would dismount, shelter themselves carefully behind the trunks of trees, and dispose in the figure of a half-moon, the favorite Indian formation. Sevier would then send out a handful of men to lure the Indians on by firing on them and scampering back to their comrades.

Such were the tactics he employed when in December 1780 he marched against the Cherokee at Boyd's Creek, beyond the French Broad River. When the redskins rushed toward them, he and his men, 170 strong, popped from their hiding places in the half-moon formation. The right horn, led by Major Jesse Walton, swung in briskly; but the left horn, under Major Jonathan Tipton, an indifferent officer, was so slow that it left an open space on the field.

The Indians, bewildered by the unexpected appearance of the dreaded Sevier and his men, rushed past them, and those who were not killed or wounded escaped in a swamp which their pursuers found impassable for horses. Sevier, on his swift white mare, chased a brave who, seeing that he was about to be run down, turned and fired at him. The bullet grazed Sevier's queue without doing any other injury. Sevier spurred his mare and, having already emptied his pistols, attempted to kill the brave with his sword. The brave parried the keen thrusts with empty gun in a contest that seemed to be going against Sevier until one of his men, a dead shot, decided it in his favor.

The Wataugans had picked off twenty-eight Indians and had taken most of their weapons and all their provisions—without losing a man. In some of the bundles Sevier found proclamations from Sir Henry Clinton and from other British officers. Despite his success, Sevier could not refrain from bantering the delinquent Tipton for spoiling his chance of winning a resounding victory. The major was a younger brother of Colonel John Tipton, whom we shall presently meet. This incident may have

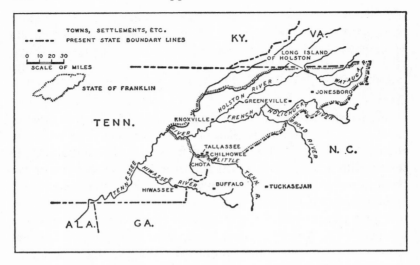

been the origin of the feud that arose between Colonel John Tipton and Sevier.

Sevier returned to the French Broad where, on an island, General Arthur Campbell and Major Joseph Martin augmented his troops by some four hundred men. The next day the entire force marched to the Little Tennessee, crossed it, swooped down on the important town of Chota, which the Cherokee had abandoned, and reduced it to ashes. From the surrounding hills where they had taken refuge, the Indians, half frightened, half enraged, watched their beloved homes crumble and disappear in smoke and flame. Up and down the Little Tennessee and then along the Hiwassee the scourge in buckskin repeated his dreadful performance again and again. Chilhowee, then Tellico, then Hiwassee, then Tallassee, then a half dozen nameless villages—each, by its destruction, lent an hour or two of summer heat to the bleak December weather. A thousand cabins, fifty thousand bushels of corn, were destroyed; twenty-nine warriors lost their lives; a score of women and children were rounded up. The Little Tennessee and the Hiwassee ran red with the blood of slaughtered cattle.

At last the braves, reduced to unbearable shame, agreed to sue for peace. They sent Nancy Ward, who in 1776, as we have seen, had given the settlers timely warning of the intended attack by her tribesmen, to placate and to treat with the furious white men. But the Wataugans remained hard of heart, for they planned to carry fire and sword to the rest of the overhill villages. They found the villages almost deserted. The only persons who remained were a Captain Rogers, four Negroes and some Indian women and children, all of whom the whites made prisoners.

Then on January 1, 1781, the army broke up in detachments which, returning home by different routes, burned more villages. The braves, cowed by Sevier's harsh measures at the beginning of the campaign, never again ventured to meet him but hid in the mountain gorges inhabited by friendly Chickamaugas.

On dead warriors and in burned towns Campbell, Sevier and Martin found letters and proclamations from British agents and commanders, inciting the Cherokee chiefs to war against the white settlers. To these chiefs the three officers now sent a written message by one of their captured braves. They accused the chiefs of starting the war "by listening to the bad counsels of the King of England, and the falsehoods told you by his agents." The officers then offered to treat for peace, "out of pity to your women and children," and instructed six of the chiefs to meet Major Martin within two moons on Long Island in the Holston. The whites offered food, clothing and shelter to the wives and children of those Cherokee who had protested the war, providing they would take refuge on Long Island until peace was restored. They warned the chiefs that, if the white leaders did not hear from them within the allotted time, they would continue to regard the Cherokee as enemies. "We will then be compelled to send another strong force into your country, that will come prepared to remain in it, to take possession of it as a conquered country, without making you any compensation for it."

Some of the old chiefs came in for a big talk with Martin, but the young braves spurned all offers of peace and continued to prowl around the settlements, stealing and murdering. Sevier, suspecting that the mischief-makers were encouraged by the Indians who had taken refuge in the mountain gorges which his troops had not penetrated, gathered a force of 130 men and after the first thaw in March advanced against the Cherokee.

Without knowledge of the terrain, without even a guide, the frontiersmen pushed 150 miles into a country of trackless forests, dangerous precipices and treacherous peaks which no Wataugan had ever seen save Isaac Thomas, the trader, who had reached it from the eastern side of the mountains.

Sometimes the mountains were too steep even for their sure-footed hill horses, which they were forced to dismount and lead up by their bridles. At last, much to their own surprise as well as to the Indians', they reached their destination. Falling like a thunderbolt on the town of Tuckasejah on the headwaters of the Little Tennessee they killed fifty warriors and took fifty women and children prisoner. Then they burned fifteen or twenty smaller villages, destroyed all the granaries of corn they could find and captured some two hundred horses.

Sevier lost only one man killed and one wounded. The braves were so amazed by the unexpected appearance of the white men, which seemed to them like an apparition, that they were unable to organize and fight. Before they fully realized what had happened Sevier and his men plunged once more into the wilderness, carrying prisoners and plunder and driving the captured horses before them. The campaign had lasted only twenty-nine days.

When he rode up to his house on the Nolichucky, Sevier found a message from General Nathanael Greene, requesting him to come to his assistance to cut off Cornwallis from his expected retreat through North Carolina. Sevier at once raised 200 men in Washington County and plunged across the mountains to Charlotte where he learned that Cornwallis had surrendered at Yorktown on October 19, 1781. Greene then ordered Sevier to turn south to the Santee River and there assist his fellow Huguenot, General Francis Marion, who was pursuing a force of several hundred Hessians under General Alexander Stewart. In November Sevier and Isaac Shelby rendered invaluable service in capturing a British post near Monk's Corner, South Carolina. This was one of the last engagements in the Revolution. Little remaining to be done, Sevier soon returned home.

Now that the end of the Revolution brought a temporary halt to Indian attacks, the Wataugans turned their attention to the problem of their relation to North Carolina. At the end of the American Revolution the Watauga country in present eastern Tennessee was still a part of the western territory of North Carolina and was composed of Washington, Sullivan and Greene counties. We will recall that Washington County at the time of its establishment late in 1777 embraced all the western territory of North Carolina, now the state of Tennessee. Less than two years later Sullivan County—named for the North Carolina hero General John Sullivan—was formed from a small strip of Washington County and from territory claimed by Virginia and later recognized as a part of that state. In April 1783 another county was set off from the western part of Washington and named Greene in honor of General Nathanael Greene.

At this time the three counties had a population of about eighteen thousand, largely of English or Scotch-Irish descent. In the early years when the Watauga and the Holston settlements were believed to lie within the boundaries of Virginia, Virginians predominated; but now Virginians and North Carolinians were about equal in number. The Scotch-Irish with their sturdiness, their restless energy and the superior education that many of them enjoyed, were the dominant group. Mingling with them and the English were Germans, Irish, French Huguenots and Welsh, all of whom eventually became good Americans by accepting the social and political ideas first expressed by the German and Scotch-Irish immigrants of an earlier day.

The blending of these stocks produced a sturdy foundation for a democratic commonwealth. The Wataugans had not been sent across the mountains as colonists by crafty "promoters or speculators interested in winning a principality for themselves under the guise of colonizing the west." They had come on their own initiative, bent on conquering the wilderness to establish new homes where they formulated and attempted to abide by their new concept of society. They were not rainbow chasers. Most of them were too primitive, too naïve, too practical, to wander far from their original settling places.

Like the settlers in the Cumberland country, the Wataugans'

... El Dorado lay not in the setting sun but in their valley, on the farm where they lived, at their very feet. If romantic unrest had brought them to the new country, it was soon exhausted. Many of them were possessed of an intense localism, a devotion to a certain spot of ground, a certain configuration of the landscape that to them meant home, freedom, wealth, that represented concretely past achievement and future progress.

In the past several years they had become increasingly dissatisfied with the treatment the state had accorded them. Their grievances were numerous and serious. Her failure to provide them with adequate protection against Indian attacks had resulted in the death of many of their relatives or friends.

On a plea of poverty North Carolina had refused to establish a Superior Court. The result was that settlements were infested with culprits of every degree of guilt and refugees who sought, in the supposed seclusion of the frontier, escape from conviction and punishment. The state had grudgingly granted the people a military force which soon proved too small to cope with the rapid growth and spread of the settlements. She had refused to appoint a brigadier general invested with the power to muster the militia of each of the three counties in case of emergency.

The representatives of the three counties reported to their constituents that North Carolina was reluctant to discharge, and sometimes openly rejected as informal or unauthorized, debts that had been contracted in guarding the settlements. The state scrutinized with unkindly eyes the claims of the Wataugans who had served her during the Revolution. The settlers' representatives in the assembly often told them that the people of the eastern counties referred to them as "off-scourings of the earth," "fugitives" and "outlaws." These same gentlemen also assailed the frontiersmen as grasping persons who seized on every pretence to "fabricate demands against the Government." Leading citizens of the eastern counties grossly insulted them by claiming that the industry and property of those east of the mountains were being converted into funds appropriated to discharge western debts.

Self-protection was the first law of the frontier. The Wataugans gradually became convinced that, since the mother state had neglected them, they must find other means, must draw on their own resources, to extricate themselves from the unexpected difficulties that surrounded them. In short, they yearned to pull away and separate themselves entirely from North Carolina.

A number of circumstances encouraged their aspirations. Their neighbors in Kentucky, with whom they were always in touch by the tide of travel which flowed forward and backward along Boone's trail through Cumberland Gap, were seeking separation from Virginia. Having lived under the Watauga Association for six years, the settlers were not inexperienced in independent government. They were confident that North Carolina, being a weak state, could offer little resistance to a separatist movement. Furthermore, many of their leaders were Virginians who felt little or no loyalty toward North Carolina, and even the North Carolinians among them were inclined to side with the Virginians in any contest against the mother state.

The movement for separation from North Carolina had its origins in the late summer of 1780 when the Continental Congress passed a resolution stating that if Virginia, North Carolina and Georgia should agree to cede their western lands, these lands would, at the appropriate time, be laid out properly in separate states. In response to this resolution, Colonel Arthur Campbell, a prominent settler of the Holston, in January 1782 circulated a document in the counties of southwestern Virginia and western North Carolina, proposing that the settlers elect delegates to a convention which should meet later in the year to take the proper steps toward creating states from the regions.

At first both North Carolina and Virginia opposed the proposal. Land speculators in the two states had no intention of surrendering their lucrative occupations to the general government. North Carolina therefore decided to wait until her citizens could avail themselves of an opportunity to appropriate the best sections of the western lands. The assembly, moreover, naturally looked to the sale of these lands to fill its coffers. It reasoned that the cession could still be made after most of the best lands had been apportioned, and that the new state could be required to assume a portion of the debt incurred in the Revolution and to guarantee payment to North Carolina soldiers in the form of land.

Virginia opposed the cession of her western lands for similar reasons, but when she reversed her decision, North Carolina followed suit. On April 19, 1784, the North Carolina assembly, meeting in Hillsboro, introduced a bill consenting to the cession. Passed on June 2, it stated that Congress, upon accepting the cession, should recognize the rights of the veterans to the lands, should consider the value of the ceded land in proportioning the Revolutionary debt, and should lay out the region into a state or states to be admitted into the Union with the provision that slavery would not be prohibited save by the assembly of the state or states thus formed. Congress was to accept the cession within a year. Some days later the assembly passed a bill which declared that no change should be made in the government of the cession until Congress adopted it.

On receiving word of this bill, the separatists in Washington, Sullivan and Greene counties jubilantly began to form plans for the organization of a government during the intervening year. The Cumberland settlers took no part in the movement. Far removed from the Holston settlements, they had no ties with them. For many years the Cumberlanders had managed their own affairs and were therefore hostile to any movement toward better government that did not originate with themselves.

The Holston efforts, on the other hand, were hastened by dreams of high offices and emoluments which the creation of a new state would make necessary, and by the restlessness of the Indians who were threatening to go to war because North Carolina had failed to send them the supplies she had promised them in an earlier treaty. On August 23, 1784, the elected delegates of the three counties convened at Jonesboro—in the present northeastern Tennessee—and resolved that they had

. . . a just and undeniable right to petition to Congress to accept the cession made by North Carolina, and for that body to countenance us for forming ourselves into a separate government, and to frame either a permanent or temporary constitution, agreeably to a resolve of Congress.

Meanwhile, North Carolina had repealed her cession act. Largely through the council of Hugh Williamson, delegate to Congress from North Carolina, Governor Martin concluded that the assembly had acted rashly in passing the cession bill. The people of the state, he argued, had not been consulted on the matter. Furthermore, North Carolina should, before ceding her western lands irrevocably to the federal government, be credited for the huge sums she had expended in the Indian campaign of 1776, and for the heavy military assistance she had extended to South Carolina and Georgia.

Williamson's attitude, however, cannot be considered a disinterested one. He knew that, as a speculator in the east, he could obtain land titles more easily under authority of North Carolina where he boasted influence, than in a new state where he would be unknown. Nevertheless, his sound economic reasoning convinced the assembly which, during the fall session of 1784, repealed the cession bill.

Before word of this action could reach the western settlements a second convention met on December 14 in Jonesboro. Sentiment was divided. Some of the delegates, believing that the bill would be repealed, genuinely wished to continue their allegiance to North Carolina. Nevertheless, the convention voted to form a separate state which eventually was named Franklin in honor of Benjamin Franklin, and not Frankland as Theodore Roosevelt and several other writers affirm.

The committee appointed to draft a course of action declared that separate statehood would "not only keep a circulating medium of gold and silver among us, but draw it from many individuals living in other states, who claim large quantities [of land] that would lie in the bounds of the new state." The statement implied that the western settlers felt money flowing toward the east with every article they purchased. To this grievance was added another. North Carolina had recently passed a law which assessed its eastern and western lands at the same value although the western lands were worth only one fourth as much. The creation of a new state would keep large sums in the west.

The constitution drawn up by the convention resembled that of North Carolina. It was, however, a temporary document. In an extraordinary resolution, the convention agreed to hold another convention which was to submit the constitution for revision, rejection or adoption.

At first John Sevier opposed the movement for statehood. For the present his chief interest was land speculation. In the previous year he had become an associate with William Blount, Richard Caswell, John Donelson and another North Carolinian in the Muscle Shoals Company. This group aimed at developing lands which lay in the Great Bend region of the Tennessee River and which were valuable for farming and were strategically located for trade with the Indians. As spokesman for the company, Blount planned to secure legal title from either North Carolina or Georgia, each of which claimed ownership of the area, and to buy the land from the Indians by private treaty with the Cherokee.

Sevier had no intention of alienating his associates—all of whom were loyal to North Carolina—by supporting or encouraging the creation of a commonwealth at the expense of the mother state. Yet he realized that this stand would be unpopular with most of the Watauga and Holston settlers. If he carried it too far, he could not expect them to support his project should the movement for statehood succeed. He extricated himself from this dilemma by adopting a policy that proved both logical and practicable: he would oppose the movement for statehood until he saw that it could succeed even without his support, then he would embrace it. Thus he anticipated complete success for his political as well as for his business plans.

In March 1785 popular clamor in favor of a separate state resulted in the first General Assembly of Franklin. Meeting in Jonesboro, it elected Sevier governor, perhaps without opposition. He reluctantly accepted the office and henceforth worked diligently to maintain the independence of Franklin. Soon afterward the assembly organized courts and chose political and military officers of every grade. Nearly all those who had held commissions under North Carolina were retained in office—a policy which minimized the friction between the two states. Four new counties were created, taxes were levied and a number of laws were enacted.

Eager to gain the friendship of North Carolina, Sevier informed Governor Martin that the three original counties across the mountains had declared their independence and had erected themselves into a separate state. Martin replied by sending

Major Samuel Henderson, brother of Richard Henderson, to Jonesboro to investigate the proceedings of the rebel government. Major Henderson also delivered to the Franklin legislature a letter by Martin asking for an "account of the late proceedings of the people of the western Country."

On the same day the governor addressed to the insurgents a spirited and elaborate manifesto in which he admonished them not to

. . . tarnish . . . the laurels you have so gloriously won at King's Mountain and elsewhere, in supporting the freedom and independence of the United States, and this state in particular, to be whose citizens were then your boast, in being concerned in a black and traitorous revolt from that government in whose defense you have so copiously bled, and which, by solemn oath, you are still bound to support.

The assembly, Major Henderson continued, would soon be convened and would discuss the "transactions of your leaders."

Let your representatives come forward and present every grievance in a constitutional manner, that they may be redressed; and let your terms of separation be proposed with decency, your proportion of the public debts ascertained, the vacant territory appropriated to the mutual benefit of both parties, in such a manner and proportion as may be just and reasonable; let your proposals be consistent with the honour of the state to accede to, which, by your allegiance as good citizens, you cannot violate, and I make no doubt but her generosity, in time, will meet your wishes.

But if in their blind ambition they continued their "present unjustifiable measures," the citizens must be prepared to suffer the consequences, for then North Carolina would be obliged to use force to "regain her government over the revolted territory or render it not worth possessing."

To the letter which Governor Martin addressed to the Frank-

lin legislature, Sevier replied by setting down in detail the reasons
for the secession. He also thanked North Carolina

. . . for every sentiment of regard she has for us, but are sorry to
observe that it is founded upon principles of interest, as is apar-
ent [*sic*] from the tenor of your letter, we are doubtful, when
the causes seases [*sic*] which is the basis of that affection, we shall
lose your esteem.

By Henderson Sevier sent Martin a private letter which said
in part:

It gives me great pain to think there should arise any Disputes
between us and North Carolina, & I flatter myself when North
Carolina be fully convinced that necessity and self-preservation
have Compelled Us to the measures we Have taken, and could
the people have discovered that No. Carolina would Have
protected and Govern'd them, They would have remained where
they were; but they perceived a neglect and Coolness, and the
Language of Many of your leading Members Convinced them
they were Altogether Disregarded.

Shortly after this letter was written Richard Caswell succeeded
Martin in the executive chair of North Carolina. The new governor, associated with Sevier in the Muscle Shoal project, made
known that he favored a more conciliatory attitude toward
Franklin. Availing himself of Caswell's friendliness, Sevier wrote
him a letter in which he voiced the determination of his people
to remain independent:

Governor Martin has lately sent up into our country a Manifesto, together with letters to private persons, in order to stir up
sedition and insurrection, thinking, thereby, to destroy that peace
and tranquility which have so greatly subsisted among the peaceful citizens of this country. . . .
The menaces made use of in the Manifesto will by no means
intimidate us. We mean to pursue our necessary measures, and
with the fullest confidence believe that your legislature, when
truly informed of our civil proceedings, will find no cause for
resenting anything we have done. . . .

Our Assembly sits again in August, at which time it is expected commissions will be appointed to adjust and consider on such matters of moment, as will be consistent with the honour and interest of each party.

Sevier's assurance seems to have satisfied Caswell that things would eventually be ironed out. He replied in a friendly letter:

. . . as you give me assurances of the peaceful disposition of the people, and their wish to conduct themselves in the manner you mention, and also to send persons to adjust, consider and conciliate matters, I suppose, to the next Assembly, for the present, things must rest as they are with respect to the subject matter of your letter, which shall be laid before the next Assembly.

When in August the Franklin assembly convened, it passed two measures aimed at winning a reconciliation with North Carolina. It returned the public money which had remained in the hands of former North Carolina officers who had become citizens of Franklin, and it appointed a commission to discuss its separate statehood movement before the North Carolina assembly. At the same time, however, it issued a call for a constitutional convention in November.

In a rich corn belt between Knoxville and Jonesboro lay the neat village of Greeneville which boasted more than forty houses built with square beams in the fashion of the old log cabins. At the center of the village stood the courthouse—a clapboard building of unhewn logs. It needed no windows, for light came in through the door and through the chinks between the logs. Here assembled the Commons of the Franklin legislature. More comfortable were the members of the Senate who gathered in one of the rooms of the village inn where some of the legislators boarded. Each guest paid twenty-five cents daily for his meals and room and twelve cents for the keep of his horse—if the animal ate only hay. A half pint of liquor or a gallon of oats cost twelve cents.

On November 14, 1785, the legislators solemnly gathered in the courthouse to provide a permanent constitution for the state of Franklin. They were by no means a harmonious group. While Sevier and his many friends were determined to maintain the independence of Franklin, Colonel John Tipton and his small coterie wished to see the region returned to the allegiance of North Carolina.

Tipton was a strong-willed, jealous, unrelenting man who had shown military ability in Lord Dunmore's War and had served as a recruiting officer in the Continental Army. Moving to Watauga in February 1782, he had settled on a farm on Sinking Creek, Washington County, about two miles south of the present Johnson City. He was one of the common run of mediocrity who know they can excel only in the absence of men of superior ability or personality.

Since Boyd's Creek Tipton had resented Sevier for poking fun at his brother Jonathan's failure in that engagement. Needless to say, Sevier's popularity and his attainment of the governorship had only increased Tipton's rancor and jealousy. Sullen and vindictive, he disavowed all connections with the new state and affirmed his loyalty to North Carolina.

Once the two men actually came to blows. At a general muster of the militia Sevier, reviewing Tipton's regiment, requested him not to summon his men under the laws of North Carolina. The governor reminded Tipton that the state of Franklin had laws of its own. One word led to another and the altercation developed into a fist fight which Tipton won. His victory made him all the more determined to defeat and humiliate Sevier and to destroy Franklin.

To this end he succeeded in getting one of his friends, a preacher named Samuel Houston, to introduce the draft of an entirely new constitution. In this Houston changed the name of the state from Franklin to Frankland because, he said, the people were as free as the ancient Franks. The constitution of Frankland adopted a unicameral legislature and excluded ministers of the gospel, attorneys at law and medical doctors. The exclusion of ministers from the legislature was simply a precaution against infringement of full religious freedom which the old constitution guaranteed. The prejudice against lawyers was doubtless the inspiration of two of the leading delegates, Samuel Houston and

William Graham, ministers who looked on lawyers "with smothered envy and admiration, but always with jealousy, suspicion, and dislike." The duty of every honest citizen, they felt, was "to prevent any man whose business it was to study the law from having a share in making the law."

The proposed constitution also declared ineligible for office all persons of immoral character, those guilty of "such flagrant enormities as drunkedness, gaming, profane swearing, lewdness, Sabbath-breaking and such like," and those denying "the existence of God, of heaven, and of hell, the inspiration of the Scriptures, or the existence of the Trinity."

In many of its provisions Frankland's constitution showed the influence of the frontier. Though it required property qualification from the members of the legislature, it granted manhood suffrage, provided for the registration of votes and election by ballot, and specified that all legislation of a general nature be referred to the people before enactment could follow. The people were to elect the governor, the executive council and all county officials. The legislature was given the power to appoint the judges of the superior courts, the secretary of state and the treasurer.

The justices of the people must be "scholars to do the business," for they were chosen for life and were to receive no pay. To discourage the possibility of suspicion among the people regarding the governmental revenue, provision was made for the assembly to publish annually full accounts of income and expenditure.

This liberalism was the weapon by which Tipton and his friends hoped to defeat and discredit Sevier. The governor, they knew, had no desire to alienate his North Carolina associates, which included Governor Caswell, in the Muscle Shoals project. Sevier's policy, therefore, was aimed at reconciling himself to the state, though not at the expense of losing the esteem of his people by surrendering the independence of Franklin. He hoped to achieve his aim by using his great influence to obtain for Franklin a constitution modeled on that of North Carolina. This, Sevier believed, would please both his countrymen and his associates. To frustrate Sevier's program, Tipton and his friends advocated a constitution that would place most of the power in the hands of the people. A democratic form of government would permit any man who had money or influence to acquire property. Thus Sevier and his North Carolina associates would eventually lose control of the Muscle Shoals project, or any future land scheme, and be overthrown.

Long and angry debates broke in the assembly over the new document. Each side issued pamphlets which, distributed among the settlers, started many fights and ended many friendships. But Sevier's popularity in the convention proved too strong for Tipton to dissipate. The legislators finally adopted the North Carolina constitution as that of Franklin. Tipton and his friends bowed to circumstances, but they would not admit defeat. Before long they began to formulate new plans to overthrow Sevier.

Meanwhile Governor Caswell of North Carolina pursued his policy of reconciliation. Five days after Franklin adopted the North Carolina constitution, the assembly at his request passed an act which stated that it wished to extend to the rebellious western counties "the benefits of civil government . . . until such time as they might be separated with advantage and convenience to themselves." North Carolina was ready to pass over, and "consign to oblivion, the mistakes and misconduct of such persons in the above-mentioned counties, as have withdrawn themselves from the government of this state; to hear and redress their grievances, if any they have, and to afford them the protection and benefits of government."

The act granted pardon to all those who might return to the allegiance of North Carolina and provided for the appointment of civil and military officers to replace the incumbents of the Franklin government. It empowered the voters of the three rebellious counties to choose representatives loyal to North Carolina. And it promised them that at the proper time they would be granted independence and be admitted as a state of the Union.

This proclamation provided Tipton with a new weapon in his relentless war against Sevier. Openly championing the cause of North Carolina, Tipton mustered the support of all those who cherished the same sympathy and called for elections to choose representatives to the assembly of the old state. Tipton himself ran for senator from Washington County and won. He and his elected friends then proceeded to reorganize the state of Franklin in the interest of North Carolina.

Tipton's activities resulted in the unsavory spectacle of two governments functioning in Franklin over the same people. Each government held court in the same county. Each government appointed some of the same men to office. Each government laid taxes on the same citizens. Father fought against son; brother, against brother. Every fresh provocation from one side led to retaliation from the other.

Between Tipton and Sevier arose a deadly hatred which found expression in furious attempts on the part of the one man to increase his support to overthrow the other. Tipton held court under the authority of North Carolina at Buffalo. Sevier held court at Jonesboro, only ten miles away. These courts frequently required the sheriff of one government to pass into the jurisdiction claimed by the other, a journey which nearly always ended in a bloody fight and sometimes in petty feuds among villagers and even among members of the same family. Needless to say, the office of sheriff required the patience of a Job and the strength of a Samson.

Sevier and Tipton themselves did their utmost to encourage the strife. Once Tipton with a few men entered the courthouse in Jonesboro, drove the judges into the street and seized the papers from the clerk. Forthwith Sevier retaliated by taking the records from the North Carolina courthouse in Washington County. At another time some of Tipton's men broke up a Franklin court sitting in Greeneville. Conditions had reached an acrimonious impasse which neither North Carolina nor Franklin could long afford to tolerate.

Meanwhile Sevier had covered himself with fresh glory in a new campaign against the Cherokee. In the late fall of 1785 commissioners from the federal government had met the Indians at Hopewell, South Carolina, and concluded with them a treaty which confirmed to them a considerable extent of territory claimed to have been previously ceded by the tribe. The treaty permitted the Cherokee to punish any settler who refused to move off land guaranteed to them and to arrest any settler whom they suspected of being guilty of a capital offense. Imagine the anger of the Franklinites when they discovered that the treaty, in addition, placed their permanent capital, Greeneville, in Cherokee territory, and that it forbade them from expanding along the rich valleys of the Holston, Nolichucky and Tennessee rivers!

Sevier, frustrated for the time being in the Muscle Shoals project, temporarily lost his customary affability in a torrent of profanity. He called a special meeting of the legislature which appointed commissioners of its own to negotiate a second treaty with the Cherokee. When this tribe responded by killing several Franklinites, Sevier early in 1786 took the field with 160 men and crossed Unaka Mountain to the Hiwassee where he burned three villages known as the valley towns and killed 15 warriors. From his headquarters he sent out spies or scouts who soon returned and reported that they had discovered a long Indian trail. Sevier immediately led his troops toward the trail. But learning that the warriors greatly outnumbered him and that they were led by John Watts, a cunning and daring commander who was probably trying to lure them into a narrow defile, Sevier and his officers saw the folly of pursuing the Indians without reinforcements. Sevier led his force homeward.

On reaching Franklin he learned that the feud with North Carolina had grown. Deploring the prevailing misery, his people in October 1786 persuaded him to make another attempt to come to some understanding with Governor Caswell. In a respectful but earnest letter Sevier announced to Caswell that the Franklin legislature had appointed a commission to present its case before the North Carolina assembly which, he hoped, would "cheerfully consent to the separation of Franklin." He was confident that the population of Franklin, though now "inconsiderable," would soon be as large as that of some of the eastern states. "I have always considered myself happy while under the government of North-Carolina, and highly honoured with the different appointments they have been pleased to offer."

The Franklin commission was originally composed of two men: Judge David Campbell—a young brother of Colonel Arthur

Campbell—and William Cocke, but at the last moment the judge became ill and remained in the west. Cocke, after leaving Boonesboro where we last saw him in 1776, had moved to the Watauga region, had taken part in King's Mountain, had become a lawyer in 1783, had served as state's attorney for North Carolina and had worked assiduously for the independence of Franklin.

A brilliant orator, Cocke now appeared before the North Carolina assembly and depicted vividly the perilous conditions which had impelled the people of Franklin to separate from the parent state. To whom could they have turned for relief from the storm? Their horizon had promised them no bright prospect. They had had no money to raise troops to defend themselves against the Indians; no authority to levy men; no power to lay taxes for the support of the government; no hope that North Carolina would defray their necessary expenditures. What, then, should they have done to stay the uplifted tomahawk? How were their women and children to avoid impending destruction? Could they have relied on Congress? No! Congress had not accepted them and was, moreover, too feeble to extend them any assistance. Should they supinely await the return of good fortune? Delay meant death, meant the yells of savages dinning through the settlements. The citizens of Franklin had no choice, said Cocke, but to turn pleadingly to North Carolina. Surely the people of that state would not harden their hearts against their western brethren who in perilous times had always heeded their cries of distress. Let them now reciprocate with the wide hand of generosity! Let them now relieve the circumstances by granting Franklin independence, remembering that all animosity should be forgotten and that the errors of their western brethren were, after all, the "off spring of the greater errors" committed by North Carolina. For it belonged to a magnanimous people

. . . to weep over the failings of their unfortunate children, especially if prompted by the inconsiderate behavior of the parent. Far should it be from their hearts to harbour the unnatural purpose of adding still more affliction to those who have suffered but too much already. It belongs to a magnanimous people to give an industrious attention to circumstances, in order to form a just judgment upon a subject so much deserving of their serious meditation, and when once carefully formed, to employ, with sedulous anxiety, the best efforts of their purest wisdom, in choosing a course to pursue, suitable to the dignity of their character, consistent with their own honour, and the best calculated to allay that storm of distraction in which their hapless children have been so unexpectedly involved. If the mother shall judge the expense of adhesion too heavily to be borne, let us remain as we are, and support ourselves by our own exertions; if otherwise, let the means for the continuance of our connexion be supplied with the degree of liberality which will• demonstrate seriousness on the one hand, and secure affection on the other.

To this appeal the North Carolina assembly listened attentively, but it would not retreat from its established policy. Cocke went home, his mission a failure.

Caswell now endeavored to end the strife in the western counties by offering the Franklinites a plan of his own. To this end he requested Sevier to receive a commissioner whom he was about to appoint and send to confer with him. Sevier consented to the proposal. Caswell then chose Evan Shelby, whom he had recently appointed brigadier general of the Washington District, as the commissioner. In selecting Shelby, Caswell acted with diplomatic wisdom. Shelby, like Sevier, had always been identified, "in all his sympathies and interests," with the Watauga country. Shelby and Sevier, moreover, were close friends. They had been neighbors for many years; they had fought at King's Mountain. Each admired the other, and each strongly desired independence for Franklin, though Shelby thought it should be achieved only with the consent of North Carolina.

Caswell felt that Shelby's remarkable candor, good sense and patriotism would assure success of his plan. On March 20, 1787, Shelby with a few officers met Sevier and a small group of his friends at Samuel Smith's house. The plan which Shelby disclosed provided that every man in Franklin should choose for himself which government he wished to acknowledge and pay his taxes to it accordingly. Sevier submitted it to his people, who accepted it. Thus was adopted a "live and let live" policy pending redress of grievances.

During this interlude of peace Sevier decided to enlist the support of the man for whom the state was named. On April 9, 1787, he wrote to Benjamin Franklin reiterating the grievances which his people nursed against North Carolina and requesting the aged statesman to champion the cause of the western state with his illustrious pen. On June 30 Franklin replied that since he had been away in Europe he was not well acquainted with conditions in the state but that he intended to study the records of Congress and to report "if anything should occur to me." In closing, Franklin advised Sevier to effect some satisfactory compromise with North Carolina:

There are only two Things that Humanity induces me to wish you may succeed in: The Accomodating your Misunderstanding with the Government of North Carolina, by amicable Means; and the Avoiding an Indian war, by preventing Encroaching on their Lands. . . . The Inconvenience to your People attending so remote a Seat of Government, and the difficulty to that Government in ruling well so remote a People, would I think be powerful Inducements with it, to accede to any fair & reasonable Proposition it may receive from you towards an Accomodation.

In accordance with Franklin's advice Sevier decided to go personally to the North Carolina assembly to seek reconciliation with that body. But before he could do so he received information that struck a fatal blow to his Muscle Shoals project and, consequently, to the state of Franklin.

The lands lying in the Great Bend of the Tennessee were by now acknowledged to be under the jurisdiction of the state of Georgia. For several years Franklin and Georgia had enjoyed very friendly relations. The governors of the two states had exchanged complimentary letters, and Georgia had made Sevier a brigadier general of militia for the region in the Great Bend, which the state had recently organized as Houston County.

When in April 1786 Georgia had declared war against the Creek Indians, she had requested assistance from her friends in

Franklin. The two states had then made a bargain. In return for 1,500 soldiers, Franklin was to receive land grants in Muscle Shoals, which Sevier and his associates had been denied by the Treaty of Hopewell. For nearly two years the alliance had occasioned much correspondence between the two states, but Georgia, financially embarrassed and short of ammunition, was unable to wage the war she had declared.

Such was her position when at the end of 1787 the Federal Constitution was submitted to the states. Georgia, wisely exchanging her frustrated plans against the Creeks for the support of a strong central government, promptly accepted the Constitution. A few months later in February 1788 she informed Sevier that Congress, assuming control of Indian affairs, had sent a commission to make peace with the Creeks and that in consequence no force would be sent against them. This meant that Georgia, requiring no military service from Sevier, would grant him no land in the Great Bend of the Tennessee.

Thus crumbled with one blow Sevier's Muscle Shoals project and, in consequence, his cherished hope of independence for Franklin. To this adversity was added the anguish of seeing his followers melt away by the hundreds. With their loss Franklin began to totter. On March 1, 1788, Sevier's term as governor would end, and no one cared to succeed him to the post. He himself had seceded reluctantly from North Carolina. He had done so because he needed the support of the western settlers to maintain the Muscle Shoals project of his associates. Now that dream had faded, and with it his desire for political separation.

The North Carolina officers eagerly took advantage of Sevier's misfortune to wrest from the falling state what vestige of governmental authority remained. This proved an easy matter. The political leaders of Franklin were happy to accept offices offered them by North Carolina, which, continuing its wise policy of reconciliation, had issued acts of "pardon and oblivion" for those who wished to return to the fold. Many members of the Franklin Council of State, of the judiciary and of the legislature found political fortune in North Carolina. Among them was David Campbell, who was appointed to the North Carolina assembly and who soon rose to the judgeship of the Superior Court for the Washington District at Jonesboro.

Tipton seized on Sevier's downfall to deal him a crushing blow. Joseph Martin, who was friendly toward Sevier, had recently succeeded Evan Shelby as brigadier general of the Washington District. But Tipton, acting quickly in Martin's temporary absence, sent Sheriff John Pugh to seize Sevier's slaves toward the payment of North Carolina taxes.

Pugh carried the slaves to Tipton's house at Sinking Creek about ten miles east of Jonesboro. When Sevier, who had been away fighting Indians, learned of this act, he flew into a towering rage. Swearing to seek out this Saul who hounded him "in all the dens and hiding places of the country," he mustered about a hundred and fifty of his followers, led them straightway to Tipton's house, and ordered him by letter to surrender unconditionally.

Though Tipton had only fifteen men with him he proved as stubborn as his enemy was angry. He promptly sent word back to fire and be damned. Whereupon Sevier arrayed his men on a sunken piece of ground about two or three hundred yards from the house and ordered them to shoot at its corners while he loudly threatened to demolish it altogether. Tipton, convinced that Sevier was in earnest, dispatched messengers during the night to his friends, Colonel George Maxwell and Colonel Thomas Love, begging them to hasten to his assistance.

The next morning, February 27, Sevier again demanded unconditional surrender. When Tipton ignored the order, Sevier posted some of his men on an eminence of limestone rocks which lay near the road that led to the house, and ordered them to resume their shooting. They accidentally wounded in the shoulder a woman who, in company with another woman, was emerging from the house.

At this juncture Colonel Love, who was hastening to Tipton's assistance with ten or twelve men—all he could gather—learned of the guard at the rocks and resolved to hold a parley with them. Leaving his companions, he pranced up, hemming and coughing, on his horse, but found the place deserted. The cold was bitter and the guards had rejoined the main force to warm themselves by the fires. When Love returned to his companions and told them that the guards were absent from their post, they let out a whoop and went in full gallop to Tipton's house. Their arrival encouraged Tipton to hold out.

At dawn a heavy snow began to fall. Sevier dispatched sentinels to the road on which Maxwell was approaching, but the cold was so intense that they soon went to warm themselves. In their absence Maxwell arrived and marched to within gunshot of Sevier's camp without being detected. When daylight made objects visible, Maxwell's troops at his command fired a volley and raised a shout that "seemed to reach to heaven." With jubilant shouts of deliverance Tipton and his men ran out of the house and joined Maxwell, who had already attacked Sevier's troops in the heavy snowfall and forced them to retreat.

Sheriff Pugh was mortally wounded. Several of Sevier's men were wounded and captured, among them his two sons who had ventured into camp in the belief that it was still in their father's possession. Sevier's troops fled in all directions, some throwing away their rifles in their desperation to get away. Tipton swore to hang Sevier's sons, but he desisted when Colonel Love convinced him that such an act would bring grave consequences on himself. Tipton then released them and even returned to their owners the property he had seized in the camp. In vain did friends of both the two men try to get them to patch up their differences. Then Joseph Martin obtained from North Carolina authority to take the Sevier tax case into his own hands, a measure which restored peace.

When on March 1 his term of office expired, Sevier tried to retrieve his popularity by winning fame in a campaign against the Cherokee who, despite their many setbacks, were still determined to drive the whites from the land assigned to them by the Hopewell Treaty. In May 1788 a brave named Slim Tom fell on Sevier's friends, the Kirk family, while Kirk himself and his son were away, and massacred eleven of them in the yard of their home. When the horrified father and son returned they gave the alarm.

Sevier hastily gathered the militia, led it to a Cherokee village on the Hiwassee River, burned the village to ashes and killed or made prisoner those who had not fled. He imposed the same punishment on some villages on the Tennessee. Among Sevier's soldiers was Kirk's son, who burned to avenge the murder of his mother and his brothers and sisters. In Sevier's absence, young Kirk went with the consent of his superior officer to the house where the Indian prisoners were lodged and tomahawked one of them while his comrades looked on. The other prisoners, five or six in number, realizing that the same fate awaited them, conveniently bowed their heads while Kirk hacked them down one by one. When Sevier returned he remonstrated loudly against the barbarous act. Kirk soon silenced him. If you had suffered the same anguish as I, he asked, would you not have done likewise? With this incontrovertible argument the young man escaped punishment. Tipton of course seized on the incident to justify further his hatred for Sevier. He accused the former governor of consenting to absent himself in order to permit the crime to take place.

One who watched Sevier's dwindling political career with intense curiosity was Don Diego Gardoqui. The Spanish chargé d'affaires was then working diligently to utilize the statehood aspirations of the Kentucky and Tennessee frontiersmen in the interest of his own country. Learning of Sevier's tussle with Tipton, which he construed as armed insurrection against the authority of North Carolina, he dispatched an emissary to sound the governor in regard to a possible understanding with Spain.

The emissary, Dr. James White, Superintendent of Indian Affairs for the Southern Department, was one of many Americans whom Gardoqui employed as his agents in his efforts to limit the United States to the Atlantic states by separating her western lands and creating them into buffer states. Gardoqui already had had occasion to write to Sevier. Alarmed over the unprovoked depredations and murders of the Cherokee, Sevier, like Robertson, had persuaded Governor Samuel Johnston of North Carolina to address Gardoqui and request him to exert his influence to put a stop to the Indian attacks. Gardoqui, sensing a rare opportunity to enlist Sevier's support in his scheme, expressed to him this dexterous sentiment: "His Majesty is very favorably inclined to give the inhabitants of that region all the protection that they ask for, and, on my part, I shall take very great pleasure in contributing to it on this occasion and other occasions."

The shrewd Spaniard now put nothing down in writing. He merely instructed White to make every effort to win Sevier over and gave White $300 to cover the expenses of his trip. Arriving in Franklin in July 1788, White found that circumstances made Sevier ready to clutch any helping hand. By his heroic exploits against Chickamauga and Cherokee in the remote western counties of Franklin, 'Chucky Jack had regained much of his old popularity. Even Tipton had to admit that Sevier's numerous followers were ready to support him in any movement that had a chance of success. With the material assistance of Spain, Sevier could wage a successful campaign to drive the supporters of North Carolina from Franklin. The United States, he believed, would not interfere, for in August North Carolina had postponed ratification of the Federal Constitution and she was, therefore, not a member of the Union. The success of his plans would enable Sevier to revive the state of Franklin and perhaps reach a new understanding with Georgia on the Muscle Shoals project.

With these objectives in mind, Sevier accepted Gardoqui's offer of help. Since he had no notion of playing the puppet of Spain a minute longer than was necessary, Sevier refrained from promising to become a citizen of that country. On September 12 he wrote two letters to Gardoqui and sent his son, James, to deliver them in New York. In one letter he revealed his intention to establish a colony at Muscle Shoals and requested Spanish intervention to prevent the southern Indians from attacking the settlers in that region. In the other letter he urgently petitioned Gardoqui for a loan of a few thousand pounds to enable him to "make the most expedient and necessary preparations for defense" against North Carolina:

. . . upon consulting with the principal men of this country, I have been particularly happy to find that they are equally disposed and ready as I am to accept your propositions and guarantees. You may be sure that the pleasing hopes and ideas which the people of this country hold with regard to the probability of an alliance with, and commercial concessions from, you are very ardent, and that we are unanimously determined to that score. The people of this region have come to realize truly upon what part of the world and upon which nation their future happiness and security depend, and they immediately infer that their interest and prosperity depend entirely upon the protection and liberality of your government. . . . Being the first from this side of the Appalachian Mountains to resort in this way to your protection and liberality, we feel encouraged to entertain the greatest hope that we shall be granted all reasonable aid by him who is so amply able to do it, and to give the protection and help that is asked of him in this petition. You know our delicate situation and the difficulties in which we are in respect to our mother State which is making use of every stratagem to impede the development and prosperity of this country. . . . Before I conclude, it may be necessary to remind you that there will be no more favorable occasion than the present one to put this plan into execution. North Carolina has rejected the Constitution and moreover it seems to me that a considerable time will elapse before she becomes a member of the Union, if that event ever happens.

James Sevier delivered this letter to Gardoqui. On October 10 Gardoqui wrote to Miró recommending to Spain's attention Dr. White and James Sevier, the emissaries of Franklin, with their plans and proposals. But a sudden change in Spanish policy ended the project before Miró could act.

By this time Sevier had been arrested by order of Governor Johnston on a charge of high treason. The man to whom the order was originally given was Judge Campbell who was to exercise his authority after he had examined the "affidavits of credible persons." Campbell's judicial opinion was that any affidavit against Sevier could not be made by a credible person. He refused to issue the warrant. It was finally issued by one of Tipton's friends, Spencer, who had been judge of the Superior Court of North Carolina in the west. Spencer sent Tipton to make the arrest.

Sevier was at the Widow Brown's Inn with some of his men when Tipton at last came up to him. The sun had just risen. Tipton and his posse were about to enter the inn when the portly and dauntless widow, surmising the reason for the visit, "drew up her chair into the doorway, plonked herself down on it, and refused to budge for all the writs of North Carolina."

Tipton blustered; Widow Brown rocked. Sevier, aroused from sleep by the noise, sprang from his bed and dressed hurriedly; looking through a crack in the door, he saw Colonel Love. He opened the door and held out his hands, saying, "I surrender to you."

At the sight of his enemy Tipton became enraged: "I'll hang you," he blurted; "I'll hang you!" Then, thrusting his pistol against Sevier, he threatened to shoot at the least show of resistance. Sevier's comrades, shouting furiously, urged him to put up a fight, but he, perhaps remembering the beating that Tipton had once given him, admonished them to respect the law. Tipton, feeling that no jail in the western country could hold Sevier for long, escorted him on horseback to Jonesboro. Fearing a riot, he left him in charge of a deputy sheriff at Widow Pugh's with orders to take him to Morganton for trial. Before Tipton departed for that town he called two of the guards aside and gave them instructions of which the more honorable among them were ignorant. When the party entered the mountains, Gourley and French were to lag behind with the prisoner until the others were out of sight on the twisting trail. Then French was to kill Sevier and assert that he had done so because the prisoner had made an attempt to escape.

The plan failed. Gourley, suffering from a qualm of conscience, informed Sevier of what awaited him and gave him an opportunity to escape. Sevier plunged down the mountainside, but became entangled in the underbrush. French overtook him and fired. Again fate interceded in Sevier's behalf: the ball had dropped out of French's pistol. So Sevier reached Morganton, but he did not go to jail. His old comrade-in-arms, General Joseph McDowell, took him home, wined and dined him, and became his security for a few days while he visited relatives and awaited trial.

Back home across the mountains Sevier's friends received word of his arrest with great indignation. Their feeling of retaliation and revenge would not have been keener had the chiefs and warriors of the entire Cherokee nation fallen on and butchered defenseless women and children. Sevier's sons, James and John, and Major Nathaniel Evans, Doctor James Cozby, Jesse Greene and John Gibson—old friends who had served him faithfully in many Indian campaigns—immediately planned to rescue him. Their intention was to secure his release by stratagem, or, that failing, to set fire to the town and in the ensuing confusion to break into the prison and rescue the prisoner.

On the day of the trial while settlers from the surrounding country filled Morganton to see the famous prisoner with their own eyes, Sevier's friends approached as near to the town as they deemed prudent. While four of them concealed themselves near the road Cozby and Evans entered the town and, tying their horses to the limb of a tree near the courthouse, mingled with the crowd. In one of the stables Evans found Sevier's white race mare and, with her bridle carelessly thrown over her head, led her up to the courthouse door.

Meanwhile Cozby had entered the courthouse, "and there, arraigned at the bar, sat the object of their solicitude; there he sat, as firm and undaunted as when charging hosts of Wyuca on the Lookout Mountain." Slowly Sevier turned his head; his eyes met Cozby's. Sevier knew that rescue was at hand, but, taking a cue from Cozby, he remained perfectly calm. Cozby waited for a pause in the trial and then, stepping forward, asked the judge if he were through with the man. Cozby's question, his manner and the tone of his voice caused every person in the courthouse to look at the speaker and then at the judge in amazement. Sevier seized this moment to make his getaway. Catching a glimpse of his mare, he sprang to the door, made one long leap to the saddle and sped away with his friends. Up in front in the courthouse sat an old man who admired Sevier intensely and who had been watching the trial with rapt attention. "I'll be damned if you ain't through with him!" he crowed to the judge, guffawing and slapping his knee.

That night Sevier and his rescuers rested at the house of a

friend, about twenty miles away. The following day they began an easy journey to their homes, happy in having achieved a bloodless victory. Nobody dared attempt to recapture Sevier and no further effort was made to prosecute him.

The capture and brief expatriation of Sevier served only to awaken in his behalf a higher appreciation of his services and a deeper conviction of his claims to the esteem and consideration of his countrymen. His return was everywhere greeted with enthusiasm and joy. In November the North Carolina assembly passed an act of pardon and oblivion with respect to Franklin. Though this act debarred Sevier from office, it automatically operated to clear him of the alleged offense of high treason.

The people of Greene County soon called on Sevier to represent them in the senate of North Carolina. He was elected without difficulty, whereupon the assembly pardoned him, let him take his seat with his colleagues and with extraordinary consideration honored him with the rank of brigadier general. Sevier had at last achieved his long sought reconciliation with North Carolina—but at the expense of Franklin, the lost state.

Kentucky:

Struggle for Statehood

Boone's HEROIC DEFENSE OF BOONESBORO AND, AT ABOUT THE same time, George Rogers Clark's brilliant campaign in the Illinois County sent waves of eager humanity to Kentucky, which by the end of the Revolution counted close to twenty thousand people. There they found much rich land but felt little security. For several years more the settlers grappled with poverty, even famine. To these sinister agents was soon added another. The representatives of a powerful northern organization known as the Grand Ohio Company, which pretended title to western Virginia and a large part of Kentucky under deeds fraudulently procured from the Six Nations of New York, spared no effort in sowing dissension among the settlers. By controlling the eastern delegates in the Continental Congress, the Ohio Company rendered that body powerless in the last years of the Revolution to execute its duties with its usual dexterity.

The new immigrants found most of the choice land of Kentucky already taken under grants from Virginia. Since many of the settlers came from Pennsylvania, they disputed these grants and sided with the land jobbers in scheming to overthrow Virginia's government in Kentucky and setting up in its stead a new state under authority from Congress. The ready puppet of the northern delegates—who, in turn, moved to the strings of the land jobbers—Congress lay claim to all of the country across the Allegheny Mountains. By 1781 it forced Virginia to cede her chartered region north of the Ohio. In surrendering this portion of her domain, Virginia hoped to satisfy the northern states, leaving her in undisputed possession of the territory which now comprises West Virginia and Kentucky. But the new claimants of this region, conniving with the help of their pawns in Congress, denied Virginia's jurisdiction over it and persuaded many settlers to their way of thinking.

Virginia, fearing that she would soon be obliged to give up Kentucky, lost interest in governing and protecting that region. Realizing this, Indians of various tribes invaded Kentucky in numerous groups, killing settlers and burning their homes. The whites were powerless to defend themselves. Virginia denied them the right to attack the Indian towns north of the Ohio where their enemies were most vulnerable.

The Kentuckians naturally resolved to protect themselves by seeking separation from a state that could not or would not guarantee them security. This was only one of their several grievances. The great distance that separated them from the state capital aggravated the dangers which constantly lurked at their thresholds. Between the Kentucky frontier and Richmond lay hundreds of miles of high mountains, poor roads and perilous wilderness, all of which they must traverse for a look at a land deed, a word with a lawyer or the scratch of a magistrate's pen. These duties often entailed the ruinous expense of a long delay in Richmond before they could return home. Thus the settlers were obliged to spend much of their time guarding their lawful land titles.

Another economic reason that impelled the Kentuckians to seek independence from Virginia was Spain's refusal to permit them to navigate the lower Mississippi where she owned both banks of the river. In the eyes of that nation the American pygmy, if properly fed, would grow into a giant which might develop an appetite for its neighbor, Louisiana. Throughout the Revolution, therefore, Spain with the help of the United States' ally, France, schemed to persuade or coerce Congress to surrender to her the region between the Alleghenies and the Mississippi. When she failed to obtain this region, Spain asserted her exclusive ownership to the lower Mississippi, thereby forbidding it to Americans. Those who defied her policy were arrested and their boats and cargoes confiscated.

The Kentuckians were naturally resentful of a state of affairs which made them paupers amid their own riches. Their fertile soil yielded an abundance of products for which they received less money than they had spent in transporting them across the mountains to the Atlantic seaports. In their fury they demanded that Congress should force Spain to reopen the Mississippi whose tributaries passed by their very doors. When Congress did nothing the Kentuckians resolved to make good, by their own efforts, John Jay's remark that God had made the Mississippi as a highway for their use.

They had to wait several years, however, before they were presented with an opportunity to take the first steps toward separation. In November 1784 Benjamin Logan, founder of St. Asaph and now colonel of militia of recently organized Lincoln County, received word that the Cherokee planned a combined attack against the Kentucky settlements. This was mere rumor but Logan mistook it for truth and accordingly decided to take vigorous measures to thwart the red men.

Convening a number of inhabitants of the region at Danville, which was then the most important town in Kentucky, Logan communicated to them the information he had received. They agreed that the situation demanded an expedition against their enemies. But how should they proceed with it? No one in Kentucky was authorized to call the militia into service. Furthermore, they had no money to purchase an adequate amount of ammunition and no arms to put it to use. Even if the militia volunteered its services and furnished itself with arms and ammunition, the convention still could give no assurance that the government would pay the men for their services or reimburse their expenditures.

The existing laws could brand an expedition a conspiracy or a criminal act or an act of merit—depending on which of the terms prejudice or sympathy dictated. Faced with this predicament, the convention recommended that the people elect another group of delegates to convene in the ensuing month at Danville to find some means of preserving their country from the destruction which seemed to them impending.

This measure the delegates adopted. On May 23, 1785, the second Danville convention unanimously passed resolutions calling for Kentucky's separation from Virginia and her admission into the Union. It also issued two papers, one as a broadside to the settlers and the other as a petition to the Virginia assembly. The broadside listed the principal grievances of the people:

We have no power to call out the militia, our sure and only defense, to oppose the wicked machinations of the savages, unless in cases of actual invasion.

We can have no executive power in the district, either to enforce the execution of laws, or to grant pardons to objects of mercy; because such a power would be inconsistent with the policy of government, and contrary to the present constitution.

We are ignorant of the laws that are passed until a long time after they are enacted; and in many instances not until they have expired: by means whereof penalties may be inflicted for offenses never designed, and delinquents escape the punishment due to their crimes.

We are subjected to prosecute suits in the High Court of Appeals at Richmond, under every disadvantage, for the want of evidence, want of friends, and want of money.

The petition declared that the remoteness of Kentucky from the seat of government, "together with other inconveniences, subjects the . . . people . . . to a number of grievances too pressing to be longer borne, and which cannot be remedied whilst the district continues a part of the state of Virginia."

Most historians believe that both papers were the brain children of General James Wilkinson. Though not a member of the convention, Wilkinson had guarded reasons for wanting to know what was going on. From a motive which, as we shall see, was far removed from patriotism, he had volunteered his grandiloquent pen in Kentucky's behalf. He was a jealous man with a large talent for intrigue which he concealed under a number of external graces and a glib intellect. His handsome face, his friendly approach, his sonorous voice, his exquisite manners and his brilliant pen—all were attractions by which he succeeded in duping even the most discerning of his countrymen.

Wilkinson's gifts for intrigue had all the polish of long and wide practice. As a young officer in the Revolution he won by his elegant manners and brilliant address the favor of prominent men. Though his ability was never more than mediocre, his personality enabled him to climb from promotion to promotion. Success bared his shortcomings. He won the confidence of his superiors, only to plot their downfall; he won the love of his friends, only to betray them to his own aggrandizement.

When Burgoyne invaded New York, Colonel Hardin discovered an important movement of that general and communicated it to Wilkinson, who reported it as his own discovery. Later General Horatio Gates sent him to report Burgoyne's surrender at Saratoga to Congress. Invited to address that body, he won its favor and the rank of brigadier general—in preference to the two real heroes of Saratoga, Colonel Daniel Morgan and General Benedict Arnold.

When Gates became President of the Board of War, an office of great power, he made Wilkinson secretary of that body. Later Wilkinson became the moving spirit in the infamous cabal by which Gates and a few of his friends plotted to overthrow Washington and make Gates commander in chief of the Continental Army. But Wilkinson, soon sensing that the cabal would not succeed in its aim, betrayed its secrets to Lord Sterling. This Scotsman, whose title was pretended, went with the information to Washington's aide, Alexander Hamilton, who confronted Gates with the plot. Gates flew into a rage and vowed to challenge his betrayer, who saved his "honor" by denouncing Sterling as a liar and by dismissing his part in the cabal as the indiscretion of a "convivial hour." With this explanation Wilkinson avoided duels with Gates and Sterling; but his fellow officers were not deceived. Forty-nine other brigadier generals requested Congress to rescind his commission. Wilkinson quickly resigned.

Within eighteen months he was back on the payroll as clothier general—a post highly congenial to one of his peculiar talents. Accused of corruption, Wilkinson resigned and again protested his innocence. To a friend he rationalized that his resignation had resulted, not from "conscious guilt and an apprehension of punishment," but from "the difficulty, if not impossibility, of obtaining a public opinion against the infallibility of George Washington."

Impoverished but ambitious, bitter but undaunted, Wilkinson moved to Kentucky where in 1784 he borrowed enough money to open a trading post and build a fine frame house at Lexington. But he was more interested in land speculation than in the store which he left in the charge of an assistant who helped himself to the money of some of the sales. Before long Wilkinson was in dire financial straits which his scheming mind hoped to relieve by the devious route of local politics. His high military rank and his vaunted courage during the Revolution won him the support of the unsuspecting settlers. He was elected a delegate to the next Danville convention.

The old convention had had no intention of acting hastily on the important matter of separation from Virginia. To have more time for the gathering of additional information and for obtaining the unity of the settlers, before it adjourned it had recommended the election of delegates to another convention during the summer.

The third Danville convention met on August 8, 1785. Wilkinson was conspicuously present. He easily dominated the convention hall. In a fiery address he charged that the domestic taxes of Virginia were as obnoxious as the British colonial taxes had been. He was so loudly applauded that he was inspired to write another address. This was directed to the Virginia assembly and taken to that body by two prominent members of the convention, George Muter, Judge of the Supreme Court, and Harry Inness, Attorney General. The Wilkinsonian flavor is unmistakable as it pleads for separation:

To recite minutely the causes and reasoning which have directed and will justify this address, would, we conceive, be a matter of impropriety at this juncture. It would be preposterous for us to enter upon the support of facts and consequences, which we presume are incontestable; our sequestered situation from the seat of government, with the intervention of a mountainous desert of two hundred miles, always dangerous, and passable only at particular seasons, precludes every idea of a connexion on republican principles. The patriots who formed our constitution, sensible of the impracticability of connecting permanently in a free government, the extensive limits of the commonwealth, most wisely made provision for the act which we now solicit.

To the sacred record we appeal. . . . 'Tis not the ill-directed or inconsiderable zeal of a few, 'tis not that impatience of power to which ambitious minds are prone; nor yet the baser considerations of personal interest, which influences the people of Kentucky; directed by superior motives, they are incapable of cherishing a wish unfounded in justice; and are now impelled by expanding evils, and irremediable grievances, universally seen, felt and acknowledged, to obey the irresistible dictates of self-preservation, and seek for happiness by means honorable to themselves, honorable to you, and injurious to neither.

We therefore . . . do pray that an act may pass at the ensuing session of assembly, declaring and acknowledging the sovereignty and independence of this district.

The delegates were so sure that this appeal would succeed that they adjourned the convention without providing for another. The next convention, they believed, would be for the purpose of drafting a constitution. One of the delegates, Judge Caleb Wallace, wrote to James Madison inviting him to become a citizen of the new state. But Madison, confessing a dislike for "your wilderness," politely refused the invitation.

The Virginia assembly lent a willing ear to Kentucky's plea. Anxious to rid itself of a region which had long proved a burden to govern and defend, it passed on January 10, 1786, an enabling act. It was willing to grant Kentucky separation, however, only on condition that she should become a part of the Union; it had no intention of permitting her to go to Spain through some intrigue or design on the part of some of her politicians.

The enabling act provided that the boundaries of the state of Kentucky should be those of the territory of Kentucky. The land claims of the new state, which were based on those of Virginia, were to be left unchanged. Kentucky was to assume a proportionate share of Virginia's Revolutionary War debt. The lands which Virginia had assigned to her soldiers were to be reserved until 1788. The Ohio River was declared free to all Americans. All disputes over the foregoing matters were to be settled by arbitration.

In addition to these terms the enabling act stipulated that the people of Kentucky should hold another convention in September 1786 and declare for separation under the terms of the enabling act. The new convention then should name a day before September 1787 when Virginia's authority over the region should cease. Thereupon the enabling act was to "become a solemn compact . . . provided, however, that prior to June 1, 1787, Congress shall assent" to Kentucky's admission into the Union in accordance with the specified terms.

Circumstances prevented the next convention from assembling at the designated time. Early in 1786 Indian tribes from north of the Ohio attacked several Kentucky settlements, compelling them to ask Virginia for military assistance. Governor Patrick Henry replied that he had informed Congress of the matter and had urged it to take measures to protect the settlements. In a private letter to Colonel Logan, however, Henry admitted that Congress had taken no account of his representation. At the same time Henry wrote to the county lieutenants ordering them to undertake expeditions against the offending Indians.

When the time for convening the fourth convention arrived, so many of its delegates were absent on military duty that it was unable to proceed with business. The delegates who remained in Danville addressed to the Virginia assembly a memorial informing it of the delay and requesting it to extend the time limit set for separation in the enabling act. After delegating John Marshall to present the memorial, the convention dissolved itself.

Not until January 1787 did a quorum of delegates present themselves in Danville. They reconvened only to learn that the Virginia assembly had repealed the enabling act. Then it had passed a new enabling act, explaining that, since unforeseen events had hindered the delegates from meeting on the date stipulated in the first act, Congress had not had sufficient time in which to deliberate on the propriety of admitting Kentucky into the Union. The new act then directed another convention to meet at Danville in September 1787 and to fix a day, not later than January 1, 1789, on which Virginia's authority should cease, provided Congress should assent to Kentucky's admission prior to July 4, 1788.

Needless to say, the people of Kentucky received information of this second enabling act with great "discomfiture and chagrin." Independence was as far away as ever. Their depressed mood envisioned every ugly possibility. What could prevent the assembly from repealing the new act as it had the old? Could it not, if it wished, find plausible pretense for so doing? In that case the "evils and inconveniences" which had impelled the settlers to seek separation would continue, and might even increase!

Upon this aggravation came another. In March after the convention had adjourned, the Correspondence Committee of Western Pennsylvania, with headquarters in Pittsburgh, informed the Kentuckians that Minister of Foreign Affairs John Jay had made a definite proposition to Gardoqui to cede the navigation of the Mississippi for a period of twenty-five or thirty years in return for granting certain commercial advantages to the eastern states. In this letter the infuriated settlers saw nothing less than the "absolute sacrifice of every interest of the Western countries, to promote the prosperity of the east." The newly organized Danville Club, which met every Saturday to discuss the current political situation in Kentucky, persuaded four prominent members of the adjourned convention, John Brown, John Sebastian, Harry Innes and George Muter, to address a protest to Congress saying, in part:

This is a subject that requires no comment—the injustice of the measure is glaring—and as the inhabitants of this district wish to unite their efforts, to oppose the cession of the navigation of the Mississippi, with those of their brethren residing on the western waters, we hope to see such an exertion made, upon this important occasion, as may convince Congress that the inhabitants of the western country are united in the opposition, and consider themselves entitled to all the privileges of freemen, and those blessings procured by the revolution; and will not tamely submit to an act of oppression, which would tend to a deprivation of our rights and privileges.

The protest was dispatched, but before it arrived in New York the Kentuckians were relieved to learn that Congress had rejected Jay's proposal.

On October 17, 1787, the fifth convention assembled belatedly in Danville. Wilkinson was not a member. The previous spring he had departed for New Orleans—for what reasons we shall presently learn. The delegates again petitioned Congress to grant Kentucky statehood and suggested December 31, 1788, as the date on which Virginia's authority should end. At about the same time they requested the Virginia assembly to appoint a delegate to plead Kentucky's case in Congress. Complying with their wish, the assembly chose John Brown, a former delegate to the convention and now a state senator from the Kentucky region.

Doubting that his mission would succeed, Brown arrived in New York where Congress was in session. Circumstances were clearly against him. The Federal Convention, sitting in Philadelphia, had been proposing an entirely new government to supplant the insolvent Confederation. It had drafted the Federal Constitution and had submitted it to the states for ratification or rejection. Ratification by nine of them would mean the dissolution of Congress.

Another problem pressed Brown. He must obtain statehood for Kentucky before July 4, 1788, as stipulated in the second enabling act, or his mission would fail even though Congress should remain in session longer. Determined to overcome these handicaps, Brown promptly presented Kentucky's petition, but Congress took no notice of it for over three months. Then, instead of giving its assent, it merely resolved on the expediency of admitting Kentucky as an independent member of the Confederation.

Accordingly, Congress appointed a committee to report the necessary act, but neither it nor the committee took action on the matter. Brown suspected with justification that the eastern members of Congress were responsible for the delay; they were, he wrote, jealous "of the growing importance of the western country" and therefore unwilling "to add a vote to the southern interest."

The eastern members anxiously awaited ratification of the Federal Constitution, an event which would preclude the possibility of admitting Kentucky into the Confederation. Their hopes were soon realized. By July 2—only two days before the limiting date set for statehood in the enabling act—nine states had ratified the Constitution. Thereupon the committee dissolved itself. Congress then passed a resolution directing its secretary to advise the Virginia assembly and Samuel McDowell, president of the Danville convention, that, in view of events, Congress was unable "to adopt any other measure." However, it recommended statehood for Kentucky "as soon as convenience will permit," and urged the Virginia assembly to change its enabling act to conform with the spirit of the Constitution.

Gardoqui quickly took advantage of Brown's disappointment to approach him with an attractive offer. The Spanish chargé d'affaires agreed to open the Mississippi to the Kentucky settlers if Kentucky would declare her independence and empower some person to negotiate with Spain. But because of commercial treaties existing between Spain and other European powers, he added he could not grant them this privilege so long as Kentucky remained a part of the United States.

Brown listened with a friendly but objective demeanor, discreetly committing himself to nothing; he neither embraced nor rejected the scheme. He replied that he would reflect on the matter and would discuss it further with Gardoqui at a later date. After the interview Brown disclosed the Spanish proposition to his old friend and fellow delegate, James Madison, who shared the same house with him. The two men favored and discussed the Federal Constitution and exchanged views on the political situation in Kentucky. Madison advised Brown to keep Gardoqui's scheme a secret. The impatience of the Kentuckians to obtain navigation of the Mississippi and their distrust of Federal policy, he feared, might induce them to support a proposition seemingly propitious to them.

Brown took Madison's advice. In a letter reporting the failure of his mission to his friends, George Muter and Samuel McDowell, he enclosed an account of his interview with Gardoqui. When a few days later he saw Gardoqui again, Brown maintained his usual discretion. He told Gardoqui that the people of Kentucky would soon elect a new convention which would doubtless resolve on the creation of an independent state. Then he disclosed his intention to return soon to Kentucky where he promised to discuss the subject of their interview with the delegates. In bidding the Spaniard good-by Brown politely thanked him for his offer in the name of the people of Kentucky.

The sixth Danville convention, meeting on July 28, 1788, had the mortification to learn of Congress' failure to admit Kentucky into the Union. Prominent among the delegates to this convention was Isaac Shelby, who had moved to Kentucky in 1783. Shelby had married a daughter of Nathaniel Hart at Boonesboro and settled down as a cotton planter. He served as a trustee of Transylvania Seminary and, in 1784, had been chairman of the first Danville convention. Affable and politically sagacious, he was to become the first governor of the state of Kentucky. Shelby now had the backing of his colleagues in resolving a firm policy.

The convention recommended to the people the election of five representatives from each county to meet in Danville on November 4, 1788, and to delegate to them full power to adopt whatever measures they deemed expedient to obtain admission for Kentucky "as a separate and independent member of the United States of America, and the navigation of the river Mississippi." The delegates closed their meeting by voting to "wait on Mr. Brown, when he shall return to the district, and in the most respectful terms express to him the obligations which the convention and their constituents were under to him, for his faithful attention to their interests."

The general dismay and confusion that prevailed in Kentucky between the fourth and fifth Danville conventions provided James Wilkinson with the conditions he needed to stage the most brilliant of his intrigues. Unsuccessful in business—and afraid of his creditors in Kentucky—he determined to make his fortune elsewhere. His scheme was as bold as it was original. Wilkinson planned to take a boatload of Kentucky products to New Orleans, confer there with Governor Miró, win his friendship and obtain from him a monopoly of trade. In return Wilkinson was prepared to offer the King of Spain his great influence to detach Kentucky from the United States and to convert it into an independent buffer state that should serve to shield Louisiana from possible American aggression.

But how was he to guard himself against arrest and the con-
fiscation of his boat and cargo? His imagination, always fertile
in such matters, promptly furnished him with the answer. He
would first send a friend to warn Miró that the arrest of such
an important person as himself would precipitate a war which
might well result in the conquest of Louisiana. Faced with this
threat, Miró would be pleased to receive Wilkinson.

The scheme worked. The Spanish river authorities permitted
Wilkinson's friend to proceed with the cargo to New Orleans,
and Wilkinson himself reached the city on July 2, 1787. He saw
a gay emporium of over five thousand Spaniards and Frenchmen
whose languages he did not understand and whose religion was
distasteful to him. He saw evidences of squalor and ignorance,
but also of wealth and culture. As he looked sensuously at the
powdered Frenchwomen, dancing the quadrille in their intrigu-
ing finery, "he must have thought ruefully of his horny-handed
wife in her homespun dress." But he did not remain a stranger
long. His friendly manner, his elegant address and his appar-
ent sincerity soon won him the friendship of the Spanish officials.

Miró, who spoke a little English, was especially delighted by
Wilkinson's handsome face and his gift of repartee. In a conference with the governor the American explained that the people of Kentucky nursed serious grievances against both Virginia
and the United States and planned to go their independent way.
That was their ultimate goal; their immediate objective was to
secure the navigation of the Mississippi by invading Louisiana
and by driving out the Spaniards. Even now, said Wilkinson, a
large American army to be commanded by George Rogers Clark
was being formed at Vincennes for that very purpose.

Wilkinson's tissue of lies impressed Miró immeasurably.
George Rogers Clark! The mention of that conqueror made the
Spaniard tremble and sent the American bounding up the lucrative path. Wilkinson hastened to assure Miró that his influence
was so great that he could prevent the invasion. Indeed, he
could do much more: he could persuade his "fellow countrymen" to repudiate the United States and ally themselves with
Spain. As a reward for his services he asked only that he be given
the exclusive privilege of trading with New Orleans in Kentucky
products. The Kentuckians, envying his good fortune and eager

to share it with him, would embrace his program. True, the exclusive trade would yield him immense profit—this was purely incidental; his primary aim, he said, was to benefit the Kentuckians as well as His Catholic Majesty.

All of which was as clever as it was untrue. Wilkinson was interested neither in obtaining benefits for his fellow countrymen nor in urging them to establish a separate state. A critical study of the writings and documents dealing with his career should convince any discerning person that he was working solely for himself. Money was his mania.

Yet several writers with more learning than understanding have, after vigorous digging into archival materials, concluded that he meant to separate the region of Kentucky from the United States and that, therefore, he was a traitor to his country. Failing to find documentary evidence, they have resorted to innuendo and inference—and have succeeded in proving only their own pedestrian vagueness. In the knowledge of the present writer only two scholars—James Ripley Jacobs and Thomas Robson Hay—have explained correctly Wilkinson's connections with the Spanish governors of New Orleans. "It is largely a matter of interpretation," says Hay in an admirable article, "to determine just what were Wilkinson's intentions, motives, and aspirations. That he was unscrupulous and of a jealous disposition, that he was an adventurer and a dissimulator is evident in many ways; that he was a traitor rather than an opportunist and a speculator, is not by any means proved." Wilkinson, continues Hay, "let the Spanish governors . . . think he was working in their interests, while he was doing the same thing with respect to his friends and associates in Kentucky and elsewhere." His motives were obviously to profit financially from both parties without siding with either.

How did Wilkinson expect to dupe Miró? By the simple procedure of making promises that he would postpone from time to time while he fattened his purse by buying Kentucky products on his own terms and then selling them in New Orleans for several hundred per cent profit.

Miró welcomed the scheme for reasons easily seen. In limiting the use of the Mississippi to the Kentuckians he envisaged the eventual downfall of the United States. Without a trade outlet the lands north of the Ohio, which the United States had acquired at the end of the Revolution, would be unsalable; immigrants from the east would by-pass them and settle in Spain's ally, Kentucky. Unable to sell her public lands on which she depended for finances to meet her expenses, the United States would eventually fall to pieces. The nation would separate into thirteen small, quarreling and lawless governments confined by the Alleghenies. Some would probably ally themselves with Great Britain, others with France and still others with Spain. Miró knew that his superiors in Madrid would like nothing better than this.

Miró was credulous but not a fool. Unwilling to rest complete confidence in Wilkinson's verbal promises, he called in Intendant Martín Navarro as a witness to their conference. The three men then contributed the ideas for a memorial which Wilkinson consented to write and sign. When the memorial was completed Miró sent it to Valdés, Secretary of State and President of the Council of the Indies.

The memorial displays all of Wilkinson's literary characteristics: his pompous and exuberant style, his ingenious dialectics and his brilliant and audacious mendacity. Wilkinson argued that navigation of the Mississippi was the fountain from which the western settlers hoped to find relief and comfort. "They will employ any means, however desperate, to attain it." In order to achieve this end they were determined "to separate themselves from the American Union." But Kentuckians wished no quarrel with Spain; indeed, they wanted to come to "an amicable agreement" with her. Her refusal to grant them this privilege might cause them to join England in hostilities against His Catholic Majesty.

Wilkinson now summoned God to the support of his arguments. The Almighty, he affirmed, made the Mississippi to help the people living on its banks:

When we cast our eyes on the country East of the Mississippi we find it of vast extension, varied in its climate, of excellent lands, the best in the New World, abounding in the most useful mines, minerals and metals; on making this examination the question naturally arises: For what purpose did the Father of the Universe create this country? Surely for the good of his creatures, for we are taught that he made nothing in vain. Does it not, therefore, strike the most limited intellect that he who closes the only gate by which the inhabitants of this extensive region may approach their neighbors in pursuit of useful intercourse, oppose this benevolent design? Is not the Mississippi this gate? The privation of its use takes away from us Americans what nature seems to have provided for their indispensable convenience and happiness.

By this celestial path Wilkinson led the Spanish government head-on to the brink of hard reality. Compare the impregnable position of the Americans with the vulnerable exposure of the Spaniards:

The American defended by the barriers of nature is absolutely inacessible to any adequate force that may be sent to reduce him, at the same time he can instantly introduce into the very heart of Louisiana any corps of troops judged necessary, which can be easily made to submit by means of the same channel by which they came down. Thus it is in his power to incommode and tire Louisiana, even with small parties, without those having to expose their wives and children and goods, and it cannot be doubted that a daring race of men, accustomed to war and familiarized with danger on account of their incessant hostilities with the savages, will not hesitate to expose their lives in a fight of so great moment to themselves and their posterity.

But Wilkinson hastened to assure the Spanish government that he had the power to obviate this evil:

If in the reply which I may receive to this memorial my propositions are admitted, I shall on my return to Kentucky proceed with careful deliberation, take advantage of my personal consideration and political influence in order to familiarize the people with whom I live with and make popular among them the aims that constitute the purpose of my present voyage, to which I have already fixed the sight of all that part that knows how to discern in this community, and I will bind myself to constantly send by confidential messenger . . . exact accounts of the measures I may have adopted in this important business, the effect they produce as also of any procedure of Congress.

Wilkinson closed this masterpiece of dissimulation by enjoining the strictest secrecy to his project. Its success, he said, would depend largely on the continuance of Miró in office, "on account of his personal knowledge that both of us have formed." He also remembered Martín Navarro, whom he recommended for the post of minister to the United States as "most advantageous for the promotion of the project."

On completing the memorial Wilkinson clinched his arguments by giving Miró a declaration of his intention to expatriate himself—to repudiate the United States and take an oath of allegiance to His Catholic Majesty. Characteristically it remained an intention; it never became a fact. This political chameleon could without the slightest qualm change the color of his faith. In New Orleans he was a Spaniard; in Kentucky, an American. He was in complete accord with any side that could provide him with an opportunity to acquire wealth. He himself always avowed that he remained at heart an American. And for once he was probably telling the truth.

When Wilkinson submitted the memorial he received a written reply, signed jointly by Miró and Navarro, in which they granted him the right to send to New Orleans a cargo of tobacco, Negroes, cattle, hogs and apples worth between fifty and sixty thousand dollars. To give proof of his good conduct, Wilkinson made arrangements to deposit the proceeds in the provincial treasury. In turn Miró and Navarro assured him that, though they were not authorized to grant him the favors he asked, they were "persuaded that His Majesty will heed the reasons in the memorial, which fact you can make known to the prominent men and the other inhabitants of the district for their satisfaction and hope."

Elated with his success, Wilkinson sailed to Charleston. Thence he traveled by land to Richmond where he lobbied against the new Federal Constitution whose passage would be detrimental to his plans, visited George Washington in Philadelphia and relatives in Maryland and hurried on to Kentucky. In February 1788 he appeared in Lexington riding in a chariot drawn by four horses and surrounded by slaves and dogs, like a Roman general returning home from a victorious campaign.

He was as close-lipped on the matter of his pretended intrigue as he was loquacious in regard to the contract he had obtained. The Kentuckians, of course, were overjoyed. In their eyes Wilkinson was the answer to their economic prayers; he had found a market for their products. Wilkinson's popularity grew with every pound of pork and tobacco he bought, with every ship he had built, with every man he hired to act as agent or oarsman to take the produce to New Orleans.

In the spring of 1788 he formed a partnership with Major Isaac B. Dunn, who, with the assistance of a young adventurer named Philip Nolan, took to New Orleans a flotilla of twenty-five boats loaded with tobacco and flour that had lain in warehouses for three years. On arriving in New Orleans Dunn signed for himself and Wilkinson an agreement with Daniel Clark making him their agent for future shipments to Kentucky. Dunn returned home by sea, leaving Nolan to take a boatload of produce up the Mississippi. The boat, however, capsized in the frozen Ohio with a loss to Wilkinson and Dunn of $8,000. Wilkinson by letter criticized Clark for sending the boat in the dead of winter and discharged him.

Meanwhile Wilkinson was sparing no effort to give Miró evidence of his loyalty. Using his popularity with certain political leaders, he got himself elected as a delegate to the seventh convention which met in Danville on November 3, 1788. From the moment the convention opened he cunningly managed to direct most of its proceedings in such a manner that record of them would convince Miró he was exerting all his influence to bring about the eventual success of their scheme.

The convention resolved itself into a committee of the whole, of which Wilkinson was nearly always chairman. The committee studied Congress' resolution recommending statehood for Kentucky and the resolution, passed in the previous convention, granting full power to the five representatives of each county to try to gain statehood and navigation of the Mississippi. The result of this deliberation was the appointment of two special committees: one was to request the Virginia assembly to grant independence to Kentucky; the other was to ask Congress "to take immediate and effective measures for procuring the navigation of the Mississippi."

John Brown offered a resolution setting forth Kentucky's desire for separation from Virginia and admission as an independent state into the Union. Needless to say, this was highly injurious to Wilkinson's pretenses, and by his contrivance, it was laid on the table. Instead Wilkinson used his old weapon of temporizing by offering a resolution which suggested that an address be distributed among the people, "urging the necessity of union, concord, and mutual concession, and solemnly calling upon them to furnish" the delegates "with instructions in what manner to proceed on the important subject" submitted to them. The resolution was unanimously adopted.

At this juncture his confidant, Harry Innes, by prearrangement, called on Wilkinson for an account of his sojourn in New Orleans. He rose and in a matter-of-fact manner stated that Miró had requested him to commit to writing his sentiments on navigation of the Mississippi. He then produced a copy of his memorial and began to read it. By carefully passing over the incriminating passages he succeeded in presenting an interesting essay in defense of navigation of the river. As he finished each page he handed it to another confidant, John Sebastian, who guarded them all as if they were treasures and disposed of them as soon as he could. The unsuspecting delegates greeted Wilkinson's version of the memorial with loud applause.

When the room was quiet again Wilkinson called on John Brown to give an account of his conferences with Gardoqui. Mindful of Madison's warning that public knowledge of the matter might arouse a mighty demand to accept Gardoqui's offer, Brown hesitated to stand. Obliged to make some sort of reply, he said that, though he was not at liberty to mention what had passed between Gardoqui and himself in their private conversations, he could assure the delegates that, if they remained united in their councils, everything they wished for would be realized.

In the last session of the convention Wilkinson resumed the chairmanship of the committee. By ingenious manipulation he obtained a resolution to approve his memorial. In return, the convention requested McDowell to present him the thanks of the delegates "for the regard which he therein manifested for the Interest of the Western Country." This motion, passed without a dissenting vote, was calculated to furnish Miró with additional proof of his influence in Kentucky. At Wilkinson's suggestion the convention ordered that the proceedings of the convention be published in the *Kentucky Gazette*.

Again Wilkinson played Miró against time. In a letter to the governor he disclosed that the people of Kentucky had been invited to adopt "all the measures necessary to secure for themselves a government separate from that of the United States because it would have been evident that Congress had neither the will nor the power to satisfy their hopes." Then he went on to explain that he had decided

... to wait for the effects which will result from the disappointment of these hopes ... The same effect will be produced by the suspension of the navigation of the Mississippi, which lies entirely in the power of Spain, and which must reduce this section of the country to misery and ruin; and as it has been stipulated that the operations of the Federal Government shall be uniform, the new Congress will have to lay taxes, without exception Whatever, over the whole country submitted to its jurisdiction. The people here, not having the means of paying these taxes, will resist them, and the authority of the new government will be set at naught, which will produce a Civil war, and result in the separation of the West and the East.

This event, Wilkinson averred, was "written in the book of destiny," though its advent must await "the natural effect of political measures." In concluding his letter he requested Miró to forbid navigation of the river to anybody save "those who understand and promote the interest of Spain in this part of the Country. . . ."

Wilkinson enclosed a copy of the *Kentucky Gazette* containing the proceedings of the convention. Thus Miró was deceived into believing he had incontestable proof that Wilkinson had read his memorial to the convention, that the delegates had been informed of the scheme to detach Kentucky, that Brown's pro-Union resolution had been rejected and that, instead, the convention had adopted Wilkinson's resolutions calling for popular instructions and for another convention—all without a dissenting vote. Miró could also learn in the newspaper that the convention had approved the memorial and had even voted its author an ovation. He would have no doubt that Wilkinson was really working to detach Kentucky from the United States and to convert it eventually into a Spanish dependency.

Wilkinson's satisfaction was short-lived, however. In the autumn of 1788 Dunn brought word from New York that Gardoqui had given Colonel George Morgan, a shrewd land speculator and veteran of the Revolution, permission to establish a colony in the southwest corner of present Missouri. This was in keeping with the Spanish policy of attempting to circumvent the United States by encouraging the establishment of American colonies in Spanish territory west of the Mississippi.

The capital of the proposed colony, New Madrid, was to be a frontier metropolis with a natural lake, straight and wide streets and sidewalks, fragrant groves and orchards, park highways, schools and churches of every denomination, for Gardoqui had promised to grant the prospective colonists the special dispensation of religious toleration. This wilderness Utopia was to be free of all taxes, poverty and white hunters. New Madrid was to thrive on agriculture and commerce alone, and the buffalo and bear in the surrounding forest were to be reserved for the neighboring Indians.

The establishment of such a colony would, of course, ruin Wilkinson's monopoly since Kentuckians could dispose of their products in nearer New Madrid where they would be detained until they could be taken to market in New Orleans. Alarmed, Wilkinson hurried to confer with Miró on the matter, arriving in New Orleans in July 1789 with a cargo of tallow, tobacco, butter, bacon, hams, lard and smoked beef. Bad news greeted him: Isaac Dunn had found his wife unfaithful and had in a moment of jealous rage put a bullet through his head, leaving his partner responsible for $10,000 in joint obligations. Depressed and bitter, Wilkinson went to see Miró, who told him he had recently held an interview with Morgan, whose project he had, for obvious reasons, disparaged.

Wilkinson demolished Morgan with a barrage of epithets which sprang from an unconscious estimate of his own character: the colonel was an opportunist, a schemer, a turncoat; he sought to ally himself with anybody who provided him with an opportunity to turn a dishonest dollar; he was completely unworthy of His Majesty's trust. Morgan's project, moreover, would do Spain no good. On the contrary, it would do immeasurable harm, for the Americans who settled in New Madrid would never become loyal subjects of Spain. By maintaining "constant contact with their compatriots in Kentucky," they would keep "all their old prejudices and principles," remaining as American as when they lived on the Ohio.

Furthermore, if Gardoqui allowed the Kentuckians to dispose of their products at the free port of New Madrid so far from the market at New Orleans, it would cause all sorts of difficulties which would lead to misunderstanding and perhaps even war between Spain and the United States. Wilkinson warned Miró that such an event would completely ruin their plans.

The governor, impressed by these arguments, assured Wilkinson that he was opposed to the project and that he would do all he could to discourage it. But Miró changed his mind completely and formed a favorable impression of Morgan when a few months later Spain reversed her foreign policy in order to gain the friendship of the United States. Circumstances external to our story, however, forced Morgan to abandon the project.

Two other important matters had sent Wilkinson southward: he expected the arrival of a reply to his memorial, and his financial circumstances were such that he was impelled to seek immediate compensation for his "services" to Spain. In pursuance of the second matter he penned a second memorial in which he informed the Spanish government that lack of funds prevented him from maintaining his personal influence and that of "many who cooperate with me." He mentioned money, he said, "with extreme repugnance," and only because he was in such "critical circumstances." He estimated his immediate need at $7,000 which he felt was due him for his services to Spain and as reimbursement for journeys he had made and was to make in his capacity as secret agent of Spain. In conclusion Wilkinson "pointed out that he had invested $14,000 in merchandize shipped from New Orleans in order to convince the people along the Ohio that merchandize could be transported to New Orleans at a lower cost than to the Atlantic seaboard across the Appalachian Mountains." Miró gave Wilkinson the sum he requested with the understanding that it should be repaid if the Spanish court refused to allow it as a pension.

The ease with which he secured the money prompted Wilkinson to ask Miró for a much larger sum. He pretended to the governor that he had obtained the support of a number of Kentucky "notables" in their scheme and that these requested bribes for their services. He drew up a list of his "supporters," each of whom was to be pensioned in proportion to his importance. "To have one's name on the list was no index of dishonesty— only an indication that Wilkinson considered the person worth mentioning." Even his bitterest political foes, Thomas and Humphrey Marshall, were included. Why not? In this windfall of Spanish dollars, Wilkinson was to be the chief, if not the only, beneficiary:

Harry Innes, attorney and counseler at law, now has
   $500.00 from the State of Virginia..............$1000.00
Benjamin Sebastian, Jurist........................$1000.00
John Brown, Member of Congress...................$1000.00
Caleb Wallace, one of our Judges, enjoys $1000.00 from
   the State of Virginia.........................$1000.00
John Fowler, zealous advocate of our cause and a man of
   influence $1000.00
The above are confidential friends, who support my plans.

Benjamin Logan, lately a Major of Militia............$ 800.00
Isaac Shelby, a planter of means and influence........$ 800.00
James Garard, Colonel of Militia and a man of influence $ 800.00
These favor separation from Virginia and an amicable agreement with Spain.

William Wood, a Minister of great power..........$ 500.00
Henry Lee, Colonel of Militia.....................$ 500.00
Richard Taylor, a planter of much influence........$ 500.00
These favor separation from Virginia, but their aims do
    not go beyond that.

General Lawson arrived in Kentucky just at the time I
    was leaving there; he is a gentleman of high attain-
    ments and Military knowledge, is my friend and
    will embrace our principles..................$1000.00
George Nicholas, has lately arrived in Kentucky; he is
    among the more wealthy gentlemen of the Country,
    of great ability and it will be a great point to attract
    him to our political aims. I have for some time been
    an intimate friend of his and I believe that he will
    offer his services...........................$2000.00
Alexander Scott Bullitt, a man of means and ability, but
    very capricious. Nevertheless he will serve our
    cause $1000.00
Thomas Marshall, Surveyor......................$1000.00
Humphrey Marshall, a villain without principles, un-
    scrupulous and may cause us much harm........$ 600.00
George Muter, has $1000.00 from the State of Virginia $1200.00
Green Clay, a private party of some influence........$ 500.00
Samuel Taylor,   ”   ”   ”   ”   ”   ....$ 500.00
Robert Caldwell, Colonel of Militia................$ 500.00
Richard Sanderson, Surveyor, Popular, but not very
    capable ....$ 500.00

Wilkinson submitted the list in vain. About this time Miró received a reply to Wilkinson's first memorial. It completely
shattered their plans.

The Council of Ministers, meeting in November 1788, had
flatly rejected Wilkinson's proposal that Spain foment a revolution in Kentucky. The Council, fearing trouble with the United
States, had declared that until the frontiersmen established their
own independence Spain could form no connection with them.
Miró was instructed to continue his correspondence with Wilkinson but was forbidden to spend any money to encourage a fron-

tier revolution or to make promises to, or even engagements with, the revolutionists.

The truth was that Spain, unsure of her European position, felt the need of American friendship and could not afford to be implicated in fomenting a revolution so close to her own dominions. Miró informed Wilkinson that the King of Spain had abandoned his unwise course of trying to conspire with the Kentuckians; indeed, he had completely reversed his former policy by encouraging Americans to migrate to Louisiana. Henceforth, by paying a 15 per cent duty, Kentuckians were to be permitted to ship their goods through New Orleans. Furthermore, they could escape this duty by migrating to Louisiana where they were promised free land, religious freedom, equal trading privileges and the right to sell tobacco at high prices to the royal warehouses. Miró explained to Wilkinson that Spain by this policy hoped to strengthen her weak colonies with a wealthy and loyal population.

Thunderstruck by this reversal of fortune, Wilkinson returned to Kentucky in the fall of 1789 to learn the fatal word that his countrymen were preparing to draw up a constitution under which they hoped to enter the Union. On December 29, 1788, in response to the address submitted by the Danville convention, the Virginia assembly had passed a third enabling act which authorized elections for a new convention to decide again on the expediency of separation. The second and eighth articles of this document were materially altered, to the detriment of Kentucky, for they proposed that she should pay a part of Virginia's state debt and was denied any right to unappropriated lands after she was made into an independent state.

The eighth convention, meeting in Danville on July 20, 1789, during Wilkinson's absence, found the terms of the enabling act "inadmissable and injurious to the people." It therefore addressed a memorial to the Virginia assembly requesting it to remove the obnoxious articles. The assembly complied by passing a new enabling act which provided for the election of delegates to a new convention at Danville on July 26, 1790, to determine for a fifth time whether the people of the region wished to separate from Virginia. If the convention decided in the affirmative, the people were authorized by the new enabling act to designate a day before the first of November 1791 on which the authority of Virginia should cease, provided the federal government should give its consent and take the necessary measures for the election of a convention to form a constitution.

In the light of these events Wilkinson saw the possibility of being discovered and branded a traitor. To avoid this he abandoned all hope of finding fortune through intrigue and resolved to seek it instead in the army. As a result of the failure of his New Orleans trade his finances were in a bad way. He had borrowed, had earned, large sums; but the more he pursued wealth, the more it eluded him. All his life he had wanted to live like a maharajah. He had entertained lavishly and speculated unwisely on land schemes. Now he was contriving either to meet or, more often, to evade his debts.

To recoup his blasted fortune and silence his creditors, Wilkinson sent a cargo of tobacco to New Orleans, but misfortune dogged its progress. One of the boats sprang a leak and three others grounded in the river. Wilkinson's misfortunes ran in pairs. From New Orleans came word that only about half the cargo had passed the royal inspection and that his contingent expenses equaled the sum he should have received from a profitable sale of all his tobacco. He found himself $6,000 in debt. In despair he sent a circular letter to his creditors, begging them to refrain from pressing their claims. They waited grumblingly.

Bankrupt and disgusted, Wilkinson professed a sudden aversion for political life. He refused to seek election as a delegate to the next convention. Instead he confined himself for the time to the management of his tottering business affairs.

Wilkinson's vanity forbade him to confess deception to Miró outright. He preferred to let himself—and the governor—down gradually. He began by making excuses for accomplishing less than he had expected. In one letter he failed to mention the "notables" whom he had hitherto represented to Miró as his confederates. In another he confessed that he "had opened myself only to the Attorney General Innes and to Colonel Bullitt," though he softened the blow to the governor by adding that he had indirectly "sounded others, whom I also found well disposed to adopt my ideas." Then he attempted to restore his own damaged vanity by obliquely blaming Spanish policy for the failure of their scheme:

The general permission to export the products of this country through the Mississippi river, on paying a duty of 15 percent. has worked the consequences which I feared, because, every motive of discontent having been thus removed, the political agitation has subsided, and to-day there is not one word said about separation. Nor are the effects produced by this pernicious system less fatal in relation to our plan of fostering emigration to Louisiana. Every year, the inhabitants and landholders of these parts had ever present in their minds the terrible prospect of seeing their produce perish in their hands for want of a market, but now they no longer have any such apprehensions on account of the ready outlet they find at New Orleans for the fruits of their labor—which circumstances has diffused universal satisfaction in this district. . . .

Eventually Wilkinson admitted that even Innes and Bullitt had deserted his "plan," and that only Sebastian remained to assist him.

Thus the deceiver gradually bared himself to the deceived. But the governor was just as reluctant to admit credulity to his superior as Wilkinson had been to confess deception to the governor. In a letter to Valdés, Miró expressed surprise at the sudden change that Spain's new policy had wrought upon the attitude of the Kentuckians, and he wavered between an expression of confidence in Wilkinson's continued services and a confession of doubt in his loyalty:

Although I thought with Wilkinson that the commercial concessions made to the Western people might deter them from effecting their separation from the United States . . . yet I never imagined that the effects would be so sudden, and that the large number of influential men, whom Wilkinson, in his previous letters, had mentioned as having been gained over to our party, would have entirely vanished, as he now announces it, since he affirms having no other aid at present than Sebastian.

I consider that I am exposed to err in expressing an opinion on the acts of a man, who works at six hundred leagues from this place, and who had undoubtedly rendered, and is still rendering services to His Majesty, as I have explained it in my other dispatches. But the great falling off which I observe in his last letter induces me to believe that, full of good will and zeal, and persuaded from the experiences of past years, that he could bring around to his own opinions the chief men of Kentucky, he declared in anticipation that he had won over many of them, when he had never approached them on the main question. . . . Nevertheless, I am of opinion that said brigadier-general ought to be retained in the service of his Majesty, with an annual pension of two thousand dollars.

Despite these apologies for Wilkinson's conduct and the recommendation of a pension for him, Miró had no intention of giving him another opportunity to dissemble with impunity. He therefore decided to pursue the only wise policy in the game of corruption: "set a thief to catch a thief, and a spy after another spy." In concluding his letter to Valdés the governor recommended that Sebastian be pensioned also, "because I think it proper to treat with this individual, who will be able to enlighten me on the conduct of Wilkinson, and on what we have to expect from the plans of the said brigadier-general."

Thus the links in this chain of infamy were completed. Wilkinson was employed to watch the Kentuckians; Sebastian, to betray his confederate, Wilkinson. In 1792 the two men began to receive their pensions. By this time Wilkinson, commissioned by President Washington as a brigadier general in the United States Army, had begun another intrigue against his superior, General Anthony Wayne. Four years later, when Wayne died, Washington made Wilkinson commander in chief of the army— a position which, despite his continuing intrigues, he held for nineteen years.

As for Kentucky, she had long before passed triumphantly into the Union. The ninth convention, meeting in Danville on

July 27, 1790, decided in favor of statehood and advised Congress, which gave its consent. Accordingly, a constitutional convention in December 1791 drew up a constitution which Congress approved on February 4 of the following year. In June Kentucky became the fifteenth state of the Union. The fourteenth state, Vermont, had been admitted the previous year.

Making

of Tennessee

AT THE FORK OF THE HOLSTON AND WATAUGA RIVERS—NEAR where the first settlement of Tennessee was planted—stood a plain, commodious and heavily comfortable house of white oak logs. Its owner and occupant was William Cobb, a farmer of substance and culture, who entertained his guests more with profusion than with plenty. His servants, his spacious grounds, his simple and unpretentious equipage were always at their bidding. His horses, dogs, rifles and traps were more in their hands than in his own. "They felt themselves at home, and never said adieu to him or his family without the parting regret and the tenderness of an old friendship."

In the fall of 1790 Cobb entertained a most distinguished guest: William Blount, Governor of the "Territory of the United States South of the River Ohio." Significant events had preluded Blount's appointment to the post. In December 1789 North Carolina at last ceded her western lands to Congress which in the ensuing spring accepted them and converted them into a federal territory. President Washington considered Blount the best qualified of all the candidates for the governorship. He had long been a loyal friend, had a good military and Federalist record and was thoroughly familiar with, and sympathetic toward, frontier affairs and leaders. Feeling confident that a man of such qualifications would calm the turbulent frontiersmen and perhaps even align them with the administration, Congress in June appointed him to the post. At the same time he was made Superintendent of Indian Affairs for the Southern Department.

Though still young—he was only forty-one—the governor was a man of wide and diversified experience. Born of wealthy parents in eastern North Carolina, he received a private education superior to that of many of his contemporaries. At the outbreak of the Revolution he supported independence and became a paymaster in the army. Entering a political career, he served first in the North Carolina assembly, twice in the federal House of Representatives and then again in the state assembly. While he pursued politics he embraced a business enterprise of no small scope. As spokesman for his associates in the Muscle Shoals project, Blount sought to secure legal titles from either North Carolina or Georgia—both of which claimed ownership to the area—and to buy the land by private treaty with the Cherokee.

Much to his chagrin, Blount soon learned that federal commissioners had chosen to treat with the Southern Indians. Armed with Richard Caswell's financial support, he hurried southward with the intention of purchasing the Muscle Shoals area before the federal commissioners should award it to the Indians. But on the treaty ground at Hopewell, South Carolina, General Andrew Pickens, federal Indian agent who had "a vast contempt for the common white settler and an interest in Indian welfare," opposed him and succeeded for the time being in frustrating his plans. Turning to federal problems, Blount represented North Carolina in the Constitutional Convention at Philadelphia, though he played no prominent part in that body. When North Carolina accepted the constitution in 1789 Blount signed it as a member of the state convention. He unsuccessfully sought election as one of North Carolina's first senators.

Pending the location and establishment of a territorial capital, Blount made Cobb's home his residence as well as his executive mansion. Comfortable in a room with such frontier luxuries as glass windows and a fireplace, he moved with an air of dignified affluence, conducting state affairs, entertaining, and beguiling idle hours by reading John Trusler's *Principles of Politeness*. Then in November just before the cold snap set in, he and Judge Campbell undertook a tour of the territory. They covered the old Washington District, stopping at every county seat, naming officers whom Campbell swore in, and receiving the encomiums of the citizenry.

Later in the month the two men journeyed to Nashville where

James Robertson proudly showed them his estate of 4,000 rich acres, his grist and saw mills, his orchards and his blooded stock. Everywhere governor and citizens scrutinized each other with intense curiosity. The citizens saw a handsome, fair-haired man in lace, buckled shoes and a coat of the finest cloth, who spoke with learned phrases that sounded almost foreign but who, nevertheless, was friendly, practical, sincere and greatly interested in them and in their country.

As for Blount, he saw a society in transition. In the East he had pictured the people whom he was to govern as drunkards, brawlers and ear-croppers. Instead, he found them to be hard-working men, behaving more or less like those in the East. Fights and brawls were few and far between, and most settlers managed to keep their ears intact. Buckskins were giving way to eastern dress. Clubbed hair, once seen only in the inns, was becoming the common custom. Religion and education was strengthening frontier morality.

As he toured the counties Blount proclaimed the new government and notified those who held commissions under authority of North Carolina. To the citizenry he read the act of Congress accepting the cession of North Carolina, mentioned his own commission as governor, and disclosed that henceforth Congress would assume and execute the government of the territory in a manner similar to that which it supported north of the Ohio. He was alluding to the Northwest Ordinance which the Congress of the Confederation had passed on July 13, 1787, as the instrument of government for the territory acquired from Great Britain by the Treaty of Paris which ended the Revolution.

Blount explained that the Ordinance—adopted in its entirety by the new Federal Congress—established three stages of government for each territory in its progress toward statehood. In the first stage a governor, a secretary and three judges appointed by Congress were authorized to enforce laws and control the militia. A territory reached the second stage when it attained 5,000 free white males of voting age. At this point it would have a legislature consisting of a House of Representatives elected by the people and a Council of five members selected by Congress on nomination of the territorial House of Representatives. Also at this stage a territory would also send a delegate to Congress, who could participate in the deliberations of that body but could not vote.

A territory attained the last stage of government when it could count 60,000 inhabitants. It would then frame a constitution and apply for admission to the Union "on an equal footing with the original states, in all respects whatever." The Ordinance granted religious freedom, guaranteed trial by jury and declared that "schools and the means of education shall forever be encouraged."

In the interest of unity, Blount shrewdly recommended for office many of the adherents of the old Franklin government. John Sevier and James Robertson were commissioned brigadier generals of the militia in the eastern and western districts of the territory, respectively. To the minor military and civil offices the governor nearly always appointed men acceptable to the people.

Blount's position called for unusual tact. The settlers constantly complained that, as a hireling of the federal authorities, he pursued their policy of favoring the Indians. On the contrary, the federal authorities often upbraided the governor for failing to stop the settlers from making incursions on Indian lands. This state of affairs seldom bewildered Blount. While he steadfastly did his best to provide protection for the settlers against Indian attacks, he applied no mean diplomatic skill to avoid a break with the federal authorities. And he always tried to instill in the settlers a feeling of loyalty for the Union.

Returning to Cobb's late in December 1790, Blount found a message from the federal government requesting him to treat with the Cherokee. Embittered against the Franklin authorities for permitting speculators to appear on the bend of the Tennessee in violation of the Treaty of Hopewell, the Cherokee had gone on the warpath in a fanatic attempt to drive the whites from the region. More recently they had derived much encouragement from word of an Indian victory in the Northwest in October 1790 over Colonel Joshua Harmar, commanding a force of American militia. With this event the Indian marauding parties in Tennessee had increased. The settlers, fearing a general attack, had appealed to the federal government for assistance.

Blount, therefore, hastened his plans for peace. He sent Major Robert King, United States agent to the Cherokee, to summon their chiefs to a conference. At the same time he did not neglect his personal interests. Eager to procure the purchase of the Muscle Shoals area, which Pickens had frustrated at Hopewell, Blount wrote Secretary of War Henry Knox, arguing in favor of scrapping the treaty and of obtaining further Indian concessions for an annuity of $1,000. The authorities gave their approval.

Meanwhile King had returned from the Cherokee with the good news that they were willing to talk peace. Still the governor found discouragement on every side. Pickens, angry with him over their differences at Hopewell, warned the Cherokee that Blount was their secret enemy and that his only ambition was to grab all their lands. At about the same time the Cherokee harkened to rumors that Blount, in summoning them to a conference, planned to have them all massacred. The governor found them so skeptical of his good intentions that he had to send Robertson to reassure them.

In June 1791 Blount departed for White's Fort where the Cherokee had finally agreed to meet him. Among the 12,000 that gathered were two of the leading chiefs of the nation, John Watts and Bloody Fellow, both of whom had been friendly to the Americans until the Treaty of Hopewell disillusioned them. Watts was an astute, strong-willed and witty man whose father had been a trader of the same name and whose mother was a daughter of Chief Old Tassel. The Chickamauga were to make Watts their chief at the death of Dragging Canoe. Bloody Fellow was not as sanguinary as his name indicates. He seems to have derived it, not from any predilection for bloodshed, but from a fondness for bloody meat.

Though the Chickamauga were absent, Blount persuaded himself that enough of the Cherokee were present to formulate a binding treaty. Aware of the Indian love of ceremony, he overlooked no detail in his plans to entertain the chiefs with respectful attention and colorful pomp. By the bank of the river in the shade of huge elms he erected a marquee under which he sat in full dress with military hat and sword. Around him, uncovered and respectful, stood his civil and military officers. Here and there were gathered small bands of settlers from the surrounding countryside. The Indian braves, decorated with eagle feathers and the insignia of their rank, and the older chiefs and medicine men in common Indian dress, approached the marquee where James Armstrong, familiar with the etiquette of European courts, acted as master of ceremonies. One of the interpreters, in Indian costume, introduced each chief to Armstrong, who in turn presented him by his Indian name to Blount.

The negotiations were conducted in the style of an Indian council. Each speaker stood alone while his colleagues sat respectfully silent and fixedly attentive on the ground in a circle around him. Blount spoke first, announcing that the purpose of the conference was to buy another piece of ground from the Indians. Watts and Bloody Fellow, thinking that the conference had been called to iron out procedural kinks in the Treaty of Hopewell, were deeply chagrined. They protested loudly, but the hard-headed governor pressed his attack, demanding that the boundary be drawn in the Cumberland region. Watts and Bloody Fellow countered with a flat no, whereupon Blount, mindful of Muscle Shoals, proposed a larger cession whose boundary he said he would enforce by settling upon it. An even more emphatic no forced Blount to retreat to his first proposal which the Indians again rejected.

The debating grew more and more acrimonious with each proposal and counterproposal until Watts flew into a rage. He denounced North Carolinians, including Blount, as treaty-breakers, warned the other chiefs that negotiations with them was useless and threatened to go to Philadelphia and appeal to the Great White Father. To Watts's torrent of anger Blount made cool replies. He claimed all the disputed lands by right of conquest in the Revolution and reminded the chiefs that they could not appeal to President Washington without money to make the journey to Philadelphia.

At last cooler tempers prevailed. The Indians agreed to cede a tract of land running from a ridge on the Holston to the North Carolina border and westward to the mouth of the Clinch. As compensation for the cession Blount offered the chiefs an annuity of $1,000 and certain valuable gifts. The chiefs scorned this paltry sum. It would not buy, they said, a breechcloth for each person in their nation, but they accepted it temporarily when Blount promised to apply to Congress for a larger sum.

The Treaty of Holston, as it was called, established "perpetual peace" and restored friendship "between all the citizens of the United States and the whole Cherokee nation." It stated that the Cherokee agreed to place their fur trade under the protection of the United States, to grant American citizens navigation of the Tennessee River and the free and unmolested use of the road running between the Washington and Mero districts, and to surrender horse thieves and other felonious fugitives to the American authorities. In return for these concessions the United States gave the Cherokee a free hand in dealing with white intruders on Indian lands, requested passports for entry into Indian territory and renounced acts of retaliation. The two parties agreed to an exchange of prisoners by the following April and to the appointment of a joint commission of whites and Indians to mark the boundary guaranteed by the United States.

From a public and private point of view the treaty may be considered a success. Though Blount failed to secure the coveted Muscles Shoals area, he succeeded in regularizing on paper the points of dispute between the Cherokee and the settlers. Further, he legalized the settlements south of the French Broad and added a considerable slice of valuable wooded ground to Tennessee. The treaty, too, included certain equivocal terminology which could be construed to favor further cessions and more squatters within Indian territory.

Convinced that he had struck the best possible agreement with the Cherokee for the present, Blount sent the treaty to Philadelphia by express. In October it was laid before the Senate which soon ratified it. President Washington was as pleased with the Treaty of Holston as was Blount. In a letter of thanks he praised the governor for his zeal in promoting the interests of the United States and in endeavoring to obtain "a peace on the basis of justice and humanity."

During his sojourn at White's Fort, Blount was convinced that there was the best site for his capital. Much of the ground belonged to General James White, who had built the fort and given it his name. White was commissioned to lay out the streets and lots for a town which Blount named Knoxville for his superior officer, Secretary of War Henry Knox. On a knoll near the river Blount planned to build a weatherboarded log cabin where he would live with his family until he could realize a more fitting residence.

Knoxville grew rapidly. Settlers, anticipating the rising value of the ground, flocked there in large numbers; within a year it became the largest town in all Tennessee. It boasted more than two hundred houses, most of which were built of wood. John Chisholm, Blount's personal Indian agent and general handyman, built Knoxville's first tavern where such dignitaries as Attorney General Andrew Jackson and former Governor John Sevier often wined and dined. Chisholm's rates were considered "steep" for his day: "one shilling for breakfast, one shilling for supper, and one and sixpense for dinner; board and lodging for a week costing two dollars, and board only for the same space of time nine shillings."

Few stores in the East were as well stocked as those in Knoxville. The merchants procured their goods in the great trade centers of Richmond, Philadelphia and Baltimore. Because of the scarcity of coin and bank notes, most of the trade was carried on by barter. The manufacturers would specify the kinds of goods they would take and the different values they placed on them. The salt works of Washington, Virginia, for example, sold their product at seven shillings and sixpence per bushel if paid in cash or in such prime furs as mink, 'coon, muskrat, wildcat and beaver; at ten shillings if paid in bear or deerskins, beeswax, hemp, bacon, butter or beef cattle; and at twelve shillings if paid in ordinary garden produce. For their articles the manufacturers also accepted cash, tallow, lard in "white walnut kegs," new feathers, good horses, corn, rye, oats, flax and depreciated Continental currency. The stores sold nails, calico, axes, broadcloths, books, silks, furniture and salt over the counter. Such articles as drapery, mercury, drugs, fine earthenware and tea were brought directly from India to the United States in American ships. The Caribees furnished coffee and raw sugar. France sent taffetas, stockings, brandies and millstones.

Tennessee's earliest newspaper, the *Knoxville Gazette*, was printed first at Rogersville in 1791 because of troublesome Indians around Knoxville. The publisher was George Roulstone, who, with the assistance of R. Ferguson, also printed the paper. It was a double sheet, each page being ten by sixteen inches in size, containing advertisements as well as reading matter. The printers introduced the first issue in this manner:

We have now the pleasure of presenting the public with the first number of the 'Knoxville Gazette'. . . . The 'Knoxville Gazette' shall be published once in every two weeks. Each subscriber to pay two dollars per annum, one-half on subscribing, the remaining half in six months.

On Wednesday, October 10, 1792, the paper announced that it had moved to Knoxville which became its permanent home.

The *Knoxville Gazette* is a gold mine of information for almost every aspect of pioneer life in Tennessee. In politics it was strongly Federalist, mirroring in an emotional manner the policies of George Washington. Roulstone, like most journalists of the time, sympathized with the French Revolution; but in 1794 he ranged himself against it when he learned of the beheading of Marie Antoinette and of the Jacobin terror in Paris. The paper was full of poignantly quaint advertisements by persons whose friends and kinsfolk had been carried off by Indians and who anxiously sought their whereabouts. The many collection notices showed that the creditors realized that the people would pay their obligations if they could possibly do so. Another type of collector as well as of debtor is presented in the following advertisement:

TAKE NOTICE ALL YE WHISKEY DRINKERS—
That I will positively sue every person indebted to me in 21 days from this date, if they do not make payment.
                                                    Benjamin White

The columns of the *Gazette* were by no means confined to the opinions of white people; even an Indian used them. Chief Red

Bird of the Cherokee put into the paper, for two buckskins, a talk to the Cherokee chief of the upper towns, warning him to desist from disturbing William Cocke, "the white man who lives among the mulberry trees," for, said Red Bird, "the mulberry man talks very strong and runs very fast." Chief Red Bird ended his letter by the expression of a rather quaint wish, "that all the bad people on both sides were laid in the ground, for then there would not be so many mush men trying to make people to believe they were warriors."

A few contractors, or "undertakers" as they were called, were busy in eastern Tennessee. In 1792 the Knox County Court appointed Thomas M'Culloch, George M'Nutt, James Cozby, Joseph Greer and John Adair as commissioners to let a contract for the building of a courthouse, prison and stocks for the county. They were authorized to give the contract to the lowest bidder, and to require the "undertaker" to make bond or give approved security before they accepted his bid. The project was advertised to the public in the following manner:

> To be let to the bidder who plays lowest fox,
> And by him to be raised from the stump,
> A house that will hold all the justices of Knox,
> And the cash will be paid by the lump.
> Not too high, nor too low, but a neat little box,
> To hold quarter-sessions and pleas,
> And to punish the rogues, both a prison and stocks
> For then we may sleep at our ease.
> The plan may be seen in the ville of Knox
> On Monday, the first day of Court,
> Where those who love fun may meet
> And thus attend business and sport.
> M'Culloch presides, & the sign is three knocks,
> When the building is taken in care
> But the bond must secure both the keys & the locks
> To M'Nutt, Cozby, Greer, and Adair.

In September 1791 Blount returned to eastern North Carolina to look after some business matters and to fetch his wife and children back to Tennessee. During his absence a printed copy of the Treaty of Holston reached the Cherokee, who, acquainting themselves with its contents for the first time, regarded it as a piece of diplomatic trickery. Its provisions, when set down from oral agreement in Cherokee to written English, had offered opportunity for honest misunderstanding as well as for deliberate chicanery. The Cherokee were greatly angered to learn, for example, that American citizens were given free navigation of the Tennessee. They also charged that Blount had deceived them in fixing the western boundary of the cession and insisted that an annuity of $2,000 had been agreed on but that only half of that amount had been inserted in the treaty.

Their anger changed to clamor for war when they received word that on November 4, 1791, the Indians in the Northwest Territory had crushed an American force under General Arthur St. Clair. This defeat, which was the second suffered by American troops in about a year, encouraged the Southern Indians to revive a confederacy to rid themselves forever of American invaders. The Cherokee, furious in the belief that they had been cheated in the treaty, took advantage of Blount's absence to send a delegation headed by Bloody Fellow to President Washington, who graciously listened to their complaints and proposed to increase their annuity to $1,500. He also changed Bloody Fellow's unpleasant name to Eskaqua or Clear Sky and conferred upon him the title of general. Bloody Fellow was perhaps the only member of his race to receive this honor prior to the Civil War. He returned with his comrades to his people sporting a scarlet match coat with silver epaulets, broad silver lace and a shining silver star, and vowing eternal gratitude and loyalty to his Great White Father and benefactor.

The young men of the tribe, however, had already gone on the warpath, killing and burning and stealing in every white settlement they could successfully attack. Even more venomous were the Chickamauga and the Creeks. The Creeks were encouraged by their half-breed chief, Alexander McGillivray, and by the English adventurer, William August Bowles, who declared that neither the Americans nor the Spaniards had any right to control the Indians and that with the help of the English their lands would be restored to the original boundaries described in the Proclamation of 1763. Another source of support was Baron Hector Carondelet, Miró's successor as governor of Louisiana and West Florida, whose policy called for nullifying all American gains in previous treaties by uniting the Creeks and whatever other tribes wished to join in an offensive and defensive coalition against the whites.

Such was the humor of the Southern Indians when in March 1792 Blount moved to his new residence in Knoxville. The month opened with renewed attacks and retaliations. All eastern Tennessee was a stage on which shifted scenes of murder, ambuscade, horse stealing and cabin burning. Blount, hearing reports of an impending alliance between Spain and the Creeks and Chickamauga, diverted the company raised to guard the Cumberland district to the Washington District and ordered another company to the Cumberland.

At this point John Watts invited the governor to visit the Indian town of Coyatee, situated at the junction of the Holston and the Little Tennessee, for the first annual distribution of gifts under the Treaty of Holston. Blount accepted the invitation for several reasons. He hoped to correct the stories which the Indians were said to have told in Philadelphia concerning his dishonesty in the Treaty of Holston. He also saw in the visit an opportunity to retrieve the friendship of those Cherokee chiefs whom the Indian trader, Joseph Sevier, had exculpated from participation in the recent attacks.

Watts spared no expense in his endeavor to make the conference one of the most brilliant in Indian annals. For Blount and his party he built a spacious hut before which flew the Stars and Stripes on a long pole. First to arrive in Coyatee were the chiefs, who were painted black and sprinkled over with flour to denote that they had been at war but that they were now for peace. When they learned that Blount was approaching they sent a well-dressed young warrior on horseback to request him to halt until he should be notified of their readiness to receive him. Eventually invited to Coyatee, Blount found some two thousand warriors arranged in two lines of about three hundred yards in length. As he entered between the lines, they began firing salutes and shouting joyously. The clamor increased when, under the flag, he greeted Watts, Bloody Fellow and other chiefs.

Indians and whites devoted the next day to drinking and eating and watching a ball game, the national sport of the Cherokee. The object of the game was for one of the teams to drive by means of rackets a ball of stuffed deerskin through the goal of its opponent. The captain of each team placed the ball in the center of the field while his twelve players took their places about twenty yards out in the opponent's ground. Amid the cheers and yells of the spectators, one of the captains lifted the ball with his racket and tossed it up thirty or forty feet. When it descended each captain, though he did not otherwise take part in the game, leaped high in the air and struck furiously in his effort to reach the ball and drive it in the direction of the opponent's goal. Back and forth flew the ball to the pounding of as many of the twenty-four rackets as could reach it. While by the rules of the game no player was permitted to strike, scratch or bruise any of his opponents, he could double him up by lifting him by his feet and pressing his head and shoulders to the ground until, disabled in the back, he was carried off the field. The breathless game went on until one side drove the ball across the goal of its opponent.

The chiefs bet the garments they wore, down to their flaps. Bloody Fellow's team lost. To recover his garments, he resorted to a bit of strategy. He got all the best players of the opposing team drunk while he kept his own best players sober. Thus on the following day he realized his aim. Only then was he ready to enter the conference.

The governor delivered a carefully written speech. While he approved the favors Bloody Fellow had obtained in Philadelphia, he gently chided the Indians for minimizing the powers President Washington vested in him. Recalling the Indian atrocities since the Treaty of Holston, Blount stated that fifty whites had been killed and hundreds taken prisoner and their properties destroyed. Yet he was careful to assure the Cherokee that they were only partially responsible for the crimes, and he asked their support in finding and punishing the guilty parties. In return for this favor he promised to submit the dispute about the boundary to the more representative Cherokee council scheduled to meet at Estanaula in the latter part of June. Bloody Fellow promised him a reply from that conference, and the Chickamauga delegates assured him that the whites would obtain satisfaction from it. Thus heartened, Blount left the division of the gifts to the Indians and departed for Knoxville.

His hopes for peace were vain. He was only a few hours out of Coyatee when Watts and Bloody Fellow received from William Panton an invitation to a conference in Pensacola.

Panton was a wealthy Scotch merchant with strong Tory sympathies. Early in the Revolution the Americans had confiscated his vast estates in South Carolina and Georgia. Embittered, he had moved from Charleston to Pensacola where he established an extensive trading house. When Spain took the town in 1781 he had formed with her a commercial treaty which enriched him and brought the surrounding tribes to an understanding with the Florida government.

In the name of Arturo O'Neal, commander of Pensacola, Panton requested Watts and Bloody Fellow to come down with ten pack horses, promising them all the arms, ammunition and supplies they needed to fight the Americans. The two chiefs hastened southward, but Bloody Fellow gradually repented his ungrateful course. The honors President Washington had conferred on the chief were too great and too recent to permit him to take the Spaniards by the hand. He went as far as the Coosa River and then, casting a longing eye in the direction of Pensacola, turned homeward. He discreetly stayed away from the council in Estanaula, which expressed dissatisfaction with the Treaty of Holston.

O'Neal received Watts with open arms and easily won him over by loading him with presents and conferring on him the title of colonel. Painting himself black, Watts raised the war whoop against the United States and summoned the chiefs to a council at Wills Town to explain his visit in Pensacola.

Wills Town was about thirty miles from Running Water where Dragging Canoe had lived. When Watts succeeded Dragging Canoe as head of the Chickamauga he made Wills Town his home, as did Bloody Fellow. Thenceforth Blount considered Wills Town the capital of the Chickamauga.

On the designated day the Cherokee assembled to hear Watts's report and to attend the annual green corn dance. The chief, standing in the circle of his seated friends, delivered an elaborate speech, explaining that O'Neal had received him like a brother and had assured him he wanted no Indian ground. Wherever the Spaniards land, said Watts, they sit down, whereas the Americans first take your land and then make a treaty by which they give you little or nothing for it. Your Spanish Father across the sea offers you all the powder, lead and arms you need to war against the United States. You young fellows—you have always wanted war. Well, now you can have as much of it as you want. The Creeks, the Choctaw and their old brothers, the Spaniards, back you to the last man.

All the Indians save Bloody Fellow greeted the speech with joyous shouts. Bloody Fellow stood alone in the circle and manfully and courageously opposed war. To go to war, he warned, was a false step; you will stumble, will fall. "Look at the flag; do you see the stars on it? They are not towns—they are nations. There are thirteen of them," he said, forgetting or ignorant of the recent admission of Vermont and Kentucky. "They are people who are very strong, and yet fight as one man."

With these words Bloody Fellow clenched the silver medal on his scarlet coat and asked: "When was the day that you went to [Colonel Stuart] and brought back the like of this?" Angered by the truth of this remark, Watts yanked off the medal and threw it to the ground.

This encouraged one of Dragging Canoe's brothers to declare for war: "My father was a man," he said to Bloody Fellow, "and I am as good a man as he was. To war I will go, and spill blood in spite of what you say."

Whereupon Watts took the brave by the hand, saying: "You are a man. I like your talk. To war we will go together."

Another chief joined them: "With these hands I have taken the lives of three hundred men, and now the time has come when I shall take the lives of three hundred more; then I shall be satisfied and sit down in peace. I will drink my fill of blood!"

To which Bloody Fellow, still standing, replied: "You go to war if you will, but I will not!"

Stripping to their flaps, Watts's party painted themselves black and danced the war dance all night long around the Stars and Stripes. At dawn they wanted to fire on the flag, but Bloody Fellow stopped them by threatening to kill some of them.

The next day Watts and his party went to Lookout Mountain, from where they planned to proceed to the Cumberland country. But they met Chief White-Man Killer, who filled them with so much firewater that Watts had to defer his plans. Then two traders, Richard Findleston and Joseph Deroque, learning of Watts's intentions and being friendly toward the whites, contrived to delay him further by pretending that they had come at the request of the British authorities to ascertain how the settlements could best be invaded. Watts saw half of September fritter away before he could organize his campaign.

As Superintendent of Indian Affairs for the Southern Department, Blount maintained, among the Cherokee, agents who furnished him with information of the planned invasion. He immediately requested Robertson to muster his brigade with which to repel the invaders should they attack the Cumberland country.

Anticipating this precaution, Watts hastened to counter it by a clever ruse. He induced Bloody Fellow, who still opposed war, and another chief named Glass to write Blount a letter calculated to throw him off his guard. They alleged that Robertson, in a meeting with the Chickasaw and Choctaw, had told them that he would sweep clean with their blood any blood they might spill in Nashville. Bloody Fellow and Glass wrote that the threat had caused the young men of the aforementioned tribes to plan an attack on the white settlements, but that they, with the aid of Watts and some other headmen, had frustrated it by sending them to their different homes to mind their hunting.

Blount's desire for peace and his faith in Watts led him straight into the trap. On September 14 he ordered the Knox Regiment and the Mero Brigade to disband; but when four days later he heard, much to his chagrin, that a large force of Indians was crossing the Tennessee, he ordered augmented by seven the number of militia companies in the Washington District under John

Sevier. Robertson, meanwhile, shared none of Blount's faith in Watts. Findleston and Deroque by their reports only supported his undying suspicions of Watts, Bloody Fellow, Glass or any other savage. He ignored Blount's order to disband the Mero Brigade.

Before long Robertson's suspicions proved well-founded. On the night of September 30 Watts with a force of between two and three hundred warriors marched silently and swiftly on Buchanan's Station, a fort which housed several refugee families and which was defended by a garrison of fifteen men. Warned by disturbed cattle, John McRory and a few other settlers fired on the Indians when they came to within ten yards of the gate. The Indians retaliated by a heavy discharge which lasted for an hour. Thirty balls passed through a single porthole of the "over jutting" and lodged in the roof within the circumference of a hat. The women, under Mrs. Sally Buchanan, assisted the defenders in every possible way. They molded bullets, distributed ammunition, loaded guns and, on pressing occasions, even killed a few Indians.

Nevertheless, Watts managed to gather around the walls of the blockhouse a goodly number of his men. One of the chiefs, a half-breed, leaped to the roof, but he was shot through the thighs and fell to the ground. Despite his wounds he managed to set fire to the walls of the blockhouse by blowing with his dying breath into the flames. The fire was eventually put out. The fitful glare of the cane torches gave proof that the black walls remained standing while countless tongues of fire streamed around them.

Before dawn the Indians became discouraged. Watts fell with a rifle shot through both thighs and was carried away on a stretcher pulled by a horse. White-Man Killer was dangerously hurt and Dragging Canoe's brother was mortally wounded. Four other warriors were wounded, two or three of whom later died. At sunrise the Indians heard the report of a swivel in the direction of Nashville, four miles away, signaling that Robertson had started to the relief of the garrison. The Indians withdrew. None of the defenders was killed. Near the blockhouse they found hatchets, pipes, kettles and a sword with a fine Spanish blade richly ornamented with martial designs.

The joy of the whites knew no bounds. Blount claimed that it "really surpassed that experienced on the surrender of Cornwallis." Through printer Roulstone he covered the settlers with glory and his critics with contempt. But all his elation found no sympathy in Philadelphia. Knox, involved in a war against the Indians in the Northwest Territory, opposed war in the Southwest. He assured Blount that the Creeks would be restrained but reminded him that, since Congress alone could declare war, any military action against the Indians must be purely defensive. They must not be attacked until Congress, which would convene in March, decided what measures might be taken.

To this unpromising letter Blount replied with long and careful arguments and explanations. He placed the blame for the attacks, not on the encroachment of the whites on Indian lands, but on the schemes of "the Officers administrating the Government of Louisiana and their Instrument Mr Panton." He enclosed a list of persons killed, wounded or carried into captivity by Creeks and Cherokee since the beginning of 1791. Most of the depredations, Blount explained, were attributable to a distortion of the Indian law of retaliation in tribal feuds: instead of killing their own people the Indians now substituted white victims.

Blount devoted considerable space to horse stealing and its bloody effects:

The Indians go into the Frontier settlements in search of Horses and if they find an unarmed person or family fall on them and if they take horses and are pursued kill in their own defense. As soon as the Indians return to the nation with the horses those who encouraged the stealing of them become the purchasers and shortly after knowing the quarter from whence they were taken carry them out of the nation in a different direction and sell them to a great profit.

The government of the Creeks and of the Cherokee, Blount continued, was such that all the chiefs of the nation could neither restrain nor punish the "most worthless fellow in it nor for a violation of the existing treaties lest the enormity of it be ever so great or evident nor if demanded by the United States dare they deliver him up to be punished." The Cherokee, he argued, had no well-founded claim to the land lying on the Cumberland River, for they had ceded it by two treaties to the United States. He concluded with a warning of rising anger among the settlers whose "thirst for revenge or, what is here termed, satisfaction, will lead them to break through the Bounds of good order and Government, nothwithstanding what can be said or done to prevent it."

These arguments and explanations and warnings drew from the indignant Knox a scathing reply. He repeated that a war with the Southern Indians must be avoided at all costs. While he admitted that the Cherokee could have received encouragement from Spanish officials, he insisted that they must have reasons for their hostility to the Cumberland settlers. He informed the governor that James Seagrove, United States agent to the Creeks, had been ordered to meet with their chiefs at the headwaters of the St. Mary's and to urge them to persuade their young men to cease their depredations. The Chickamauga, who "seem the germ of the evil," should then be bought off.

Knox admitted that the militia Blount had called into service in times of danger was necessary, but he urged the governor to retain it only as long as circumstances required, for it was a great expense to the public and, moreover, its members were exposed to unnecessary dangers. After a long lecture on economy, Knox announced the imminent appointment in Philadelphia of a new quartermaster and paymaster, David Henley, who was to "have rules and regulations prescribed to him which will be communicated to you and by whom all expenditures must be conducted. This arrangement will greatly tend to your ease and prevent all anxiety about the settlement of Accounts." Knox also announced the impending dispatch of two brass cannon which, however, needed repairs, and a company of volunteers from North Carolina.

Blount could give as much as he could take. He wrote Knox an even longer letter than Knox had written him, denying the Indian claims and justifying his own expenses and measures with characteristic vehemence. Yet, in the face of loud and angry protests, he carried out Knox's orders. He requested Robertson and Sevier each to disband his entire brigade save for a company of infantry and one troop of cavalry. In the Cumberland country where relentless fire, theft and murder had driven scores of hapless settlers to the protection of the forts, the reaction was so violent that Robertson had to strain every modicum of his influence to maintain order.

Meanwhile Blount's reputation sank lower and lower as the toll of dead, wounded and captured mounted. The governor was bombarded from all sides with proposals for securing peace and with demands for an offensive expedition against the Creeks, who were accused of committing most of the depredations. Small wonder that Seagrove's assurances of their pacific disposition brought down on him a torrent of scorn and irony. The *Gazette* each week applied to the local situation the words with which Cato was wont to close every speech before the Roman senate— *Delenda est Carthago*—and added for the benefit of unlearned settlers, "The Creek nation must be destroyed."

The newspaper seethed with letters attacking the governor and ridiculing Congress for sending corn to the distressed parts of the Creek nation, thus "invigorating" them to carry on their murdering raids. "Where," asked one of the settlers, "will all these mischiefs end? What are the blessings of government to us? Are we to hope for protection? If so, when?"

Some settlers spurned mere words for efficacious action. John Morris, a Chickasaw warrior visiting Knoxville as a guest of the governor, was killed by an unknown assailant. To soothe the feelings of the Chickasaw Blount gave Morris the military funeral due to a warrior of a friendly nation. In the procession to the local graveyard for white people, Blount and Morris' brother walked together as chief mourners. The governor vainly offered a reward for the apprehension of the assassin or assassins.

Early in February 1793 Secretary Knox, in the interest of peace, requested Blount to accompany Watts and other leading chiefs to Philadelphia for a conference with President Washington. Anticipating such a move, Blount had sent Watts's bosom friend John McKee to persuade him to bury the hatchet. The two men embraced like long-separated brothers at Chattooga, about twenty miles from Wills Town, and began to entertain one another with lively conversation.

Over cups of the whisky brought by McKee to assist in his mission, Watts inquired about Blount's health and spoke pleasantly of the war which, he said, several chiefs had tried unsuccessfully to induce him to renew. Far from feeling bitter about his failure at Buchanan's Station, Watts treated it as a joke on himself. He was recovering from his wound, he said, and had no intention of risking another. He laughed as he told how the village of Nickajack had sent a runner to him to ascertain whether his wound still hurt, and how, when he answered in the negative, the runner had replied tauntingly that he did not expect it would be well so soon. But he broke off this geniality when McKee stumbled on the question of peace. Watts wanted, he said, to ruminate on an answer in solitude. As he left, he accepted McKee's invitation to meet him on March 8 at Spring Hill.

At that time and place, however, Watts failed to appear. McKee waited until March 16 and then sent a messenger to him. The chief replied that an important ball game, about to be played, kept him from coming. The truth was that he had been detained not by a ball game which was scheduled for later in the month, but by a quarrel between him and another chief over his meeting with McKee. Watts was so incensed that he packed up and left Wills Town, but young warriors of his tribe overtook him and persuaded him to return.

McKee had just returned to Knoxville when Watts appeared on the border and sent Blount word that he was at Hanging Maw's village with other chiefs and that they wished to talk with him in Knoxville or anywhere he deemed safe. Blount went to near-by Henry's Station and summoned the chiefs. After filling them with food and drink and good cheer, he made known to them Knox's desire that they go to Philadelphia for a conference with the President. Watts, as spokesman for the chiefs, replied that in twenty-one nights they would hold a full council at Running Water and he would then let him know their answer.

No council took place. Watts, unsure of what course he

wished to pursue, remained wisely noncommittal. But the chiefs assured Blount of their pacific disposition and agreed to proceed to Philadelphia under McKee, whom the governor had employed for the purpose.

On June 7 Blount, satisfied with his arrangement with the chiefs, departed for Philadelphia, leaving General Daniel Smith, secretary of the territory, in charge as acting governor. Printer Roulstone rode in Blount's coach as far as Jonesboro and Sevier later joined for a ten-mile ride and "a very long Talk" on the possibilities of pacifying the Indians. But peace, if he envisioned it, proved only a chimera. On June 16 while he was still traveling in the territory, Blount received word that Captain Hugh Beard and a company of Indian-hating militia had four days before raided Hanging Maw's town, killing eight or ten Indians and their white friends and wounding Hanging Maw, his wife, his daughter, and Betty Martin, the daughter of Nancy Ward and wife of General Joseph Martin. Smith, fearing that this assault on the most influential pro-American chief among the Cherokee would precipitate a general war, wrote to the chiefs Hanging Maw, Doublehead and Watts, pleading with them to restrain any retaliatory act and to go to Philadelphia and talk with their Great White Father who, he assured them, would give them satisfaction if they forbore to take it themselves.

John Watts assumed a stony silence, but Hanging Maw and Doublehead were too angry and aggrieved to be mollified by mere words. They demanded that Smith arrest Beard and his party. "I am still among my people," wrote Doublehead, "living in gores of blood. I shall not go from this place until I get full answer from you." Hanging Maw sarcastically pointed out in his reply that nothing had happened as long as Blount was present in the territory. "Surely," he wrote, "they are making fun of you. If you are left in the place of the Governor you ought to take satisfaction yourself." To the Great White Father he dispatched a note curtly announcing that the chiefs would not go to Philadelphia at this time. Smith had Beard arrested and tried before a court-martial, but most of the settlers regarded him as a hero, and he was acquitted. Smith admitted with shame that he was powerless for the present to punish Beard by law.

Blount, dwelling on the possible results of the assault, had a notion to turn back; but he persuaded himself that Smith had done all he could to stay Indian wrath until the President could act. On the night of July 19 he reached Philadelphia.

Knox received him with cool courtesy. This changed to angry disappointment when he learned of Beard's attack and of the consequent refusal of the chiefs to come to Philadelphia. A good part of his irritation was caused by the fact that he was just then grappling with a weightier problem than that of the Indians. The French minister to the United States, Edmond Charles Genet, was endangering American neutrality by fitting out privateers to prey on British shipping in the conflict between France and England. Preoccupied with this situation, Knox could see Blount only intermittently. The governor for once enjoyed the support of Andrew Pickens, who had also been summoned to confer, and the two men, by conference and correspondence, worked hard to win Knox to their views. They urged that the government establish a military and trading post at the mouth of Bear Creek near Muscle Shoals. Such a post would serve to divert Chickasaw trade from Spain to the United States, to secure Chickasaw and perhaps Choctaw assistance in a common war against the Creeks, and to protect the Cumberland country. Last but not least, it would preclude the possibility of an alliance between the Northern and Southern tribes.

These were strong arguments, but they failed before the determination of Congress and the President to avoid punitive measures against the Creeks. On August 5 Knox, bowing to the wishes of Congress, asked Blount and Pickens for suggestions as to how a Creek war might be postponed. On the following day they replied wearily that "sending some Person of Address and knowledge of Indian affairs" disguised as a trader to distribute gifts to the Creek headmen might induce them "to commit fewer Murders and Robberies than they otherwise would." They added wishfully that the trader "might collect much Information that would be useful in the War with that Nation." With this they brought their futile conference with Knox to a close. As the governor made his way homeward, he reflected ironically that all he had gained by his journey was the painful duty of having to inform his people that they must continue to suffer. Eventually, he hoped, the government might experience a change of heart. Wayne's possible success against the Indians in the Northwest could result in a subsequent diversion of troops against the Creeks and Chickamauga.

During his absence from the territory, Indian affairs had gone from bad to worse. Beard's attack on Hanging Maw had precipitated many bloody reprisals. In retaliation the settlers invaded "Indian territory and killed Indians usually innocent of the immediate outrage which had provoked the attack." The climax came on September 24 when Watts and Doublehead led a force of 700 Creeks and Chickamauga across the Tennessee with the intention of surprising Knoxville. When they came to within eight miles of their destination, they heard the report of a cannon fired by United States troops in the town. Construing this as evidence of their expected approach, they turned instead on near-by Cavet's Station. By promising to spare its defenders, Doublehead induced them to surrender. Scarcely had they emerged from the building than the chief and his party fell on them and butchered thirteen men, women and children. Among them was Alexander Cavet himself. He had just put seven bullets into his mouth to expedite the loading of his gun and gone to his garden to defend himself. After plundering and burning the station the Indians withdrew.

On learning of the massacre Acting Governor Smith ordered John Sevier to pursue the Indians to their own country. Sevier immediately marched southward with 700 men and on October 14 reached Estanaula. Finding the town deserted and full of supplies, he made it his temporary headquarters. That night he repulsed some Indians attempting to surprise the camp and took several prisoners who told him that a few days before the main Indian force had passed Estanaula on its way to Etowah near the present site of Rome, Georgia, on the river of the same name. After refreshing his horsemen he approached the river and learned that the Indians had entrenched themselves on the opposite bank to hinder his passage. Had he attempted to ford the river he would have faced a deadly fire and perhaps defeat, but a fortunate mistake on the part of his guides saved the day for him. The guides led Colonel Kelly and a few of his men about a half mile below the ford to a ferry where they immediately swam the river. The Indians, discovering this movement and construing it as evidence of a design against their town, abandoned their intrenchments and rushed down the river to oppose Kelly. The rest of Sevier's army, however, discovered the mistake and forded the river with the intention of riding to the town and attacking it. They advanced so rapidly that the Indians, having no time to regain their trenches, found themselves scattered and hemmed in on the riverbank. The whites dismounted and, shielding themselves behind trees, mowed down many young warriors with deadly accuracy. One of the chiefs, King Fisher, resisted bravely and made a daring sally, but he soon fell and his warriors fled to the fastnesses of the adjacent country. Sevier burned Etowah, rescued Colonel Kelly and his horsemen from the place where they had concealed themselves and returned home. The dejected Watts put down his hatchet and never took it up again.

The Creek and Chickamauga attacks against the Cumberland settlements temporarily ceased. The calm permitted Blount, who had returned to the territory early in October, to reduce the militia, though through Seagrove he warned the Creeks that he could no longer restrain the infuriated settlers from taking retaliatory measures against fresh attacks. He was not retreating but advancing by another road. The settlers had long demanded the second stage of territorial government which, in accordance with the Ordinance of 1787, called for a legislature composed of a council and representatives. Such a body, Blount believed, might persuade the government to undertake a military campaign against the Indians. In addition, the second stage of territorial government must inevitably lead to the third—statehood— in which Blount hoped to reap a senatorship as the reward for his services. The opportunity he sought came in October when the grand jury of Hamilton County complained of Indian attacks and demanded a legislature as a means of stopping them. Blount replied by calling for elections of representatives for late December. In February 1794 the successful candidates assembled in

Knoxville and in accordance with the Ordinance nominated the ten councilors from whom Congress was to choose five. Blount had good reasons for selecting this early date. He wanted to make sure that Congress would be in session when record of the meeting of the representatives reached Philadelphia, for it was to include a demand for offensive measures against the Creeks.

After nominating the councilors, the representatives passed a resolution to send Congress an address in which they demanded a war against the Creeks. Reminding Congress that the Indians had killed 200 settlers and destroyed property valued at $100,000 since the Treaty of Holston, they warned that self-preservation might induce the settlers to take unauthorized measures against their enemies. They claimed they were "as much entitled to be protected in their lives, their families and little property, as those who were in luxury, ease, and affluence in the great and opulent Atlantic cities." They sent the list of nominees to Congress by express and delegated Dr. James White to deliver the address.

The ensuing months saw a renewal of Indian attacks in the Cumberland country. Again Blount was forced to revoke his late orders and enlarged the militia; again his popularity sank as the toll of murders, assaults and thefts rose. In the face of this new storm he maintained his usual equilibrium; he urged patience and practiced it himself in waiting the outcome of Dr. White's mission to Congress. But as usual he was doomed to disappointment. On May 29 the House passed a bill authorizing the President to build in the Southwest Territory a chain of forts with permanent garrisons and scouts, and to call out 10,000 militia for offensive operations against the Creeks and Chickamauga; but the Senate made such heavy amendments in the bill that the House rejected it. The best that Knox could do, therefore, was to build a post at Cumberland crossing and to permit a small increase in the Cumberland militia. In a last-minute gesture of generosity he threw in for Nashville six small iron howitzers and about two hundred old muskets that needed repairs.

Enraged by this niggardly treatment, the Cumberland settlers resolved to take matters into their own hands. Heeding the popular clamor, Robertson, in defiance of federal policy, planned an expedition against the Chickamauga. Blount gave unofficial approval to the project and then pressed Knox for authorization of an attack. When Knox refused it, public sentiment flared. The legislature, convening in August, was constrained to address Congress another petition demanding punitive measures against "those two faithless and bloodthirsty nations, the Creeks and the Cherokee." The petition included a painstaking account of the murders, captures and stolen horses from February to September 1794, denounced the policy of gifts to Indians and assured the government that "fear, not love, is the only means by which the Indians can be governed."

In accordance with this conviction, Blount and Robertson proceeded with their plans. The governor sent Major James Ore with sixty-nine men to the Cumberland country for a scouting expedition under Robertson's orders. Robertson himself sent Sampson Williams, former sheriff of Davidson County, to invite Colonel William Whiteley of Kentucky to join the intended expedition. Colonel Whiteley had often expressed to Robertson readiness to assist him in any movement against the Indians and promptly responded with 100 militia. Robertson later justified the expedition on the ground that "a man of as much veracity as any in the nation" had advised him of an impending Chickamauga invasion of the Cumberland country. He could thus claim that he had struck first in self-defense.

Robertson and Blount agreed that the governor should give no official sanction to the proposed attack. Indeed, Robertson, long weary of his official duties and desirous of relinquishing them, was happy to assume full responsibility for the expedition. Anticipating Knox's wrath, he sought to appease it by tendering his resignation—actually written by Blount—and by helping the governor choose his successor. But Robertson was so enthusiastic about his scheme that he revealed it to his friends with the result that it soon became common knowledge. So many settlers volunteered for the campaign that when on September 6 he held a meeting of his force at Brown's Blockhouse, he found himself at the head of nearly four hundred men. He entrusted the chief command to Ore because that officer commanded the only federal troops and could, therefore, claim pay for their services.

Robertson ordered him to march against the Creeks and Chicka-mauga before they could threaten the Cumberland country. Ore wasted no time in realizing his mission. He fell on the towns of Nickajack and Running Water on Muscle Shoals, crushed all resistance, captured nineteen women and children and killed scores of braves. After burning the two towns to the ground in one day, he returned in triumph to Nashville. His only losses in the expedition were three men wounded, two slightly and one mortally.

The Cherokee and Chickamauga soon made peace. This, how-ever, was due to other factors as much as to the destruction of Nickajack and Running Water. In the previous June the Chero-kee signed with the federal government the Treaty of Philadel-phia by which their annuity was raised from $1,500 to $5,000 in goods but was subject to a deduction of $50 for every horse they stole and failed to return within three months. Less than two months later the martial designs of the Chickamauga were frustrated by General Wayne's victory over the Indians at Fallen Timbers in the Northwest Territory. At the same time Blount strengthened the possibilities of a permanent peace, and certainly prevented the repetition of such occurrences as the Beard attack and the Etowah expedition, by erecting in the Indian country five blockhouses which were garrisoned not by militia but by regular federal troops. Finally in November the governor, availing himself of the aforementioned factors as well as the Nickajack expedition, held a conference with the Chicka-mauga and Cherokee at Tellico Blockhouse where Watts and Hanging Maw each pledged his people to a lasting peace and friendship with the United States.

The Creeks still remained at war. Throughout the fall of 1794 they not only attacked various settlements but deepened their hostilities against the Chickasaw, who since 1783 had been at peace with the United States. Blount, however, was now confident that the Creeks could be easily handled. The suppres-sion of the Whisky Rebellion in southwestern Pennsylvania and Wayne's victory convinced him that the Southwest Territory would now receive the support it had long been denied. He therefore resolved on the bold scheme of sowing discord among the tribes for the purpose of getting the Chickasaw and the Cherokee to join the United States in a war against the Creeks. While Robertson egged on the Chickasaw, Blount at Tellico Blockhouse in December 1794 and January 1795 pressed the Cherokee to keep the Creeks from crossing their towns and therefore from striking at the white settlements, to join the Chickasaw and to permit sixty of their young warriors to serve with pay in the militia of the Cumberland country. In letters to Knox he argued the inevitability of war against the Creeks and the practicality of obtaining for it the support of the Cherokee, the Chickasaw and even the Choctaw. The destruction of the Creeks by the assistance of these tribes, he reasoned in one letter, would not only be accomplished much cheaper than by an army of whites but would have the added advantages of preventing a coalition of the Southern tribes against the United States in the future. "If the Citizens of the United States," he concluded, "do not destroy the Creeks, the Creeks will kill the Citizens of the United States, the alternative is to kill or be killed."

Blount's scheme early bore fruit. On January 2, 1795, a force of about seventy Chickasaw under the half-breed Billy Colbert scalped five Creeks. Going to Robertson with the scalps, they begged him to permit them to join the whites and to build and defend blockhouses on the Tennessee River. They also requested him to inform Blount that they had been waiting "to see you retaliate on the Creeks for the many injuries done your people." Robertson reported these sentiments in a letter to Blount, who replied that war was now certain between the Chickasaw and the Creeks, "and thereby it is highly probable, the Southwestern frontiers will, for a time, be relieved from the tomahawk and scalping knife." He relayed a copy of Robertson's letter together with a copy of his reply to the Secretary of War. He was in a happy mood. He immediately spread word among the Cherokee that what the Chickasaw had done was proof of their love for the people of the United States. At the same time he advised Robertson to accept the services of sixty Chickasaw to protect the frontier and to dismiss an equal number of militia.

On February 13 the Secretary of War received, read and forwarded the Robertson-Blount letters to the President, who in turn directed them to Congress for its decision. The Senate, dominated by high Federalists, opposed the frontier and therefore passed a bill rejecting war against the southern tribes. The House, being anti-Federalist, rejected the bill and attempted to substitute a milder measure which, however, failed in the rush of business that swamped Congress just before it adjourned. This meant a victory for the opponents of the Creek war. The high Federalists, suspecting that the governor's motives in desiring war were related to his well-known Muscle Shoals and other extensive land speculations on the frontier, disapproved of his and Smith's military acts. On March 19 territorial delegate White had the unpleasant duty of informing Blount that, despite his strong representations, Congress deemed the Etowah expedition of 1793 not defensive but offensive and that, therefore, it had refused to appropriate the money with which to pay the soldiers who had served under Sevier in it. Referring to the governor's representations, White wrote: "Pardon me if I inform you that your candid & generous Statement of the necessity of Congress resenting the outrages committed against your Government by the Creeks, occasioned a Person high in office to observe that the ardor you Showed for that object indicated a disposition interested for that Purpose: which mistaken idea I had the mortification to hear uttered in my own presence."

This was mild compared to the devastating attack which was soon to come from the Secretary of War. On December 31, 1794, Henry Knox had resigned his office and had a few days later been succeeded by Timothy Pickering. The new Secretary had early formed an unfavorable impression of the governor. William H. Masterson in his excellent biography of Blount states that David Henley, the paymaster whom Knox in 1792 had appointed to supervise territorial expenditures, charged the governor with

. . . duplicity toward the Indians, with using his office for private gain through illegal contracts for supplies, and with disregard

of United States policy in the interest of his private land speculations. From his first days in office, therefore, the Secretary was
convinced that Blount was a self-seeking swindler, and he refused to consider rationally any Blount suggestion, whatever
its merits.

Repudiation of Blount's Indian policy by Congress furnished
Pickering with a golden opportunity to administer official censure on the man he disliked. On March 23 he informed Blount
that Congress had refused to declare war against the Creeks and
that, therefore, "all ideas of offensive operations" were "to be
laid aside and all possible harmony cultivated with the Indian
Tribes." In pursuance of this aim Congress had appropriated
$50,000 on measures of peace and $130,000 "for the Defensive
Protection of the Frontiers." All of the Indians, Pickering
averred, were at peace save "small parties of plundering Creeks,"
whom Seagrove would be instructed to restrain by "some pointed
declarations." The angry and rambling pen then heaped censure
on the governor and Robertson for promising assistance to the
Cherokee and the Chickasaw in a war against the Creeks. This
error he ordered the governor to correct as soon as possible and
he warned him to refrain henceforth from encouraging the Cherokee to attack the Creeks. "It was not necessary for you," he
scolded, "in your answer, pointedly to commit the United
States" at Tellico Blockhouse. The Secretary could not "discern"
the inevitability of a war between the Creeks and the Chickasaw,
unless the governor incited them to further hostilities, and this he
must stop doing in the cases of both the Chickasaw and the Cherokee. As for the governor praising the Chickasaw in the presence
of the Cherokee for killing five Creeks, Pickering asked sarcastically: "Was not this saying—you Cherokee Chiefs and Warriors
go and do likewise?" His anger grew as his stilted pen ran over
the paper:

In your letter . . . to General Robertson you express your opinion
that Congress will order an army, in the course of the ensuing
Spring or Summer, Sufficient to humble, if not destroy the Creek
Nation: but the General has acted very unadvisedly in expressing

and repeating the same opinion to the Chickasaws. . . . Upon the whole, Sir, I cannot refrain from saying that the complexion of some of the Transactions in the South western territory appears unfavorable to the public interests.

He ordered the governor to dismantle three and to reduce the garrison of another of the forts he had built if they displeased the Indians, and to remove all white encroachers on Indian lands by Federal troops if necessary. The settlers, continued Pickering, had no good reason to complain of horse stealing which Blount had represented as "a great source of hostility" so long as they robbed the Indians of their lands. With this thought his anger seems to have subsided. He brought his letter to a conclusion in a philosophic tone: "One Species of robbery affords as just ground of hostility as the other."

The governor had no choice but to extricate himself from his difficulties "as best he could and to convert the territory into a state as soon as he could." Fortunately for both him and Pickering, a series of well-directed measures brought the long Indian problem to a peaceful conclusion. Seagrove, by his judicious handling of the Creeks, persuaded them to refrain from warring on the Chickasaw. In June 1795 their chiefs, Mad Dog and Big Warrior, assured him that all they wanted was satisfaction. At Blount's request, Robertson conferred with the Chickasaw and persuaded them to return all the Creek prisoners they had taken during the short period of hostilites. Blount then apologized to the Creeks in behalf of the Cumberland settlers who had joined Billy Colbert. Later in the summer Colbert visited President Washington, who expressed strong disapproval of Robertson's doings. The general, he said, "was wrong in telling your nation last year that the United States would send an army against the Creeks last summer." That fall Seagrove was instrumental in getting the Creeks to hold a full council in which they ratified proposals of peace with the Chickasaw. Finally Captain John Chisholm, acting as agent for both the United States and the Creeks, carried peace overtures to the Chickasaw who accepted them. At last the territory enjoyed peace for the first time in several years.

It was soon to become the state of Tennessee. With the solution of the Indian problem, Blount pushed his great objective: statehood for the territory and the Senate for himself. Without waiting for Congress to pass an enabling act, he convened the territorial legislature on July 11, 1795, and ordered it to have a census taken and, if this showed the requisite 60,000, as set forth in the Ordinance of 1787, to proceed with steps for the election of a constitutional convention. The final returns of the census showed a population of 77,262, of which 10,613 were slaves. Whereupon Blount proclaimed an election of constitutional delegates who met on January 11, 1796, with Blount as president of the convention. The delegates soon drew up a constitution which was submitted to the Secretary of State. On March 28 the first state assembly met and the next day chose John Sevier, the most popular man in the region, governor of Tennessee, and William Blount and William Cocke senators. The admission of Tennessee as the sixteenth state of the Union on June 1, 1796, brings to a close the epic of the pioneers in the Appalachian Frontier.

Notes

Text to which the notes refer is indicated below by page and paragraph, the number of the page followed in parentheses by the *final word* of the paragraph. When a paragraph carries over from one page to another, the number of the second page is given here.

Notes referring to passages longer than a single paragraph are located by the numbers of all pages involved and by the final words of all paragraphs covered.

CHAPTER 1 (pages 13-23)

14 (trinkets): Clarence W. Alvord and Lee Bidgood, eds., *The First Explorations of the Trans-Allegheny Region by the Virginians, 1650-1694*, pp. 32-33.

14 (abundance): Edward Bland, "The Discovery of New Brittaine," in *ibid.*, p. 120.

15 (King, Henry): *Ibid.*, pp. 49, 117, 126.

16 (parts): Sir William Talbot, "The Discoveries of John Lederer, etc.," in *ibid.*, pp. 141, 148, 160.

16 (Region): Lyman Carrier, "The Veracity of John Lederer," in *William and Mary College Quarterly*, XIX (1939), 445, 437, 444.

17 (Herman): Alvord and Bidgood, p. 69. Carrier, p. 438.

17 (colony, expedition): Alvord and Bidgood, pp. 170, 76, 71.

17 (line): John Clayton, "Transcript of the Journal of Robert Fallam," in *ibid.*, pp. 183-193. Draper MSS, 503. Alvord and Bidgood, p. 74.

18 (Ocean, oblivion): *Ibid.*, pp. 192, 20.

19 (Henry): Abraham Wood to John Richards, August 22, 1674, in *ibid.*, p. 210.

19 (Kanawha): *Ibid.*, pp. 85, 87.

20 (Chickasaw): John Spencer Bassett, ed., *The Writings of Colonel William Byrd*, pp. 184-185, 101-102 (hereinafter Bassett, ed., *Writings of Byrd*).

20 (shelter): Frederick Jackson Turner, *The Frontier in American History*, p. 88.

20 (reverence, America): Bassett, ed., *Writings of Byrd*, pp. 356, 358.

20 (quartermaster-general): Charles H. Ambler, *West Virginia, The Mountain State*, p. 44.

21 (mountains): "John Fontaine's Journal," in W. W. Scott, *A History of Orange County, Virginia*, pp. 104-106. Draper MSS, 503 (10).

21 (Catawbas): Scott, p. 110.

22 (Horseshoe): Some historians give it as *Sic Jurat Transcendere Montes*.

22 (acres, Virginia, established): Bassett, ed., *Writings of Byrd*, p. xix.

CHAPTER 2 (pages 24-42)

24 (charge): Walter Allen Knittle, *Early Eighteenth Century Palatine Emigration*, p. 38.

24 (Pfalz-Neuberg): *Ibid.*, p. 41. Albert Bernhardt Faust, *The German Element in the United States*, I, 74-75. Knittle, p. 41.

25 (carts): *Ibid.*, pp. 4-5. Duke de Saint-Simon, *Memoirs*, II, 537-538.

25 (transportation): Knittle, pp. 67, 69. Faust, I, 78. Lucy Forney Bittinger, *The Germans in Colonial Times*, pp. 85, 68.

25 (measure): Narcissus Luttrel, *A Brief Historical Relation of State Affairs, 1678-1714*, VI, 488.

26 (air): Knittle, pp. 71-72.

27 (themselves): *Ibid.*, pp. 111-134, 188. Faust, I, 87-88.

27 (thousand): Knittle, p. 195.

28 (health): John Mason Brown, *Brief Sketch of the First Settlement of the County of Schoharie by the Germans*, p. 12.

29-30 (treatment, Rhine, cattle, less, 1734): Bittinger, pp. 85-87, 92, 115.

30 (Mountain): Charles E. Kemper, "The Settlement of the Valley," in *Virginia Magazine of History and Biography*, XXX (1922), 172-173. See petition of Adam Müller and his seven friends, in Harry Miller Strickler, *Massanutten Settled by Pennsylvania Pilgrim in 1726*, pp. 26-27.

30 (City, Frontier): Samuel Kercheval, *A History of the Valley of Virginia*, p. 41. See also Herrmann Schuricht, *History of the German Element in Virginia*, I, 86, 93.

31 (work): Edward Rondthaler, "The Doctrinal Position of the Moravian Church," in John Henry Clewell, *History of Wachovia in North Carolina*, p. 305.

32 (through): *Ibid.*, pp. 4, 6. Faust, I, 231. Adelaide L. Fries, ed., *Records of the Moravians in North Carolina*, I, 14-15.

32-33 (trees, better, wound, Brethren): "The Spangenburg Diary," December 5, 14 and 20, 1752, in Fries, I, 55, 57-59.

33 (property): January 8, 1753, in *ibid.*, I, 59. Clewell, pp. 9-10, 12.

34 (region): *Ibid.*, p. 12.

34-35 (trees, safely, place, heads): "Bethabara Diary," October 16, 21 and 30, and November 17, 1753, in Fries, I, 77, 79-80.

36 (anise, miles, sides): Clewell, pp. 24, 21 (list), 25.

37 (night): *Ibid.*, p. 31.

38 (cheese): See Ian Charles Cargill Graham, *Colonists from Scotland*, p. 13, for a discussion of Scotch-Irish exports.

38 (Ireland): Henry Jones Ford, *The Scotch-Irish in America*, pp. 183-185.

38 (imprisonment): *Ibid.*, pp. 185, 187. Wayland Fuller Dunaway, *The Scotch-Irish of Colonial Pennsylvania*, p. 29.

38 (world): *Ibid.*, p. 264. *Pennsylvania Gazette*, November 20, 1729. Charles Knowles Bolton, *Scotch-Irish Pioneers in Ulster and America*, p. 283.

39 (Bedford): Dunaway, pp. 51-65.

39 (years): Archibald Henderson, *The Conquest of the Old Southwest*, p. 11 (hereinafter, Henderson, *Old Southwest*).

39 (superiors): For a penetrating study of the influence of poverty on Scotch character, see Wallace Notestein, *The Scot in History*, pp. 55-66. For the cultural pattern of the Scotch-Irish, see Frederick B. Tolles, *James Logan and the Culture of Provincial America*, pp. 159-185.

40 (courage): W. L. Saunders, ed., *The Colonial Records of North Carolina*, VII, 100-101.

41 (withstand): *The Scotch-Irish in America* (Scotch-Irish Society, 1889), pp. 78-79.

41 (pocket): Bolton, pp. 302-303.

CHAPTER 3 (pages 43-63)

43 (history): Francis Parkman, *La Salle and the Discovery of the Great West*, p. 52.

46 (settlements): This account is based on George M. Wrong, *Rise and Fall of New France*, I, 477ff.

46 (Lancaster, territory): Albert T. Volwiler, *George Croghan and the Westward Movement, 1741-1782*, pp. 39, 36.

47 (men, region): Kenneth P. Bailey, *The Ohio Company of Virginia and the Westward Movement, 1748-1792*, pp. 27-31, 64-82.

48 (River, French): Francis Parkman, *Montcalm and Wolfe*, I, 36-62, 128-133, 135.

49-50-51 (wounded, expedition, Ohio, French, him, expected): Douglas Southall Freeman, *George Washington*, I, 370-373, 385-394, 398-401.

52 (wounded): *Ibid.*, I, 402-411. Parkman, *Montcalm and Wolfe*, I, 159.

52 (begun): *Ibid.*, I, 161.

53-54 (days, it): Saunders, V, 560-617.

54 (Catawba): *Ibid.*, V, 604. Henderson, *Old Southwest*, p. 62.

55 (French): Andrew Lewis to Governor Lyttelton, September 30, 1756, in Saunders, V, 612-614. Philip M. Hamer, "Anglo-French Rivalry in the Cherokee Country, 1754-1757" (hereinafter Hamer, "Anglo-French Rivalry"), in *The North Carolina Historical Review*, II, (1925), 312.

55 (completed): Henderson, *Old Southwest*, pp. 66-67. Hamer, "Anglo-French Rivalry," p. 313. Saunders, V, 585, 612-614, 635.

55 (River): *Ibid.*, V, 610. James G. M. Ramsey, *The Annals of Tennessee*, p. 57. W. Neil Franklin, "Virginia and the Cherokee Indian Trade, 1753-1775," in East Tennessee Historical Society *Publications*, V (1933), 25.

57 (nation): *Ibid.*

57 (home): Draper MSS, Life of Boone, pp. 65-66. Jared Sparks, ed., *The Writings of George Washington*, II, 322.

57 (Loudoun): Draper MSS, 2C67 (2).

58 (homes): *South Carolina Gazette*, January 12, 1760.

59 (Keowee): Draper MSS, Life of Boone, p. 75. Philip M. Hamer, "Fort Loudoun in the Cherokee War," in *The North Carolina Historical Review*, II (1925), 450.

60 (failure): *South Carolina Gazette*, August 2 and 13, 1760.

60 (ammunition): *Ibid.*, August 23, 1760.

61 (months): *Ibid.*, September 6, 1760. The reasons for the rescue of

Stuart are given in Mary V. Rothrock, "Carolina Traders Among the Overhill Cherokee, 1690-1760," in East Tennessee Historical Society *Publications*, I (1929), 16. *South Carolina Gazette*, April 3, 1762.

61 (destroyed): *Ibid.*

63 (Kentucky): See Clarence W. Alvord, *The Mississippi Valley in British Politics*, I, 82.

CHAPTER 4 (pages 64-82)

64 (historians): Robert S. Cotterill, *History of Pioneer Kentucky*, p. 15.

64 (carriage): Jared Sparks, ed., *Works of Franklin*, III, 346-350.

65 (rivers): "Doctor Thomas Walker's Journal," in J. Stoddard Johnston, ed., *First Explorations in Kentucky*, p. 48 (hereinafter Johnston, ed., *First Explorations*).

65 (dissolved): Draper MSS, 5C12. "Doctor Thomas Walker's Journal," June 19, May 26, April 28 and May 1, 1750, in Johnston, ed., *First Explorations*, pp. 70, 64, 55-56. Alvord, I, 160-161.

66 (Kanawha): Draper MSS, 5C12. "Christopher Gist's Journal," in Johnston, ed., *First Explorations*, pp. 149-150, 155-166.

67 (Company): C. A. Hanna, *The Wilderness Trail*, II, 216.

67 (it): Quoted in Henderson, *Old Southwest*, p. 106.

68 (River): *Ibid.*, pp. 120-122.

68 (eaten): Lyman C. Draper, *King's Mountain and Its Heroes*, pp. 429-430 (hereinafter Draper, *King's Mt.*).

68 (name): Henderson, *Old Southwest*, pp. 123-124.

68 (home): Draper MSS, 5C18.

69 (underground, Cumberland): Draper MSS, 3B47-51, 3B53-84.

70 (trigger, manners): Draper MSS, Life of Boone, pp. 13, 24-26.

71 (shooting): John Bakeless, *Daniel Boone*, pp. 25, 11 (quoted).

71 (cabin): Draper MSS, 1C24, 35.

71 (forest): Bakeless, p. 25.

71 (Bryan): Draper MSS, 3C3-4.

72 (Yadkin): Draper MSS, Life of Boone, p. 58.

72 (pleasures): Joseph Doddridge, *Notes on the Settlement and Indian Wars of the Western Parts of Virginia and Pennsylvania*, pp. 155-156 (hereinafter Doddridge, *Notes*).

73 (Creek): William K. Boyd, ed., *William Byrd's History of the Dividing Line Betwixt Virginia and North Carolina*, pp. 156, 158 (hereinafter, Boyd, ed., *Dividing Line*). Henderson, *Old Southwest*, pp. 131-132.

73 (River): Draper MSS, 2C53-57.

73 (wilderness): MSS, Draper 8C17, 93, 98.

74-75 (water, market, expensive): Bakeless, pp. 37-39.

76 (routes): L. P. Summers, *History of Southwest Virginia*, p. 76. Draper MSS, 3C72.

76 (thoughts): Draper MSS, 2C18.

77 (cash): Draper MSS, 22C5, 2C19-20, Life of Boone, p. 156.

77-78 (Kentucky, Kentucky, River): Henderson, *Old Southwest*, pp. 147-148.

78 (Valley): *Ibid.*, p. 149. Bakeless, p. 48.

79 (severely, ha): Henderson, *Old Southwest*, pp. 151-152.

79 (escaped): Draper MSS, 6S49-52.
80 (went): Draper MSS, 2C24-26.
80 (holds): Draper MSS, 2C34, 4C89.
80-81 (nowhere, day): Bakeless, pp. 55-56.
81 (Indians): Henderson, *Old Southwest*, p. 156. Draper MSS, 3C67 (9).
81 (county): Draper MSS, Life of Boone, p. 217.
82 (hence): Draper MSS, 3C58.

CHAPTER 5 (pages 83-102)

83 (country): Saunders, ed., VII, 248.
85 (himself): John Spencer Bassett, "The Regulators of North Carolina," (hereinafter Bassett, "The Regulators"), in American Historical Association *Annual Report* (1894), pp. 148-149, 151.
86 (tax): E. W. Caruthers, *The Old North State in 1776*, pp. 21-22.
86 (fees): Bassett, "The Regulators," p. 152.
87 (merchant): George Sims, "An Address to the People of Granville County," in William K. Boyd, ed., *Some Eighteenth Century Tracts Concerning North Carolina*, p. 189. The original manuscript is in the possession of the North Carolina Historical Association; it was first printed by Archibald Henderson in the *American Historical Review*, XXI (1916), 325-332.
87 (America): See Alonzo Thomas Dill, "Tryon's Palace: A Neglected Niche of North Carolina," in *The North Carolina Historical Review*, XIX (1942), 119-167, for history and maps. See William Spence Robertson, ed., *The Diary of Francisco de Miranda*, pp. 5-6.
89 (Majority): Saunders, ed., VII, 672-673. Archibald Henderson, ed., "Hermon Husband's Continuation of the Imperial Regulation," in *The North Carolina Historical Review*, XVIII (1941), 48-81, throws added light on the Regulator movement and describes Husband's efforts to obtain legal help in his case.
89 (paid): B. J. Lossing, *Field Book of the Revolution*, II, 571. E. W. Caruthers, *Life and Character of the Rev. David Caldwell*, p. 575 (hereinafter Caruthers, *Caldwell*). Julian P. Boyd, "The Sheriff in Colonial North Carolina," in *The North Carolina Historical Review*, V (1928), 151-180, describes the establishment of the office of sheriff, the appointing of the sheriffs, their embezzlements as pointed out by Tryon and their control of elections.
90 (court): Bassett, "The Regulators," pp. 169-170.
91 (gold): Caruthers, *Caldwell*, pp. 116n, 130n.
91 (service): Bassett, "The Regulators," p. 181.
92 (governor): Saunders, ed., VII, 767-771.
92 (proclamation, hands): *Ibid.*, VII, 801-803.
93 (court): *Ibid.*, VII, 805-806.
93 (homes): Bassett, "The Regulators," p. 179.
93 (town): *Ibid.*, p. 181. Saunders, ed., VII, 847, 884.
94 (register): Bassett, "The Regulators," p. 181.
94-95-96-97 (assembly, learned, place, home, belongings, hellward, apprehended, law, leader): Saunders, ed., VIII, 231-234, 260, 241-244, 236-240, 268-270, 356, 388, 390, 494.

97-98 (homes, purpose, accused): George Bancroft, *History of the United States*, III, 399-400.
98 (faces): Walter Clark, ed., *State Records of North Carolina*, XIX, 837-839 (hereinafter Clark, ed., *Records of N. C.*).
99 (men): William Edward Fitch, *Some Neglected History of North Carolina*, pp. 196-197. Caruthers, *Caldwell*, p. 145.
99 (columns, laws): Saunders, ed., VIII, 608-610, 642.
100 (joined): Fitch, p. 220.
100 (spot): Bassett, "The Regulators," p. 204.
101 (overturned): Caruthers, *Caldwell*, p. 165. W. H. Foote, *Sketches of North Carolina*, p. 64.
101 (farms): Henderson, *Old Southwest*, p. 175. Saunders, ed., VIII, 655.
101 (them): Bassett, "The Regulators," p. 211.
102 (British): George Bancroft to D. L. Swain, quoted in Ramsey, pp. 101-102.

CHAPTER 6 (pages 103-119)

103 (Robertson): A. W. Putnam, *History of Middle Tennessee*, p. 21. Ramsey, p. 664. Theodore Roosevelt, *The Winning of the West*, I, 204. Samuel Cole Williams, *Dawn of Tennessee Valley and Tennessee History*, p. 370 (hereinafter, Williams, *Dawn of Tenn.*) Philip M. Hamer, ed., *Tennessee, A History*, I, 12 (hereinafter Hamer, ed., *Tenn.*), says Robertson came to Watauga in 1768; he may have confused "the father of Tennessee" with a James Robertson who lived in Fincastle County, Virginia, and served under Preston in Lord Dunmore's War. See Thomas Perkins Abernethy, *From Frontier to Plantation in Tennessee*, p. 3n.
104-105 (horses, settlements): Roosevelt, I, 206.
106 (obtained): Draper MSS, 16DD4. Alfred Proctor James, "The First English-Speaking Trans-Appalachian Frontier," in *Mississippi Valley Historical Review*, XVII (1930), 55-70, shows that the first settlements were made in western Pennsylvania.
106 (Holston): Draper MSS, 11DD19, 10DD14.
107 (region): Carl S. Driver, *John Sevier, Pioneer of the Old Southwest*, pp. 6-10.
107-108 (agreement, Indians): Saunders, ed., XIX, 314.
108 (river): Hamer, ed., *Tenn.*, I, 67.
109 (home): Roosevelt, I, 217-218.
109 (business): Hamer, ed., *Tenn.*, I, 68.
109 (authority): Dunmore to Dartmouth, May 16, 1774, quoted in Philip M. Hamer, "The Wataugans and the Cherokee Indians in 1776" (hereinafter Hamer, "Wataugans and Cherokee"), in East Tennessee Historical Society *Publications*, III (1931), 112-113.
110-111 (them, formed, power, remedies, army, colonel): Ramsey, p. 107. Williams, *Dawn of Tenn.*, p. 369, 373-374, 376.
112 (grounds, move): Saunders, ed., 763-785. Hamer, "Wataugans and Cherokee," pp. 114-115. Hamer, ed., *Tenn.*, I, 74-75.
112 (more): Printed in Philip M. Hamer, ed., "Correspondence of

Henry Stuart and Alexander Cameron with the Wataugans" (here-inafter, Hamer, ed., "Correspondence of Stuart and Cameron"), in *Mississippi Valley Historical Review*, XVII (1930).

112 (Cherokee): Hamer, "Watuagans and Cherokee," pp. 120-121.
113 (witnesses): Printed in Hamer, ed., "Correspondence of Stuart and Cameron," p. 186.
113 (Carolina): Draper MSS, 4QQ39.
114 (command): Ramsey, p. 34. Hamer, ed., "Wataugans and Chero-kee," p. 126.
115 (recovered): John Haywood, *Civil and Political History of the State of Tennessee*, p. 60. See also A. V. Goodpasture, "Indian Wars and Warriors," in *Tennessee Historical Magazine*, IV (1918), 29.
115 (husband): See Driver, pp. 19-20.
116 (pardon): Draper MSS, 30S351-355, 30S140-143.
116 (neighbors): Ramsey, p. 38.
116 (towns): Draper MSS, 2DD29, 3DD339, 3DD186.
117-118 (homes, nation, Moore, Chickamauga): Ramsey, pp. 165-170.
118 (treaty): See Haywood, pp. 501-514, for the Treaty of Long Island.
118 (disputes): Williams, *Dawn of Tenn.*, p. 382.
119 (Chota): *Ibid.* Draper MSS, 11DD82. Ramsey, p. 183.

CHAPTER 7 (pages 120-142)

120 (Pitt): Dunmore to Dartmouth, December 24, 1774, in Draper MSS, 155J4-48.
120 (Kentucky): Randolph C. Downes, *Council Fires of the Upper Ohio*, p. 158.
121 (year): Randolph C. Downes, "Dunmore's War: An Interpretation" (hereinafter Downes, "Dunmore's War"), in *Mississippi Valley Historical Review*, XXI (1934), 314.
121 (them): E. B. O'Callaghan, ed., *Documents Relative to the Colonial History of the State of New York*, VIII, 462.
122 (Creation): Dunmore to Dartmouth, December 24, 1774, in Draper MSS, 15J4-48.
123 (resentment): Johnson to Dartmouth, June 20, 1774, in O'Callaghan, ed., VIII, 460.
123 (Nations): Peter Force, ed., *American Archives*, Fourth Series, I, 468.
124 (frontiersmen): Dunmore to Dartmouth, December 24, 1774, in Draper MSS, 15J4-48.
124 (Trail): John Floyd to William Preston, Little Guandot, April 26, 1774, in Draper MSS, 3QQ19.
124 (advice): Downes, "Dunmore's War," p. 320.
125 (themselves): Consul W. Butterfield, ed., *The Washington-Craw-ford Letters*, p. 40.
125 (boats): O'Callaghan, ed., VIII, 463.
126 (home): Draper MSS, 2D15-19.
127 (Territory): Reminiscences of Judge Henry Jolly, in Draper MSS,

6NN22-24. Michael Cresap, Jr., to Lyman C. Draper, 1845, in Draper MSS, 2SS33-35. George Edgington to Lyman C. Draper, 1845, in Draper MSS, 2SS34.

127 (children): Draper MSS, 2SS37.

127 (myself): Enclosure of Logan's letter, somewhat torn, in Arthur Campbell to William Preston, in Draper MSS, 3QQ118. Reuben Gold Thwaites and Louise Phelps Kellogg, eds., *Documentary History of Dunmore's War*, pp. 246-247.

128 (men): Force, ed., I, 469. *Pennsylvania Archives*, IV, 497-498.

128 (manner, vengeance): Downes, "Dunmore's War," pp. 325-326.

129 (Monongahela): Virgil Lewis, *History of the Battle of Point Pleasant*, p. 17. See also Butterfield, pp. 48, 85.

129 (Enemies): Quoted in Lewis, p. 18.

130 (corn): Angus McDonald to John Connolly, in Thwaites and Kellogg, eds., pp. 151-154.

130 (Lords): Lewis, p. 23.

130 (camps): Dunmore to Andrew Lewis, in Draper MSS, 3QQ141.

131 (warfare): Lewis, p. 29.

131 (behind): William Christian to Preston, September 7, 1774, in Draper MSS, 3QQ92.

131 (Kanawha): Draper MSS, 1DD118, 120-121.

132 (wilderness): Christian to Preston, September 7, 1774, in Draper MSS, 3QQ92, 1DD196.

133 (Religion): William Fleming to Nancy Fleming, Mouth of Elk River, Virginia, September 27, 1774, in Draper MSS, 2ZZ5.

133 (him): Roosevelt, I, 276.

134 (died): Christian to Preston, Point Pleasant, October 5, 1774, in Thwaites and Kellogg, eds., pp. 261-262.

135 (years): Fleming to William Bowyer, in Draper MSS, 2ZZ7-9.

135 (now): Preston to Patrick Henry, October 31, 1774, in Draper MSS, 3QQ128.

136 (clubs): Isaac Shelby to John Shelby, Camp opposite to the mouth of the Great Canaway [Kanawha], October 16, 1774, in Draper MSS, 7ZZ2, 1DD179.

136 (over): Dunmore to Dartmouth, official report, Williamsburg, Virginia, December 24, 1774, in Draper MSS, 15J4-48, 1DD192. Christian to Preston, Camp at Point Pleasant, October 15, 1774, in Thwaites and Kellogg, eds., 261-266.

137 (Dunmore): Lewis, p. 54.

137 (chiefs): Christian to Preston, Smithfield, Virginia, November 8, 1774, in Draper MSS, 3QQ130.

138 (homes): Lewis, pp. 58-59.

138 (confirmed): Thwaites and Kellogg, eds., p. xxiii. Lewis, p. 62.

138 (Mountains): Roosevelt, I, 291.

139 (Revolution): Lewis, p. 69.

139 (Michilimackinac): Samuel Flagg Bemis, *Diplomacy of the American Revolution*, p. 219n.

141 (countrymen): Force, ed., I, 962-963.

142 (one): Roosevelt, I, 372-373, 289, 288. Joseph Doddridge, *Logan, The Last of the Race of the Shikellimus*, p. 66.

CHAPTER 8 (pages 143-157)

143 (sovereignty): Draper MSS, 2CC34-37.
144 (posterity): Draper MSS, 1CC2-5.
145 (trinkets): Saunders, ed., IX, 1129.
145 (colony): William Stewart Lester, *The Transylvania Colony*, p. 21.
146 (sixteenth): Draper MSS, 1CC3-9.
146 (well): Draper MSS, 4CC1.
146 (Virginia): Preston to George Washington, January 31, 1775, in Draper MSS, 15S100.
147 (purchased, Undertaking): *North Carolina Gazette*, February 24, 1775. Saunders, ed., IX, 1122-1125.
147 (goods): Robert Lee Kincaid, *The Wilderness Road*, pp. 95-96.
148 (end): Draper MSS, 4QQ7.
148 (prophetic): Felix Walker, "Narrative of His Trip with Boone from Long Island to Boonesborough in 1775," in *De Bow's Review*, February 1854.
149 (purchase): Lester, p. 37.
149 (unfolds): John Clement Fitzpatrick, ed., *The Writings of George Washington*, III, 279.
149 (Henderson): Quoted in Lester, pp. 39-40.
152 (America): Quoted from the original manuscript in Henderson, *Old Southwest*, pp. 233-234.
152 (Sam): Bakeless, p. 91.
153 (them): Boone to Henderson, April 1, 1775, in Draper MSS, 17CC166-167.
153 (plain): Walker.
154 (Deer): Abraham Hanks was the uncle of Nancy Hanks, Abraham Lincoln's mother. Lewis H. Kilpatrick, ed., "Journal of William Calk," in *Mississippi Valley Historical Review*, VII (1921), 367.
154 (salt): Henderson to associates, April 8, 1775, in James Hall, *The Romance of Western History*, pp. 169-170.
154 (assistance): Kilpatrick, p. 367.
155 (alone): Henderson's Journal, in Draper MSS, 1CC21-102.
156 (sound): Kilpatrick, ed., p. 368.
156 (saw): Bakeless, p. 98.
157 (all): Kilpatrick, ed., p. 369.

CHAPTER 9 (pages 158-180)

158-159 (mischief, scheme): Henderson's Journal, in Draper MSS, 1CC21-102.
160 (support): *Ibid.* Kathryn Harrod Mason, *James Harrod of Kentucky*, pp. 80-81.
161 (faithfully): *Ibid.*
162 (undertaking, immorality): George W. Ranck, *Boonesborough*, pp. 196-212.
162 (contemplation): Quoted in Lester, p. 91.
163 (long): Ranck, p. 29.
163 (acres, appropriations): Lester, p. 93-98.
164 (Kentucky): Bakeless, p. 104.

164 (persons): Quoted in Lester, p. 100.
164 (corn): Kilpatrick, ed., pp. 369-370.
165 (cleared): Lester, p. 103.
165 (down): Henderson's Journal, in Draper MSS, 1CC21-102.
166 (thirty): *Ibid.*
166 (fortnight): Draper MSS, 1CC195-197.
166-167-168 (acres, duplicity, fear, lives, proprietors, abilities): Saunders, ed., X, 256-262.
168 (reproached): Quoted in James Hogg to Richard Henderson, January 1776, in Ranck, p. 225.
168 (schemes): Edmund Cody Burnett, ed., *Letters of the Members of the Continental Congress*, I, 306.
169 (life): Hogg to Henderson, January 1776, in Ranck, p. 228-229.
170 (men): Henderson's Journal in Draper MSS, 1CC21-102. John Williams to the Transylvania associates, January 3, 1776, in Saunders, ed., X, 382-384.
170 (Falls): Ranck, pp. 230-232. Saunders, X, 384.
171 (Colony): Force, ed., VI, 1528-1529.
172 (year): James Rood Robertson, ed., *Petitions of the Early Inhabitants of Kentucky*, pp. 49-50 (hereinafter Robertson, ed., *Petitions*).
173 (Jones): George Rogers Clark to James Madison (Clark's Memoir), in Draper MSS, 47J2. Printed in James A. James, ed., *George Rogers Clark Papers, 1771-1781*, in Collections of the Illinois State Historical Library, VIII, 208ff, Virginia Series (III).
174 (interests): Robertson, ed., *Petitions*, pp. 36-38. Mason, pp. 94-96.
175 (settlements): Robertson, ed., *Petitions*, pp. 39-41. Draper MSS, 14S2.
176 (States): Force, ed., VI, 1573.
176 (officers): Lester, p. 139.
177 (October): *Journal of the Virginia Convention*, June 24, 1776, p. 63.
178 (disposal): Draper MSS, 47J5-7.
179 (America): Draper, MSS, 47J8.
180 (Kentucky): *Journal of the Virginia House of Delegates*, December 20, 1776.

CHAPTER 10 (pages 181-206)

181 (family): Ranck, pp. 40-41.
182 (mystery): *Ibid.*, pp. 45-46.
182 (warriors): Draper MSS, 11C11 (39). Ranck, p. 46.
182 (forest): Draper MSS, 12CC201-208, 4C20. *Kentucky Commonwealth*, January 14, 1834.
183 (them): Draper MSS, 6S78-79, 11CC11-15, 17C171-176.
183 (free): Draper MSS, 6S301-302.
183 (progress): Draper MSS, 6S96, 11CC11-15, 23S199-216.
183 (them): Bakeless, p. 130. Draper MSS, 12CC201-208, 4B83-84.
184 (retreat, again): Draper MSS, Life of Boone, pp. 466-469.
184 (lap): Draper MSS, 23S199-205, 7C67, 11CC51.
185 (sputtered, Jemima, rescuers, Indians, death): Draper MSS, 11CC75, 14C84-85, Life of Boone, p. 474.
186 (people): Draper MSS, 17CC171-175.

186 (Harrodsburg): Draper MSS, 11C44, Life of Boone, p. 493.
186 (moment): Draper MSS, 48J10-12, 4CC30-36.
187 (cattle): Draper MSS, 12C26-29, 48J10.
187 (scalped): Draper MSS, 4B118, 48J10.
187 (man): Bakeless, p. 151. Draper MSS, 48J10, 26CC55.
188 (home): Draper MSS, Life of Boone, p. 513.
188 (area): Ranck, p. 64.
189 (by): Bakeless, p. 158. Ranck, p. 64. Draper MSS, 4B147-151.
189 (winter): Draper MSS, Life of Boone, pp. 528-529.
189 (killed): Draper MSS, 4B151-155.
190 (delivered): David Trabue's Diary, in Draper MSS, 57J27.
190 (surrendered): Draper MSS, 4B155-157.
191 (you): Draper MSS, Life of Boone, pp. 533-535, 11C62-68.
191 (saved): Draper MSS, 11C62.
192 (admiration): Draper MSS, Life of Boone, p. 541.
192 (rumor, Indians, it): Quoted in Bakeless, p. 173.
192 (them): Draper MSS, 23C36, 4B162-167.
193 (back, sound): Bakeless, p. 170.
193-194 (smoked, repair, Chillicothe, doing, you, angry, alarm, days): Draper MSS, Life of Boone, pp. 557-558, 571, 566-567.
194-195 (away, lap, recovered): Bakeless, p. 185.
195 (defenses, them): Draper MSS, Life of Boone, p. 579.
196 (on, warfare): Draper MSS, 4B204, Life of Boone, pp. 580-581, 4C79.
196 (them): Draper MSS, 4C79-80.
196 (home): Draper MSS, 11C62, Life of Boone, pp. 584-585, 4B204, 4C79-80.
197 (before): Draper MSS, 4B210.
197 (authority): Account of Josiah Collins, in Draper MSS, 12CC74.
198 (gravely): Draper MSS, 11CC94, 12CC205.
198 (on, easy, fort): Draper MSS, 19C79. Bakeless, p. 203.
198 (away): Draper MSS, 12CC75.
199 (proposition): Draper MSS, 12CC201-210. Ranck, p. 85.
199 (here, true, peace): Draper MSS, 22C5 (16), 6S141, Life of Boone, p. 600.
200 (him): Draper MSS, 11C98-99, 12C5 (8-9).
200-201 (noise, comrades): Ranck, p. 91.
201 (dirt, river, mine): Draper MSS, 11CC11-15, 4B235-240. Ranck, pp. 97-100.
201 (revenge): Trabue's Diary, in Draper MSS, 57J27.
202 (end, cheers): Draper MSS, Life of Boone, pp. 613-624.
202 (cabin, out): Draper MSS, 11CC13. Ranck, pp. 95-96.
202 (banter, Shawnee, do, bitches): Draper MSS, 6C143.
203 (house, horse, water, river): Bakeless, p. 222.
203 (words): Draper MSS, 11CC14, 6S143.
203-204 (daylight, ruse, rest): Ranck, pp. 99-102.
204 (resentment): Bakeless, p. 229.
205 (itself): *Ibid.*, p. 232.
205 (commyssion): Draper MSS, Life of Boone, pp. 630-632. Bakeless, p. 234.

206 (warpath): Ranck, p. 105. Draper MSS, 57J44, Life of Boone, pp. 630-632.

CHAPTER 11 (pages 207-234)

208 (waters): Quoted in Ramsey, p. 718.
208 (honor): Doddridge, *Notes*, pp. 185-186.
209 (doubled): *Ibid.*, p. 186.
209 (for): Ramsey, p. 725.
209 (kettles): Constance Lindsay Skinner, *Pioneers of the Old Southwest*, p. 34.
210 (grease): *Ibid.*, p. 35. Draper MSS, 48J10.
210 (grease): Skinner, p. 46. M. J. Spaulding, *Sketches of the Early Catholic Missions in Kentucky*, p. 31.
211 (size): For a vivid account of frontier furniture, see Doddridge, *Notes*, pp. 135-140.
211 (ground): See John G. W. Dillin, *The Kentucky Rifle*, pp. 17-26.
211 (wear): Draper MSS, 4B143.
212 (flannel): John Mason Brown, "The Kentucky Pioneers" (hereinafter Brown, "Ky. Pioneers"), in *Harper's Magazine*, LXXV, June 1887.
212 (cloth): Draper MSS, 4B106.
212 (clothing): See Abernethy, p. 148.
212 (neighbors): *Ibid.*, pp. 148-149. Ramsey, p. 715.
213 (barefooted): Doddridge, *Notes*, pp. 140-141.
214 (him): J. F. D. Smythe, *A Tour of the United States of America*, I, 222-223. Trabue's Diary, in Draper MSS, 57J27.
214 (Months, Prayer): Boyd, ed., *Dividing Line*, pp. 250, 252.
215 (themselves): Lester, p. 245.
215 (Denton): Draper MSS, 4B106.
215 (calf): Doddridge, *Notes*, p. 147.
215 (petition): Robertson, ed., *Petitions*, pp. 43-44. See Thomas D. Clark, "Salt, a Factor in the Settlement of Kentucky," in *Filson Club History Quarterly*, XII (1938), 42 passim.
216 (year, family): William Flynn Rogers, "Life in East Tennessee Near the End of the Eighteenth Century," in East Tennessee Historical Society *Publications*, I, (1929), 32-33.
217 (hand): Daniel Drake, ed., *Pioneer Life in Kentucky*, pp. 45, 63.
217-218 (two, proportioned, Native, America): Boyd, ed., *Dividing Line*, p. 4.
218 (truth): Ramsey, p. 717. Doddridge, *Notes*, pp. 154-155.
218 (fire): *Ibid.*, pp. 157-160.
219 (filled): Draper MSS, 4B103-104.
219-220-221 (air, turnips, upward, certain, gunpowder, joints, money, bewitched, incantations, coals): Doddridge, *Notes*, pp. 168-172, 180-181.
222 (Southwest): Walter Brownlow Posey, *The Development of Methodism in the Old Southwest, 1783-1824*, p. 1 (hereinafter Posey, *Methodism*).
222 (brows): Roosevelt, I, 195.
222 (president): C. W. Heiskell, *Pioneer Presbyterianism in Tennessee*,

pp. 17-21. Lucius S. Merriam, *Higher Education in Tennessee*, p. 227.

223 (clubfooted, throat): William Warren Sweet, ed., *The Rise of Methodism in the West*, p. 51. David Benedict, *Fifty Years Among the Baptists*, pp. 92-96. Peter Cartwright, *Autobiography*, pp. 133-136. Robert S. Semple, *A History of the Rise and Progress of the Baptists in Virginia*, p. 15.

224 (civilization): W. T. Thom, *Struggle for Religious Freedom in Virginia: The Baptists*, p. 73.

224 (baptism): See John Taylor, "Extracts from the History of Ten Baptist Churches," in William Warren Sweet, ed., *Religion of the American Frontier: The Baptists*, pp. 141-143.

225 (man): Quoted in L. A. Weigle, *American Idealism*, p. 150. Posey, *Methodism*, p. 42.

225 (log): Nathan Bangs, *History of the Methodist Episcopal Church*, I, 272. Moses M. Henkle, *The Life of Henry Bidleman Bascom*, p. 70.

225 (preachers): W. M. Gewehr, "Some Factors in the Expansion of Frontier Methodism, 1800-1811," in *Journal of Religion*, VIII (1928), 103.

226 (exposure): Posey, *Methodism*, p. 22.

226 (life): Sweet, ed., *Rise of Methodism in the West*, pp. 55-56.

227 (souls): Francis Asbury, *Journal*, II, 342.

228-229 (life, them, another, approval, Amen, brother, it, God, Lord, guilt, Lord, Lord): Posey, *Methodism*, p. 19, 21-22, 24-25.

229 (Lord, came, ecstasy): Richard McNemar, *The Kentucky Revival*, p. 21.

230 (heaven, rapidity, unconscious, singing): Posey, *Methodism*, pp. 26-27.

231 (madly): John W. Monette, *History of the Discovery and Settlement of the Valley of the Mississippi*, II, 29. Lorenzo Dow, *History of Cosmopolite*, p. 184. Posey, *Methodism*, p. 28.

231 (children, Beelzebub): Quoted in *ibid.*, p. 29.

231 (infirmity): Quoted in Walter Brownlow Posey, *The Presbyterian Church in the Old Southwest, 1778-1838*, pp. 26-27.

231 (Am): Asbury, p. 294.

232 (wished): James Phelan, *History of Tennessee*, p. 127. Doddridge. *Notes*, p. 176.

232-233 (mates, chestnut): Phelan, p. 128.

235 (diligence): Ramsey, pp. 722-724.

CHAPTER 12 (pages 235-251)

237 (duty, encounter): Quoted in Draper, *King's Mt.*, pp. 52-53.

237 (death): *Ibid.*, p. 66.

238 (weapon): *Ibid.*, p. 51.

238 (proficient): Skinner, p. 197. Draper, *King's Mt.*, p. 55.

238-239 (Carolina, flight): *Ibid.*, pp. 71, 73, 82.

239 (followed): Draper MSS, 4DD103-117.

239 (Shelby): Draper, *King's Mt.*, p. 169.

239-240 (King, country, soldiers): *Ibid.*, pp. 151-153.
240 (threat): *Ibid.*, p. 170.
240 (before): *Ibid.*, pp. 104-122.
240 (lead): *Ibid.*, p. 175n.
241 (trail): *Ibid.*, p. 176. Skinner, p. 207.
241 (column): Draper, *King's Mt.*, pp. 177-180.
242 (hour, it): Draper MSS, 4DD81-84.
243 (soldiery): Skinner, p. 211.
243 (liberty): Draper, *King's Mt.*, p. 187-188.
243 (fervent): Ramsey, p. 229. Draper, *King's Mt.*, pp. 378-387.
244 (men): Virginia *Gazette*, November 11, 1780.
245 (it): See Isaac Shelby's "Narrative of King's Mountain," in *American Review*, December 1848.
245 (victory): Draper MSS, 32S504.
245 (rifles): Draper, *King's Mt.*, p. 233.
246 (rocks): Draper MSS, 4DD41-43, describes the route taken by the Americans.
246 (first): Draper MSS, 5DD20.
247 (artery): Draper, *King's Mt.*, p. 258.
247 (hilt): *Ibid.*, p. 274.
247-248 (him, rifle, stirrup): *Ibid.*, p. 275.
248 (cease): General De Peyster's account of the battle, in Draper MSS, 4DD10.
248 (supplies): Reports conflict as to the actual number of Americans killed. See Banastre Tarleton, *Campaign in the Southern Provinces*, p. 128. See also Draper MSS, 5DD22, which states forty-one Americans lost their lives.
248 (watch, battlefield): Draper, *King's Mt.*, pp. 307-308.
249 (blankets): *Ibid.*, p. 318.
249 (Carolinas): *Ibid.*, p. 322.
250 (pardoned): Anthony Allaire's Diary, in Draper MSS, 4DD85. Draper MSS, 4DD91-98.
250 (homes): Draper, *King's Mt.*, pp. 349-356.
251 (independence): *Ibid.*, p. 374, 377.
251 (Yorktown): Skinner, p. 222. Draper MSS, 5DD25-28.

CHAPTER 13 (pages 252-279)

252 (Creek): See Lester, p. 255. Archibald Henderson, "Richard Henderson: The Authorship of the Cumberland Compact and the Founding of Nashville," in *Tennessee Historical Magazine*, II (1916), 161.
252 (colony): James A. James, *The Life of George Rogers Clark*, p. 187 (hereinafter James, *Life of Clark*).
253 (Cherokee): Marquis James, *The Life of Andrew Jackson*, p. 49 (hereinafter James, *Life of Jackson*).
253 (corn): Haywood, p. 95.
253 (migration): James, *Life of Clark*, p. 187.
254 (Day): Saunders, ed., XIV, 354-355. Lester, p. 259.
255 (Lick, frontier, water): *Ibid.*, p. 262.
255 (fame): Henderson, *Old Southwest*, p. 282.

256 (river): James, *Life of Jackson*, p. 50.
256 (type): See Donald Davidson, *The Tennessee* [River], I, 155-156.
256-257-258 (snow, baggage, rain, cargo, river, legs, family, them, danger, attack, tragedy): John Donelson, "Journal of a Voyage Intended by God's Permission in the Good Boat Adventure from Fort Patrick Henry on Holston River, to the French Salt Springs on Cumberland River" (hereinafter Donelson's "Journal") in Ramsey, p. 197ff.
259 (could, sound): *Ibid.* Haywood, p. 102.
259-260-261 (forest, exertion, troubles, campfire, country, delicious): Donelson's "Journal," pp. 199-202.
261 (expedition): The exact number is disputed. See Davidson, *The Tennessee*, I, 166.
262 (before): Goodpasture, p. 113.
263 (regulations): Hamer, ed., *Tenn.*, I, 105-106.
263 (commodities): Haywood, pp. 126-127.
264 (final): *Ibid.*
264 (laws): *Ibid.* Hamer, ed., *Tenn.*, I, 105-106.
264 (injured): *Ibid.*
264 (government): Quoted in Lester, p. 268.
265 (needs): Roosevelt, III, 24.
265 (lifeless): *Ibid.*, III, 27-28. Haywood, p. 125.
265-266 (game, sentinels): Roosevelt, III, 30.
266 (others): Haywood, p. 131. Ramsey, p. 451.
267 (scalp, enemies): Haywood, pp. 133-134.
268 (arrive): Roosevelt, III, 40. Ramsey, p. 458.
268 (troops): *Ibid.*, p. 492.
268 (2,560): Albert Campbell Holt, *Economic and Social Beginnings of Tennessee*, p. 76.
269 (gallon): Hamer, ed., *Tenn.*, I, 110.
269-270 (rock, age): Holt, p. 121.
270 (States): *Ibid.*, p. 125.
271 (Nashville): *Ibid.*, p. 70.
273 (troops): Phelan, p. 141-143.
273 (heavy): Roosevelt, III, 174-175.
274 (immigration): Clark, ed., *Records of N. C.*, XX, 703-705, 771-773, 786-787.
274 (attacks): Arthur Preston Whitaker, "The Spanish Intrigue in the Old Southwest" (hereinafter Whitaker, "Spanish Intrigue"), in *Mississippi Valley Historical Review*, XII (1925), 172.
276 (offered): Gardoqui to Robertson, New York, April 18, 1788, in Gardoqui MSS, Durrett Collection.
276 (assembly): Alexander McGillivray to Robertson and Bledsoe, April 1788, in Archibald Henderson, "The Spanish Conspiracy in Tennessee" (hereinafter Henderson, "Spanish Conspiracy"), in *Tennessee Historical Magazine*, III (1917), 239.
277 (with): Andrew Jackson to Daniel Smith, February 13, 1789, in John Spencer Bassett, ed., *The Correspondence of Andrew Jackson*, I, 7.
277 (Spain, September): James, *Life of Jackson*, p. 57.

278 (elsewhere): Whitaker, "Spanish Intrigue," p. 175.
279 (minds): *Ibid.*, p. 171.

CHAPTER 14 (pages 280-310)

281 (forest): Driver, p. 24. Roosevelt, II, 357.
282 (Sevier): Ramsey, p. 264. Roosevelt, II, 361.
283 (it): Ramsey, pp. 267-268.
284 (days): Roosevelt, II, 362-365. Ramsey, pp. 265-268.
284 (home): *Ibid.*, p. 254.
285 (Greene): Austin Powers Foster, *The Counties of Tennessee*, pp. 14, 40.
285 (day): Holt, p. 49.
285 (places): Samuel Cole Williams, *History of the Lost State of Franklin*, pp. 269-270 (hereinafter Williams, *Lost State*).
286 (progress): Whitaker, "Spanish Intrigue," pp. 175-176.
286 (debts): Sevier to Governor Martin, Jonesboro, March 22, 1785, in Williams, *Lost State*, p. 61.
287 (state): *Ibid.* Ramsey, pp. 282-286.
287 (regions): Williams, *Lost State*, pp. 5, 6-7 (Campbell's circular).
287 (land): *Ibid.*, p. 18.
288 (it): Clark, ed., *Records of N. C.*, XIX, 712. Williams, *Lost State*, p. 24.
288-289 (Congress, Georgia): *Ibid.*, pp. 28-29.
289 (bill): *Ibid.*, p. 35.
289 (affirm): For a clarification of the controversy over the names Franklin and Frankland, and for the boundaries of Franklin, see J. T. McGill, "Franklin and Frankland: Names and Boundaries," in *Tennessee Historical Magazine*, VIII (1924), 248-257.
289 (west, adoption): Williams, *Lost State*, pp. 38-40.
290 (Cherokee): For a detailed account of this project, see Arthur Preston Whitaker, "The Muscle Shoals Speculation, 1783-1789" (hereinafter Whitaker, "Muscle Shoals"), in *Mississippi Valley Historical Review*, XIII (1926), 365-386.
290 (plans, enacted): Driver, p. 88.
291 (wishes, possessing): Alexander Martin to the Inhabitants of the Counties of Washington, Sullivan and Greene, April 25, 1785, in Williams, *Lost State*, pp. 68-69.
292 (esteem, Disregarded): Sevier to Martin, in *ibid.*, pp. 71-74.
293 (party, Assembly, November): State of Franklin to Governor Richard Caswell, Washington County, May 14, 1785, in *ibid.*, pp. 71-74, 76.
293 (cents): Roosevelt, III, 258. Ramsey, pp. 334-335.
294 (Franklin): Roosevelt, III, 254. Williams, *Lost State*, p. 91. Driver, p. 91.
295 (law): Ramsey, p. 324. Williams, *Lost State*, p. 91. Roosevelt, III, 257.
295 (Trinity): *Ibid.*, III, 256.
295 (treasurer, expenditure): See constitution of Frankland, in Ramsey, pp. 326-334.

296 (overthrown): Abernethy, p. 79.
296 (Sevier): Roosevelt, III, 257-258.
296 (Union): Clark, ed., *Records of N. C.*, XXIII, Chap. 46.
297 (Carolina): Roosevelt, III, 259.
297 (tolerate): Williams, *Lost State,* pp. 104-107. Clark, ed., *Records of N. C.,* XXII, 678-679.
298 (homeward): Ramsey, p. 341.
298 (offer): Sevier to Caswell, Mount Pleasant, Franklin, October 28, 1786, in *ibid.,* pp. 348-349.
300 (other, failure): Williams, *Lost State,* 113-114.
301 (grievances): *Ibid.,* pp. 138-139.
301 (Accomodation): Sevier to Franklin, April 9, 1787, Mount Pleasant, State of Franklin, in Sparks, ed., *Works of Franklin,* X, 270. Franklin to Sevier, Philadelphia, June 30, 1787, in Franklin Papers, VIII, folio 1803, MSS Division of Library of Congress. In Williams, *Lost State,* pp. 161-162, the same letter is somewhat changed in sentence structure and spelling.
301 (County): *Ibid.,* pp. 184-188.
302 (declared): See *Maryland Journal,* December 11, 1787.
302 (Tennessee): Williams, *Lost State,* pp. 187-188.
303-304 (Jonesboro, taxes, unconditionally, assistance, house, out): Ramsey, pp. 402, 407-408.
304 (peace): *Ibid.,* pp. 409-410. Draper MSS, 9DD47.
305 (place): Draper MSS, 5XX40.
306 (occasions): Diego Gardoqui to Sevier, April 18, 1788, in Gardoqui MSS, Durrett Collection.
306 (project): Clark, ed., *Records of N. C.,* XXII, 695-696. Henderson, *Old Southwest,* p. 336. Whitaker, "Spanish Intrigue," pp. 161-162.
307 (happens): Sevier to Gardoqui, Franklin, September 12, 1788, in Gardoqui MSS, Durrett Collection.
307 (act): Henderson, "Spanish Conspiracy," p. 236.
307 (arrest): Clark, ed., *Records of N. C.,* XXI, 484.
308 (Carolina): Skinner, p. 241.
308 (trial): Ramsey, p. 427.
309-310 (knee, him): MSS, William Smith, printed in *ibid.,* pp. 428-429.
310 (state): *Ibid.,* pp. 432-433.

CHAPTER 15 (pages 311-339)

311 (dexterity): Arthur Preston Whitaker, *The Spanish-American Frontier,* p. 26, says Kentucky in 1785 counted less than 30,000 people.
312 (thinking, vulnerable, titles): Temple Bodley, ed., *Littell's Political Transactions, etc.,* pp. iv-vi.
312-313 (confiscated, use): H. P. Johnston, ed., *The Correspondence and Public Papers of John Jay,* I, 395.
313 (impending): Bodley, ed., pp. 11-12.
314 (money, Virginia): Draper MSS, 11J37. Bodley, ed., p. 64.
317 (district): *Ibid.,* pp. 69-70.
317 (invitation): Quoted in Thomas D. Clark, *History of Kentucky,* p. 117.

317-318 (arbitration, terms): William Waller Hening, ed., *The Statutes at Large of Virginia*, XII, 37-40.

318 (itself): Bodley, ed., pp. 15-16.

318 (1788): Hening, ed., XII, 45.

319 (increase): Humphrey Marshall, *History of Kentucky*, I, 254.

319 (privileges): Bodley, ed., p. 17. Draper MSS, 14SS88. Circular letter directed to the different courts in the Western Country, March 29, 1787, in Bodley, ed., Appendix, p. 78.

319 (proposal): Thomas A. Bailey, *A Diplomatic History of the American People*, p. 48.

320 (region): Marshall, I, 275.

320 (interest): Brown to Muter, New York, July 10, 1788, in Bodley, ed., p. xxxi-xxxii.

321 (Constitution): See minutes of Congress, in *ibid.*, pp. 88-91.

321 (States): John Mason Brown, *Political Beginnings of Kentucky*, p. 146.

321 (them): Samuel McDowell, in *Western World*, August 9, 1806. Brown, *Political Beginnings of Kentucky*, p. 146. Bodley, ed., p. xxii. James Madison to Mann Butler, Montpelier, October 11, 1834, quoted in Richard H. Collins, *History of Kentucky*, I, 328.

322 (Kentucky): Bodley, ed., pp. xxv, xxviii.

322 (interests): *Kentucky Gazette*, September 6, 1788. Bodley, p. xxxviii.

323 (Wilkinson): *Ibid.*, p. xxxix.

323-324 (purpose, Majesty): James Ripley Jacobs, *Tarnished Warrior: Major-General James Wilkinson*, pp. 78-79. See also Bodley, ed., p. xl.

324 (mania): Thomas Robson Hay, "Some Reflections of the Career of General James Wilkinson," in *Mississippi Valley Historical Review*, XXI (1934), 473.

324 (either): *Ibid.*, 474, 476.

324 (profit): Bodley, ed., p. xl.

325 (this): *Ibid.*, p. xli.

325 (Indies): See Whitaker, *Spanish-American Frontier*, p. 98-99.

325-326-327 (Majesty, happiness, posterity, Congress, project): Wilkinson's Memorial, printed in Bodley, ed., pp. cxxii, cxxviii-cxxix, cxxxiv-cxxxv, cxxxvii.

327-328 (hope, campaign): Thomas Robson Hay and M. R. Werner, *The Admirable Trumpeter: A Biography of General James Wilkinson*, pp. 87-89.

328 (him): *Ibid.*, pp. 91-92.

329 (Mississippi): Bodley, ed., p. lvi.

329-330 (adopted, applause, realized, *Gazette*): Brown, *Political Beginnings of Kentucky*, p. 259. Bodley, ed., pp. lvii-lxii.

330 (East, Country): Wilkinson to Miró, August, 1788, in Charles Gayerré, *History of Louisiana, Spanish Domination*, pp. 227-234.

331 (Indians): Max Savelle, "The Founding of New Madrid, Missouri," in *Mississippi Valley Historical Review*, XIX (1932), 30-56.

332 (Ohio, plans): Hay and Werner, p. 94. Jacobs, p. 95.

332 (project): Savelle, pp. 55-56.

333 (pension): Jacobs, p. 97. Whitaker, *Spanish-American Frontier*, p. 117.
334 (plans): Jacobs, p. 97. See list in Bodley, ed., pp. xlvi-xlvii.
335 (population): Whitaker, *Spanish-American Frontier*, pp. 101-102.
336 (constitution): *Kentucky Gazette*, August 29 and September 5, 1789. Bodley, ed., pp. 111-114.
336 (debts): *Ibid.*, p. lxviii.
336 (grumblingly): Jacobs, p. 106. Wilkinson to Rees and Clark, May 20 and June 20, 1790, in *American State Papers*, Misc. II, 121-122.
337 (him): Wilkinson to Miró, January, 1790, in Gayerré, p. 224.
338 (dollars): Miró to Valdés, in *ibid.*, pp. 277-278.
338 (brigadier-general): *Ibid.*, pp. 285-286.
338 (years): *Ibid.*, p. 287.

CHAPTER 16 (pages 340-372)

340 (friendship): Ramsey, p. 542.
340 (Department): Hamer, ed., *History of Tenn.*, I, 151-152.
341 (welfare): Whitaker, "Muscle Shoals," pp. 365-386.
341 (senators): Hamer, ed., *History of Tenn.*, I, 152.
342 (morality): P. L. Cobb, "William Cobb—Host of Governor Blount," in *Tennessee Historical Magazine*, IX (1926), 241-263. William H. Masterson, *William Blount*, pp. 189-190, 192-195.
344 (assistance): Mary Mitchell to Isaac Shelby, May 1, 1793, in Draper MSS, 11DD19c.
344 (approval, them): Henry Knox to George Washington, March 10, 1791, in Clarence Edwin Carter, ed., *The Territorial Papers of the United States*, IV, 50-52.
345 (Blount): Ramsey, pp. 555-556.
345-346 (Philadelphia, sum): Masterson, p. 205.
346 (States): See the Treaty of Holston, in Carter, IV, 60-67.
346 (humanity): Masterson, p. 214.
347 (residence): Ramsey, pp. 558-560.
347 (shillings): Knoxville *Gazette*, June 1, 1793.
347 (stones): F. A. Michaux, "Travels to the West of the Allegheny Mountains," in Reuben Gold Thwaites, ed., *Early Western Travels, 1748-1846*, III, 261-265. Knoxville *Gazette*, January 14 and February 11, 1792. Reuben T. Durrett, ed., *The Centenary of Kentucky*, pp. 76-77.
348 (home): Knoxville *Gazette*, November 5, 1791, and October 6, 1792.
348-349 (White, warriors): *Ibid.*, January 16, 1793.
349 (Adair): *Ibid.*, March 9, 1792.
350 (treaty): Masterson, p. 206.
350 (benefactor): Walter Lowrie and M. S. C. Clark, eds., *American State Papers, Class II, Indian Affairs*, I, 268.
351 (whites): Whitaker, *Spanish-American Frontier*, p. 153-154, 163-166.

351 (attacks): William Blount to Daniel Smith, April 27 and 29, 1792, in Draper MSS, 4XX28. Samuel Newell to Arthur Campbell, February 1, 1792, in *ibid.* Masterson, p. 222.

352 (chiefs): Lowrie and Clark, eds., I, 269.

352 (conference): *Ibid.*, I, 267.

353 (Knoxville, government): Goodpasture, IV, 187-188.

353-354-355 (Holston, Pensacola, Chickamauga, man, man, ground, say, together, blood, not, them, campaign): Lowrie and Clark, eds., I, 288-290.

355 (hunting): Goodpasture, p. 191.

356 (Brigade): Masterson, pp. 231-232.

356 (Indians): Lowrie and Clark, eds., I, 294.

357 (designs): *Ibid.*, 331.

357 (taken): Henry Knox to Blount, October 9, 1792, in Carter, ed., IV, 194-195.

358 (it): Blount to Knox, November 8, 1792, in *ibid.*, 208-216.

358 (Carolina): Knox to Blount, November 26, 1792, in *ibid.*, 220-226.

359 (assassins): Knoxville *Gazette*, January 12, April 6, May 18 and June 1, 1793. Ramsey, pp. 576-577.

360 (Hill): Lowrie and Clark, eds., I, 435, 445.

361 (themselves): Draper MSS, 4C22, 4XX32.

361 (law): Lowrie and Clark, eds., I, 460.

362 (tribes): Carter, IV, 283-289.

363 (Chicamauga): Blount and Pickens to Knox, Philadelphia, August 6, 1793, in *ibid.*, IV, 295.

363 (withdrew): Masterson, p. 253. Ramsey, pp. 580-581.

364 (again): *Ibid.*, pp. 584-589. Lowrie and Clark, eds., I, 469.

365 (Creeks): Carter, ed., IV, 319.

365 (address): Ramsey, pp. 621-622. Knoxville *Gazette*, March 13 and 27, 1794.

365 (repairs): Masterson, pp. 259-260.

366 (governed): The petition is reproduced in Carter, ed., IV, 354-355.

366 (self-defense): *Ibid.*, IV, 358.

367 (mortally): Goodpasture, pp. 273-280. "Correspondence of General James Robertson," in *American Historical Magazine*, I (1895), V (1899).

367 (States): Carter, ed., IV, 364, 377. Lowrie and Clark, eds., I, 536.

368 (killed): Blount to James Robertson, October 8, 1794, January 6 and February 2, 1795, in "Correspondence of General James Robertson," p. 365. Carter, ed., IV, 370.

368 (militia): Lowrie and Clark, eds., I, 556-557. Randolph C. Downes, "Indian Affairs in the Southwest Territory, 1790-1796," in *Tennessee Historical Magazine*, Series 2, III (1937), 265.

369 (presence): Carter, ed., IV, 385.

370 (merits): Masterson, p. 272.

371 (other): Tobias Pickering to Blount, March 23, 1795, in Carter, ed., IV, 386-393.

371 (years): Downes, "Indian Affairs in the Southwest Territory, 1790-1796," p. 267.

Selected Bibliography

PRIMARY WORKS

MANUSCRIPTS

LYMAN C. DRAPER COLLECTION, Wisconsin State Historical Society, Madison, Wisc.:

Series B	Life of Boone
Series C	Daniel Boone
Series CC	Kentucky
Series D	Border Forays
Series DD	King's Mountain
Series J	George Rogers Clark Papers
Series QQ	Preston Papers
Series S	Draper's Notes
Series SS	Shepherd Papers
Series XX	Preston Papers
Series ZZ	Virginia Series

GARDOQUI MSS, REUBEN T. DURRETT COLLECTION, University of Chicago
FRANKLIN PAPERS, Library of Congress, Washington, D. C.

PRINTED SOURCES

Newspapers

Kentucky Commonwealth, 1834.
Kentucky Gazette, 1788-1789.
Knoxville *Gazette,* 1791-1795.
Maryland Journal, 1787.
North Carolina Gazette, 1775.
Pennsylvania Gazette, 1729.
South Carolina Gazette, 1760-1762.
Virginia *Gazette,* 1780.
Western World, 1806.

Books

ALVORD, CLARENCE W., and BIDGOOD, LEE, eds. *The First Explorations of the Trans-Allegheny Region by the Virginians, 1650-1694* (Cleveland, 1912).
ASBURY, FRANCIS. *Journal* (3 vols., New York, 1852).

393

BASSETT, JOHN SPENCER, ed. *The Writings of Colonel William Byrd* (New York, 1901).

——. *The Correspondence of Andrew Jackson* (6 vols., Washington, 1928).

BODLEY, TEMPLE, ed. *Littell's Political Transactions, etc.* (Louisville, 1926).

BOYD, WILLIAM K., ed. *Some Eighteenth Century Tracts Concerning North Carolina* (Raleigh, 1927).

——, ed. *William Byrd's History of the Dividing Line Betwixt Virginia and North Carolina* (Raleigh, 1929).

BURNETT, EDMUND CODY, ed. *Letters of the Members of the Continental Congress* (8 vols., Washington, 1921-1936).

BUTTERFIELD, CONSUL W., ed. *The Washington-Crawford Letters* (Madison, 1882).

CARTER, CLARENCE EDWIN, ed. *The Territorial Papers of the United States* (17 vols., Washington, 1934-1950).

CARTWRIGHT, PETER. *Autobiography* (New York, 1857).

CLARK, WALTER, ed. *State Records of North Carolina* (16 vols., Raleigh, 1896-1907).

DODDRIDGE, JOSEPH. *Notes on the Settlements and Indian Wars of the Western Parts of Virginia and Pennsylvania* (Albany, 1876).

FITZPATRICK, JOHN CLEMENT, ed. *The Writings of George Washington* (39 vols., Washington, 1931-1944).

FORCE, PETER, ed. *American Archives*, Fourth Series (6 vols., Washington, 1837-1853).

FRIES, ADELAIDE L., ed. *Records of the Moravians in North Carolina* (8 vols., Raleigh, 1922-1954).

HAYWOOD, JOHN. *Civil and Political History of the State of Tennessee* (Nashville, 1891).

HENING, WILLIAM WALLER, ed. *The Statutes at Large of Virginia* (10 vols., Richmond, 1810-1823).

JAMES, JAMES A., ed. *George Rogers Clark Papers, 1771-1781* (Springfield, 1912).

JOHNSTON, H. P., ed. *The Correspondence and Public Papers of John Jay* (New York, 1891).

JOHNSTON, J. STODDARD, ed. *First Explorations in Kentucky* (Louisville, 1898).

Journal of the Virginia Convention (Richmond, n. d.).

Journal of the Virginia House of Delegates (Richmond, n. d.).

LOWRIE, WALTER and CLARK, M. S. C., eds. *American State Papers, Class II, Indian Affairs* (2 vols., Washington, 1832-1834).

LUTTRELL, NARCISSUS. *A Brief Historical Relation of State Affairs, 1678-1714* (6 vols., Oxford, 1857).

MARSHALL, HUMPHREY. *History of Kentucky* (2 vols., Frankfort, Ky., 1824).

MICHAUX, F. A. "Travels to the West of the Allegheny Mountains" in REUBEN GOLD THWAITES, ed., *Early Western Travels, 1748-1846* (32 vols., Cleveland, 1904-1907).

O'CALLAGHAN, E. B., ed. *Documents Relative to the Colonial History of the State of New York* (15 vols., Albany, 1853-1887).

Pennsylvania Archives, First Series (12 vols., Philadelphia, 1852-1856).
RAMSEY, JAMES G. M. *The Annals of Tennessee* (Chattanooga, 1926).
ROBERTSON, JAMES ROOD, ed. *Petitions of the Early Inhabitants of Kentucky* (Louisville, 1914).
ROBERTSON, WILLIAM SPENCE, ed. *The Diary of Francisco de Miranda* (New York, 1928).
SAINT-SIMON, DUKE DE. *Memoirs* (3 vols., New York, 1910).
SAUNDERS, W. L., ed. *The Colonial Records of North Carolina* (10 vols., Raleigh, 1886-1890).
SMYTHE, J. F. D. *A Tour of the United States of America* (2 vols., Dublin, 1784).
SPARKS, JARED, ed. *Works of Franklin* (10 vols., Chicago, 1882).
——, ed. *The Writings of George Washington* (12 vols., Boston, 1834-1837).
SWEET, WILLIAM WARREN, ed. *Religion of the American Frontier: The Baptists* (New York, 1931).
——, ed. *The Rise of Methodism in the West* (New York, 1920).
TARLETON, BANASTRE. *Campaign in the Southern Provinces* (Dublin, 1787).
THWAITES, REUBEN GOLD, and KELLOGG, LOUISE PHELPS, eds. *Documentary History of Dunmore's War* (Madison, 1905).

Magazines

CALK, WILLIAM. "Journal of William Calk," *see* KILPATRICK, LEWIS H., ed.
"Correspondence of General James Robertson," *American Historical Magazine,* I (1895), V (1899).
KILPATRICK, LEWIS H., ed. "Journal of William Calk," *Mississippi Valley Historical Review,* VII (1921).
SHELBY, ISAAC. "Narrative of King's Mountain," *American Review* (December 1848).
WALKER, FELIX. "Narrative of His Trip with Boone from Long Island to Boonesborough in 1775," *De Bow's Review* (February 1854).

SECONDARY WORKS

Books

ABERNETHY, THOMAS PERKINS. *From Frontier to Plantation in Tennessee* (Chapel Hill, 1932).
ALVORD, CLARENCE W. *The Mississippi Valley in British Politics* (2 vols., Cleveland, 1916).
AMBLER, CHARLES H. *West Virginia, The Mountain State* (New York, 1949).
BAILEY, KENNETH P. *The Ohio Company of Virginia and the Westward Movement, 1748-1792* (Glendale, Calif., 1939).
BAILEY, THOMAS P. *A Diplomatic History of the American People* (New York, 1946).
BAKELESS, JOHN. *Daniel Boone* (New York, 1939).
BANCROFT, GEORGE. *History of the United States* (6 vols., New York, 1888).

BANGS, NATHAN. *History of the Methodist Episcopal Church* (4 vols., New York, 1857).

BEMIS, SAMUEL FLAGG. *Diplomacy of the American Revolution* (New York, 1935).

BENEDICT, DAVID. *Fifty Years Among the Baptists* (New York, 1860).

BITTINGER, LUCY FORNEY. *The Germans in Colonial Times* (New York, 1901).

BOLTON, CHARLES KNOWLES. *Scotch-Irish Pioneers in Ulster and America* (Boston, 1910).

BROWN, JOHN MASON. *Political Beginnings of Kentucky* (Louisville, 1889).

CARUTHERS, E. W. *The Old North State in 1776* (Raleigh, 1856).

———. *Life and Character of the Rev. David Caldwell* (Greensboro, 1842).

CLARK, THOMAS D. *History of Kentucky* (New York, 1937).

CLEWELL, JOHN HENRY. *History of Wachovia in North Carolina* (New York, 1902).

COLLINS, RICHARD H. *History of Kentucky* (2 vols., Louisville, 1874).

COTTERILL, ROBERT S. *History of Pioneer Kentucky* (Cincinnati, 1917).

DAVIDSON, DONALD. *The Tennessee* [River] (2 vols., New York, 1946-1948).

DILLIN, JOHN G. W. *The Kentucky Rifle* (Washington, 1924).

DODDRIDGE, JOSEPH. *Logan: the Last of the Race of the Shikellimus* (privately printed, Buffalo Creek, Va., 1823; rev. ed., Cincinnati, 1868).

DOW, LORENZO. *History of Cosmopolite* (New York, 1881).

DOWNES, RANDOLPH C. *Council Fires of the Upper Ohio* (Pittsburgh, 1940).

DRAKE, DANIEL. *Pioneer Life in Kentucky* (Cincinnati, 1870).

DRAPER, LYMAN C. *King's Mountain and Its Heroes* (New York, 1929).

DRIVER, CARL S. *John Sevier, Pioneer of the Old Southwest* (Chapel Hill, 1932).

DUNAWAY, WAYLAND FULLER. *The Scotch-Irish of Colonial Pennsylvania* (Chapel Hill, 1944).

DURRETT, REUBEN T. *The Centenary of Kentucky* (Louisville, 1893).

FAUST, ALBERT BERNHARDT. *The German Element in the United States* (2 vols., Boston, 1909).

FITCH, WILLIAM EDWARD. *Some Neglected History of North Carolina* (New York, 1914).

FOOTE, W. H. *Sketches of North Carolina* (New York, 1846).

FORD, HENRY JONES. *The Scotch-Irish in America* (Princeton, 1915).

FREEMAN, DOUGLAS SOUTHALL. *George Washington* (6 vols., New York, 1949-1954).

GAYERRÉ, CHARLES. *History of Louisiana, Spanish Domination* (4 vols., New Orleans, 1903).

GRAHAM, IAN CHARLES CARGILL. *Colonists from Scotland* (Ithaca, 1956).

HALL, JAMES. *The Romance of Western History* (Cincinnati, 1857).

HAMER, PHILIP M., ed. *Tennessee, A History* (4 vols., New York, 1933).

HANNA, C. A. *The Wilderness Trail* (2 vols., New York, 1911).

HAY, THOMAS ROBSON and WERNER, M. R. *The Admirable Trumpeter: A Biography of General James Wilkinson* (New York, 1941).

HEISKELL, C. W. *Pioneer Presbyterianism in Tennessee* (Nashville, 1891).

HENDERSON, ARCHIBALD. *The Conquest of the Old Southwest* (New York, 1920).

HENKLE, MOSES M. *The Life of Henry Bidleman Bascom* (Nashville, 1860).

JACOBS, JAMES RIPLEY. *Tarnished Warrior: Major-General James Wilkinson* (New York, 1938).

JAMES, JAMES A. *The Life of George Rogers Clark* (Chicago, 1928).

JAMES, MARQUIS. *The Life of Andrew Jackson* (Indianapolis, 1938).

KERCHEVAL, SAMUEL. *A History of the Valley of Virginia* (Richmond, 1902).

KINCAID, ROBERT LEE. *The Wilderness Road* (Indianapolis, 1947).

KNITTLE, WALTER ALLEN. *Early Eighteenth Century Palatine Emigration* (Philadelphia, 1937).

LESTER, WILLIAM STEWART. *The Transylvania Colony* (Spencer, Ind., 1935).

LEWIS, VIRGIL. *History of the Battle of Point Pleasant* (Charleston, 1909).

LOSSING, B. J. *Field Book of the Revolution* (2 vols., Louisville, 1866).

MASON, KATHRYN HARROD. *James Harrod of Kentucky* (Baton Rouge, 1951).

MASTERSON, WILLIAM H. *William Blount* (Baton Rouge, 1954).

McNEMAR, RICHARD. *The Kentucky Revival* (Cincinnati, 1807).

MERRIAM, LUCIUS S. *Higher Education in Tennessee* (Washington, 1893).

MONETTE, JOHN W. *History of the Discovery and Settlement of the Valley of the Mississippi* (2 vols., New York, 1846).

NOTESTEIN, WALLACE. *The Scot in History* (New Haven, 1947).

PARKMAN, FRANCIS. *La Salle and the Discovery of the Great West* (Boston, 1919).

——. *Montcalm and Wolfe* (2 vols., Boston, 1891).

PHELAN, JAMES. *History of Tennessee* (Boston, 1888).

POSEY, WALTER BROWNLOW. *The Presbyterian Church in the Old Southwest, 1778-1838* (Richmond, 1952).

——. *The Development of Methodism in the Old Southwest* (Nashville, 1933).

PUTNAM, A. W. *History of Middle Tennessee* (Nashville, 1859).

RANCK, GEORGE W. *Boonesborough* (Louisville, 1901).

ROOSEVELT, THEODORE. *The Winning of the West* (4 vols., New York, 1904).

The Scotch-Irish in America (Scotch-Irish Society, 1889).

SCOTT, W. W. *A History of Orange County, Virginia* (Richmond, 1907).

SCHURICHT, HERRMANN. *History of the German Element in Virginia* (Richmond, 1898-1900).

SEMPLE, ROBERT B. *History of the Rise and Progress of the Baptists in Virginia* (Richmond, 1894).
SKINNER, CONSTANCE LINDSAY. *Pioneers of the Old Southwest* (New Haven, 1919).
SPAULDING, M. J. *Sketches of the Early Catholic Missions in Kentucky* (Louisville, 1856).
SUMMERS, L. P. *History of Southwest Virginia* (Richmond, 1903).
THOM, W. T. *Struggle for Religious Freedom in Virginia: The Baptists* (Baltimore, 1900).
TOLLES, FREDERICK B. *James Logan and the Culture of Provincial America* (Boston, 1957).
TURNER, FREDERICK JACKSON. *The Frontier in American History* (New York, 1948).
VOLWILER, ALBERT T. *George Croghan and the Westward Movement, 1741-1782* (Cleveland, 1926).
WEIGLE, L. A. *American Idealism* (New Haven, 1928).
WHITAKER, ARTHUR PRESTON. *The Spanish-American Frontier* (Boston, 1927).
WILLIAMS, SAMUEL COLE. *History of the Lost State of Franklin* (Johnson City, Tenn., 1924).
———. *Dawn of Tennessee Valley and Tennessee History* (Johnson City, Tenn., 1937).
WRONG, GEORGE M. *Rise and Fall of New France* (2 vols., New York, 1928).

Monographs and Magazine Articles

BASSETT, JOHN SPENCER. "The Regulators of North Carolina," American Historical Association *Annual Report*, 1894.
BOYD, JULIAN P. "The Sheriff in Colonial North Carolina," *The North Carolina Historical Review*, V (1928).
BROWN, JOHN MASON. *Brief Sketch of the First Settlement of the County of Schoharie by the Germans* (n. d.).
———. "The Kentucky Pioneers," *Harper's Magazine*, LXXV (June 1887).
CARRIER, LYMAN. "The Veracity of John Lederer," *William and Mary College Quarterly*, XIX (1939).
CLARK, THOMAS D. "Salt, a Factor in the Settlement of Kentucky," *Filson Club History Quarterly*, XII (1938), Louisville.
COBB, P. L. "William Cobb—Host of Governor Blount," *Tennessee Historical Magazine*, IX (1926).
DILL, ALONZO THOMAS. "Tryon's Palace: A Neglected Niche of North Carolina," *The North Carolina Historical Review*, XIX (1942).
DOWNES, RANDOLPH C. "Dunmore's War: An Interpretation," *Mississippi Valley Historical Review*, XXI (1934).
———. "Indian Affairs in the Southwest Territory, 1790-1796," *Tennessee Historical Magazine*, Series 2, III (1937).
FOSTER, AUSTIN POWERS. *The Counties of Tennessee* (Nashville, 1923).
FRANKLIN, W. NEIL. "Virginia and the Cherokee Indian Trade, 1753-1775," East Tennessee Historical Society *Publications*, V (1933).

GEWEHR, W. M. "Some Factors in the Expansion of Frontier Methodism, 1800-1811," *Journal of Religion,* VIII (1928).

GOODPASTURE, A. V. "Indian Wars and Warriors," *Tennessee Historical Magazine,* IV (1918).

HAMER, PHILIP M. "Anglo-French Rivalry in the Cherokee Country, 1754-1757," *The North Carolina Historical Review,* II (1925).

——. "Fort Loudoun in the Cherokee War," *The North Carolina Historical Review,* II (1925).

——. "The Wataugans and the Cherokee Indians in 1776," East Tennessee Historical Society *Publications,* III (1931).

——, ed. "Correspondence of Henry Stuart and Alexander Cameron with the Wataugans," *Mississippi Valley Historical Review,* XVII (1930).

HAY, THOMAS ROBSON. "Some Reflections on the Career of General James Wilkinson," *Mississippi Valley Historical Review,* XXI (1934).

HENDERSON, ARCHIBALD. "The Spanish Conspiracy in Tennessee," *Tennessee Historical Magazine,* III (1917).

——. "Richard Henderson: The Authorship of the Cumberland Compact and the Founding of Nashville," *Tennessee Historical Magazine,* II (1916).

——. "Hermon Husband's Continuation of the Impartial Regulation," *The North Carolina Historical Review,* XVIII (1941).

HOLT, ALBERT CAMPBELL. *Economic and Social Beginnings of Tennessee* (Nashville, 1923).

JAMES, ALFRED PROCTOR. "The First English-Speaking Trans-Appalachian Frontier," *Mississippi Valley Historical Review,* XVII (1930).

KEMPER, CHARLES E. "The Settlement of the Valley," *Virginia Magazine of History and Biography,* XXX (1922).

McGILL, J. T. "Franklin and Frankland: Names and Boundaries," *Tennessee Historical Magazine,* VIII (1924).

ROGERS, WILLIAM FLYNN. "Life in East Tennessee Near the End of Eighteenth Century," East Tennessee Historical Society *Publications,* I (1929).

ROTHROCK, MARY V. "Carolina Traders Among the Overhill Cherokee, 1690-1760," East Tennessee Historical Society *Publications,* I (1929).

SAVELLE, MAX. "The Founding of New Madrid, Missouri," *Mississippi Valley Historical Review,* XIX (1932).

STRICKLER, HARRY MILLER. *Massanutten Settled by Pennsylvania Pilgrim in 1726* (Strasburg, Va., 1924).

WHITAKER, ARTHUR PRESTON. "The Muscle Shoals Speculation, 1783-1789," *Mississippi Valley Historical Review,* XIII (1926).

——. "The Spanish Intrigue in the Old Southwest," *Mississippi Valley Historical Review,* XII (1925).

Acknowledgments

A book of this scope is seldom the work of the author alone. It was made possible only by the experience, knowledge and patience of many persons. I want to thank the staff members of the following institutions for their cheerful and invaluable help: Wisconsin State Historical Society; Library of Congress; Library of the University of Chicago; Carnegie Library of Pittsburgh; Public Library of New York City; Library of the Organization of American States, Washington, D.C.; Library of West Virginia University; Kanawha County Library, Charleston, West Virginia; Carnegie Library of Parkersburg, West Virginia; and Ohio County Public Library of Wheeling, West Virginia.

For many kinds of help I am grateful to Charles Shetler, Floyd W. Miller, Jennie Boughner, Ruth Blodgett, Virginia Perry and Virginia Ebeling.

I am especially indebted to Robert F. Munn, Librarian, West Virginia University, for doing me the great favor of obtaining microfilm of those volumes of the Draper Collection of Manuscripts which I had not examined in their originals.

My thanks go to Robert Y. Zachary, Editor, Louisiana State University Press, for permission to quote from William H. Masterson, *William Blount*.

The late Dr. Charles Henry Ambler, Professor Emeritus of History, West Virginia University, carefully read ten chapters in the book and made many invaluable comments. I regret that he is not alive to see what I have done with what he taught me.

I am grateful to Dr. Ruel E. Foster, Professor of English, West Virginia University, who read the first seven chapters, offered his experience as an author in countless ways and suggested many paragraph changes which invariably proved sound.

Last but not least, I owe a debt of gratitude to my editors, Barbara Johnson and Andrée Fé Coers, for their encouragement, wise editorial guidance and infinite patience, and for making order out of chaos in many paragraphs and putting me straight on a number of facts and opinions.

Morgantown, West Virginia

JOHN ANTHONY CARUSO

Index

Current boundary lines have been observed in locating towns, villages, forts, etc., within states.